OX 4/02 . . . . translated [from
Russian] by Guy Daniels edited
by David H. Appel. . . .

1. Prokofiev, Sergei, 1891-
1953. = Title.

PROKOFIEV BY PROKOFIEV

SERGEI PROKOFIEV

PROKOFIEV BY PROKOFIEV

A COMPOSER'S MEMOIR

EDITED BY DAVID H. APPEL  TRANSLATED BY GUY DANIELS
DOUBLEDAY & COMPANY, INC., GARDEN CITY, NEW YORK
1979

BOOK DESIGN BY BEVERLEY GALLEGOS
ISBN: 0-385-09960-6
Library of Congress Catalog Card Number 77–25605

CONTENTS

EDITOR'S EXPLANATORY NOTE

For his thirteenth birthday Sergei Prokofiev's mother gave her son a bright green, cardboard-bound notebook.

"Sergushechka," Maria Prokofieva advised Sergei, "write down everything that passes through your little head. Don't miss a thing. Don't skip anything."

Sergei was not the type of boy to disregard parental advice. Over the years he became an obsessive diarist, developing a vowelless secret code designed to frustrate anyone who intruded on his sacred diary pages. He also became a compulsive collector of correspondence, so that when the time arrived to write his memoirs the documentation was not only abundant, it was overwhelming. In addition Sergei was seemingly endowed with powers of total recall.

This detailed memoir of childhood and early youth, covering the composer's life until he was seventeen, was assembled over two different periods. First there was a two-year span from 1937 to 1939; second, a six-year term starting in 1945, when Prokofiev worked with his wife. The chronicle enlarges on the author-composer's previous *Brief Autobiography,* incorporating material available for the first time in English.

Prokofiev's *Childhood*—the first part of this book—is a remarkable picture of rural life in the Russian Ukraine at the turn of the century, when the boy grew up amid the special joys of a childhood spent on a large estate.

At thirteen, young Prokofiev, armed with four operas, a symphony, and several piano pieces of his own, was admitted to the prestigious St. Petersburg Conservatory. There, with Rimsky-Korsakov, Lyadov, and Glazunov as his teachers, Prokofiev was part of a significant turning point in Russian musical history.

Throughout these pages, in the city and in the country with Sergei, there is ample evidence of that wit and charm that came to mark such later musical works as his *Classical Symphony, The Love for Three Oranges, Peter and the Wolf* and *Lieutenant Kije.*

The literary groundwork for these memoirs was established by the Russian editor M. Kozlova, who verified and correlated the Prokofiev materials for the original Russian edition. Kozlova's perceptive commentary can be found on page 327. The effort was placed in its proper framework by Dmitri Kabalevsky, noted Russian composer and musical editor, whose views appear on page ix.

Editor's Explanatory Note

My undertaking was to fashion these chapters for American readers. The guidelines were clear enough. Prokofiev's youthful perspective of his two worlds, country and city, is vital to any understanding of him as a composer. His insights into the process of musical composition are essential to this narrative, as are his views of his composer contemporaries. But his total recall, adding a heavy burden to the memoirs, often had to be curtailed, albeit carefully, for this edition.

For assistance in my task I enlisted the help of Dr. Peter J. Schoenbach, formerly dean of the Curtis Institute of Music in Philadelphia, and currently assistant to the president and associate dean of the New England Conservatory of Music in Boston. He was helpful and enthusiastic.

But the largest share of thanks is reserved for Maria Prokofieva, who so long ago, with her clear view from Sontsovka, urged her Sergei to keep the records complete.

David H. Appel
Philadelphia, 1978

PREFACE

Hundreds of books and innumerable articles have been written about Sergei Prokofiev. His music has been the subject of many theses and dissertations. But the best account of Prokofiev's life, of his complex and unique inner world, was written by Sergei Prokofiev himself.

In addition to being a composer of genius who exercised a tremendous influence on twentieth-century music, and an outstanding pianist and conductor, Prokofiev had an inimitable literary flair.

Just as one can glimpse the future innovator in the earliest music Prokofiev wrote as a child (they were usually witty, pungent, and biting pieces, and he called them "puppies"), so in his childhood letters to his relatives one can easily discern the origins of the mature Prokofiev's writing style: the language sharp-edged, the descriptions laconic and accurate with biting humor throughout.

For its significance and style, Sergei Prokofiev's autobiography can be compared to such masterpieces as the *Memoirs* of Hector Berlioz or Rimsky-Korsakov's no less celebrated *Record of My Musical Life.*

The role played by Prokofiev in the music of our century is a significant one. An enthusiastic celebrant of life, sunshine, and youth, he brought to the harsh, cruel, and anxiety-ridden twentieth century that joy and light the times so often lacked.

Although Prokofiev's life was not very long—he lived to age sixty-two—it was a very full one. He traveled over most of the world. He met almost all the well-known musicians, actors, writers, and directors of his day.

Prokofiev's *autobiograhy* covers that period of his life least known to the general public—from his earliest years to his graduation from the composition department of the St. Petersburg Conservatory. This volume is a lively account of the childhood and youth of one of the towering figures in Russian culture, who has rightfully taken his place among the great masters of Russian music.

Dmitri Kabalevsky

November 14, 1971

INTRODUCTION—AND APOLOGY

How to begin? With an old joke, of course.

"How marvelously I played tonight!" said the musician to his friend. "The melody flowed in such an inspired way! And the passage work was irreproachable!"

The musician talked on and on for a good fifteen minutes. Then, suddenly, he became embarrassed and exclaimed, "Forgive me! That was very impolite. I've been talking about myself all the time. Let's talk about something else. After all, you were in the audience. Perhaps you could tell me what *you* thought of my concert tonight."

That joke came to mind when I sat down to write this autobiography. Is it worthwhile to write one's autobiography—and a long one at that? Of course it's not worthwhile. The only trouble is that if I don't write it others will; and they will no doubt get things wrong—in all good conscience. If I may so express it, they will lie in good conscience; that is, not maliciously, but for want of information—on the basis of logical premises.

It's probably just as well that they go ahead and write. That really isn't so frightful, and my music won't suffer because of it. But there is one other problem. I have kept quite a number of papers—diaries, letters, and notebooks. And I'm unwilling to see those papers mutilated.

There is one great advantage if I go through them myself: I can remember between the lines—shadings that even the friendliest biographer can't discern. Thus sometimes in the case of failure, my diary bears the notation "Didn't come off—no go." But actually I was heartsick.

Or there may be some recorded conversation that recalls a whole chain of circumstances much more interesting than the conversation itself.

Why did I accumulate so many papers? The inclination to put things into writing has been a trait of mine since early childhood. My parents encouraged it.

At the age of six I was already writing music. At seven, after learning how to play chess, I kept a notebook and began to jot down games. The first game, which I titled "Pastoral," was a checkmate in four moves.

At nine I was writing histories of the battles fought by my tin soldiers, keeping track of their losses and making diagrams of their movements. At eleven

I surreptitiously observed how my music teacher kept his diary. It seemed most remarkable, and I began to keep my own, in great secrecy from everyone, sometimes even recording events while sitting on the toilet.

Later my mother gave me a thick bound notebook, saying, "Sergushechka, write down everything that passes through your little head. Don't skip anything."

I kept that first diary for six months and then abandoned it. My enrollment at the Conservatory at the age of thirteen produced so many new impressions and contacts that I resumed my diary. But I soon had to abandon it a second time because it was impossible to keep up with events.

At sixteen I went back to the diary yet once again. By now images of girls from the Conservatory were beginning to skip through my mind. It was frightfully important not to miss anything.

At about this time I began to keep the letters I had received and rough drafts or copies of those I sent. I arranged them in chronological order and bound the letters for each year in separate volumes.

At twenty-one, having read Rimsky-Korsakov's *Record* and a long biography of Tchaikovsky, and feeling that I was a composer in whom people were beginning to take an interest, I decided that in time I would write my autobiography.

Someone had said in my presence, "I would compel all remarkable people to write their autobiographies." I thought, I already have the material. All I have to do now is become famous. And I decided: by forty I'll have composed enough that I'll want to take a rest. At that point I'll be able to take up my autobiography.

But when I reached forty my youthful braggadocio had vanished, and my view of life was more sensible. So the question arose: Is it worthwhile to write at such length about oneself? By that time I had lost interest in keeping my diary at all, and the idea of writing an autobiography no longer appealed to me.

But what to do with the papers? Abandon them? Throw them away? Perhaps Gogol's greatness lay in the fact that he was bold enough to burn his own manuscripts.*

Is not that person capable of creating a masterpiece who is ready, without blinking an eye, to destroy his work if its right to exist is not clear to him? I vacillated.

But in the end two arguments prevailed. First, I have managed some achievements in my lifetime, so my autobiography might be useful to someone. Second, I have met many interesting people, and accounts of them might be interesting.

---

* A few days before his death in 1952, Nikolai Gogol burned the manuscript of the second part of *Dead Souls*. (Translator's note.)

PART ONE

CHILDHOOD

MY father, Sergei Alekseyevich Prokofiev, was born in Moscow on July 8, 1846. This date is given according to the Old Style calendar. To convert to New Style, one has to add twelve days to dates in that century, making his birthday July 20. But that date means nothing to me. The date fixed in my memory as a child was July 8. On that day guests came to visit us, and the first muskmelon ripened. If it had ripened earlier, we would have saved it for the big day. If it had been late in ripening, we would have said that the melon had failed us.

I have but slight information on my father's parents. They died when he was fourteen. Furthermore, I was a late-born child, my father being almost forty-five when I was born. It was not until almost a half century after the death of his parents that I began to inquire seriously about the context of my life. It is only natural that by that time my father's memory had grown dim.

Today, for example, it astonishes me to realize that I don't know my grandmother's first name or her maiden name. My grandfather's first name was, I believe, Aleksei, and his patronymic was Nikitich.

The Prokofievs were propertied people, but hardly cultured. I believe they owned a small factory.

On the same day in 1860 both of my father's parents died of cholera, which was epidemic in Moscow at the time. Their bodies lay together on the table.* They left my father, aged fourteen, his brother, Peter, aged eleven, and their older sister, Nadezhda, who was already married to Mikhail Smirnov, by whom she had four daughters, Nadezhda, Catherine, Maria, and Anna. (Some of these children were born later, as I recall.) I knew them when they were middle-aged women.

Since my father's older sister married young and had children early, and since her daughters did the same, this line of the family had already produced two generations before I was born. As a result, at the age of seven I already had grandnephews, and proudly called myself "Grandpa."

After the death of their parents, my father and his brother went to live with

---

* A reference to the custom of laying out the body of the deceased on a table in the home before the funeral rites. (Translator's note.)

the Smirnovs. Both boys studied at a commercial school. At this time a difference in their characters became plain. My father, the older of the two, liked schoolwork. But his brother, Peter, tried to get it over with as soon as possible so as to begin an independent life, for which he had many plans. These plans did not succeed. He started up a business, but it failed; and he spent the rest of his life managing the business affairs of his nieces, the Smirnov sisters.

Meantime, my father, dissatisfied with the commercial school, transferred to a *Realschule* and then went on to college. He was uncertain as to what specialty he should take up. For a time he wanted to be a doctor, and he was also attracted by chemistry. But he finally chose the Petrovsko-Razumovskaya Agricultural Academy near Moscow—a choice made easier by the fact that the academy had a well-equipped chemistry laboratory.

There were some student riots while my father was at the academy. He took no direct part in them, but in the subsequent repressions he refused to betray his comrades. For this he was punished. Either he was arrested, or he was deprived of some of his rights upon graduation from the academy—an event that took place in the early 1870s. In any case, this made an impression on him, and from then on he always tried to avoid any friction with the authorities.

2

Meantime, in the Smirnov family Father's four nieces were growing up. And while my father, serious and already bearded, was poring over his books, the laughter of these high school girls and their friends could be heard from the adjoining rooms.

As it happened, the Smirnov family, with its four girls, had become friends with the Zhitkov family, in which there were also four girls: Barbara, Maria, Catherine, and Tatyana. One of these would later become my father's wife and my mother.

The Zhitkovs were originally peasants from Tula Province—from the village of Serebryanye Prudy, adjacent to Leo Tolstoy's estate of Yasnaya Polyana.

My mother's grandfather, Nikita Andreyevich Shilin, had been sent to Saratov Province because of his obstinate disposition. There he became a serf of Count Sheremetev. But his son Cyril later showed up in the Sheremetev household on the Fontanka in Petersburg as superintendent of the storerooms containing precious metals (gold and silver). He was followed to Petersburg by two of his brothers, Paul and Grigory, the latter being my grandfather.

For reasons that have never been explained they took the last name of Zhitkov (from the word *zhito,* meaning "rye"), whereas the brothers who remained in Saratov kept the name of Shilin.

My grandfather, Grigory Nikitich Zhitkov (his brother Paul lived to be a hundred), at first worked in the Sheremetev household. Probably at the time the serfs were emancipated in 1861, he became a petty clerk at the Winter Palace. And later he worked as a *stryapchiy,* that is, one who handled legal affairs without having a degree in law. His wife, Anna Vasilevna, nee Inshtetova, was a kindhearted, friendly woman with fine features, beautiful hands, and small feet. Tradition has it that the Inshtetovs were descended from the Swedish Count Instedt, who had immigrated to Russia.

Grigory Zhitkov's affairs did not prosper. He had a big family, and they were so poverty-stricken that one of his daughters, Olga, who at the time was a teen-ager, poisoned herself. She did it not out of unrequited love but because of the burden of poverty. The family kept moving—first to Moscow, then back to Petersburg. Grigory often lived alone. Yet his wife and daughters still aspired to some social life. Two of the girls, Maria and Catherine, went to an academic high school, and the other two studied at home.

Once, when they had managed to sew some new dresses, the whole family started out to visit friends in the country. But at the railroad station, a locomotive which had pulled in let out a big burst of greasy steam which ruined the dresses. My mother told me about this incident some fifty years later, yet her distress was still so great that she could not talk about it calmly.

In Moscow the two Zhitkov girls who were going to high school made friends with the Smirnov girls attending the same school. The Smirnovs, who were well-to-do, looked down on the impoverished Zhitkovs, not noticing that the latter were much more refined and cultivated than themselves. Perhaps it was precisely this that attracted the pampered Smirnov girls to Maria and Catherine Zhitkov. Maria was fun-loving and witty; Catherine was pretty, with a sweet disposition.

All of these bubbly young girls made a hubbub in the Smirnov house, interfering with the homework of the student Prokofiev, who would open his door to cast angry glances at the girls. They would be intimidated by his stern appearance, his beard, and his gold-rimmed glasses. But when Maria Zhitkova was finally graduated from high school with a gold medal, she went up to young Prokofiev, also a new graduate (from the academy), and with her hands clasped defiantly behind her back, announced, "Sergei Alekseyevich, I'm not afraid of you any more." That was the beginning of their love story.

3

A friend of my mother describes her in those years: "Manyusha (Maria) Zhitkova was not pretty. She had a turned-up nose and full lips. Her jaw was somewhat prominent, and her hair was straight and cut short. She became pretty later, after her first child and after she had typhus, when her hair began to curl. But even before then she had a good figure, small feet, which she liked to show to advantage, a fresh complexion, and, above all, wit and liveliness. She was a good dancer, but her future husband was attracted to her intellectually."

How did their romance progress? There is very little information on this, but in all likelihood it didn't go smoothly. First, because the Zhitkov family again moved to Petersburg, while my father, after his graduation, bought a small farm and went there to take charge, so that it became more difficult for them to meet. Second, because of the Smirnov family. They were very fond of the lively, fun-loving Zhitkov sisters so long as they were just friends who brought gaiety into the Smirnov home. But when it turned out that my father, the oldest male in the household and the hope of the family, wanted to marry a girl without a dowry, that was another matter. They frankly said they preferred that he choose a propertied girl who would not only come into the family but contribute something to it.

The fact that my father had his training at an agricultural academy naturally shaped his life plans. When he was graduated and had come into the small sum bequeathed him by his parents (I don't really know how much it was—perhaps 15,000 gold rubles), he bought a property called Nikolayevka in Smolensk Province and decided to apply to it the training he had acquired. But the new-style farming required expenditures: one had to buy machinery and put up buildings. Moreover, the property was small, with rather unfertile soil, and didn't yield much income.

My father placed his hopes in a friend who had gone to China to test business plans and had taken money from him, the idea being that the two of them would subsequently split the profits. But this friend never sent any profits and never even wrote. My father was bitterly disillusioned.

I still have in my possession a letter from mother to my father, dated November 10, 1876, written when they were engaged but foresaw many obstacles to their marriage.

As I glance through it, this is a strange, touching experience for me to imagine my mother as a girl in love; to see that handwriting, not yet fully developed, rather like that of a high school girl, but in which one can discern the origins of her future script, beautiful and vigorous, and so familiar! It may not have been fully developed, but its character was completely mature: the letter was full of love—and some sarcasm and references to calculations, and quotations—and, most important, unswayable purpose.

> To my bitter sorrow, I can offer you nothing but myself, and I wish the same from you. I repeat what I have said before: I am not enticed by your future wealth. It repels me, since it now separates me from you. . . .

And at the end, as though she were suspecting the reasons for his hesitation, a quotation (a bit garbled) from Griboyedov: "What will society say? What will Princess Maria Aleksevna say about me?"

Yes, there were obstacles, but love was triumphant. They were married on April 25 (May 7), 1877.[1]

I note, not without secret pride, that in her family my mother was the most intellectual, as my father was in his. They were mutually attracted.

4

The newlyweds set up housekeeping at Nikolayevka, my father's place in Smolensk Province. He was then thirty years old. I do not know exactly what my mother's age was, probably about twenty-one. She kept her age a secret all of her life. And she did it so skillfully that, even after her death, her passport showed her to be fifteen years younger than her actual age. It was only indirectly, through questioning and comparisons, that I was able to ascertain that she was born in 1855, in Petersburg, on December 25, the first day of Christmastide, according to the Old Style calendar, corresponding to January 6, New Style, which makes for an additional difficulty in determining the year.

My father was tall, with a large cranium, a nose that might have been painted by an iconographer, and a light-colored, spade-shaped little beard—sometimes a big beard. His glasses made him look serious, but even in old age he could laugh irrepressibly, like a child.

Before they were married he was extremely cautious about money, reckoning that his financial circumstances did not yet permit his taking on the burden of a family. And when the marriage had taken place, he had to face up to the question of what to do about the property at Nikolayevka, which wasn't providing any income but required additional investment.

During this period of uncertainty he received from the rich landowner Dmitri Sontsov an offer to become manager of the latter's large estate in the Ukraine.

Dmitri Sontsov had been a student at the academy when my father was there. They had a high opinion of each other. Sontsov lived on an estate of his near Kursk. His other estate, a huge chunk of uncultivated land, sprawled somewhere in the Ukraine. It was in charge of a steward who couldn't take things in hand, and sent him no income. This gave Sontsov the idea that what he needed in the Ukraine was not a semi-literate employee, paid fifty rubles a month, but an educated soil engineer who could develop a large-scale agricultural enterprise; that he should pay such a professional a decent salary, give him extensive rights, and make it worthwhile for him to increase the income from the estate.

My father vacillated. On the one hand, he felt the urge to apply his know-how on a large scale. On the other hand, he was reluctant to bury his youth on the Godforsaken Ukrainian steppes.

Wouldn't it be better to stay at Nikolayevka, his own place, even if it yielded no income, than to become manager for another landowner, even if he seemed to be a decent fellow?

Sontsov promised not to meddle in the management of the estate. As for Nikolayevka, it required more and more money. So my parents decided to go to Sontsov's estate for a trial period of perhaps three years. They sold Nikolayevka. They stayed in the Ukraine all their lives.

5

The estate of Sontsovka, which comprised more than 15,000 acres, was in Ekaterinoslav Province, Bakhmutsky District—names which have disappeared into the past.

If you raise a one-hundred-kilometer perpendicular from the Sea of Azov— in particular, from Mariupol—it will come within several kilometers of the loca- ton. In the spring of 1878, my parents took the train as far as the station of Kon- stantinovka, on the as yet incomplete main line from Kharkov to Rostov, and traveled the remaining sixty kilometers by carriage. There was one other station, Yuzovka (later renamed Stalino),[2] forty kilometers from Sontsovka, but for some reason they preferred Konstantinovka.

When the carriage drawn by four horses brought my parents to Sontsovka, they were astonished by the beauty of the flowering steppe.

I can still remember that countryside as it was a quarter century later. Even then, on the estate of Sontsovka alone, there were many acres—perhaps even 250 acres—of virgin land, steppeland untouched by the plow.

In late April and May this land came alive with thousands of wild flowers, and later, in the summer, the gray feather grass stood tall in the wind.

At the time when my parents arrived the tracts of virgin land were of course much larger, and the carpets of flowers alternated with green strips of wheat as far as the distant, flat horizon.

In those fields were small mounds, relics of the earliest nomads who had roamed the steppes. Utensils and some ancient coins had been found in them. This was a completely different world from Smolensk Province where my par- ents had lived.

Sontsovka was situated at the confluence of two streams, the Solenenkoi and the Shurov. In the summer they wound quietly along the bottoms of rather deep gullies. Occasionally, the rivulets dried up. But in the spring they turned into torrential streams, carrying away dams and homemade bridges. The streets of the village extended along the banks of these gullies, which had thick growths of poplar, willow, and cherry trees. The huge manorial orchards stretched out along the bottomland where the two streams came together.

The manor house with its outbuildings stood some distance away, on a slope. Around it ran a small orchard of three or four acres protected by a low stone wall.

When I try to describe Sontsovka, I get double vision: I see it as it was early in the twentieth century, and yet I want to tell what it was like thirty years before that.

At the beginning of this century—that is, when I was ten or fifteen years old—Sontsovka was a large village with a population of a thousand. Five streets, each two kilometers long, extended from the center in different directions, like a spider's web. The church stood on a little rise of ground, and the school on another slope. Our house was a squat, one-story building painted white, with a green roof. It was shaded on one side by a chestnut tree under which I loved to play on hot days, and on the other by several false acacias.

The rooms had white walls with yellow trim. They were not really small, but they had low ceilings. The furniture was protected by slipcovers because the upholstery was old. Rubber plants, philodendron, and a small palm grew in tubs in the corners. There were nine rooms in all, not counting the office, the maids' quarters, and the storerooms.

The kitchen was in a separate building. Beyond were three stables (the Sontsovs were horse breeders), four granaries, outbuildings, a forge, and a pigsty. Still farther beyond were sheepfolds and smokehouses. In each of the orchards there was a bathhouse, an apiary, a raspberry patch, and an irrigated kitchen garden.

Sontsovka was a very out-of-the-way place. The railroad was twenty-five kilometers away, the doctor and hospital twenty-three. We had to go eight kilometers to get our mail, and the post office was open only two days a week. There was no highway, and there were no neighbors who could be called intelligentsia. One can easily imagine what kind of wilderness it was in the year my parents arrived.

6

Upon taking over management of Sontsovka, my father had the estate accurately surveyed. The entire area was marked off in sections. This was by no means a simple job, since the survey had to be done not only on paper but on the land itself. That is, peg stakes had to be driven, ditches dug, and pathways laid out. Then the peg stakes were stolen, and the ditches disappeared during the spring floods or the rainy autumn.

The agreement with Sontsov was that my father should get 20 per cent of the income from Sontsovka plus a salary of 1,200 rubles. When, toward the end of my father's life, Sontsovka began to yield from 40,000 to 60,000 rubles a year, that 20 per cent amounted to a considerable income, and the 1,200 rubbles was merely a kind of bonus.

During the first years, however, the estate yielded nothing, and the 1,200 rubles should have been Father's basic means of subsistence. But knowing that Sontsov was a bit stingy and not wanting to disquiet him, my father took no salary during that time.

There must have been considerable initial outlay for expenses. The surveyor had to be paid. Also, the system of farming had been neglected. Or, more accurately, it did not exist. It was necessary to set up a staff of employees—overseers, clerks, and horse trainers.

Gradually, the number of agricultural implements was increased. We required mowing machines, then reapers, and a threshing machine with two steam engines.

New granaries were built, and a new story added to our house. Roses bloomed in the orchard, as did lilacs, yellow and false acacias, lilies, and irises. We cultivated one part of the land and turned the rest over to the peasants. Hay was mowed on the virgin tracts and in the meadows; and after the haying, cows and sheep were pastured there.

We had 4,000 head of sheep. They were sheared in the spring. This was a big event, and peasant women from the village came to take part. A peasant woman would take a sheep in her lap. It would bleat and struggle while its wool was cut off with a big pair of shears. Then the animal would run off, naked and confused, and the peasant would hand the wool to a clerk, who would make a mark opposite her name on a list. In the evening the marks would be totaled up, and the women would be paid a ten-kopeck piece for each mark. When all the sheep had been sheared, the wool, sewn into great bags, would be hauled to the railroad station in eighty *britzky*. From there it would be sent to the fair at Kharkov, to which city my father would also go. He would scrupulously enter one ruble in the Sontsovka account as the price of his hotel room, although in fact he had paid more.

7

Most of our neighbors lived fifteen or twenty kilometers away. They were few in number, and not interesting, being hardly more than semi-educated. The relationships that developed between them and us were ambivalent. After my parents had spent "three and thirty years" at Sontsovka (by coincidence, this is the precise figure), their only good friends were the doctor and the veterinarian.[3]

My mother was much more sociable than my father. She enjoyed friends, was fond of lively and interesting conversation.

Becoming a kind of cultural leader among the peasants provided a natural outlet for her intellectual proclivities. I don't know whether even the beginnings of a school had previously existed at Sontsovka, or whether the school we had was founded by my parents. But during the first years my mother herself did the teaching there. When one considers that such concepts as "enlightenment," "progress," "science," and "culture" were honored above all else by my parents, it is obvious that my mother got great satisfaction from teaching at the school. But there was a considerable gap between principles and practice, since teaching young children turned out to be a job requiring stamina and patience. Finally, my mother, having worn out her voice, gave up teaching. But she did remain the sponsor of the school, in which role she confined herself to general supervision, giving breakfast and lunch to the teacher when she came, monitoring exams, and awarding red calico shirts to the graduates. She herself was awarded a gold medal for doing twenty-five years' work of this kind.

Another of my mother's activities was caring for the ill. Mother knew something about medicine, as did my father, and would consult medical books as the occasion demanded.

Treatment was confined to such elementary remedies as quinine, castor oil, iodine, and mild sedatives. Yet my mother had a rather extensive "pharmacy," including poisonous substances entrusted to her by the district physician.

8

After a few years a daughter, Maria, was born to my parents. She lived only two years, dying from encephalitis when she was cutting her teeth. A second daughter, Lyubov, lived only nine months. She, too, died of complications from teething.

While Sontsovka was a pretty place in the spring and summer, it was melancholy in the autumn, when the fields were black after having been plowed to make ready for sowing winter wheat. Then came the *rasputitsa* (the season of the bad roads), when the black earth roads were so deep in mud you could negotiate them only on horseback or in a two-wheeled cart, or sometimes only on foot; and when you had to wear high boots even for walking around the estate.

During December and January, Sontsovka was buried deep in snow. When it melted, there was another *rasputitsa*. It was not until late March and April that spring again burst into bloom.

9

My mother loved music, and my father respected it. No doubt he, too, loved it, but on a philosophical level, as a manifestation of culture, as a flight of the human spirit. On one occasion in my boyhood when I was playing the piano, my father paused near me, listened, and said, "Noble sounds." That was the key to his attitude toward music.

My mother's attitude toward it was much more practical. She played the piano rather well, and her rustic leisure enabled her to devote as much time to it as she wished. It can hardly be said that she had musical talents. Technique was difficult for her to master, and her finger pads did not extend beyond her nails. She was too timid to play for an audience. But she had three musical virtues: persistence, love, and taste.

Mother strove for the best possible execution of the pieces she was learning; she worked at it lovingly; and she was interested only in serious music, a fact which played a very important role in developing my taste in music.

From the day I was born I heard Beethoven and Chopin; and I recall that at twelve I was genuinely scornful of light music. While she was pregnant with me, my mother played the piano as much as six hours a day. The future homunculus was formed to the accompaniment of music.

I was born in 1891. Borodin had died four years earlier, Liszt five years earlier, Wagner eight, and Moussorgsky ten. There were two and a half years of life remaining to Tchaikovsky. He had completed his *Fifth Symphony* but had not yet begun the *Sixth*.[4]

Alexander III reigned in Russia. Lenin was twenty-one, and Stalin was eleven.

I was born on Wednesday, April 11 (Old Style) at five in the afternoon. It was the one hundredth day of the year.[5]

Because of the dangerous complications from teeth-cutting in the cases of my sisters, Mother's friend Olya Philimonova persuaded her not to nurse me herself but engage a wet nurse. In her opinion, the threat would be lessened if I got my milk from someone else. My wet nurse was a healthy peasant girl with an illegitimate child. She had enough milk for two.

I had no trouble when it came time to cut my teeth. But I sometimes wonder whether a certain sternness in my character cannot be traced to the milk I took from that peasant girl.

At six weeks I almost died of dysentery, and was weaned on Nestlé pabulum. Thus my parents had nearly lost their third child in succession. Nonetheless, my mother made ready for her usual two-month sojourn in Petersburg, leaving me with my father and grandmother, because the winters in Sontsovka were dull and monotonous.

I was a disagreeable baby. I would hit my mother in the face when her pince-nez bothered me, and piercingly shout, *"Makaka!"*—meaning *moloka* (milk).

Until I was three I was kept in a little dress—a reminder of my dead sisters. Once when my parents took me to church and it was crowded, my mother quietly nudged me up toward the altar so I couldn't be jostled. The priest frowned angrily since girls weren't allowed near the altar. My mother whispered, "A boy, a boy . . ." And Father Andrei nodded indulgently.

My earliest memory dates from that period; that is, when I was three. I was tumbling about on my father's bed as the family looked on. Then the doorbell rang, signaling the arrival of guests. Everyone hurried to greet them. I went on tumbling about, fell off the bed, and hit my head against an iron trunk. I let out a terrible yell, and everyone came running back.

It was a hard blow. I had a knob on my head throughout my youth, and it didn't go completely away until my thirties. I recall that when I was conducting in Paris as a young man, the painter Larinov touched the knob with his finger and said, "Perhaps all your talent lies there!"

A trip to Sevastopol was my first venture away from Sontsovka. It took place in October 1894, when I was three and a half. By then many new railroad lines were crisscrossing the south of Russia, and the station nearest to Sontsovka (Grishino, which after the Revolution was renamed Krasnoarmeiskoye) was only twenty-five kilometers away.

In Sevastopol my parents were met by their old friends, the Lyashchenkos. Then, after hiring two carriages, we all went to Yalta. We stayed in a hotel at the Baidarskiye Gates. While Lyashchenko was eating lunch, I sat next to him. I spit on his bald head and then very seriously spread the saliva around with my finger. When my father noticed my actions, he was filled with consternation. But Lyashchenko said good-humoredly, "Don't bother him. He's very lovable."

We made the last leg of our return journey to Sontsovka in a phaeton drawn by four horses through the night. It was pitch-dark, and our way was lighted by a man on horseback carrying a torch giving off a red flame that was rather terrifying.

My second trip was one we made the following summer to visit the Rayevskys (my Aunt Katya's family) in Kaluga Province. It was time to take my grandmother back there (she stayed first with one daughter, then another), and my mother took me along at the same time. In the manor house I was pleasantly astonished to find a ballroom. It had a parquet floor, polished and slippery (there were no such floors at Sontsovka). I dashed into the room with a shout of joy, and in the middle I sprawled at full length. From then on I made my way gingerly around the dangerous room, hanging onto chairs.

10

I began to show an aptitude for music quite early, probably at about age four. I had heard music in our home since infancy. When I was put to bed at night, I never wanted to sleep. I would lie there and listen as the sound of a Beethoven sonata came from somewhere far off, several rooms away. More than anything else, my mother played the sonatas of Volume I.

Next came Chopin's preludes, mazurkas, and waltzes. Sometimes there was a piece by Liszt—something not too difficult. Her favorite Russian composers were Tchaikovsky and Rubinstein. Anton Rubinstein was at the height of his fame, and my mother was convinced that he was a greater phenomenon than Tchaikovsky. A portrait of Rubinstein hung over the grand piano.

My mother would begin her piano practice with Hanon's exercises and Czerny's études. At this point I would try to find room for myself at the keyboard. Since she was using the middle register for her exercises, Mother would sometimes let me use the two upper octaves, on which I would tap out my childish experiments. This might seem a rather barbarous ensemble at first glance. But her thinking proved to be correct: I was soon sitting down at the piano by myself, trying to pick out a tune.

Mother had a pedagogic talent. Unobtrusively, she tried to guide me and explain how to use the instrument. I was curious about what she played, and critical. Sometimes I would say, "I like that tune. I want it to be my own."

From time to time there would be an argument between me and my grandmother as to what piece Mother was playing. Usually I was right.

As a result of listening to music and improvising at the keyboard, I began to pick out my own tunes.

At this stage my creativity developed, rather piquantly, along two different lines. On the one hand, I would work out little motifs that I was as yet unable to jot down. On the other hand, while sitting at the piano I would jot down notes that meant nothing. I drew them as ornaments, the way children draw people and trains, simply because I had always seen music on the piano.

One day, as my mother told it, "Sergushechka came to his mother with a sheet of paper covered with notes and declared, 'I have composed Liszt's *Rhapsody.*'"

She had to explain that one couldn't compose a Liszt rhapsody because it was a piece of music that Liszt himself had composed. Also, one could not write music on nine lines without bars, because music was, in fact, written on five lines with bars. All of this prompted Mother to give me a more systematic explanation of the principles of musical notation.

Meantime, I had put together a tune that took on a completely acceptable form. I played it several times, and Mother decided to write it down. No doubt she had some difficulty doing it, since she was new at such an assignment.

It is hard to imagine a more absurd title than the one I gave this composition: *Indian Galop*. As it happened, there was a famine in India in those days, and the adults read about it in the newspapers and discussed it while I listened. The lack of a B-flat should not be attributed to a sympathy for the Lydian mode.* Rather, the inexperienced composer had not yet decided to touch the black keys. But my mother explained that it would be better with a black key, and without further argument she put in a B-flat.[6]

All of this happened in the summer of 1896, when I was five years and a few months old. The process of writing down music made an impression on me, and I soon learned how to do it, more or less.

My ideas did not always accommodate themselves to the bars, and the rhythmic figures gave me trouble, but the pieces got written somehow, and they could be read.

In this way I wrote three pieces in the spring and summer of 1897: a *Waltz,* a *March,* and a *Rondo.*[7] We didn't have any music paper in the house, so a clerk named Vanka lined some regular paper for me. All three pieces were in C major, and in style were close to *Indian Galop.* The fourth piece, a *March* in B minor, was a bit more complex.[8]

Then Catherine Lyashchenko—the wife of that Lyashchenko on whose bald head I had spat—came to Sontsovka. She played the piano well, and even worked with my mother a little. They played four-hand arrangements and I liked the idea very much. Each was playing something different, yet it didn't come out at all badly!

"*Mamochka,* I'm going to write a march for four hands."

"That's hard to do, Sergushechka. You can't pick out a tune for one person and for another at the same time."

Nonetheless, I sat down to compose, and the march came out well. It was a pleasure to play it together with another person at the keyboard, and to hear how things composed separately sounded when played together.

In any case, this was my first partitura (orchestral score).[9] The time was February 1898; my age was six years and ten months.

Aunt Tanya, my mother's younger sister, enraptured by her young nephew's accomplishments, took all these scribblings to Petersburg and turned them over to a skillful copyist. When they had been copied neatly and prettily, the pieces were bound in an album upon which was inscribed in gilt letters: "Compositions of Serezhenka Prokofiev."

This album contained everything done during the first eighteen months of my creative career, representing three stages of development: music of mine written down by someone else; music written in the hand of the composer; and music for four hands—that is, the kind that could not be picked out at the piano but had to be composed in one's head.

The album still exists.[10] The copyist discarded the originals as useless.

* A span of eight notes, from F to F, in which the B is not flatted as it would be in the modern major scale. (Editor's note.)

II

As a child I would sit for long periods jotting down music and drawing people. When my parents noticed that I was "writing with my nose," they decided to take me to an eye doctor.

This accounted for my trip to see the famous oculist Girshman, in Kharkov. My father had gone to sell wool in Kharkov, and one of my aunts was returning my grandmother to the Rayevskys in Pokrovskoye. They took me along and turned me over to my father at the railroad station in Kharkov.

Oculist Girshman found nothing wrong. He advised, "Make sure that when he writes, the light always comes from the left." Since then I have always made sure to do this, and I am so accustomed to having the light over my left shoulder that I cannot write otherwise.

12

My parents laid great stress on my general education. One of the points in their program was an early familiarity with foreign languages. At seven I already understood a bit of French. What was needed now was a genuine Frenchwoman with a good pronunciation. In the last analysis, it would not cost very much, since, given the abundance of food at Sontsovka, she could be kept for very little, and with room and board a salary of fifteen rubles a month was considered sufficient.

But my mother's regular winter visit to Petersburg did not yield a satisfactory candidate. The governesses were either "repulsive," as she put it, or defective in the matter of pronunciation. Mother knew French well enough to judge these things. Finally, it developed that in Warsaw there was a special agency connected directly with Paris and that recruited "fresh material" with a pronunciation guaranteed 100 per cent. Without giving it a second thought, my mother boarded a train for Petersburg, and from there went to Warsaw. This involved an extra 1,000 kilometers of travel, but her son's education was worth more than that.

And as a matter of fact, in Warsaw she was offered a young Frenchwoman named Louise Roblin, just arrived from Paris. Her father had died of wounds incurred in the defense of Paris in 1871, but the family had been left with decent means. Later their fortunes took a turn for the worse: they lost their money, and at seventeen Louise had to go off to the "land of the white bears" to earn a living.

Louise was counting on going to Petersburg and did not even want to consider such a remote place as Sontsovka. In order to persuade her, my mother offered her two inducements: she would be taught to play the piano; and in the summer she could go horseback riding, perhaps even gallop across the steppe on a stallion. In all likelihood my mother's personality also made an impression, since she was an intelligent woman who knew how to charm people. So Louise agreed to come to Sontsovka.

In those days there were no direct railroad connections between Warsaw and Sontsovka. Mother and Louise traveled for three days, with five or six changes of train, then a sleigh for another two hours.

Finally, one January evening in 1899, the whole family plus the new *mademoiselle* gathered in the living room at Sontsovka for tea. I was sitting next to Louise. Astounded at the idea that there could be a person who didn't understand a single word of Russian, I was teaching her:

"Eléphant—slon. Lion—lev."

And Louise, still bewildered by the unfamiliar surroundings, would repeat: *"Slon, lev . . ."*

At that point she was offered some caviar. She put it in her mouth with pleasure, but then made a terrible face, not knowing whether to spit it out or eat it anyway. She had thought it was some kind of preserve, and it had turned out to be a salty abomination.

However, Louise acclimated rather quickly. I was forbidden to teach her Russian. Instead, I was made to read *Les Malheurs de Sophie* aloud. I had trouble reading, and didn't quite understand whether it was a lesson or for pleasure.

My mother spoke fluently with Louise. Father knew French theoretically, and even had French books on gardening in his library, but his pronunciation was ghastly. Nonetheless, he sometimes made jokes. In the evening, when everyone was going to bed and the lamps had to be put out everywhere in the house, he would say, *"Agacez* les lampes."* And when a lamp was smoking, he would say, *"Une lampe captive."*†

Everybody would laugh but Louise.

Before long, in imitation of *Les Malheurs de Sophie*, I began writing *The Adventures of Mademoiselle*, setting it down in large, childish letters on lined paper. I wrote about caviar mistaken for preserves, a galosh lost in the deep mud of Sontsovka, and an unsuccessful attempt to cross a stream on a plank. There was also another, more curious episode that I failed to understand because I was too young.

One morning three priests came to call on us. Louise saw their fur coats and fur caps when she came out to the entrance hallway. She was told they were three young officers who would stay for breakfast. She went to her room, powdered her nose, and came to the table. There she found three fat village priests with big beards, one of whom had his hair in braids. Her look of amazement

---

* A pun on the Russian *gasit*. (Translator's note.)

† A pun on the Russian *koptit*, meaning "to smoke." (Translator's note.)

was greeted with a hearty laugh. Everybody found it funny that the mademoiselle had been deceived.

I didn't quite understand what was going on. But when breakfast was over and the adults had gone into the living room, I came back to the dining room and drank the wine left in all the glasses. For this I got punished.

But I was not often punished. Only when I didn't want to do my French lessons and tormented my mother, who invariably supervised the lessons. Then she would shout, "Matrena, bring the lash!"

13

My childhood companions, I recall, were Serezha, Stenya, Sasha, Kolya, Marfusha, and Egorka. The first four were the children of Elena Vlasova, our housekeeper. Stenya was a capricious little girl, always neat in her appearance, about six months younger than I. Her brother Serezha, my namesake, had a big head, was a year and a half younger than I. Sasha and Kolya were small fry who didn't count at first but later came into their own.

They all called me *barchuk* ("young master") and addressed me with the formal *vy*. I called them by their first names and used the familiar *ty*.

They had strict orders to behave properly toward me, the *barchuk*, and not do "anything stupid."

Elena's sister, Marfusha, was my mother's maid. She was a clever girl, interested in everything, and was my only more or less serious opponent at chess. Egorka Shumeiko, two years older than I, was the brother of Vanka the clerk (the one who had lined the music paper for me) and the son of the chief overseer. The latter had a revolver; and when my father went off somewhere, it was he who came to sleep in the pantry so that there would be a man in the house.

One of my childhood passions was the *Granat Encyclopedia*. I would climb up on my father's desk and, from the shelf above it, take down one of the eight volumes of the encyclopedia.

The flags of all nations, reproduced in color, caught my young imagination. I nagged my mother until she sewed some flags for me: the Russian, French, and Italian. The most interesting flag was, of course, that of the United States, with its stars; but it was a difficult one to sew. One day I slipped into the room where my mother and aunt were sewing something. Mother promptly said, "Go away. You mustn't come in here."

"Why not?"

"Because the window is open," she said, quickly opening the window. Since she had first said the window was open, and then opened it, I felt that an injustice was somehow being practiced on me. But she just took me by the shoulder and propelled me into the next room.

The next day I learned that my mother and aunt were sewing an American flag for me, keeping the *Granat Encyclopedia* open beside the sewing machine as a guide. On the following morning it was given to me as a birthday present. I triumphantly flew it from the highest corner of the fence. By evening, it had been stolen by the village boys.

Another interesting flag was that of Morocco—all red without any stripes or other decorations. It was a very easy one to make. Thus many years before the Revolution, Sontsovka had its first red flag—the fruit of a little boy's fantasy.

14

My mother was very attentive to my musical development, and very cautious. Her main objective was to sustain her son's interest in music and not (God forbid!) alienate him with drudgery. Consequently, she spent the least possible time on my exercises and the greatest possible time familiarizing me with the literature, an excellent approach, and one that all mamas should remember.

At first (i.e., when I was about seven) she would have me practice twenty minutes a day, making sure I did not exceed that time limit. Later, when I was nine, the practice period was gradually increased to one hour.

For my practicing, she bought the Strobel *School Library,* in which the pieces were arranged by degree of difficulty. I read music easily, and when I had played a piece several times, it usually went smoothly.

Mother feared drudgery above all else, and she would shift me to a second piece, and then a third. Also, in order to build up my repertory, she subscribed to both the von Arc *School Library* and the Czerny. In this way I went through a tremendous amount of music.

Before giving the pieces to me, Mother would play through all of them herself; and if any struck her as dull she would discard them. Those she approved would be given to me to play, and then we would discuss them: I would tell her what I liked, and what I didn't like, and why. In this way I early developed independence of judgment; while the ability to read music well, and my familiarity with a lot of music, helped me to judge pieces easily.

But this coin had another side: I didn't learn any piece thoroughly, and tended to play carelessly. And I was sloppy in another way: in positioning my fingers on the keys. My thoughts would run ahead, and my fingers would follow somehow or other.

This lack of polish in details and impurity of technique remained my *bête noire* all the time I was at the conservatory. It was a fault I began gradually to overcome only after I was twenty.

On the other hand, at age ten I had my own viewpoint on musical compositions and could defend it. This early musical maturity was a guarantee that I could cope with my faults when they became obvious.

Because of the importance of music in our home, my parents decided to buy a new grand piano. And so, after one of my mother's winter trips to the capital, a Schroeder piano arrived at Sontsovka. It had cost seven hundred rubles and had been brought from the Grishina Station with the greatest care, the horses having covered the entire distance of twenty-five kilometers at a walk. This piano was much better than our old one, with a fuller and richer sound, although the tone was a bit muffled since it had not been played.

"The Prokofievs have gone completely mad," the neighbors said. "Why do they need another grand piano?"

But the new piano was a source of tremendous pleasure to my mother. As for the old one, she sold it to the district doctor for two hundred rubles. The appearance of the Schroeder was soon followed by that of the piano tuner—a rare phenomenon in our backwoods area. He had such a long beard that if you came up behind him while he was tuning the piano, you could see it hanging down below his hands.

Meantime, the new century had begun, and in January 1900 my parents made ready to go to Moscow for a few weeks. This time they had decided to take me with them.

This trip marked a new stage in my musical life. During the preceding period, whose beginning was marked by the bound album containing the "Compositions of Serezhenka Prokofiev," I had composed two waltzes for two hands (one of which had an introductory section in 4/4 time) and three pieces for four hands: two marches and one piece with no title.

My fond aunts had already become accustomed to their nephew's creative outburst, and they did not have these pieces copied in a beautiful album, with the result that the original manuscripts were destined to survive.

Thus the first of my manuscripts that have been preserved dated from the time I was seven. It begins with a polka in twelve measures. Then the polka is dropped and is followed by the above-mentioned waltz for two hands. On the verso there is a march for four hands.

The paper on which this music was written was yellow, or perhaps it turned yellow with time. In any case, it is miserable paper of the kind that can't take ink. The writing, sometimes in ink and again in pencil, is sloppy, with blots; and there are numerous mistakes in meter. Thus in the polka the rhythm didn't work out: in the left hand there are five eighth notes in one measure, as against four in the right.

Waltz No. 2, with an introduction in 4/4 time, was written in the summer of 1899, when I was eight. Here again, the paper was of poor quality, and the inked notes spread. On the top "Waltz" is written in my own hand; on the bottom (in French) *"Valse"* in Louise's hand.[11] The untitled piece for four hands[12] was written in November 1899, and consists of five related episodes. It marks a considerable step forward relative to the others.

At age eleven I decided to draw up a catalogue of my compositions, jotting down the first bars of each and indicating the year when it was composed.[13]

This childish whim has proved very useful now for orientation. But the manuscript pages also include unfinished fragments that did not get into the catalogue. Apparently, from the exalted viewpoint of an eleven-year-old, I did not
consider them worthy of attention.

15

In Moscow I was taken to the opera. *Faust* was being performed. When we
were seated in our box at the Solodovnikov Theater (after the Revolution it became a branch of the Bolshoi), my mother gave me some preliminary explanations.

"You see, once there was a man named Faust, a scholar. He was already
old, and was always reading books. Then one day the Devil came to him and
said, 'If you sell me your soul, I'll make you young.' Well, Faust sold him his
soul, the Devil made him young, and then they began to have fun . . ."

We had come to the opera house long before curtain time, and I was getting bored with waiting. I had no clear idea of what kind of place they had
brought me to, or why, and I was skeptical about what was in store for me. But
suddenly, an interesting prospect loomed ahead: "The Devil would show up,
and they would begin to have fun."

The orchestra struck up the overture, and the curtain rose. Mother had
been right. There was Faust with his beard, among all kinds of books. He
would read from a dusty old tome, and sing something; then read again, and
sing again. When would the Devil show up? It all went so slowly. At last! But
why was he in a red costume? Why was he wearing a sword and looking so elegant? For some reason I had anticipated that the Devil would be black like a
Negro, that he would be half naked and perhaps have hooves. Later, when "they
began to have fun," I recognized the waltz and the march I had heard my
mother play at Sontsovka.

Mother had chosen *Faust* because she wanted me to hear some music I
knew. I didn't understand much of what they were up to when they were "having fun." But the duel with swords and the death of Valentine impressed me.
Also, I must have taken in a good deal more, either consciously or subconsciously, because when we got back to the hotel I kept asking my mother, "Did
you notice such-and-such?"

"No, I didn't."

"Well, I did."

Or, "Did you pay attention to such-and-such?"

"No, I didn't."

"Well, I did."

It wasn't entirely clear to me why a white spotlight sometimes shone on
Marguerite, whereas a rich red light was used on Mephisto, especially when he

was singing for a long time. But perhaps I didn't know all there was to know about devils, and it was quite proper for him to be bathed in red light . . .

The second opera I saw was *Prince Igor*. It impressed me less, although I was very sorry for Igor when he fled to Yaroslavna in the last act.

In Moscow we were constantly in the company of my Uncle Peter and his nieces—those same Smirnov girls in whose home my mother had met my father. But since those days these *jeunes filles de famille* had married, become Burovs, Sezhenskys, and Faleyevs, had children, and become widows or divorcees. Some of their children had been married and produced offspring, making me a great-uncle. Others were my own age. We played host to all these families and were entertained by them in turn.

January 26 was my mother's name day. All the relatives conferred as to how to celebrate the occasion. They finally decided to get seats in two boxes at the Bolshoi Theater, where Tchaikovsky's *Sleeping Beauty* was being performed. To the mind of a child, this was a great occasion: some fifteen familiar people, including quite a few children, were gathered together in two adjoining boxes. Several boxes of candy made their appearance, and you could take as much as you wanted from them. Then baskets of tangerines and other fruits were opened. All of this no doubt made a greater impression on me than the ballet itself.

But when they—that is, some of the cast in the *Sleeping Beauty*—were moving along in a boat while the stage set moved toward them, your gaze, after having been glued to the spectacle for a time, involuntarily shifted. And as you looked around, it seemed that the theater was also moving, until finally you couldn't tell whether it was the stage, or the theater, or your own head that was spinning.

16

I came back to Sontsovka with a rich store of impressions. The fantasies they produced followed two directions.

I began to stage plays. The plots were wretched and invariably included a duel with swords. In terms of form, this was *commedia dell'arte*: we would think up a skeletal plot, and then the actors would improvise.

The second thing was that I came to my mother and announced, "Mama, I want to write my own opera."

"How can you write an opera?" she objected, without the slightest respect for me. "Why talk about things you can't do?"

"Just wait! You'll see!"

To all appearances, that was the end of it. Just about that time, the family went into mourning. My grandmother had died. As late as the preceding autumn she had been in good health and spirits, and we had taken long walks together. When we got back from Moscow she was beginning to feel sickly, but she recovered.

Late one afternoon she was in her room getting ready for tea, trying to put on a knot of moiré ribbons. "Heavens!" she said. "What a sinner I am! An old lady still thinking about prettying herself up!"

With those words, she lay down with her head on a pillow and died.

The whole household was in a turmoil. "Anna Vasilevna is sick!" Artificial respiration was attempted. They tortured the poor body for almost an hour, then left it in peace.

Father Andrei showed up. With his beard he looked a bit like Leo Tolstoy. "How sad!" he said, and crossed himself.

I took up a position behind the door where I could pray, though I didn't quite know about what. From there I could see the icon, although I myself couldn't be seen. My father came by. When he noticed me, he said, "What are you doing here?" Then he walked past without waiting for a reply.

Later I watched him sit down beside the bed on which Grandmother was laid out, and heard him moan loudly. Then he stopped and went out. I was frightened. The mirrors were covered. The funeral rites were performed. The clinging odor of decomposition spread through the house, and more and more often I was sent out for long walks with Louise. Louise once said, "The weather is dry and sunny. That's good for burying your grandmother." I was astonished that she could talk that way about such things.

Before Grandmother's death I had slept in my parents' room. Afterward I was shifted to her room, which had a connecting door with my parents' bedroom. The low window, which looked to the south, was half filled with a large lilac bush.

17

I came back to the idea of composing my own opera. Or rather, the idea had never left me, but circumstances had interfered. My first opera, *The Giant,* began with this overture:

In writing it, I immediately ran into difficulties. First, the first bar. In what part of the measure does the music begin? I couldn't work it out, and started the first figure one beat later. Then the fourth and fifth bars. They were written as follows:

Meantime I, of course, wanted things the way they are in the first example. My skill at notation lagged behind my ideas, which in *The Giant* made a leap ahead of my earlier pieces.

At the end of the first example—that is, in the ninth measure of the overture—I felt the need for a modulation, for a new key but I hadn't the slightest notion of either one or the other, and couldn't figure out where to go. It was a curious sensation: to feel that you want to express something, but to be unable to find precisely what it is. Even today I cannot imagine what key I wanted. Perhaps it was:

Or perhaps it was something altogether different. In a word, I couldn't figure out how to continue. And although I wrote something, I didn't use it; and when I played the piano score, I usually made a hash of that passage.

The metronome was set at that same time. The overture lasted thirty or forty bars, and then came Act I, Scene 1. There was another four-bar introduction to the first scene:

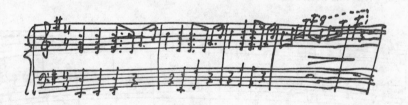

Another problem: what kind of meter? Sixteenths didn't work, and God only knows what part of the measure the chords fell in. The first variant was:

But I felt that something was wrong, and reworked it several times. Finally, I wrote a variant in 2/4 time with grace notes instead of sixteenths, and eliminated the first two chords. This introductory section was followed by an episode in 6/8 time. Stenya, our housekeeper's daughter, is sitting reading a book. The Giant appears. Stenya: "Who is that?" The Giant: "It's me!" The Giant tries to catch her. In the right hand, a tremolo in the upper register; in the left, descending fourths. Stenya is supposed to scream on the high notes, along with the tremolo. Egorka, also a child of the housekeeper, and I enter. This lively bit was invariably successful.

"Stop! Wait! Look! Look!" I stop Egorka as The Giant flees. Stenya falls in a faint. Gallant gentlemen put her on the divan. She sighs. Modestly they leave, accidentally dropping their calling cards. Stenya sings an aria:

Curtain. The unexpected conclusion that it was time to go to bed gave the grown-ups more than one moment of laughter. I had often heard: *Ya zdes sama* ["I'm here alone"]—the influence of the Ukrainian *ya tutochki usovsem sama*

[the same as *odna*—alone]*. All the music was written in the form of a piano score for two hands, without a separate vocal part. I had seen scores like this in my mother's library.

Scene 2. Same set, but the action takes place the following morning. Stenya is drinking tea. To the accompaniment of waltz-like music, she sings, "Shall I have a cup?" She pours it out and burns herself. She rushes to the washbasin to put her hand in the cold water, then comes back and sits down to write invitations to her deliverers. To the accompaniment of music rather like a polka, she sings:

> I've finished. Now I'll go
> To take them to the post office.

(I was bedeviled by the urge to write a libretto in verse.)†

She leaves for the post office. The Giant appears and sings a threatening aria:

My idea was that the aria, with prolonged notes, four fortes, and a clearly defined accompaniment, would produce a terrifying impression. But the level of feeling drops somewhat:

> No? All right,
> [If I can't eat *you*]‡
> I'll eat *your* dinner.

He eats it and leaves. Stenya, suspecting nothing, returns. Guests show up, in the person of Egorka and me. A rather ceremonious scene of gratitude follows:

> STENYA: Good sirs,
> I must thank you.
> WE: What? What do you mean?
> What did we do?

---

*Translator's interpolations. This refers to the words of the aria in the third figure on this page. (Translator's note.)

† In Russian these two lines rhyme. (Editor's note.)

‡ Translator's interpolation. Otherwise bracketed interpolations are Prokofiev's.

And right at this point, as a background for this scene, comes a theme which is probably the best I composed during this entire period:

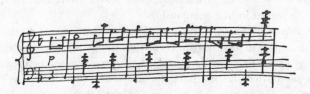

Today I can't remember the words, or whether there were any at all but I can recall the theme exactly. I also remember that I liked the theme but paid no attention to it and that under the influence of the words I began to pride myself on other moments, such as: "Well, shall I shoot?" "No, wait." Yet that theme was incomparably finer and more significant. And from it one could tell that the composition of music was no longer merely an amusement.

Stenya wants to entertain her deliverers, but suddenly notices that everything has been eaten and broken. Surmising that it was The Giant who was responsible, she falls into a second faint. This time the guests are more attentive, and revive her. Whereupon I declare that things cannot go on like this—that we must tell the King about The Giant. Curtain. End of Act I.[14]

18

Early in the summer of 1900, when I was nine, I brought my mother the manuscript and told her, "Mama, you said that I couldn't write an opera. But I've written one!"

At first she wondered when I had managed to do it. We went to the piano and the music came off well—it was even entertaining.

Mother said, "Your Aunt Tanya is coming to see us soon. She is still grieving over Grandma's death. If you dedicate your opera to her, it will make her feel good."

"What does 'dedicate' mean?"

"Why, it means to give something."

"But I don't want to give her my music."

"You'll keep your music. But it will turn out as if you had composed it for Aunt Tanya. After all, last year you gave me your piece for four hands."

"But I didn't compose *The Giant* for Aunt Tanya."

Dedicating *The Giant* to Aunt Tanya might bring her pleasure, and at the same time it wouldn't mean any personal loss for me, so I consented. Since the score was written on pieces of paper that were frightfully dirty, Mother decided to see whether Louise could copy it neatly.

Louise wrote a good hand, and under Mother's guidance she made good progress in music. The question was: Could she suddenly cope with copying music? She sat down to work—first with a piece for four hands, and then with *The Giant*—and she coped. By the time Aunt Tanya arrived, the first act of the opera had been copied in fine penmanship.

But before the manuscript was turned over to Louise, my mother sat down with me at the piano to look it over, correcting things that were patently absurd; e.g., bars in 3/4 time that had three and a half quarter notes, or episodes written on different sheets that did not hang together. The four fortes in The Giant's aria also came in for trouble. My mother thought two were enough, but I took offense, being convinced that in this case the aria would be less impressive. After a heated argument and a few tears, we compromised on three fortes.

Next came the matter of the characters' names. I immediately came up with "Sergeyev" and "Egorov." As for the heroine, "Stenya" did not sound operatic, somehow; and her full name of "Ustinya" was ugly. (Imagine an operatic heroine named Ustinya!) We consulted with my father, who suggested using a completely different name. But the composer was thinking in absolutely concrete terms. "Still, she *is* Stenya," I said. "How can we call her by another name?"

So we kept "Ustinya," reassuring each other that before Pushkin's *Eugene Onegin,* "Tatyana" was regarded as the kind of name that was not really "presentable," whereas afterward it became a favorite; and that even *The Giant* was dedicated to a Tatyana.

My mother had correctly evaluated the situation: Aunt Tatyana was in tears when she arrived. But when she had seen the score of *The Giant,* dedicated to her by her remarkable nephew, and heard it played (with a running commentary on the plot), her tears gave way to a smile.

19

Emboldened by the success of the first act of *The Giant,* I went to work on Act II. Here, new musical elements made their appearance. I had come to know the sweetness of the chromatic scale, and began to use it.

The music for the beginning of the act consisted of chords with rather boring chromatic runs between them.

The first scene took place in the forest. Along with the chromatic introduction and the singing of birds rendered by grace notes, it had three numbers: an *arioso* for Sergeyev, one for The Giant, and a finale. For some reason I had decided that each character had to be given one *aria* and one *arioso.*

Sergeyev enters and sings that he has come to track down The Giant. And indeed, the latter appears:

> I am king
> And sovereign over everything.
> She alone
> Disobeys me.

This is an allusion to Ustinya. Just how she disobeyed him was not clear. I myself felt that something was wrong with this bit but since I couldn't think up anything better, I left it as it was.

After singing his *arioso*—which, incidentally, was less impressive than his aria in the first act—The Giant disappears. Sergeyev then emerges from the forest and sings a brief conclusion:

> What? No!
> Why let her be killed?

The grown-ups found this very romantic.

Scene 2. At the palace. An adjutant reports that Sergeyev has come on important business. The King receives him. Sergeyev tells him about The Giant in the following informal language:

My parents smiled at the awkward phrase "to us from unknown lands." They pointed out that it was not really appropriate to address a king in this way. But for me the lively little motif was intertwined with the text, and I was unwilling to change either of them. Then my mother suggested that Sergeyev sing this bit while onstage alone, waiting for his audience with the King.

When the King has heard Sergeyev's report, he agrees to provide him with a detachment of troops for an expedition against The Giant. Here a contrapuntal device is employed. While the King is singing about the troops, The Giant passes by, hears him, and sings at the same time, "They want to kill me."

Objections were raised to this. I was asked how The Giant could possibly have gotten into the palace. But I could not be persuaded to discard the scene: I was too pleased with my contrapuntal achievement.

We finally settled on a compromise: the King is sitting on a balcony when he receives Sergeyev, and The Giant walks past below the balcony. He walks, in this case, precisely where Sergeyev was walking while awaiting his audience and singing, "What's this? This is a bad place."

I shall not quote the duet, since I don't remember it well. (I do recall that the King's music was in the right hand, and The Giant's in the left.) It can't really be said that the duet came out well, but it came out nonetheless. In conclusion, the King sings an aria threatening to destroy The Giant.

Scene 3. The forest again. Sergeyev and Egorov are leading a detachment of troops. The music is a march. At the time I was convinced that the most important numbers in operas must be marches and waltzes. This conviction derived from *Faust*. I had known the march and waltz from *Faust* before I had seen the opera, so that during the performance the impression they made was especially vivid. In addition to them, I knew the waltz from *Eugene Onegin* very well; and unless I am mistaken, I was familiar with the waltz from *Aïda* or *The Prophet*.* I tried especially hard to write a good march.

The Giant appears, and a battle takes place. The Giant rushes in amid the troops, disperses them, and then dashes off. Sergeyev, together with the remaining troops, beats a rapid retreat, leaving some dead soldiers and the wounded Egorov on the field of battle. Next to the scene of gratitude in Act I, the battle music is perhaps the best of the whole opera. One senses in it a certain fascination with the battle:

Egorov revives and sings an aria of complaint at having been abandoned, wounded and alone. What kind of friend is Sergeyev if he could leave him at such a time? But Sergeyev returns with reinforcements. He lifts Egorov from the ground, and explains to him that only military necessity compelled him to abandon him temporarily. This aria of friendship concludes the second act.

Act III starts with a party at Ustinya's house. When the curtain goes up, she is alone, singing an *arioso*. The doorbell rings—once, twice, three times—and in come Sergeyev, Egorov, and other guests. The main number is a long waltz in F major. When the party is in full swing, the King appears. He is disheveled and has a dagger in his hand. He sings that he can no longer combat The Giant, and he curses everyone. Then he stabs himself. At first everyone is shaken. But then they all sing "Long Live Our Giant!" Final curtain.

This turn of events was rather unexpected. And another kind of objection came from my father, who still remembered the unpleasant things that had happened to him as a student.

There was no need, Father said, for his nine-year-old son to thoughtlessly play at being a revolutionary. Very tactfully, he talked it over with me, asking whether I couldn't give the opera a different ending. For example, why couldn't the King make peace with The Giant? But that was not the kind of thing I had in mind: it struck me as stale. Moreover, what would I do with the King's touching recitative, which I was unwilling to discard? This interference threw me off the track, with the result that the text was never written for the third act.

* Presumably Meyerbeer's *Le Prophète* (libretto by Scribe). (Translator's note.)

I had taken the same great pains with the waltz as with the march. The former began as follows:

I discerned a certain elegance in those sixteenth notes. At the end of the opera, when all the guests are singing "Long Live Our Giant!" the right hand ascends higher and higher until finally, with the concluding tremolo, it reaches F in the five-line, which does not exist on the piano keyboard. In going over the score my mother wanted to delete that F. But then she manifested her liberalism, saying that the limits of the keyboard should not be allowed to stifle the fantasy of a young composer. So the F remained, although of course it could have been dispensed with.

Louise copied *The Giant* out completely. Then Aunt Tanya took the score to Petersburg and had it bound in red with gilt letters:

THE GIANT
An Opera in Three Acts
COMPOSITIONS OF SEREZHENKA PROKOFIEV

20

While I was writing my opera, life at Sontsovka followed its usual course: sowing was succeeded by the harvest, and the harvest by the deep mud of autumn. The farming system was further developed by my father, the income from Sontsovka increased, and with that increase came an improvement in my parents' financial situation.

Every evening the steward would come to the house, bringing the keys to the barns. Overnight, my father kept the keys near his bed, on that same iron trunk I had bumped my head on.

In the morning, at first light, the men would come and knock on the wall outside my father's bedroom, saying, "For the keys." Father would go out and give them the keys, sometimes giving a few instructions—projects that had occurred to him during the night—in addition to those assignments he had issued the evening before when the men came "for orders." Then he would go back to bed. Once in a while I, too, would be awakened by the knocking on the wall. After hearing "For the keys," I would immediately go back to sleep.

At night the house and farm were protected by the watchmen, Gavrila and Mikhaila, who whanged away with a wooden clapper as they made their rounds. On warm, dark evenings I would slip down to the orchard to look for sparrows. Someone had told me that at night they perch in bushes and sleep on branches, so that you could catch them with your bare hands. But for all my peering around and getting pricked by dry branches, I never even so much as saw a sparrow—to say nothing of catching one.

After such a venture, I would seek out Gavrila or Mikhaila, grab him by the sleeve, and make the rounds with him, whanging with the clapper. Gradually, we would step up the pace. After a while my father, having heard the frantic whanging and the sound of scurrying feet under the windows, would come out onto the balcony and say, in a voice full of irritation. "Stop that at once! You'll be going to bed soon, but Gavrila has to keep making his rounds at night. You shouldn't wear him out."

But Father's humane attitude toward the watchmen was subject to change. Late in the evening, for instance, after he had listened in vain (once or twice) for the sound of the clapper, he walked into the orchard and found Gavrila or Mikhaila fast asleep on a bench.

"Son of a bitch!" he would shout, with a great crescendo toward the end.

"*Papochka,* what does 'son of a bitch' mean?" I would ask the next morning.

Whereupon he would frown and ask, "Where did you hear such an expression?"

Yet for all of this, the gentle manner prevailed. When speaking to a peasant, Father usually called him *bratets.**

My mother did not share his views in this manner. "He's not your brother!" she would object.

At this point I must note a difference of character between my father and my mother. Father, who came from a family that was rather well-to-do but not overly cultivated, made every effort to overcome his background. For him, matters of culture and humaneness were basic: they were his guidelines.

My mother had been born into a family without means and had made something of herself thanks to her personal qualities (a gold medal upon graduation from high school; joint work with my father). Therefore, she valued intellect and talent above all else. Placed by fate in permanent contact with peasants, who at that time lacked culture and education, she longed for the company of people who could think—and express their thoughts—on a high plane. As for those whose development was inferior, she quite simply regarded them as inferior. Hence her remark "He's not your brother!"

In late summer came the big moment of the agricultural season: threshing. For several weeks in advance, the blacksmiths, Pimen and Nikifor, had been working on the threshing machine and the ten-horsepower steam engine that

* The general sense of the word (and it is usually so rendered in English) is "old chap, old fellow," etc. But the literal meaning is "little brother." (Translator's note.)

drove it. Then came the triumphal procession to the scene of the threshing. Heading the vanguard was the steam engine, drawn by four pairs of oxen at a slow pace. It was followed by the threshing machine, also drawn by four pairs of oxen, after which came an "elevator" for building the straw into big stacks, a kind of trailer on four wheels and then several *britsky* and carts that housed the "office," the scales, etc.

Marching in front of this whole procession, with hands folded across his chest, was either Pimen or Nikifor (depending upon which one was sober that day), on the lookout for holes and ditches to be avoided so that his "baby" could reach its destination undamaged.

Pimen and Nikifor were the general handymen: it was they I ran to when the wheels had come off my toy carriage and had to be welded on again. One day one of them put up a hook in the living room ceiling for a new kerosene lamp. My father expressed doubts as to how solid the ceiling was: if it didn't hold, and the lamp fell, the whole house would go up in flames. Pimen (or perhaps it was Nikifor) began to argue. Then, to show he was right, he grasped the hook with both hands and pulled himself up toward the ceiling. At that moment the hook broke loose and he fell heavily on the dining room table, amid a cloud of dust from rotted wood. There was nothing more to argue about. A hole was cut in the ceiling. Another hook, twice as big, was bolted to a beam in the attic.

After a gentle, warm September (and sometimes October) the cold would set in, and early in the morning Gavrila would come to the house to start a fire in the furnace. While still half asleep I could hear him shoveling coal into the furnace. Then the fire would start up with a roar. I would snuggle into the blankets up to my ears and go back to sleep with the pleasant thought that when I woke up everything would be snug and warm.

I was given a pair of skates, but for a long time I couldn't decide to go out on the ice. Finally, my parents persuaded me that falling wouldn't be so bad if I wore warm pants and a quilted jacket. I decided to take some falls and count them. When I had counted ninety of them, I started carefully down the frozen stream, moving rather like a spider.

My father built a wooden toboggan slide in the orchard. It was drenched with water, which then froze. The toboggan had high sides; it tipped over, and I bumped my head on the corner of a plank. After that, the toboggan slide was no longer popular.

In January and February it was cold, with heavy snows. Then the cold let up, the snow began to melt and the deep black mud began to dry up. Despite the cold winds from the steppes, the marvelous southern Russian spring burst forth. My father taught me the names of the flowers and stars.

Easter came, and at 11:30 at night I was awakened for Easter services. I was sleepy and chilled to the bone, but I could tell that something very interesting was in store. We went out onto the porch. The night was absolutely black, but the air was already warm.

The church, which stood on a small rise of ground, was illuminated by lampions, and along the fence there were two or three barrels of tar. Stumbling through the dark, we arrived at the church. It was packed with people, and the stale air was full of asphyxiating smells from the peasants. But out here in the country, we were privileged Orthodox, and our places were in the front part of the church, in the choir. The service was brief. Then, at midnight, came the most interesting ceremony: a procession that went around the church three times, bearing gonfalons and singing, past the smokily flaring barrels of tar and the flickering lampions.

One spring was very rainy, with regular cloudbursts during which water from the steppes formed into streams that swelled and carried away bridges. Especially hard hit was the so-called big orchard, located in the bottomlands. In it was the apiary, my father's pet hobby for a time. There were about a hundred hives: pretty little houses of various colors with a top half that was removable so one could get at the inside. Afloat on the water, they were carried through the trees and up against the fence, through which the current was raging. There they capsized, losing their tops, and sank. The frightened watchman saved himself from the water and the bees by climbing a tree.

June 29, Peter's and Paul's Day, was a holy day. Church services were held, a bullock was slaughtered, and a feast was served in the square. My father was invited for breakfast in the official tent where the Sontsovka aristocracy were gathered: the village elder, the village policeman, the priest, the deacon, and the teacher. As for me, I stood at the orchard gate and watched, from far off, the wrestling matches among the village strong men that marked the end of the feast. The prize was the bullock's head. To win it, a wrestler had to throw three others three times.

In this way the annual cycle was completed, and year followed year. I had contrived a tear-off calendar that covered an entire month, and had drawn pictures on the cardboard to which it was fastened. At the top I had drawn a winged chariot with the caption "Time flies." No doubt I had drawn the chariot from some model or other, but my parents were touched. They said, "Yes, that's true. Time flies!"

21

My parents undertook my general education systematically and seriously. My father was the teacher for Russian, arithmetic, geography, and (later) history; my mother for foreign languages and the Old and New Testaments. Louise had gone back to Paris after spending two years at Sontsovka. She was replaced first by one German girl, then by another: four in all, over a short period of time, since I didn't get along with them as I had with Louise. Also, German girl Number 2 had tried to flirt with my father, and he chased her out of the house with a shout. I didn't like German as well as French, so I had a harder time trying to learn it. But I was fond of a few words, such as *Knospe* (bud) or *zwischen* (between).

My music lessons went forward. Mother kept herself in form and took piano lessons when she went to Petersburg. She told me, with evident approval, a story she had heard about Anton Rubinstein. It seems that he would mark in pencil some passage in a student's sheet of music and write under it, "Repeat three hundred times" or "Repeat five hundred times."

But with me, Mother stuck to her own system: to make things interesting, to expand my horizons, to develop skills gradually, and above all not to alienate me with drudgery.

By nine I was playing some Mozart and two of Beethoven's easier sonatas. I would transpose the simplest pieces into another key—or several keys.

Then Mother, by way of developing my independence of judgment, would ask me which sounded best. It most cases it turned out that the piece sounded best in the key in which it had been written.

I would willingly play what I had learned for an audience, but if someone asked me to improvise, there was no stopping me. The fantasies would pour forth endlessly. At such times my mother or father would sidle up to the piano and whisper in my ear, after which I would reluctantly stop playing the endless piece.

In late 1900, at the age of nine and a half, I began work on a new opera, *Desert Islands*.[15] Since *The Giant* I had composed a few trifles, but *Desert Islands* was conceived on a broad scale and gradually swallowed up most of the other material.

I still have the penciled mss. of two little pieces written as a present for my father on his name day in September 1900. One of them has an interesting first bar though why it should be in 12/8 time I simply cannot imagine:

Another fragment in pencil no doubt belongs to that same period.[16] Likewise unfinished was a fragment for piano (four hands) and zither. (We had a zither in the house, although I didn't so much play it as merely strum on it.) In any case, since this was my first piece of chamber music, things got out of hand, and the fragment has more experimentation than music in it.[17]

The story line of *Desert Islands* was utterly childish. A ship is wrecked in a storm, and the characters find themselves on desert islands. The dramatis personae were the same as the *The Giant*, except for the little boy Vasya, who had replaced Egorka. But now they had new names: Sergeyev was called Serezhin, and Vasya was named Vasin. I don't remember what Stenya was called; it may have been Stenina. In short, none of this was very inventive. Also, the story was less dramatic than that of *The Giant.* On the other hand, the music includes attempts at portraying the elements (a storm, etc.) and the scope of the opera was tremendous. I worked on it for eighteen months, composing only the overture and the first act, which had three scenes. But each scene was almost as long as the whole of *The Giant.*

The overture was likewise much longer than the overture to *The Giant.* But it was rather loose in structure, since I was not familiar with the form. It began as follows:

The action of the first scene—the departure of the ship—has something in common with that in the first act of *Prince Igor,* but it is shifted to the seashore and involves no military factors.[18] The beginning is rather solemn:

I don't remember why the scene was a long one; i.e., what its content was. The second scene opens with a violent storm. Here is an excerpt from it:

The first fragment shows the influence, to some extent, of Chopin's *Etude Number 12*. In the second there are certainly some echoes of Beethoven, and his influence is evident in other passages of *Desert Islands*. But as compared to *The Giant*, it represented an advance. There are no more mistakes in meter, and diminished sevenths make their appearance (in the second fragment from the storm music: from B-natural to B-flat). At the same time, there were comic discoveries. For example, I had heard for the first time of double sharps. Not really knowing how they should be used, I put them in at random. This yielded major triads with an F-double sharp:

I completed writing *Desert Islands* before I was eleven. Naturally, I wasn't at it all the time. I would begin, drop it, come back to it, and work on other things at the same time. During this period I was developing. As a result, some parts of it were rather simple and rough; others were more complex and ambitious.

At the end of the second scene there is a passage in C-minor portraying a shower, with reiterated notes. I don't recall the content of the third scene. In general, despite the great step forward I made with *Desert Islands,* I recall *The Giant* more distinctly.

22

Along with the local children, some of the servants also took part in the plays—especially Marfusha, who was more cultivated than the others. In fact, I often had talks—and sometimes quarrels—about music with her. One of the pieces I was especially fond of at that time was Suppé's *Poet and Peasant* overture. We had a four-hand arrangement of it. After playing this arrangement with Mother, I learned how to study it on my own, and considered it a remarkable composition. I shared my impressions with Marfusha, and she agreed.

Before coming to us, Marfusha had been in service as a maid with a neighboring landlord, Bakhirev. She told me that in the evening, when he was all alone, Bakhirev would sit down at the piano and play for a long time. He would play one piece after another, for an hour or two. Then he would go to the cupboard and get out a big box of chocolates. He would eat one after another, as though he would never stop.

After this he would go back to the piano and play on and on, loudly, until late at night. . . . I listened as if spellbound. I very much wanted to hear Bakhirev play, but he had never come to our house. I didn't know—and if I had,

I would not have been able to understand it—that Bakhirev had an illegitimate family. Also, that as soon as he got some money he went off to Kharkov to squander it; that he had often had his agricultural implements sold off at auction to pay his debts: and that the carriage we rode in had been bought through a middle man at one such auction.

Thus even though Bakhirev lived only some eight miles away—a short distance in the southern steppes—we had never struck up an acquaintanceship with him.

But one fine day he did come to Sontsovka—on some business he had with my father. He was a middle-aged man with a gray streak in his hair and pleasant manners. I was full of anxiety: Would he play or not? My parents showed him our new Schroeder, and he sat down at it. But he only struck a few chords and played some scales and arpeggios. My mother, knowing how eager I was and being in the mood to hear some music herself, said to me in his presence, "Is there something you'd like to tell our neighbor?"

Bakhirev turned around to face me. Embarrassed, I whispered brokenly, "They say you play . . . play the piano very well."

He laughed, and began to play a German march called *Die Wachtparade kommt*. His playing was not without a certain brilliance. But just when I had begun to listen closely, he broke off and stood up from the piano. Then he sat down again, held down the practice pedal and began to play loud chords as hard as he could.

My mother, worried about her beloved piano, could not bear it. She went into the next room and said, "I don't understand why he holds down the practice pedal if he wants to play so loudly!"

Bakhirev soon departed, having only whetted my appetite. When he had gone, I asked my mother to write out the music for *Die Wachtparade kommt*.

23

Sontsovka was flourishing and my father, prepared for any eventuality, had saved up his commissions. It was my mother's idea that this money should be used to buy government bonds (the most reliable) and put them in a fireproof box. My parents also bought lottery tickets, but they never won. At night, before locking the doors and going to bed, my father would look under the bed, under the divan, and behind the curtains. And he always slept with a revolver beside him. That part of Russia where we lived was still pretty wild, and such precautions were not superfluous.

At about this time, our maid Marfusha began to show a proclivity for religion. She had saved her salary for a year and, taking this money with her, she went off to visit the holy places—the Monastery of the Caves in Kiev, Novyi Afon (New Athens), and other famous monasteries. Six months later she returned and went back to work for us. She would always wear black. And when my parents were not at home, she would sing church tunes consisting of long, sustained notes with great crescendos and unexpected downward skips—apparently recalling the singing of choirs under the vaults of the monasteries.

That summer my mother took me to visit our relatives the Rayevskys at their estate of Pokrovskoye. Aunt Tanya was there, and she had brought with her *The Giant,* newly bound.

My boy cousins played the piano rather well, and Cousin Katya was studying voice, so we decided to perform *The Giant.* The casting went as follows. Aunt Tanya was The Giant, I was of course Sergeyev, Cousin Katya was Ustinya, and my cousin Shurik (six years older than I) was Egorov.

My older cousin, Andryusha, a high school student of nineteen accompanied us at the piano, representing an orchestra. We spent the whole day learning the music, improvising costumes, and trying them on. I was out of my mind with excitement.

By evening we had learned the first act. My mother said, "They'll have to perform what they've learned. Otherwise, he'll get so nervous he'll fall ill."

We put on our makeup and our costumes, with The Giant in high hunter's boots. The audience took their seats in the big hall (the same one where I had taken a pratfall on the parquet floor). Andryusha struck up the overture and the show began.

My Cousin Katya was sitting there with a book in her hands. Then The Giant stomped his feet loudly and Katya, embarrassed, sang, "Who is it?" But Aunt Tanya immediately set the pace, and the bit where The Giant chases Ustinya made the audience laugh.

Now the rhythm shifted to regular 4/4 time, and Egorov and I entered, with cap pistols and daggers. I had directed the rehearsals and taught everyone how to sing. But up there on the stage, the excitement was too much for me. Without waiting for Egorov to sing his words ("Well, shall I shoot?") I sang them myself.

"That's wrong," whispered Shurik, and took over his own part. I sang, "No, wait"—and everything was back in order.

The rest of this scene went off smoothly. My aunts felt that Cousin Katya had sung Ustinya's aria very, very nicely, and that she should definitely continue her voice lessons.

The second scene didn't go so well because we hadn't learned it thoroughly. But Act I was brought to a successful conclusion. Everyone applauded and was delighted. My uncle (Rayevsky) was very pleased with the production. Laughing and rubbing his nose, as was his habit, he said, "Well, Serezha, when they produce your works at some Imperial theater, don't forget that your first opera production took place at my house."

In saying this, he certainly wasn't thinking seriously of the future—only joking. Twenty years later (my uncle was no longer alive, and there weren't anymore Imperial theaters), when another opera of mine was premiered in Chicago,[19] I remembered his words.

The next day our operatic ardor diminished, so we never learned the other two acts. But every morning, when I came to tea, my uncle would invariably sing (slightly off key), "Well, what do you say? Shall I shoot?"

And every time I would methodically correct him. "No, Uncle Sasha. It's not 'Well, what do you say? Shall I shoot?' It's just 'Well, shall I shoot?'"

24

In September 1901, I composed a rather long untitled piece for piano (two hands) and dedicated it to my father for his name day. The manuscript of this piece, in pencil, has been preserved.[20]

By that time a tradition had been established that for the birthdays and name days of my parents I would write congratulatory letters, even though we were living under the same roof. For the most part, these letters were of negligible content. But they were written in good penmanship, often in gilt ink; and apparently they gave pleasure to their recipients. However, the piece I dedicated to my father established a new tradition: instead of writing a letter, I would compose something for one of my parents and dedicate it to him or her. Subsequently, this tradition was strictly observed for at least five years.

As for my new piece, it was of motley content, being a suite consisting of seven separate episodes, some of them interrelated, others *tirés par les cheveux*. One of them was a tarantella, rather well done. Several months later I wrote a note on the cover: "Except for the tarantella, all of these themes have been used in *Desert Islands*." *Desert Islands* continued to swallow up my slighter pieces.

My parents had an ariston—a mechanical musical instrument in the form of a rather large box that played music when you turned the crank. For the musical pieces, holes were cut in a disc of heavy pasteboard, which was placed in the instrument. When you turned the handle, a bellows within swelled up, and at the same time the disc with the piece on it revolved, passing over a mechanism somewhat like a comb, each tooth of which corresponded to an individual note.

When a tooth went into a hole, a note sounded; when it hit the pasteboard, the note did not sound. We had a lot of these discs. For this purpose I composed a special piece of music. I sketched it out on the disc, and then cut the holes with a knife. It was tedious work, and I didn't cut all the holes on the disc. But what I had done made a distinct sound. True, it didn't last long, since the pasteboard I used was friable and the holes got jagged—especially where the notes were repeated.

Later on—I seem to recall that it was in the autumn, but it may have been earlier—we acquired a better instrument. When my father's brother came to visit us, he brought with him a phonograph and six cylinders—fragile and wrapped in cotton. We put on the first one—and a piece of it immediately broke off. It was a lively march. We glued the piece back on several times, but it didn't work. The phonograph was scarcely audible, and you had to listen to it through rubber earphones. But it wasn't an ariston. Through the hissing and wheezing you could hear a genuine human voice—"like something devilish," as they said in the kitchen. But the cylinders quickly wore out, so they had to be used sparingly. We couldn't listen to them every night.

25

That autumn I almost lost an eye. Gavrila, the watchman, had a dog—disagreeable, but a good watchdog. He was called Ryabichik. Once when my favorite dog, Joujou, was gnawing a bone, Ryabichik came up, showed his teeth, snatched the bone, and began to gnaw on it himself. Someone had told me that dogs don't like it when you blow on their muzzles, and I decided to make things unpleasant for the villain. I puffed up my cheeks and blew. Ryabichik, thinking I wanted to eat his bone, snapped at me, and then went on with his meal. But when he snapped at me, his lower teeth caught me under the eye and his upper teeth bit into my eyebrow. I was lucky his aim wasn't either higher or lower; otherwise, one of his teeth would have hit me in the eye.

Face bloodied, I was taken to my mother, who after her first fright washed out the wound (there was only a scratch on my eyebrow, but a deep cut under my eye), held it together with her fingers, and poured collodion on it. The doctor was sent for. But since he lived twenty-five kilometers away, he didn't come until the next day. "If you washed out the wound well," he said, "everything will be all right. If not, we'll see what happens in a few days."

The wound had been washed out cleanly and gradually began to heal. Some six months later, however, it began to take on a reddish look. When the doctor saw it, he said it was a "cockscomb," or proud flesh.

Actually, I was rather glad to have a cockscomb, but my parents were not pleased with it. Later it gradually subsided, although the scar remained for a long time thereafter and did not entirely disappear until some ten years later. From then on I distrusted dogs. There was good reason to fear them. Most of the local variety were sheepdogs, used to guard the flocks. When someone passed by, they would rush at him, seemingly converted into a ball of fur. The children playing with me knew about my fear of dogs, and they would take advantage of the situation to throw even more fright into me. Eyes bulging with feigned fright, they would tell me, "A dog has run up to the gate. He has a rope around his neck, and another around his tail."

I would feel that something was wrong. A rope around the neck was one thing. But why another around the tail? Nonetheless, I would head for the house. And while my parents were taking afternoon tea, I would stick as close to them as possible.

26

In December 1901 my parents took me to Petersburg, and then to Moscow. They made it a point to take me to the opera, since I demonstrated talents as a composer in that genre. In this way I heard *A Life for the Tsar (Ivan Susanin)*, *Russalka,* The Demon,* Traviata,* and *Carmen.*

The Rayevsky girls, my cousins, whom we visited, gave me all kinds of tid-bits—sardines, sprats, and white salmon—until one fine night I got so sick to my stomach that my temperature jumped to 104. This frightened Mother and Aunt Tanya, with whom we were staying, and henceforth my appetite was kept under control.

Aunt Tanya took me to a photographer, who posed me before a pasteboard piano with a blank sheet of paper on the music rack. When the photographs were ready, they were taken to a colleague of Aunt Tanya's who wrote a very fine hand. On some of them he inscribed: *"The Giant:* an Opera by Serezha Prokofiev." On others: *"Desert Islands:* an Opera." But there were only two or three of the latter, since *Desert Islands* was less popular, and besides the title was too long to fit easily in the little square.

Noticing that my love for chess was blooming, Aunt Tanya took me to see an acquaintance of hers, Solovyev, who played rather well and was already a chess club member. I lost the first game. In the second game, he advanced his Queen and Knight, and I won. Again he advanced his Queen and Knight, and again I won. Enraptured by my own skill, I asked him, "Are you the best player in the club?"

"No, I'm in the fifth category."

"You mean you're the fifth best player in the club?"

"The fifth category, not the fifth best player."

"Well, it's all the same," I said, not surmising that the fifth category comprised the worst players in the club.

Since Solovyev had discovered that I knew the names of the squares by heart, we played the next game *l'aveugle.* I won and went off in triumph, carrying with me a gift—a bound volume of old chess journals. Subsequently, I played the games in those journals over and over. The Chigorin-Tarrash and Steinitz-Lasker matches are still fresh in my memory, although at the time I had only a superficial understanding of their meaning.

In January 1902 we again visited Moscow, and our sojourn there marked a

* *Russalka*—an opera by Dargomyzhsky, based on a work by Pushkin. *The Demon*—an opera by Anton Rubinstein, based on a narrative poem by Lermontov. (Translator's note.)

new stage in my development. I made contact with the world of professional composers.

A family named Pomerantsev, friends of my parents, were living in Moscow then. When my mother complained how inconvenient it was to be staying at a hotel, they invited us to stay with them. My mother did not think it proper to take advantage of their offer. But she did pay them a visit, in the course of which she recounted my musical accomplishments. At this, one of the Pomerantsevs exclaimed, "But you have to bring him to see our Yurochka! Yurochka will be graduating from the Conservatory soon. He is studying the theory of composition. Taneyev likes him very much."

My mother didn't have a very good idea of who Taneyev was, but the opportunity was not one to be missed. So a few days later my compositions were assembled in a cardboard portfolio, Mother put a new sailor collar on me, and I was taken to the Pomerantsevs' to meet Yurochka.

Yury (Yurochka) Nikolayevich Pomerantsev was a pleasant young man a little over twenty years old. He was indeed studying theory of composition in one of the upper classes at the Conservatory, from which he was graduated a year or two later with a silver medal. He never did become a great composer. But he went to Leipzig to study conducting with Nikisch, and later worked at the Bolshoi, conducting ballets.

My mother advised me to play something from *The Giant* for him, but I preferred to play music from *Desert Islands*. Then Pomerantsev sat down at the piano and had me call out the notes and chords he played. I named them accurately, and it turned out that I had absolute pitch. Next he jotted down a few bars and told me to look them over carefully, and then play them from memory. This I did, making a few mistakes. The next thing he had me do, as I recall, was just the opposite: to pick out a few bars on the piano, then go to the desk and write them down.

Pomerantsev had some words of praise for me, and said he would try to arrange for me to audition with Taneyev, the greatest professor in Moscow.

He was as good as his word. And a week later, on a bright winter day, Mother and I, carrying the cardboard portfolio, were walking through the side streets of Moscow on our way to see Taneyev, who lived in a little one-story house—located, as I recall, on Mertvi Pereulok ("Dead Man's Lane"). In the meantime, Mother had found out who Taneyev was, and had been worried how such a famous man would receive us. But Pomerantsev had reassured her, telling her that Taneyev was kindness itself and very attentive.

I have only a vague recollection of this first meeting with Taneyev but I was favorably impressed when he immediately picked up a bar of chocolate from the table and offered it to me.

The door to his study has been opened for us by his nurse, who waddled so much she resembled a boat riding the waves. On the music rack was a sheet of paper on which a theme had been written in huge round notes, one per measure. Apparently it was some *cantus firmus*.

When Taneyev saw the gilt letters on the binding of *The Giant*, he asked, "Why 'Compositions of *Serezhenka* Prokofiev'!"

Mother tried to justify the pet name. "Because he's a little boy. Besides, his aunt, who dotes on him—"

" 'Sergei, Sergei.' Or 'Serzha' at the very most," Taneyev said.

I began to play the overture to *Desert Islands*. It was rather loosely structured, and of course not the best part of the opera. If I had known that I would be allowed to play only something the length of the overture, I would have chosen some other part; e.g., the storm music. But Taneyev went on to *The Giant*, and then started to talk to my mother. He told her that she should take advantage of our sojourn in Moscow and have me take some lessons in the theory of composition—with Pomerantsev perhaps.

He said that although her son was only ten, he must begin to learn harmony as correctly taught; otherwise the youthful composer would acquire bad habits he would find hard to break later on.

27

Such was the beginning of my lessons with Yury Nikolayevich Pomerantsev. He explained the four-voice style and the relationships among the scale degrees, and had me do assignments from Arensky's textbook.

I can't say that I liked it. I wanted to compose operas with marches, storms, and complicated scenes, but now I was being held back. Parallel octaves were ruled out, as was a fifth voice. Instead, I had to write boring stuff of no use to anyone. Sometimes, after he had explained a new rule, Pomerantsev would tell me to write an example of it. I rebelled and showed poor results. Then Pomerantsev would get angry and say, "How stupid you are, Serezha!"

But when the lesson had turned out well, he would take me into the playroom. There his nephew, Volodya Bryansky, a boy of my own age, would be sitting at a table, concentrating on lining up his tin soldiers. He had about five hundred of them, and full-scale battles would be fought on that table. Once he had about a hundred soldiers lined up in a row, close together. Pomerantsev got out his leather purse, took a five-kopeck piece out of it, and said, "Volodya, I'll give you this coin if you let me knock down just one of your soldiers."

But knocking down "just one soldier" would mean that all one hundred of them would go down. Volodya, however, couldn't be bribed. He just shook his head in the negative and went on, very seriously, setting up the next rank.

Before we left Moscow for Sontsovka my mother again visited Taneyev, who told her the lessons I had taken from Pomerantsev were only a small beginning. He said that in order to get me started on composition in a serious way, it would be a good idea to invite a genuine composer—a conservatory graduate—to Sontsovka for the summer. He could work with me for three months, not only giving me harmony lessons but explaining and developing the procedures of composition, making me acquainted with musical literature, and in general broadening my outlook.

"He could also give him piano lessons," put in my mother, to whom the advantages of composing over performing were not entirely clear.

Taneyev agreed. My mother said she was afraid Sontsovka might be too ramshackle a place for such a composer, but Taneyev reassured her. He said he would try to find a sufficiently pleasant person whose tastes were simple enough —one who, moreover, would pay close heed to my interests.

"The main thing is to make careful use of your son's energies," said Sergei Ivanovich (Taneyev). And my mother often recalled that bit of advice.

My mother was completely charmed by Sergei Ivanovich's solicitude, and thanked him. Then we headed home.

Before leaving for Sontsovka we attended a rehearsal of a symphonic concert. It was not open to the public, and there were only a few people in the hall, including Taneyev. I like Tchaikovsky's *Second Symphony,* and we bought a four-hand arrangement of it. As I recall, that was still a novelty at the time.

A serious unpleasantness occurred before we got home. The train had just left the station of Mezhevaya. I was standing in the corridor. Suddenly the car began to lurch violently, and the floor dropped away from under my feet. With a shout, I managed to dash into our compartment, where Mother took me in her arms.

"You'll be all right, Serezha," she said, trying to calm me even though she herself was frightened.

Passengers were thrown from their seats, and suitcases flew into the air. The lurching of the car became slower, and the train stopped.

Three cars had left the rails as a result of a spreading of the tracks. The first part of the train had managed to negotiate the bad section of track, but our car had gone off the rails. The next one had stayed on, but the one after that had been derailed; and so on for three cars. There were no serious injuries. But you could see marks on the crossties ten centimeters from the edge; and the embankment, although not really high, was high enough for a car to capsize.

The passengers were shifted to the front part of the train, and we went on to Grishino. We arrived late but with heaps of impressions. And I had an axle nut I had picked up as a souvenir of the accident—a real accident!

For some time after our return to Sontsovka, my parents discussed whether they should invite a music teacher for the summer. On the one hand, the salary of seventy-five rubles a month seemed inordinate—especially when compared to the fifteen rubles paid to Louise or the German girls. On the other hand, since such an important musician as Taneyev had taken an interest in their son, his advice should be thought over carefully. After pondering the matter, they wrote

Taneyev in the affirmative. Sometime later he replied, saying he could probably arrange for the services of a talented young composer by the name of Golden-weiser, who had been graduated from the Conservatory with high marks in two specialties, piano and theory of composition, for which he had been awarded the gold medal.

My parents were both glad and worried. They were worried because the man who was soon to arrive was so famous and entitled to such deference that they wouldn't know how to cater to his whims. But somewhat later they received still another letter from Taneyev, who was taking exceptionally great interest in this whole matter. The arrangement with Goldenweiser hadn't worked out, but he could be replaced by Glière, also very good, who had himself won a gold medal. The Pomerantsevs also sent an explanation: Goldenweiser was in fact a man of rather difficult temperament, while Glière was simpler and more pleas-ant. True, he was not a professional pianist, but he played rather well; and as a composer he showed even greater promise than Goldenweiser. (Goldenweiser spent part of the summer of 1902 as a guest of Leo Tolstoy at Yasnaya Polyana.)

28

Reinhold Moritsevich Glière came to Sontsovka early in the summer of 1902, when I was eleven and he was twenty-eight. At first I paid no attention to my mother's talk about his impending arrival. But when I saw that Mother and Marfusha were making ready a good room for him, and that the whole business was becoming a reality, I gradually got it into my head that this man was com-ing to work with me and not somebody else, and I began to get a little excited.

My parents knew that Glière had been graduated from the Conservatory with a gold medal, that some of his compositions had been published, and that he had even won a prize. Still, they felt it would not be right if the whole family came out on the porch to greet him. Decorum had to be preserved so they had instructed me to greet him.

The four-horse carriage my parents had sent to the station drew up in front of the porch, and out of it stepped a mustachioed young man. "Serezha?" he inquired.

I nodded and said hello, being mostly interested in the violin case he was carrying. While the luggage was being unloaded by Nikita, who served as both clerk and footman, I showed Glière to his room. All the time I was thinking, "But he's going to work with me on the piano. So why does he have a violin?"

I went back to my parents for further instructions. My mother said, "Let him get his bearings and wash up after his trip. In about ten minutes you can go and invite him to lunch on the terrace."

Glière turned out to be a pleasant person, one who fitted in well and wasn't obtrusive. In addition to the two or three hours of lessons with me every day, he worked hard on his own projects. In the morning he would work on his string quarter, and in the evening he would rewrite what he had composed, or would sit in his room, reading. In a word, he was busy.

My piano lesson came at eleven, after Glière's morning's work. Mother asked permission to sit in so that in the autumn, when he had left, she could continue with his system. She was very interested in my switchover from one piano teacher (herself) to another—much more than in my composition lessons. Her attitude toward Glière's teaching was repectful, critical—and a bit jealous.

To begin with, the tutor chose one of Beethoven's G major sonatas, which I came to like very much. After lunch came my lesson on the theory of composition and, above all, harmony—although Glière was more flexible than Pomerantsev and didn't get so far away from practical composition. Then he acquainted me with musical literature. He would sit at the piano and play Beethoven sonatas, making a gradual beginning at explaining their form. I especially liked two stormy, dramatic finales: from the *First Sonata* and from the "Moonlight." Our relationship was such that I would willingly come to him with all kinds of questions about music and would always receive a thoughtful answer.

In his free time, Glière was glad to play croquet or chess, or even take up a challenge to a duel with dart pistols—which won me over even more. He always came to see our plays, considering them to be something more serious than a game and seeing in them the embryo of future works for the stage by a composer.

On quiet summer evenings Glière would call me to the piano, then take up his violin and we would play Mozart sonatas together. As soon as the first chords were struck, we could hear my father close the door to his study. He would come on tiptoe into the living room and sit down on the divan. And my mother, who was making jam outside ("We must send a jar to Katya"), would tell Marfusha to keep an eye on the saucepan and would sit down on a bench under the window.

On one occasion when Dr. Reberg came to see us, he said he had read somewhere that great composers would sit down at the piano and improvise entire fantasies, and wanted to know if it was true. Glière answered with complete modesty that he would be glad to improvise if anyone were interested. Taking a

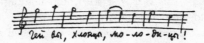

Ukrainian theme, he improvised for quite a long time, first lyrically then stormily, with glissandos across the whole keyboard.

Everyone was enraptured. But he quickly sat me down at the keyboard and said, "Now, Serezha, you improvise too."

I was not reluctant. "But I want to use my own theme," I said.

"All right, but just don't make it too long."

This proclivity toward working with my own materials has stayed with me ever since, and when it came to my own improvisations or compositions, I would bypass the folklore and use my own melodies.

I had the same attitude toward the folk songs they sang at Sontsovka. On Saturday nights and Sundays I often heard the village girls "singing."

But for whatever reason—whether because the Sontsovka region was lacking in good folk songs or because I was annoyed by the "squawking" of the village singers— I never listened closely to those songs and didn't remember a single one. It is possible, or course, that subconsciously I absorbed those songs despite all that. At any rate, some twenty-four years later when I first tried to make my music Russian, the material—my own, but in the Russian mood—came easily and naturally.[21]

29

Since Glière was a good teacher, he tried to avoid any unfavorable reactions on my part to the teaching of harmony. I was eager to compose and could not understand the purpose of those boring assignments. And yet they were necessary, since harmony was providing a foundation for my work. Without it, I wouldn't have known what I was doing, or why, or how.

One evening Glière sat me down at the piano (my mother was present) and began to explain to me what musicians call a "phrase" and a "period."

"Just try this," he said. "Compose four bars of music, but in such a way that instead of ending in the basic key they end in, say, the dominant."

I began to pick out something. I picked it out and wrote it down.

Glière continued, "Now compose another four bars in such a way that they begin roughly like the others but end in the tonic—in a full cadence."

That wasn't hard, since the first four bars were already composed. I wrote it down.

"Now," Glière said, "you must write another four bars in a related key—in the sixth scale degree, for example—but in such a way that they end in the dominant, like the first four bars."

I didn't understand this clearly. I tried, and nothing came out. Glière sat down at the piano and composed for me.

"You see," he explained, "now we have approached the second four bars just as we did the first time, and we can repeat them."

We repeated them and wrote them down.

"And so," he said, "the main part of the piece is finished. All we have to do now is write a trio in another, related key." And he explained a few things about how a trio is written.

I immediately got the feel of it and wrote a trio with pleasure. Qualitatively, it also turned out better.

When the trio was done, Glière said, "And now we must repeat everything from the beginning."

"With no changes?"

"It can be done with no changes, but it's better if you think up some new figuration that's more intricate. Let me show you."

Glière rewrote the first measure, employing diminution and introducing passing tones. "Continue in the same way," he told me. "But it's already late now. You can do it tomorrow."

I was very interested, and so was my mother. The next day I worked hard on the figuration (Glière had even canceled the harmony lesson), and with his help I finished the piece. My parents came into the living room—along with Aunt Tanya, who was visiting us—and I played the new work. The success was complete: the four-bar exposition, the repetition of fragments, and the figuration of the earlier statement—all this made for a clarity that I had lacked.

"What do you call your new piece?" Mother asked.

"What is this form called?"

"Song form," Glière said.

"Then call it a 'Little Song,'" Mother suggested.

I objected. "But it's not a song!"

Mother agreed that her suggestion was perhaps not a good one. We cast about for another label, but we didn't come up with any. At that point our gathering broke up.

The next day I had a harmony lesson. The day after that Glière suggested that I write a few more "little songs" or "ditties," indicating different variants in what he had explained before—chiefly in the cadences. He said that to start I should write several main phrases. I sat down full of enthusiasm, and in a short time I had thrown together five phrases.

Glière was disappointed. "Don't just toss in everything that comes into your head the first minute. Try to do it better."

"I *did* try," I objected. "And that *wasn't* the first thing that came into my head."

Glière began to explain patiently how, and on what basis, one should add the following phrase in each particular case. If, he said, you had to repeat one of the earlier bars, you didn't have to write it out. You just numbered the bars, and you put a number in a blank measure, indicating a repetition of an earlier one. This procedure made the work easier. You marked out four measures, put four numbers in them, and *voilà!* The piece had progressed.

"But you mustn't abuse this device," Glière warned me. "It's better to use some figuration when you repeat something, rather than to leave it unchanged."

Nonetheless, I did abuse it.

By the end of the week I had already composed six pieces, though for some reason the piece with which the whole business had begun was numbered "5."

I didn't come up with any new generic name for these pieces so that the old one ("little songs" or "ditties"), for all its absurdity, was retained.

These six pieces laid the foundation for a long series of piano works written in my childhood and youth. After six years I had written almost seventy of these "little songs." Some of them were marches or "romances,"* but they were all numbered as "ditties." My ear got used to this name, and I no longer noticed how inappropriate it was.

30

When Glière saw that I had learned the song form, he began to guide my development along another line and familiarized me with orchestration, explaining the nature of the instruments and their grouping, range, and use.

I already had a more or less clear notion of some of them, such as the flute, the trumpet, the violin, and the cello. But I had only a foggy notion of others, such as the clarinet, the trombone, and the double bass.

As for the oboe, the bassoon, the French horn, the tuba, the kettledrums, and viola, it was the first time I had heard of them. Glière described their timbres and gave me examples. If, while working with me on the piano in the morning, he noticed in a Beethoven sonata or some other piece a chord, passage, or melody characteristic of some instrument, he would stop and point out that if one were orchestrating the piece "that loud chord should be given to three trombones, that pastoral melody to the oboe, and that cantilena middle voice to the cello."

Of course it was difficult teaching orchestration when one lived a thousand kilometers away from an orchestra. And yet his method was so vividly descriptive that I grasped quite a bit. A corrective through contact with a live orchestra was necessary but I was now well prepared for making that contact.

But there were also some misunderstandings. For example, Glière showed that the main theme of Mendelssohn's G minor *Song Without Words* should be played by two clarinets in parallel thirds. I liked this, but I immediately decided that clarinets do not play except in double thirds. That evening I explained to my mother what a clarinet was like and played endless passages on the piano in thirds, not taking the register into account.

Glière lost his patience and shouted from the next room, "Not so high! Besides, just because it's a clarinet it doesn't mean that you absolutely have to use double thirds!"

Apropos of the horn he explained that it had the softest timbre of the

* A "romance" is a kind of Russian art song roughly equivalent to a lied. (Translator's note.)

brasses, and that it was often given tender melodies pianissimo. To me this meant that the French horn never played anything but tender music, and for a long time I avoided giving it forte passages.

When he saw that I had some knowledge of the instruments and had orchestrated a couple of examples for string quartet, Glière agreed—not without pressure from me—that I should score something from one of my own compositions for a full orchestra. I chose the storm music from *Desert Islands*. It was a bit complex for my first attempt. It would have been better to choose something less intricate but I insisted on the storm music. Glière did not object and with his help I finished the score. As it happened, I decided not to use any French horns in it, although because of their timbre, horns were just what I needed for the very first chord.

"Now I'm going to write a symphony," I announced to Glière.

"It's still too soon for that. You'd do better to score one of your little songs for orchestra."

"But why orchestrate a little song written for the piano when I can compose something especially for an orchestra?"

It was a well-grounded argument. Glière said, "Well, write, say, an andante for orchestra. Or a rondo."

"I want to write a symphony."

After three days of arguing, Glière yielded. I plunged into composing, and a few hours later I brought him the main theme, written in the form of an orchestral score.

The nineteen-bar (!) theme with which the symphony began was in general not bad, and even the orchestration should have yielded a decent sound, despite the awkwardness of the accompaniment. The digression into the superdominant had undoubtedly been written under Glière's influence, and he approved it.

I had no idea of how to continue the symphony, and went to Glière for advice. He explained that at first I should write a few more bars to consolidate the main theme, and then write a "bridge passage," i.e., one modulating through several tonalities to the secondary theme, which would be more broad and flowing. True, it would be in a related key—in D major. But the problem was that I first had to digress into several nearby areas before coming to rest in the key of the subordinate theme.

We composed the bridge passage together. While we were working on it, Glière explained what a "modulation plan" was. The music turned out to be mediocre, but we did arrive at D major. I composed the subordinate theme on my own, and it came out even worse. Then Glière explained why we needed a closing theme, and I added one. But the first theme proved to be the best.

While working on the first movement, I began to write a second, slow movement. When I had it in good shape, Glière exploded, because it was in the wrong key. It was in F major, which, was in no way related to the basic key of the symphony, G major. Should I transpose it? But into what key? From the experience I had acquired with my mother I knew that the original key is usually the best. We pondered the matter, tried this and that, and finally left it as was. But Glière was unhappy that a mistake had been made in the symphony.

The first theme of the slow movement was in no way distinguished but the second theme, somewhat in the manner of Beethoven, was more interesting:

By way of reconciling the keys of the first and second movements, Glière advised writing the third movement, a scherzo, in A minor, which was related to both. The Scherzo began as follows:

The fourth movement, the Finale, was again in G major, in 2/4 time, with a waltz-like third theme in triple meter. I have no recollection of this music.

Glière explained that to write out the full orchestral score forthwith would be a slow and awkward business, since except for the beginning of the first movement I had written the whole thing in the form of a preliminary sketch. And of course I hadn't the slightest notion of how to write a development.

Glière showed me examples from Beethoven sonatas, and helped me to develop the material of the first movement. The Finale—which was written in five-part rondo form at his suggestion—also required a short development section. He began to demonstrate it, and got so carried away that he wrote it himself.

By the end of the summer the music for the symphony had been composed, the first movement orchestrated, and the second and third movements half orchestrated. Before Glière left he instructed me to finish the orchestration and make a four-hand arrangment of it.

31

Glière's stay at Sontsovka had a tremendous influence on my musical development. It was not merely that I had acquired a grasp of harmony and learned something about such new spheres of composition as form and instrumentation. Of prime importance was the fact that I had passed from the hands of my mother—who, although a natural-born teacher, was an amateur and not a composer—into the hands of a professional who had a totally different attitude toward music and, without even being aware of it himself, opened up new horizons for me. Also important was the fact that Glière was gentle and always took an interest in my work, thanks to which I unconsciously felt its importance and distinguished it from other pastimes such as croquet, building summer houses, or fighting tin-soldier wars with other children.

But Glière also implanted other, harmful influences that I didn't outgrow until much later, in my maturity. For example, it was a good thing that he taught me the song form and explained the "square" structure: four bars plus four more. This brought order into my musical thinking. But he didn't take into account that this should be learned only to be forgotten later.

The four-bar structure makes for order; but if an entire long piece is built on $4+4+4+4$, that order becomes intolerable, and $4+5$ is like a breath of fresh air. My earlier themes had varied greatly in length. "Well, shall I shoot?" was six bars long; the theme of gratitude from *The Giant* was three; the main theme of the symphony was nineteen; the others were four or eight.

The second harmful influence involved stereotyped modulations that Glière himself was a victim of; e.g., digressions into VI and III. Previously they had never entered my head. But after I had worked with Glière they appeared both in my symphony and in subsequent works. Fortunately, my fondness for them didn't last long.

Finally, the third influence involved sequences, which I likewise had not known about before. One should know about sequences but one should also know enough to be wary of them. In all three cases—four-bar structure, digressions into VI, and sequences—what Glière should have done after explaining them was to warn me that they should be used with caution.

At first glance it would appear that a sequence heightens the emotional effect and gives the motif a new coloration by repeating it on another pitch level. Many composers have been trapped by that. Actually, the effect yielded by sequences is cheaply bought and as something cheap, it should be avoided. I myself used sequences for quite a long time after working with Glière but the day came when I began to hate them.

In any case, these minuses were negligible as compared to the pluses, great leaps ahead I made as a result of working with Glière. I had reason to be grateful to him. As a young boy, of course, I was hardly aware of this. If I felt grateful toward him it was rather because, when he was getting ready to leave, he entrusted me with planning his itinerary to Kiev. (There were no direct connections; three changes of trains were involved; and various routes were possible.)

"And can you take an express train?"

"Yes."

I was delighted, and acquitted myself well.

One of the sports we engaged in at Sontsovka was horseback riding. We used only gentle horses. But one day when out for a ride with my mother (the day he was to leave), Glière took a fall and returned highly embarrassed. But he didn't get hurt, and everyone joked that he had put a period with his head to his stay at Sontsovka. He not only left happy memories but took some away with him. On one occasion some thirty years later he told me, "It was really fine at Sontsovka!"

32

After Glière's departure, life returned to normal, which above all meant more work on academic subjects. Also, Louise had reappeared. She had been living in Paris, but things hadn't gone well in her family. She exchanged letters with my mother and came back to us. My work at the piano was again being supervised by my mother, who tried to continue Glière's way of teaching. She herself no longer played.

Later she said, "I gave up playing when I saw that Serezha had caught up with me."

Probably several factors were involved here: three months of not playing while Glière was staying with us, the new ideas he had introduced and the fact that I could grasp quickly what she had to labor over.

All this made for a new approach to music in our house, and it seemed to my mother that the time for her work on the piano had passed. She did, however, continue to play four-hand arrangements of Haydn and Beethoven symphonies with me. She would play the bass part, having worked on it in advance. I would sight-read, sometimes with pleasure, at other times without. Actually, what with five or six hours of lessons a day, I could scarcely wait for Sunday; and even then I would have to play a symphony. I would rather have played marbles.

Still, I did like the Haydn and Beethoven symphonies and usually played them with pleasure. My mother had chosen Beethoven's *Fifth* and *Seventh* symphonies. Haydn was represented by a volume of six selected symphonies.

My harmony lessons with Glière continued by correspondence. Before leaving he had given me assignments in Arensky's textbook. In the completed assignments I sent to Moscow, I would leave two blank staves under the two I had filled in. Glière would make corrections and send them back. He was conscientious about these exercises, but I was not.

I would select the easiest problems, the ones involving passing tones, and was not very thorough in my work. Glière would correct it, often underlining several measures and reworking the harmony. But I never studied his corrections, so that the whole point of the exercises was lost.

My mother would ask, "Did you look over Reinhold Moritsevich's corrections and try to understand why you made mistakes?"

I would reply, "I *did* look them over!" And so as not to disappoint my parents, I would sit down at the piano and play Glière's variants. But I did it while thinking of something else, not trying to understand the meaning of his corrections. Besides the fact that I didn't see the use of harmony lessons, there was another reason for my neglect: the very system of correspondence lessons was faulty. During the ten days it took for the manuscript to reach Moscow and be sent back, the problem would grow stale and be forgotten, having yielded its place to the succeeding problems I had been working on during that time.

I had a totally different attitude toward my symphony, which I very much wanted to put into final form. But it became clear that I would scarcely be able to complete both the orchestral score and the four-hand arrangement before our trip to Moscow, which was scheduled for November. I asked my mother for advice as to which one I should concentrate on. If I had asked a composer, he would have said that a symphony is a composition for orchestra and hence must first take the form of an orchestral score.

But Mother was used to playing four-hand arrangements of symphonies. An orchestral score? In her eyes that was something incomprehensible. There was no question of its being played by an orchestra, whereas a four-hand arrangement was something real and tangible.

So she said, "Of course, Sergusha, arrange it for four hands." And I willingly agreed, since I had already written several pieces for four hands and knew what I could do. An orchestral score, on the other hand, was terra incognita, and work on it was bound to involve much that was not clear to me.

At first I arranged the score of the first movement, then what I had orchestrated of the Andante and the Scherzo, writing what remained of them for four hands. Then I wrote a four-hand version of the Finale, using the sketches I had made that summer which thus never grew into an orchestral score.

As I had done with *The Giant,* I wrote rather sloppily, using odd pieces of paper, working first on one and then on another. Fortunately, however, Louise was again with us and she copied the music neatly. On the manuscripts I had drawn imps, monkeys, and little men waving their hands. I had put them there for a purpose: they indicated queries, places to be skipped, and corrections that had been made.

It was about that time, as I recall, that I attempted to draw up a catalogue of my works, giving the first few bars of each. That past summer, when Glière was acquainting me with Beethoven's sonatas, he would sometimes check in the back of the volume, where you could find the first few bars of each sonata with its number and the page reference. I liked this, and I decided (not without pride) to do the same with my own compositions.

As for extramusical interests, I had a few hobbies. For one thing I collected stamps. But since the stamps that came on the mail from the Sontsovka post office didn't offer any variety, I collected them "for quantity," soaking off about 250 of them and putting them in envelopes. I also took a great interest in the camera obscura I had tried to make from a box, a magnifying glass, and a piece of ground glass. Nothing came of it, and I was deeply disappointed. So my father, on one of his trips to Bakhmut, got me a real camera obscura. I aimed it at a path in the garden, and a charming image appeared on the ground glass. But for all my efforts to sketch it on the tracing paper I had put over the glass, only rough streaks were the result.

33

We left for Moscow in November 1902. I had completed the four-hand arrangement of the symphony, and Louise had made a fair copy of it. We took Louise along with us, figuring that the expense would not be great, and that she might prove useful, since my French lessons would not be interrupted.

We reached Moscow at four in the afternoon. Having left Louise at the station with the luggage, we, mother and I and Uncle Peter, who had come to meet us—set out in a horse-drawn cab to find lodgings. We went around until eight o'clock, going to eight different hotels in various parts of the city, and finally decided to take two rooms at the Hotel Nice, at the Nikitskiye Gates. Sixty rubles a month was a bit expensive but the rooms were decent, and there was also a place (behind a partition) for Louise. The piano we had rented arrived the next day. Glière showed up that same day.

We played the four-hand arrangement of the symphony, which bore the dedication "To R. M. Gliere." He was sorry that the orchestral score was not ready, but praised the piano score: it was clear and easy to play.

Glière promised to introduce me to the musical circle at Goldenweiser's, where I was expected to appear. All we had to do by way of preparation was run through some of the "ditties" and polish up the symphony. But at the Pomerant-sevs they had told me, "It's a good thing you didn't get Goldenweiser as a teacher! He is much taken up with his own looks, and assumes important airs. He's unpleasant to deal with."

> From me to my father in Sontsovka
> Moscow, November 17 (30), 1902.[22]

Dear Papa:

Last night mama and I went to a concert at the Nobles' Club. We did not have reserved seats, which meant that the sooner you got there, the better seat you'd have. Since the concert was to begin at nine, we left at seven. We got there at seven-thirty, but the best of the unreserved seats were already taken. Chaliapin was singing, so a great many people came. I saw S. I. Taneyev there. He introduced me to Arensky, who wrote the harmony textbook I am using. . . .* When we left the club the weather was terrible: it was snowing (small flakes, but falling thickly) and a strong wind was blowing. . . .

> Kisses from
> Your loving
> Sergei Prokofiev

I had signed "Sergei Prokofiev" because Father had said I should do so as a grown-up. My mother added a note: "Bring your quilt and felt slippers because your bedroom is cold—especially the floor."[23]

In her own letter of that same date, Mother wrote:

At the concert, after thinking it over a bit, I went up to Taneyev and chatted with him. I'll give you the details of the talk when we see you. . . . Right now we are waiting for the teacher [i.e., Glière]† who is coming to give a lesson, and he will tell us when Serezha should be taken to see Taneyev. Meantime that sonata [apparently a mistake: she should have said "symphony"] is becoming a problem; it's time to finish it. I was very

---

* In the letters, unless otherwise specified the elipses indicate deletions made by Prokofiev. (Translator's note.)

† In the letters, as in the diary excerpts quoted later, brackets indicate insertions made by Prokofiev. (Translator's note.)

pleased to see how people introduced our little *shishik** to musicians, saying, "This is Serezha," and how those he was introduced to would ask, "What key is your sonata [compare the above] in?"—meaning they had already heard of him. He was introduced that way to Arensky, Konyus, and other people of less importance.[24]

They asked not only what key the symphony was but also what key the second theme was in. At this point I began to get worried. The second theme was in the right key but if they asked about the second movement, I'd have to acknowledge that it was not in a related key. Earlier, Glière had been cross with me because I had ruined the whole symphony in that way. Now, when grown-ups were talking so seriously with me, would I really have to answer, blushingly, that the second movement was in F major—an unthinkable key for a G major symphony!

In another letter to my father (whom we were expecting in Moscow) two days later, Mother said, "Also bring along the mailing wrappers with Serezha's assignments. His teacher wants to explain his mistakes."

Apparently, Glière had got word of my lax attitude toward the assignments and, conscientious as always, had decided to show me why he had made certain corrections. For that matter, the word "wrapper" sounded suspect. Could it be that I hadn't even opened some of them?

That winter Glière was giving lessons to the widow of the composer Serov, who had died thirty years before. "First an old one and then a young one," my mother said with a laugh, comparing my youth to Mme. Serova's advanced years.

It was said that Mme. Serova was studying orchestration and counterpoint so that she could put in order the mss. her husband had left—manuscripts she was unwilling to entrust to others. But that wasn't true. She herself was a composer. Serov had got her started composing and now she wanted to finish her own opera, *Ilya Muromets*. Glière told us that the old lady was of short stature with goggle-eyes, and that she sang her own compositions in a low tenor.

34

The main event of our stay in Moscow was the visit to Taneyev. This took place on November 20 (December 3), 1902. Glière accompanied me. In my portfolio were the symphony and a bound notebook with seven "little songs." (I had composed the seventh[25] at Sontsovka after Glière's departure.) I had wanted to write a piece in the grand style, but it had come out rather stilted.

Taneyev was his usual affectionate, kindhearted self, though his tone was occasionally bantering. An unwrapped bar of chocolate lay on the table.

* This pet name apparently involves a play on words. The basic meaning of *shishka* is a "bump" or "knob" (compare the childhood accident), but it also has the slang meaning of "big shot." (Translator's note.)

He and I played the four-hand arrangement of the symphony, Taneyev modestly taking the bass part. I was amazed at the liveliness with which he played the accompaniment in the middle section of the Finale, written in the form of a fast waltz.

When Glière drew his attention to the contrapuntal development in that movement, I was embarrassed, since Glière himself had written most of the counterpoint.

When we had played the symphony, Taneyev said, "Bravo! Bravo! But the harmonic treatment is a bit simple. Mostly just . . . heh, heh . . . I, IV, and V progressions."

That little "heh, heh" played a very great role in my musical development. It went in deep, stung me, and put down roots. When I got home I broke into tears and began to rack my brains trying to think up harmonic complexities. But other reactions happened much more quietly and unnoticeably. An eleven-year-old boy had visited a professor; he had remembered some of his comments and paid no heed to the others. Yet the microbe had penetrated the organism and required a long incubation period. Only four years later my harmonic inventions were attracting attention. And when, eight years later, I played one of my most recent compositions[26] for Taneyev, he muttered, "It seems to have a lot of false notes. . . ."

At this, I reminded him of his "heh, heh." He put both hands to his head and exclaimed, not without humor, "So I was the one to nudge you onto such a slippery path!"

After we had played the symphony, Taneyev had me play a couple of the ditties for him, and he looked over the rest. He said it wasn't enough to give only one hour a week to harmony, that it would be better to take some of the time I was using for piano lessons and devote it to harmony. And he advised me to become familiar with classical scores. It would be a good idea, for example, to buy the score of the overture to Weber's *Der Freischütz,* which I could play on the piano under Glière's guidance. ("That is," Mother wrote to my father, "he should play on the piano, works written for various instruments.")

"Go back to Sontsovka next summer," Taneyev said to Glière.

"I don't see how I can do it. I need a certain ambience for composing, and it's not to be found there."

"Why? Does Serezha shout and give you so much trouble that it interferes with your work"

"No, he's very quiet. But I don't have any music library available there."

So nothing was decided as a result of that talk. As he was seeing us to the door, Taneyev told Glière to bring me to him once again before I left Moscow.

A few days later I was taken to the Conservatory to hear an organ concert. The organ was new—a fine one, in the opinion of musicians—and a famous organist was playing. But the sonority struck me as monotonous, and I was bored.

After the concert my mother said, "The organ plays but they don't give you any pancakes," referring to a restaurant where Uncle Peter used to take us to eat pancakes, and where they had a barrel organ.

I didn't approve of the witticism. After all, on the one hand you had a genuine artist, and on the other a barrel organ playing some kind of trash. But the concert *had* been boring, so I didn't raise any objections.

My father soon came to Moscow. He spent about ten days with us and then went back to Sontsovka, being unwilling to leave the estate unattended even in the winter, when no field work was being done. After his departure, I wrote him (on December 14):

> It is now one o'clock in the morning. We have just come back from a concert under the baton of Nikisch [a famous and elegant conductor who was all the rage in both of our capitals]. The concert was splendid. Nikisch was presented with two wreaths and three or four baskets of flowers. . . .
>
> In my opinion, Nikisch conducted the overture to *Ruslan and Lyudmila** more smoothly and generally better than Safonov. I knew a little of the first movement of the Tchaikovsky concerto. We liked the Grieg suite very much. You could see that everyone else liked it too, because they made him repeat the third and fourth movements. We also liked the Beethoven symphony.
>
> Reinhold Moritsevich [Glière] played a viola in the orchestra. [He very much wanted to play under Nikisch, but since all the violin desks were occupied, they offered him a viola desk.] After the concert, Nikisch was called back eight or ten times. People applauded so much that he bowed in every possible way and even blew kisses at them. They waved handkerchiefs, military caps, fur caps, and programs, offered him bouquets, and shouted "Bravo!" Even Mama shouted, and I clapped until my hands were sore.[27]

The Moscow public really adored Nikisch, and his concerts were always a festive occasion. Before the concert, as my mother was sitting on the divan (not noticing that I was in the room), she said dreamily, "Artur Nikisch. *Nikisch-kukish.*"†

I liked that. Throwing open the door of our hotel room, I rushed into the corridor and ran down the stairway shouting, *"Nikisch-kukish! Nikisch-kukish!"* My mother ran after me, stumbling because of her nearsightedness, and brought me back to our room.

"But maochka, you yourself said *'Nikisch-kukish!'* "

"I said it inadvertently. But you mustn't repeat it, understand?"

I didn't really understand. But her tone of voice was stern, and I had to submit.

I had written the letter to my father at one in the morning. Apparently my mother was indulgent about my staying up late. But she kept a close check on

---

* An opera by Glinka. (Translator's note.)

† *Kukish* means "fig," as in "to give someone the fig." (Translator's note.)

The Zhitkov sisters, Maria and Catherine, in 1867.

My mother, Maria Grigoryevna Zhitkova. St. Petersburg, 1876.

A friend of my mother describes her as follows: "... Manyusha was not pretty. She had a turned-up nose and full lips. Her jaw was somewhat prominent, and her hair was straight and cut short."

"My father was tall, with a large cranium, a nose that might have been painted by an iconographer, and a light-colored, spade-shaped little beard—sometimes a big beard."

The village of Krasnoye—formerly Sontsovka. (Contemporary photograph.)

Mother, Father, and I (age one) in the orchard at Sontsovka. Taken by a traveling photographer.

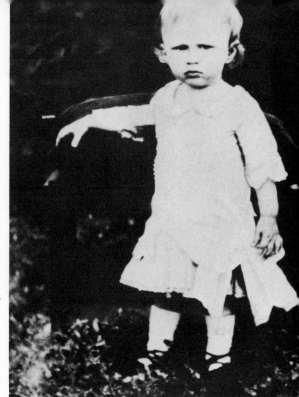

The author at the age of one.

My maternal grandmother, Anna Vasilevna Zhitkova, in 1892, when I was two.

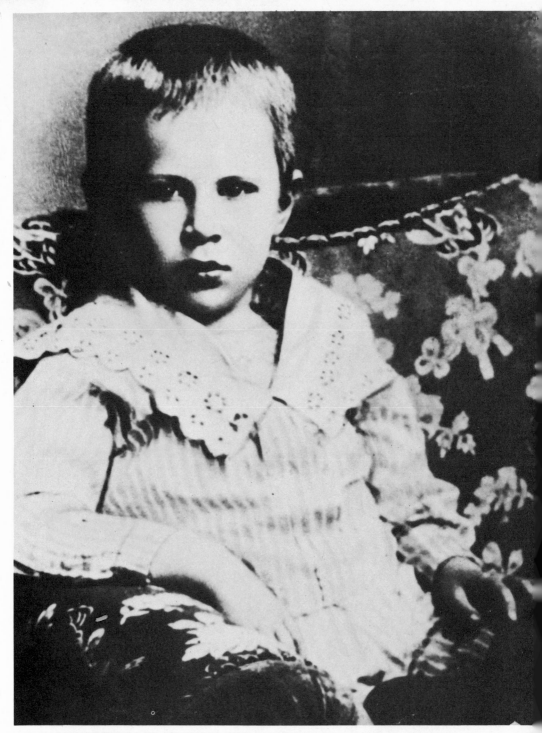

The author at the age of four. Taken in Kaluga, on the occasion of our visit to the Rayevskys' estate.

Tatyana Grigoryevna Zhitkova (Aunt Tanya), my mother's sister.

Katya Rayevskaya and her children, who were considerably older than I, visited Sontsovka.

Anton Rubinstein.

the schedule for meals and walks. "Sergushka is looking well," she wrote my father. "I am fattening him up on eggs, milk, and wine, and not overburdening him with work. He works about three hours a day."

Wine was included among the desirable elements of my diet. A spoonful of cognac was mixed in my milk but I didn't like the aftertaste.

For exercise, I was taken out for skating. But since I was afraid of falling, a teacher was taken along on two occasions. From a letter from my mother to my father: "I'm very glad that Sergushka had begun to skate. He moves along with his legs bent, like a spider, but he manages."

From a letter from me to my father, dated December 17, 1902: "On Monday the 16th Ekaterina Mikhailovna [my father's niece] took me to the Bolshoi Theater to Wagner's *Die Walküre*—a terribly boring opera without motifs or action but with a great deal of noise."[28]

It was quite natural that I should not have understood the music of *Die Walküre* at first hearing. My interest in it developed later. It is also understandable that I was bored because of the lack of stage action. But I undoubtedly picked up the phrase "a great deal of noise" from the people around me, because the loud orchestration must surely have intrigued me more than it frightened me.

This critical contact with Wagner marked the end of our stay in Moscow. In late December we left for Petersburg.

While in Moscow and Petersburg I composed several more ditties (one of them in 5/4 time), so that by New Year's Day I had twelve of them.

"That's fine," my mother said. "They can make up your first series. Next year you can compose another twelve."

"And they'll make up my second series," I agreed.

By the end of January 1903 we had returned to Sontsovka.

35

Back at home I demonstrated new skating tricks. Then I settled down to work on the violin sonata that Glière had assigned me. Special music paper had been bought for this purpose.

I worked enthusiastically and in some five weeks I had written a rather long sonata in three movements. The first was a Sonata Allegro, of a rather ballad-like character, in C minor; the second was a Minuet; the third was a C major Prestissimo in 3/4 time.

The manuscript of this sonata has been preserved, but I remember that it marked a great step forward as compared to the symphony. Another thing representing an advance was the fact that I worked on my own with the sonata form, the development, and the counterpoint.

Ten years later I used the main theme of the first movement for my *Ballade for Cello and Piano,* Opus 15. The three bars of the introduction and the first five bars of the first theme are identical with the earlier music, although from that point on, in the *Ballade,* I went in for great complexity. Thus among my published works bearing opus numbers, the first theme of the *Ballade* is the earliest written music, having been composed when I was eleven.

There is also a certain ballad-like quality in the first "little song" of the second series[29] composed in Petersburg in January. It shows the influences of Brahms and Liszt, which had not been noticeable earlier:

Or of Chopin:

But the classical style again appears in others; e.g., in the sixth ditty,[30] composed in March:

Of the two composers whose music I had heard my mother play since early childhood, Beethoven and Chopin, the former's influence was permanent and the latter's incidental. I was indifferent to Chopin's waltzes, and did not like his nocturnes. No doubt I would have felt more affinity for his études and sonatas, but my mother didn't play them. I would become especially irritated when my mother would say, "Why don't you write something tender—something more melodious? How marvelous Chopin's nocturnes are!"

When I wrote my seventh "little song"[31] I was yielding to these pressures—and also to advice I had had in Moscow from Goldenweiser, who said my style would become more pianistic if I would write the accompaniment in the form of broad arpeggios sweeping from the left hand to the right, with the melody flowing in between.

This music was tender and melodious and had broad arpeggios but qualitatively it was more stereotyped than the other little songs. I felt myself much freer when I had not been persuaded to do this or that; for example, in the eighth little song[32] (May 1903):

Or in the second,[33] in which I experimented: seven sharps in the key signature, double sharps, meters of 7/4 and 5/4, etc.

36

A new problem had to be faced by my parents: it was time to send me to high school. It was not a pleasant prospect. We had been living a quiet family life in the country, and now the even tenor of that life had to be broken.

The first question was: What high school should I go to? The nearest one was in a district town. But the district high schools were poor, and the towns themselves were Godforsaken holes. The most likely place was the provincial seat of Ekaterinoslav (now Dnepropetrovsk), eight hours away by railroad. But in proportion as the Moscow musicians took an increasing interest in me, it was natural to look farther afield—to Moscow.

My attending school in Moscow, more that two days' travel away, would mean an even greater disruption of family life. But on this point my parents disagreed. Mother was bored and restless in snowbound Sontsovka, where she had so little contact with people on her own cultural level. If I were at school in Moscow, it would give her a way out. It was not yet clear whether I would be sent to boarding school or would stay at the home of relatives where Mother could come to visit; or (finally) whether Mother and I would take lodgings together.

In the last-named case, Father would come to visit us, and during the Christmas holidays we would come back to Sontsovka. But one way or another, this would mean a more interesting life for my mother and long months of loneliness for my father.

Their discussions must have been not altogether harmonious. One morning when I woke up early (the door between my room and my parents' bedroom was always left open), I heard a stormy discussion, and my father saying, "In that case there's nothing for me to do but shoot myself."

I took him seriously and began to howl. Mother and Father were dismayed. They took me into their bedroom and tried to calm me down. Finally my father began to cry, too. Then he got up and went to his study.

The problem of where I should go to school was further complicated by the fact that it was not a simple matter to be admitted to an academic high school. The students to be admitted were selected from the preparatory form, but I had been prepared for the second or third form, where the openings were minimal. The examinations were rigorous, and the examiners often flunked a candidate for no reason at all. Besides, terrible things were told about the barbarous teachers. It was said there were sadists who experienced pleasure when a boy failed.

Actually, the causes were of a different order. There was a shortage of academic high schools in Russia, and there were more candidates than could be admitted. If there were five places open in the third form, and twenty-five candidates were taking the exam, the teacher would have to fail twenty even if he were an angel. Or even if he didn't fail them, he couldn't admit them to the class, which amounted to the same thing. After making inquiries (in Moscow), my mother wrote to my father: "If he passes the examination in the autumn but is not accepted owing to the lack of openings, he receives no papers. All he has to show for it is the pleasant realization that he passed the exams."

In March 1903, with a view to making more precise inquiries, my mother again went to Moscow. She made the rounds of the high schools, the government offices, and the tutelary authorities of the district, but the results were hardly encouraging. About the only possibility was that of sending me to a private school. She also paid a call on Glière, who (as before) wouldn't say yes or no about coming back to Sontsovka. He did, however, send me a box of stamps and the sketch of a sonata. My mother mentioned it in her letter, but I can remember nothing about the sketch. According to my notes and some faint memories, the violin sonata was by this time finished or very nearly so. It may be that this was a sketch not of the entire sonata but of the development section of the sonata allegro. Or perhaps it was a sketch of the piano sonata I didn't begin to work on until six months later.

37

In June 1903, Glière arrived at Sontsovka to spend his second summer. He was twenty-nine, and I was twelve. It turned out that his vacillation had had nothing to do with the lack of a library or of a creative atmosphere at Sontsovka. The fact was, he now had a fiancée, and he had thought a long time before deciding to seclude himself for three months in distant Sontsovka.

For starters, he looked over my violin sonata and my new ditties. He made several corrections in the sonata but left the latter unchanged. Then arose the question as to what large-scale composition I should work on during the summer. The symphony had been completed, as had the violin sonata.

Glière, who himself had written a good deal of chamber music, suggested a string quartet or sextet. But I wanted to write an opera. He protested that such a work was too complex. But I had my own point of view: this wouldn't be my first opera.

Finally Glière went to my father and came back with several volumes of Pushkin's *Collected Works*. He spent two days going through them in search of a subject, then suggested *A Feast in Time of Plague*. It was not really a very good choice, since the *Feast* offered few events likely to stimulate my youthful imagination. But it did offer some pluses. First, it was a play, hence there was no need to write a libretto. All I had to do was make some cuts here and there. Second, there was no love intrigue, so that it could be turned over to an eleven-year-old without hesitation. Third, it had only one act, hence I could finish it in the course of the summer without too much trouble.

Glière said, "Use the best themes in the overture. And do it right—in sonata form."

As a teacher, Glière realized at the outset that I had to be encouraged not only along the lines of operatic writing but also along those of symphonic composing.

The first words of the play were: "Honored Chairman, I bring up the name / Of a man very well known to us." Glière explained that it would be best to use *recitativo secco* for them, with chords separating the phrases.

The chairman as the main character would be a tenor; the young man who spoke those words would be a baritone; and the priest would be a bass. He also told me the range of each of the voices. Having learned that a baritone could reach G in the one-line octave, I wrote the whole recitative in the upper register.

"That's too high," Glière said.

"But you yourself showed me the range."

"The upper register is used only at the most tense moments."

"But the young man is singing that tensely."

"You don't understand me. The baritone's high G is used only at the end of an aria or at some dramatic moment. For example, just before the curtain in *Eugene Onegin:* 'Shame, anguish, O my miserable fate!' It is not used in ordinary recitative. Otherwise the singer would have to shout it."

Nonetheless, the recitative was for some reason left unchanged, although it would have been easy to write it a third lower.

Next (with two lines cut for brevity) came the words: "He whose jokes and funny stories / . . . Enlivened our table talk. . . ."

"At this point," said Glière, "you should depict his jokes in the accompaniment."

I couldn't do it, so Glière wrote it for me.

"And here you depict the plague: '. . . and dispersed the gloom which the Plague / Our guest, is now inflicting / Upon the most brilliant minds.' Try hard with the plague, because we're going to use this music in the overture."

I tried hard and built the plague music on diminished sevenths and chromatic scales in triplets:

In this way, the opera progressed, and after beginning cautiously, I gradually got the feel of it. When half the act was completed, Glière said I had enough material to begin the overture. It began with the plague music—the introduction. I couldn't find the right material in the opera for the main theme, so I wrote it from scratch. It proved to be negligible. For the subordinate theme we chose the following fragment:

When I was writing it in the opera, Glière had said, "Try to make it a bit more melodious. If this passage comes out well, we'll use it in the overture."

And so it happened. The fragment came out well—although further on, under Glière's influence, it went into a rather stereotyped sequence.[34]

As to the roles played by Mary and Louise in the action, and why they were called "fallen but charming creatures," I paid little attention, and Glière made it a point not to go into the question.

My piano lessons took up one hour a day, as they had the year before.

Whenever a phrase characteristic of some orchestral instrument showed up in a piano piece, Glière would say, "Now, if you were going to orchestrate this piece, this melody would have to be given to such-and-such an instrument."

This method was still fruitful, even though during the past year I had learned more about orchestras, having had the opportunity that past winter to verify a good deal at concerts and rehearsals.

As we were working on Schumann's *Warum,* Glière would say, "This first phrase would be played by the clarinet, and the horn would answer."

In this unobtrusive way we marked out all the entries—something in which *Warum* was especially helpful.

"And who will play the chords in the accompaniment?"

"The string quintet, of course."

After that, everything was clear. I sat down to work at the score, and orchestrated the whole thing without difficulty.[35]

In the evening my mother would insist that I give her a summary of what I had done during the day.

"Well, what did you do today?" she would ask—often in the presence of Glière.

Then another question: "Are you satisfied with what you did?"

Glière respected her for it. Many years later he recalled those questions she would ask in the evening.

In view of my father's impending birthday on July 8, when he would be fifty-seven, I decided to compose a piece for violin and piano that we could play when guests had assembled for the festivities. The piece was rather decent, and Louise copied it out in her beautiful handwriting.[36]

Louise was on hand most of the time and gave me a lot of help with French. When the three of us—she, Glière, and I—would go walking, I sometimes thought, "She gets fifteen rubles a month, and he gets seventy-five. That means he costs five times as much." And I would give him a respectful look out of the corner of my eye.

38

The mail came twice a week, on Tuesdays and Fridays. On those days the post boy would set off early in the morning in a droshky for Andreyevka, seven kilometers away, and come back with a leather bag full of letters and newspapers.

The bag also contained a little account book in which the postmaster would record all the letters and the number of newspapers, so nothing could get lost. For this he was sent a lamb or pig on Christmas and Easter. The day before mail day, everyone who wanted to send off a letter would give it to Father, who would record it in the same little account-book. Glière never failed to give him a thick letter to be registered, always addressed to his brother, Morits Moritsevich Glière, in Kiev.

I often heard Mother and Aunt Tanya whispering, not without womanly curiosity (a child would not understand), as they wondered about what "he" could write so much to his brother about, and what kind of brotherly love he must feel to send off a thick envelope twice a week—and a registered letter at that!

Actually, his brother never opened a single envelope: he just passed them on to Glière's fiancée, of whose existence we at Sontsovka knew nothing yet.

Once when I came into Glière's room to ask him something I found him sitting at his desk writing. The page was headed "Friday, July 11." Then came some text. I went out of the room frightfully interested. Just imagine a man's writing down everything that happened during the day. That was very important and interesting! Why shouldn't I do the same thing?

Usually, children are natural-born and accurate chroniclers. For example, a child will write: "The guests came at four o'clock and left at six-thirty." For him it is more important to note the exact time than to write who came and why. Such, roughly, was my approach to my future diary.

This idea coincided with another, which had preoccupied me for some time. At Sontsovka we would occasionally be visited by a distant relative named Rein, who boasted that he could forecast the weather. Someone once asked him how he did it. He smiled knowingly and said, "Every day I jot down a description of the weather, and in a hundred days it repeats itself."

I was dumb-struck. You're always hearing people asking what the weather will be like tomorrow, and whether they should start to thresh or whether it will rain. Yet the whole thing was really so simple!

I decided to combine the two things: I would jot down a description of the weather and at the same time tell everything that happened that day. As one does with every near and dear plan, I jealously guarded it from the others—no doubt fearing that someone would sully it with a careless hand. I wrote in pencil on small scraps of paper that I always carried in my pocket so they wouldn't come into anyone else's possession. As a result, the scraps became crumpled and the writing was blurred here and there.

I shall quote here some of the entries.*

JULY, 1903

TUESDAY, THE 15th. [I am preserving the Old Style here because dates have their own physiognomy—one that they lose when transposed into another style of calendar, even if the latter is more accurate.] Fine weather. In the morning, walked with Aunt Tanya in the big orchards. After my music lesson [that is, playing the piano] we wanted to play croquet, but the rain

---

* All square-bracketed interpolations in these entries were made subsequently by the composer.

hindered us. The temperature then was 71.6. The rain soon stopped, and we [Reinhold Glière, Louise, and I] played one game. Mlle. won. In the evening a huge moth got into the living room and laid several eggs while we were trying to catch it. Went to bed at ten o'clock.

WEDNESDAY, THE 16th. Hot weather. Threshing has begun, and Papa and I went out to where the grain is being threshed. The temperature at four o'clock was 86. At three o'clock, Reinhold, Louise, and I played croquet. Reinhold won. In the evening, Reinhold and I went horseback riding. I began to write the overture to *A Feast in Time of Plague*.

THURSDAY, THE 17th. Rather warm. Got up early and strolled for a while. In the evening we played croquet: Mama won. It rained in the evening. I have begun to orchestrate the overture I started on yesterday.

FRIDAY, THE 18th. Weather the same as yesterday. Got up at 6:45 and strolled until nine. In the morning Reinhold and I played croquet. Reinhold won. [Each day's entry gives the results of the croquet game, but I never once won. History does not record the fact that I took this very hard, and once left the game howling.] Toward evening we went out to the threshing. Shango, the puppy, has an infected ear.

SATURDAY, THE 19th. Clear weather. Shango's ear was washed out with opium in order to kill the worms that are supposed to be in there, but it didn't help much.

SUNDAY, THE 20th. Hot weather. Played with my tin soldiers in the morning. M. I. Reberg [the doctor's wife] came on a visit. Of the two tin soldier battles I fought with Reinhold, he won one and I won the other. In the evening, Shango's ear was laved.

MONDAY, THE 21st. Rather good weather. Before lunch we all went out to the big orchard to finish apple picking. We spent an hour there, and then came back to breakfast. Shango's ear has been laved twice more: he is better.

TUESDAY, THE 22nd. Pleasant weather. I got some paper and began to write a story. [I have no recollection of either the paper or the story.]

WEDNESDAY, THE 23rd. Sky overcast. Papa went to Bakhmut. We all went with him as far as the gate. It began to rain at one o'clock and continued until six.

THURSDAY, THE 24th. Overcast. Got up at 7:30. Went for a walk. We played croquet during the day. In the evening we went out to see the haymaking and threshing.

FRIDAY, THE 25th. It rained during the night. Weather clear but windy. We played croquet. Papa came back in the evening. He gave me some candy after I had already gone to bed.

SATURDAY, THE 26th. Sky overcast. Got up early and finished sketching the assignment I hadn't finished yesterday. [When I left, my father had given me assignments to do. But I had loafed and was now catching up.]

SUNDAY, THE 27th. Clear weather. Got up early and began to prepare for the war of the tin soldiers. The map represented South America. The belligerents included Aunt Tanya (Argentina), Reinhold (Bolivia), Mlle. (Peru), Serezha (Brazil), Marfusha (Venezuela), and I (Colombia). Had a music lesson with Reinhold [on the piano], since Monday we are going to the doctor's.

MONDAY, THE 28th. We went at two o'clock. We played croquet there. Reinhold and I played the harmonium. We came back at one in the morning. I read through Pushkin's *Dubrovsky*.

TUESDAY, THE 29th. We had musk-melon for the first time. [They were late that year; usually they were ripe by July 8.] Began to read Pushkin's *Kirdzhali*.

WEDNESDAY, THE 30th. Finished orchestrating Schumann's *Warum*.

THURSDAY, THE 31st. Marvelous weather. Got up at seven. Toward evening we made a game of knocking the croquet balls around, then went to the big orchard to pick apples.

AUGUST

FRIDAY, THE 1st. During a croquet game I quarreled with Mlle. Later we made up.

SUNDAY, THE 3rd. Got up late. A rather warm day. Before lunch Reinhold and I pretended to quarrel, and I challenged him to a duel. His second was Mlle., and mine was Nikita. We used crossbows with rubber balls, shooting in turn. [The duel, which had been begun according to all the rules, degenerated into a kind of general entertainment.]

WEDNESDAY, THE 6th. Sent a money order to Moscow for music paper. Have composed a charade and am putting it into verse so as to send it to a magazine I take, *The Heartfelt Word*.

SATURDAY, THE 9th. Got up early and immediately went to work on my lessons with Papa. Aunt Tanya [left at three o'clock] in the afternoon. Mama and I took her to the station. On the way we hit a bump in the road, and part of my upper left incisor broke off. [I was sitting on the front seat. I turned toward the coachman and hit my teeth on the iron bar framing his seat.] At Grishino, when I started to eat an apple, the broken tooth began to hurt from the acid.

SUNDAY, THE 10th. Worked on the lessons I missed yesterday.

MONDAY, THE 11th. Ivan Antonovich Platkevich, an examining magistrate, came to see us. [He was courting Aunt Tanya, but he came too late: she had already left for Petersburg.]

TUESDAY, THE 12th. Splendid weather. [No doubt I had heard my elders say, "What splendid weather!"] Reinhold got cross with me.

WEDNESDAY, THE 13th. I made up with Reinhold.

FRIDAY, THE 15th. Assumption Day. We went to church. Finished composing *A Feast in Time of Plague*. Reinhold left at midnight.

It was remarkable how the completion of the opera coincided with Glière's departure. But it had been completed only in the form of sketches; there was still a lot of work left by way of orchestrating it and preparing a decent piano score.

The most important part was the overture, long by comparison with the short opera—like a big head on a small body. It was written in sonata form and represented a considerable step forward as compared to my symphony, written the year before. From a technical point of view, it remained unsurpassed for several years. It had been done under Glière's guidance, whereas during the following years I worked on my own.

While staying with us, Glière had worked on his second octet, which he did not complete. Later, he made a symphony of it (his second). At my request he wrote out all the themes for me, and I was pleased to see that the main theme, upon repetition, turned out to be an excellent canon.

On his return trip Glière once again took the express train, for which I respected him.

39

AUGUST

SATURDAY, THE 16th. A splendid day. Got up late. Learned that my daily lessons would be cut by half an hour. Up until today I have had three hours of music, two and a half with Papa, and one with Mama, which adds up to six and a half hours. Now I'll have two hours of music, three hours with Papa, and an hour and a half with Mama. [This is poor mathematics, since the two totals are the same. In any case, six and one half hours per day is quite a bit for a boy of eleven, considering that there were no vacations. On the other hand, if you deduct the two hours of music, it leaves four and one half hours for general schoolwork, which is not a lot. I worked for one hour on the piano, and on the opera for another hour.]

SUNDAY, THE 17th. Got up rather late. Felt weak during the day. Shot dart pistols.

MONDAY, THE 18th. Began work on four-hand arrangement of the overture.

TUESDAY, THE 19th. Rainy weather. In the evening Mama started teaching how to play the card game called *vint*.*

WEDNESDAY, THE 20th. Very rainy weather. Played *vint* in the evening.

FRIDAY, THE 22nd. Began to read *Leatherstocking*. Played *vint* in the evening.

SUNDAY, THE 24th. We started a war of tin soldiers, but the doctor's family came to visit. In the evening Mama, Papa, Mlle., and I played two rubbers of *vint*.

MONDAY, THE 25th. Mlle.'s birthday. I picked a bouquet of flowers for her. Mama cut my hair. Had a bath.

TUESDAY, THE 26th. Reinhold mailed us the sheet music of Cui's *A Feast in Time of Plague*. A waltz by Zhenya Vedrinskaya, a fourteen-year-old girl, has been published in a magazine. It has a lot of strange things in it.

In that passing remark one can see the first manifestation of my jealous attitude toward other composers—a feeling that, unfortunately, I often had even in later years. But I showed even greater jealousy toward Cui. I played his opera music belligerently. It was ugly; mine was better. And what an itsy-bitsy overture: mine was long, and the real thing. As it happened, both he and I had written Mary's song in G minor, and even the beginning of the melody was similar.†

When you're setting to music the kind of poetry that has a strong rhythm, there is always a danger that the rhythm will get into the music. I say "danger"

* Apparently vingt-et-un.
† The notations read: top fragment—"my version"; next fragment—"Cui's version." (Translator's note.)

because a rhythm that is pleasing and natural in the poem can become monotonous and obtrusive in the music. Being too young to know any better, I had taken the bait and written the whole song as it began, using the rhythm:

But Cui, as an experienced craftsman, had made it a point in the very first bars to avoid the cliché. I didn't understand that and hence did not approve of his refinements.

"This passage of his is rather ugly," I told my mother. "Shall I play my version? Do you like it?"

"Yes, of course," she said, out of politeness. "But just don't play his opera too badly."

"It's not that I play it badly. It's a bad opera."

AUGUST

THURSDAY, THE 28th. Began to compose the ninth "little song" of the second series.[37] Gathered apples. Finished transcribing the overture.

FRIDAY, THE 29th. Holiday. Windy weather. Got up late. Began to transcribe scenes from the opera *A Feast in Time of Plague* for voice and piano. We played *vint.*

SATURDAY, THE 30th. Began to read the *Root of Evil* [by Polevoi].[38] Wrote down the names of all the kings of Portugal and England.

SUNDAY, THE 31st. Papa went for the mail. Mama, Mlle., and I went on a visit to the doctor's house. I. I. Kramer was there too. He had heard Cui's opera, *A Feast in Time of Plague,* and hadn't liked it. Copied a list of some of the Turkish sultans.

SEPTEMBER

MONDAY, THE 1st. Got up rather late. Played croquet.

TUESDAY, THE 2nd. I was given a month-old puppy named Bobrik. I built him a kennel, but since it was not pretty and was in a prominent place, I had to build another one. [A diplomatic account. The kennel was very ugly and was on the terrace. My mother objected in the strongest terms, ordered me to dismantle it. I wept.]

WEDNESDAY, THE 3rd. I asked Marfusha to wake me up at seven o'clock, but she was so quiet about it I didn't hear her. Got up at eight. Shango's right ear has begun to hurt again. We wanted to wash it out again. Finished Ditty No. 11. [This points up an error in the *Catalogue* I drew up as a child, where this little piece is dated July.]

WEDNESDAY, THE 3rd. Weather windy and very unpleasant. We went for a walk. Bobrik ran along with us.

SUNDAY, THE 7th. Weather rather cold. Wrote a letter to Aunt Tanya. Bobrik was brought into the house. [When he got to be too much, he was taken outside again.]

MONDAY, THE 8th. We went to church. Vasya came to the house. We played blindman's buff. In the evening a mouse was caught under my father's desk.

THURSDAY, THE 11th. Nikolai Yakovlevich Klenov, the veterinarian, came to visit us. We played *vint* with him. We played three rubbers. [That meant progress: Klenov was a good *vint* player.]

SUNDAY, THE 14th (September). Splendid weather. The doctor's family came on a visit. We took a walk with them. We saw a hare.

The doctor had three daughters. Vera was a bit older than I, and the brightest of the three. She was lame and used a walking-stick. The next oldest, Nina, a very lively girl, was my age. The youngest, Zina, was the prettiest and at the same time the most taciturn.

Five years before, when the doctor had first brought them to Sontsovka, he asked me, "Well, which one do you like the most?" According to his report (I don't remember it), I went up to Nina and kissed her. I was seven or eight at the time. My relations with the girls from then on were comradely, with no hint of flirtation.

WEDNESDAY, THE 17th. We had wanted to go to the doctor's house at eleven, but some officer came to visit us. At lunch he broke a wineglass. We left at one. Papa didn't get there until six.

THURSDAY, THE 18th. At 3:30 Papa left for Kharkov for the livestock exhibit. I began to survey the big orchard. [My father let me use the transit compass and told me how to do it.]

FRIDAY, THE 19th. Got up at 7:30. Went to survey the fence: difficult, but I surveyed part of the creek. We played *vint*.

MONDAY, THE 22nd (September). Griner, the surveyor, came to see us. I showed him my plan of the orchard. He left in the evening. [Griner approved of the plan in general but advised me to use a larger scale for the width of the paths than for their length.]

TUESDAY, THE 23rd. Papa came back from Kharkov at three o'clock, along with the veterinarian, Nikolai Yakovlevich Klenov. In the evening we played *vint,* and Father gave me a very good pencil. Yesterday I wrote Ditty No. 10.[39]

THURSDAY, THE 25th. Weather windy, with overcast sky. Papa's and my name day. This morning when I woke up, Mama gave me a box with "Siu Pastries" written on it. She said, "Here are some pastries for tea from me and your Aunt Tanya." While I was congratulating Papa, Mama opened the box, and there were tin soldiers in it! Then she gave me a wind-up steamer—a gift from Aunt Tanya. She gave Papa some special cuff links. I dedicated Ditty No. 10 and *A Feast in Time of Plague* to Papa. Papa gave me the book *Vanity of Vanities*,[40] three other books, a little microscope, a very interesting and peculiar top, a portable chess set in the form of a notebook, and ten rubles for my money box. Nikolai Yakovlevich [Klenov] gave me the opera *The Queen of Spades*. He liked the top very much and set it spinning several times.

The ditty dedicated to my father (No. 10) did not suffer from *longueurs,* like its predecessor, No. 9; but the two of them had one fault in common: following the rules for the song form, I had repeated entire fragments without variation. The trio showed a certain classical influence:

FRIDAY, THE 26th. Karl Fedorovich [Rein] and Uncle Hunter went hunting. [I followed them and saw Rein wound a partridge in the wing. Then it ran off, and Rein followed it. It stopped in the shelter of a bush. From a long way off, Rein took aim and shot its head off.] In the evening Karl Fedorovich showed Mlle. and me how to play open *vint*.

40

OCTOBER

WEDNESDAY, THE 1st. I have begun to keep a record of what pieces I play on the piano, and how many times I play them. [A bad kind of statistics: because of it, I would not take time over difficult passages but go on ahead, in order to make the figures higher.]

SATURDAY, THE 4th. Miserable weather. Wrote the first movement of a sonata in B-flat major.[41]

That is, I began to write it, and finished it on the eighth. Glière had assigned me the project of a piano sonata—to be written, of course, after I had finished the orchestral and piano scores of *A Feast in Time of Plague*. But I couldn't restrain myself. The sonata began directly with the main theme:

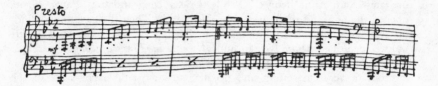

THURSDAY, THE 9th. Finished the second movement of the sonata.

SATURDAY, THE 11th. Mama is getting ready to go to the Caucasus. [To see dear Olechka in Sukhumi. Naturally, since we were starting to get autumnal weather in Sontsovka, but in Sukhumi the weather was marvelous.] I finished the book *The Adventures of Rougemont*[42]—interesting—and began the story "To the New World for Happiness."[43]

SUNDAY, THE 12th. Finished the story I started yesterday. Mama left for the Caucasus at ten o'clock in the morning. Vasya and Serezha came to the house and we played various games.

TUESDAY, THE 14th. Measured the orchard. Wrote Ditty No. 11.[44]

Again a classical influence in the trio:

But the introduction is not without tartness. Apparently Taneyev's remark about overly simple harmonies had begun to put down some rootlets.

WEDNESDAY, THE 15th. Set Lermontov's "Twig from Palestine" to music.[45] *Twig from Palestine* was my first art song ("romance"). The ms., rather sloppily written, has been preserved. My father had advised me to go deep into the content, with the result that I fell sentimentally into:

SATURDAY, THE 18th. Finished orchestrating the action [!] of *A Feast in Time of Plague.*

MONDAY, THE 20th.[46] Began to write Ditty No. 12.[47]

THURSDAY, THE 23rd. Resumed orchestrating the overture to the opera.

SATURDAY, THE 25th. Received a telegram from Mama: "Plan to arrive Tuesday at 6 P.M."

MONDAY, THE 27th. Continued work on Ditty No. 12. Am thinking of dedicating it and *Twig from Palestine* to Mama.

TUESDAY, THE 28th. Finished Ditty No. 12. At 8:30 P.M. I first saw a flaming point on the horizon—a torch. It was dark outside, and Mama's carriage was preceded by a torchbearer. I dedicated Ditty No. 12 and *Twig from Palestine* to her. She liked Ditty No. 12 better than No. 11 and *Twig from Palestine.*

One evening about this time, when the family was taking tea and my parents were praising me for having done a lot of work, my father said, "You could keep a record of when you began your compositions and when you finished them."

"It would be a kind of diary," my mother added.

I don't know whether they said that quite by chance or whether, having noticed that I was keeping a diary in secret, they had decided to legitimize my undertaking. In any case, it hit home.

"I'm already keeping . . . a kind of . . ." I stammered, and got so worked up that I left the table and went into another room.

When I came back, somewhat calmed down, my parents did not continue the conversation. As for the diary, I went on keeping it in secret.

NOVEMBER

SATURDAY, THE 1st. Received from Aunt Tanya a package containing the tin soldiers she had promised me. There were four boxes of them.

SUNDAY, THE 2nd. We had a heavy snowfall. Mlle. has finished copying the orchestral score of *A Feast in Time of Plague*.

SUNDAY, THE 9th. Thaw. Terrible mud. At 2:30 Mama and Papa went to Selitovka to a wedding [to my Uncle Stefan's house].

MONDAY, THE 10th. Mud, like yesterday. Mama and Papa came back at 3:30 in the morning. We are not going [to Moscow] today—only getting ready. Mlle. has finished copying the orchestral score of my opera [that is, the overture] and was rewarded with chocolates. She gave me a book—*La Soeur de Gribouille*. I dedicated the ninth [ditty] to her. Couldn't get to sleep until one o'clock [at night].

This had to do with our impending departure: finishing work, getting things together, agitation, insomnia. Louise, who had completed her second sojourn, was going with us. She had decided not to go back to Paris but rather to go to Petersburg to teach French. My own French lessons would be taken over by my mother, who had theoretically improved her French from being with Louise.

The matter of the weather repeating itself every hundred days was something I completely forgot in the process of keeping my diary. I didn't become interested in checking it until just now—thirty-six years later. I counted off one hundred days from July 15 and got October 23. The July notation was "Good weather." The October notation was "Cold weather." For the next day in July it was "Hot weather." And in October "Cold." Such is forecasting.

41

NOVEMBER

TUESDAY, THE 11th. Clear but muddy. We have spent the whole morning since 2:00 A.M. getting ready to leave. My moneybag had thirty-five rubles in it: Mama must have put the ten rubles that Father gave me into it instead of into the money box. I set aside ten rubles in the casket. [The distinction was rigid: anything put into the moneybag was for my own use as a child, but anything put into the money box or casket was for an indeterminate future time, when I would be grown up, and hence not so interesting.] We were traveling in a coach drawn by six horses. At Bakhirevka [the estate of that same Bakhirev who played the piano so well] we couldn't use the ford, so we started across the dam. But four horses abreast couldn't get across. Then a couple of muzhiks showed up and helped to reharness the horses, for which they got a tip of ten kopecks. We reached Grishino an hour and a half before the train was due to leave. I write Papa a letter. We had some tea. Forty-five minutes before train time, Nikolai Yakovlevich Klenov arrived. He said that the stationmaster would be very pleased if we would pay him a visit and I would accompany him. Mama gave her approval there. I accompanied him while he sang two pieces. He sang very unevenly, and it was hard to accompany him. He said that the trains on the Ekaterininsky line went as fast as fifty-four miles per hour, and promised to show me some locomotives, both dismantled and assembled. We got good seats in the railroad car.

WEDNESDAY, THE 12th. When we got to Kharkov we drank some coffee. Then Mama and Mlle. went to send a telegram, and I wrote a letter to Papa. We found good seats [in the train we changed to]. I kept track of the train's speed.

THURSDAY, THE 13th. When I woke up we were not far from Tula. When we were getting close to Moscow, Mama began looking for our baggage check but couldn't find it. In Moscow there was no one to meet us. Mama called the gendarmes, and we soon got our luggage even without having checks. Mama hired a cabby to take Mlle. to Nikolayevskaya Station: she was going to Petersburg, where she had found a job. I mailed my letter to Papa. We hired a two-horse cab and went to Tverskaya Boulevard to look for hotel rooms. From there we went to Nikitskiye Gates and took rooms in the Hotel Nice, No. 5 on the third floor. But we were only staying there temporarily, since the manager didn't allow a piano in the suite, and the bedroom was dark. Mama wrote Reinhold Glière a note saying we had arrived.

FRIDAY, THE 14th. It snowed. Reinhold came at one o'clock. He said I had composed a great deal. [At the Falz-Fein Hotel on the Tverskaya] they showed us a large suite of two rooms plus a bedroom and vestibule, with electric lighting. But it cost ninety rubles a month. We were very tired and started back to the Hotel Nice. On the way we stopped off at a barbershop and I got a haircut.

SATURDAY, THE 15th. This morning, half the people in Moscow were riding in sleighs and the other half on wheels. But by three o'clock the sleighs got the upper hand. Today I worked. We went to the Falz-Fein. Mama offered seventy rubles a month, but the owner himself, N. I. Mikheyev, said the very lowest rate was seventy-five rubles. Mama agreed to this, and we went back to the Nice to make preparations for moving.

MONDAY, THE 17th. Glière came in the morning, and I worked with him. We got tickets for the evening performance at the Bolshoi of *Dubrovsky*.[48] Then we went by streetcar—at first a horse-drawn one, then an electric one—to Dolgorukovskaya Street, where Mama wanted to look at a cloak. She put me in a cab and sent me home.

I liked the second part of the *Dubrovsky* overture and Dubrovsky's aria.

TUESDAY, THE 18th. The streets were wet and slippery. We went to see the Pomerantsevs on the Bolshaya Molchanovka, but it turned out they had moved to Dolgorukovskaya Street in Efimov's building. So went there by streetcar—first in a horse-drawn one, and then in an electric one. But it turned out that they were living in another of Efimov's buildings near the Butyrki. [In those days buildings were still identified by the names of their owners, rather than by numbers.] We walked there. They have two very fine dogs. We had dinner there. Nikolai Dmitrievich says that war with Japan is inevitable, and that a whole corps—i.e., 60,000 troops—has been sent from Moscow to Manchuria.

WEDNESDAY, THE 19th. I worked at home until five in the afternoon. In the evening we went to *Nero*[49] at the Solodovnikov Theater.

THURSDAY, THE 20th. Reinhold came, and I worked with him. We played the overture to *A Feast in Time of Plague*. I'll have to change the accompaniment in the main theme, which is hard to play on the piano. Toward evening, when Mama had gone out and left me home alone, Reinhold came and suggested a German language teacher. But since Mama wasn't there, we played chess, and I won.

FRIDAY, THE 21st. In the morning they called Mama to the telephone, but since she wasn't dressed she sent me. It was my first telephone conversation, and a great event. The call was from Valentina Dmitriyevna, a relative of that Pomerantsev who had taught me harmony. She invited Mama and me to her home for this evening. Soon after we got there, other guests began to arrive. [The provincials had shown up first.] I played my "little songs," and the one they liked best was No. 5 of the first series.[50] I played it five times.

SATURDAY, THE 22nd. It is not snowing, and the Muscovites are on wheels. We went by streetcar to the Kursk Station to meet Papa.

SUNDAY, THE 23rd. Reinhold came in the morning and said he would take me to a concert that would begin at one o'clock. Mama gave me permission. The concert consisted of art songs by Cui, Rimsky-Korsakov, Moussorgsky, Rachmaninov, Arensky, Dargomyzhsky, and Goldenweiser. When I got back home, Uncle Peter was there, and we went to the Moskovsky Restaurant.

MONDAY, THE 24th. We got up at eleven. My father and I went to buy toys: locomotives, railroad cars, rails. The total price was thirteen rubles and seventy kopecks. They reduced it to thirteen rubles, but Papa said the toys weren't worth more than twelve, and we got ready to leave. Then they reduced the price to twelve. Papa said he would pay six rubles and I should pay six. At home the locomotives went very fast, pulling the cars behind them, and didn't go off the tracks even on the turns.

WEDNESDAY, THE 26th. Mama and I went to the tailor's, where I was measured for a suit. Glière and I went to Goldenweiser's and his sister suggested I play chess with her, while her brother played against Reinhold. Goldenweiser won quickly. I almost beat his sister, but was careless with my queen and lost. Then their cousin arrived. I played him. Toward the end of the game, his position was scarcely better than mine, but Goldenweiser and some other chess players present intervened and directed my moves, and we lost.

Goldenweiser and I did the overture to *A Feast in Time of Plague.* Then he played the opera itself and looked over the orchestral score. After this he played my little songs. He said I wrote as if for the right and left hand and not as for a single instrument; also, that I wrote better for the orchestra. He said I should write twelve different accompaniments to certain of the little songs, chosen by him, and bring them to him on December 1 at 11:30 in the morning. After that we went into the dining room, where we drank tea and had a snack. Then Reinhold and I set out for the Falz-Fein Hotel and arrived here at midnight.

THURSDAY, THE 27th. Reinhold came for our music lesson. I asked him what I should compose. He said I should set Pushkin's "I'm Not the Same" to music.

FRIDAY, THE 28th. I have written the accompaniments to the little songs that Goldenweiser assigned to me. This evening we went to the Art Theater to see *Julius Caesar,* the Shakespearean play. Very good but too long: from 7:30 to 12:30!

DECEMBER

MONDAY, THE 1st. Papa and I went to Goldenweiser's. He took me there and then went back home. I was asked to take tea. I had brought the twelve accompaniments. Goldenweiser didn't like some of them, but others he liked. He looked over Ditty No. 12 of the second series and didn't like it. For next Monday he assigned me a set of variations on a theme by Beethoven.

TUESDAY, THE 2nd. Reinhold came and worked with me. I worked on the art song "I'm Not the Same."[51] Uncle Peter came, and we all went to the circus. It was boring, and half the seats were empty.

WEDNESDAY, THE 3rd. The thermometer is at 6.8 above zero. Papa left at five in the afternoon. Finished the art song.

THURSDAY, THE 4th. Reinhold said the accompaniment to the art song should be changed. We went to the Conservatory to hear some chamber music. They played Haydn's G major quartet, Gedike's G minor trio, and Schubert's G major quintet. Pretty pieces, but boring.

(Chamber music didn't get to me: I was looking for bright colors and dramatic moments.)

FRIDAY, THE 5th. I bought two more pieces of track and a toy cannon. We got tickets for Siloti's eighth concert.* The cannon doesn't shoot, and we want to take it back.

SATURDAY, THE 6th. We went to a matinee concert. The things they played the best were Beethoven's *Seventh Symphony* and Liszt's *E-Flat Major Concerto*. The cannon shoots splendidly.

SUNDAY, THE 7th. We went to visit the Tikhonovs on the Nikolo-Yamskaya. Tikhonov was a colonel and he said that if I would write a march for a band he would have it played in his regiment.

42

MONDAY, THE 8th. Rather warm weather. Worked during the day, and in the evening we went to the Nobles' Club for the Siloti-Ysaye† concert. During intermission we ran across Sergei Ivanovich [Taneyev]. After we had shaken hands, he asked me, "Where is your mama?" Then he said, "I'll be expecting to see you on Friday—you and your compositions." And he went off.

TUESDAY, THE 9th. I bought a toy pistol and a stamp album.

WEDNESDAY, THE 10th. Maria Mikhailovna came to see us in the evening, and the Tikhonovs arrived later. Colonel Tikhonov brought a list of the instruments in his regiment's band, and said that if I would write a march or something else, he would have it played and I could conduct.

FRIDAY, THE 12th. At three we went to Taneyev's. First he looked over the B-flat major sonata (i.e., the parts I had completed), then had me play the overture to *A Feast in Time of Plague* while he looked over the orchestral score. He said it was very well written and well orchestrated—better than last year's symphony. "It's so smoothly written," he said, "that you could write out the parts and have it performed right now!" Then Reinhold showed up, and Taneyev offered him tea. Afterward, I played and (on instructions from Taneyev) sang *A Feast in Time of Plague*. What he liked best of all was the second theme of the overture. He also liked the orchestration of *Warum*. We left after spending more than two hours with him.[52]

FRIDAY, THE 12th. After dining at home, we went to the Tikhonovs'. A girl who is studying at the Conservatory was there. She played the piano well (*korosho*).

That's the way I wrote it: *korosho*, not *khorosho*. My hand was trembling. I was overwrought.

* Alexander Ilich Siloti (1863–1945), pianist, conductor, and impresario, whose concert series were extremely popular at this time. (Translator's note.)
† Eugène Ysaye (1858–1931), Belgian composer and violinist. (Translator's note.)

It happened like this. At the Tikhonovs' I was asked to play my new march, and was praised for it. In addition to the march I played some little songs. They, too, were praised, and I felt I was a success. But I was not the only musician there. A girl studying at the Conservatory, a student of Safonoff, was also present. She, too, was asked to play. When she had finished, my mother said, "See how impeccably some people can play? Your own playing is often sloppy."

The girl sat down again to play the last movement of Beethoven's *Fifth Sonata* in C minor. I knew that movement and loved it. It struck me as stormy and full of excitement. And I believed Beethoven had intended it to be so. But the girl played it smoothly, neatly, and carefully. Everybody clapped, and someone asked me, "Well, did you like it?"

"No," I said. "That finale should be played in a completely different way."

"If you can do better," the girl said, "play it yourself."

"Go ahead and play it!" shouted Tikhonov, very pleased at the prospect of a musical tournament. And he dragged me to the piano.

I sat down to play, and immediately realized I had half forgotten the sonata. For that matter, I had never really learned it well. Attempting to convey the music's exaltation and stormy quality, I frequently pushed too hard, so that I didn't have time enough for the scale passages and played them sloppily.

At one point I failed to hold a sustained note long enough, and in another I skipped a bar. When I was through the audience was silent, but in that silence I could sense disapproval.

The girl decided to finish me off. "Safonoff worked with me on that finale," she said, "and he said I play it correctly."

The evening was ruined. Inspiration sans skill had clashed head-on with skill sans inspiration. I couldn't explain this to myself, hence it was difficult for me to write in my diary about the visit to the Tikhonovs. But fairness comes first. The girl played neatly, without mistakes. And I wrote: "A girl who is studying at the Conservatory was there. She played *korosho.*" It was not my fault if my hand trembled when I was praising her. But in the depths of my soul I felt injured for a long time thereafter.

SATURDAY THE 13th. Reinhold came to work with me. In the evening, Mama, Reinhold, and I went to buy toys.

SUNDAY, THE 14th. Uncle Peter came and gave me fifteen rubles [three gold pieces]. We got tickets for *Werther* tonight. A very beautiful opera.

It occurred to me that upon coming home from a concert or opera I should jot down the themes or fragments that I liked and remembered. Or perhaps some musician suggested it to me, since it is of course a useful exercise for a beginning musician. So it was that I jotted down the horn theme from Massenet's *Werther,* when Werther wants to shoot himself.

MONDAY, THE 15th. Finished the march. Reinhold said it was a concert march for good musicians and not one for soldiers to march to.

TUESDAY, THE 16th. Got up at seven, and about nine we went to the dress rehearsal of Berlioz's *Damnation of Faust*. During the last part of the program, Reinhold and I went behind the orchestra. From there one can see how the musicians play their instruments. But I recorded not a single impression of the opera. No doubt I had little understanding of the *Damnation of Faust*. In the evening we went to another Berlioz concert. We saw Taneyev. He said if I wanted to I could get his orchestral score of *Eugene Onegin* and take it to the country with me.

WEDNESDAY, THE 17th. I took the orchestral score of *Ruslan and Lyudmila* and went to Taneyev's. I gave it back to him, took the full score of *Eugene Onegin,* and brought it home with me. Mama spent the whole morning getting ready for our departure, and at one o'clock we checked out of the Falz-Fein. When we got to the Kursk Station, we had lunch, and a short time later the train was ready to leave. There were so many people on it that we scarcely managed to get a compartment, one we had to share with two ladies going to Rostov.

THURSDAY, THE 18th. One of the ladies showed me a waltz she had composed. She said she didn't know harmony, and in fact there were certain parts that weren't worked out as they should have been. In the evening we reached Kharkov.

FRIDAY, THE 19th. We reached Sinelnikovo at six in the morning. All the way from Sinelnikovo to Grishino I kept track of the train's speed. At Grishino we drank tea. A carriage had been sent for us. Papa was very glad that we arrived at the exact time stated in the telegram. Very tired.

MONDAY, THE 22nd. I have begun working seven hours a day: one hour of music [i.e., piano], one of German or French, one of religion, one of counterpoint, and three with Papa.

It would seem that while in Moscow I had worked with Glière on two-voice counterpoint, and perhaps some three-voice; and now I had to do assignments. From my work schedule it appears that free composition was not included among my projects. If you want to compose, do it in your spare time.

THURSDAY, THE 25th. Christmas. Mama's birthday. Dedicated *I'm Not the Same* to her. We went to church. Mama and Papa gave me Altayev's book, *The Lamps of Truth*,[53] and twenty *cartes postales.*

FRIDAY, THE 26th. Cold: 14 degrees below zero.

So ends the diary I kept as a child. I had kept it up until January 1, 1904, but the last page was lost.

43

After New Year's Day, 1904, I went to work scoring my march for a military band. I don't remember the score, but I'm sure it wasn't very good, since I was not familiar with bands. I merely had a superficial notion of the instruments, and knew their range. I was also busy with the third and fourth movements of my piano sonata. The third movement proved to be a rather awkward E-flat minor adagio, not in the style of the first two movements. The last movement was lively, but I don't remember it. My mother, meanwhile, was sitting and making a fair copy of my twelfth little song [of the second series] in the bound notebook in which Louise had copied the twenty-three others.

We didn't stay at Sontsovka long. In mid-January, Mother set off for Petersburg and took me with her. We were there when the Russo-Japanese War broke out. I remember the Rayevskys' apartment and Aunt Katya wringing her hands and saying, "How terrible! How terrible!"

Soon after our arrival, Mother fell ill and took to her bed. Her illness took such a serious turn that my two aunts sent Father a telegram asking him to come. When Aunt Tanya and I met him at the station, his first question naturally was, "How is Mama?"

"Better—much better," I hastened to assure him.

Actually, things weren't better: they were talking about an operation—something I hadn't known. But I turned out to be a good prophet, and she soon started to get better.

My father rented—for the two of us—two rooms in a private apartment. It was in a building on Nevsky Prospect, overlooking the second courtyard. Altogether that building had four courtyards—all of them spacious and clean. When Father went back to Sontsovka, after my mother's recovery, she moved there.

At the price of her illness she had gained an important point. The time had come to send me to school, but in what city? Father still favored Moscow: his brother and nieces lived there; Moscow was closer to Sontsovka; and our contacts with Moscow musicians had already been established.

My mother preferred Petersburg: her relatives lived there, and they were more interesting than our Moscow relatives. Also, they could give us entree to more privileged circles than was the case in Moscow. As for making contact with musicians, this matter was being taken in hand by Aunt Tanya, who very much wanted her dear sister Marishecka (my mother) to settle in Petersburg. Whereas Moscow could offer us Taneyev, Petersburg could balance the scales with Glazunov, to whom Aunt Tanya had a certain entree. My father, reluctant to quarrel with a person who had just escaped from death, also began to favor Petersburg.

We did not manage immediately to see Glazunov. Either he was busy or he had gone off somewhere. But finally he named a day and an hour, and Mother and I went to see him.

I remember that visit only vaguely. It was one o'clock in the afternoon when we arrived at his apartment, a spacious one in a building near the Kazan Cathedral. We got there early, and he wasn't at home. After a while he showed up, and I played *A Feast in Time of Plague* for him. He praised it, and then had a long talk with Mother.

When we got home, Mother seemed disappointed: Glazunov was nothing like dear, solicitous Taneyev! But a few days later, when I was home alone, Glazunov suddenly showed up, filling the whole room with his bulk.

I was embarrassed because the room was in a mess: on the table was the *kasha* I had not finished eating, together with an arithmetic text and a notebook in which I had written a problem, and a rubber pistol. There was a pile of sheet music on the upright piano we had rented. My sailor blouse was short one button, and my hair was disheveled, since I had been taking a nap on the sofa.

Glazunov expressed regret that he had not found my mother at home, and said he would come back two days later at the same time.

"Don't forget to tell her that," he added.

Then, having noticed a four-hand arrangement of a Beethoven symphony on the piano, he asked who played it.

"Mama and I."

"And what other symphonies have you played?"

"Haydn's."

"Have you played any Schumann?"

"No."

"Then buy Schumann's."

Glazunov went out. Mother came home a short time later. She was excited to learn that Glazunov had paid us a call and would come back again. The preparations began. She decided to serve tea, and bought some fine pastries and expensive fruits. The Rayevskys donated some pretty teacups, and the owner of the apartment provided a big vase for the fruit.

Glazunov arrived promptly at the designated hour. He begged off from the refreshments, saying he had but little time, and asked Mother to listen to him attentively. "I have come," he said, "to try to persuade you to send your son to the Conservatory."

Mother voiced her doubts. It would be fine, she said, if my musical abilities developed and I became a great artist. But if not? What were the prospects? To be a second-rate music teacher all one's life? Therefore, she and my father preferred that I become, say, a civil engineer or an architect—a profession that would require staying permanently in the city, which would give me an opportunity to involve myself in music on the side, while going to concerts and getting to know musicians.

Glazunov objected. "If a child with abilities like your son's shouldn't be sent to the Conservatory, then who should be? At the Conservatory his talent will be fully developed, and there is every chance he will become a genuine artist. But if he is trained as a civil engineer he'll be an amateur musician, and he'll never be able to realize his potential completely.

"Do you really want your son to become a good engineer? To do that, he'll have to become involved in his new profession; that is, relegate music to the background. But if he continues to be as much involved in music as he is now, he'll scarcely be able to devote enough time to other subjects to make a good career."

It should not be thought that this line of argument swayed my mother immediately. There were other factors: the question of matriculating at a high school; whether there would be an opening; whether I would pass the nagging entrance exams; the fear of "barbarous" treatment of her son.

And Glazunov continued, "We'll admit your son into the composition class, and along with that he can take general academic subjects at the Conservatory. They aren't as well covered there as at an academic high school, but no doubt you can have him tutored at home."

After all the worries about high school, Glazunov's words were like manna from heaven. Mother had already found out that Glazunov had great influence at the Conservatory, and in the absence of a director was its *de facto* director. Consequently, what he said counted.

"Think it over," Glazunov said, getting up. "Will you be staying in Petersburg long?"

"For a few weeks. For that period of time, I wanted to ask you to recommend a music teacher for lessons in counterpoint."

"All right, I'll try to find one. But it would be better if your son studied harmony rather than counterpoint, and then took the entire composition course with us. We teach harmony differently from the way they do it in Moscow. It won't be a loss of time, because it will provide good groundwork."

For some time after Glazunov's visit Mother vacillated, exchanging letters with Papa on the subject, and taking counsel with relatives. But in essence my matriculation at the Conservatory had been decided upon. Mother's letter to Father (not the first on this subject), dated March 14 (27), 1904, began as follows:

Since Glazunov, seconded by Rimsky-Korsakov [through Glière, who had come to Petersburg for the performance of his symphony], said that

Serezha should go to the Conservatory, all our relatives and acquaintances have begun to drone in unison: "To the Conservatory, of course!" Reinhold Moritsevich [Glière] was at Rimsky-Korsakov's, and told him a lot about Serezha—about the plays he and the other children put on, about the verse libretto for *The Giant,* and about chess—so that Rimsky-Korsakov threw up his hands in amazement. I thanked Glière for his recommendation and good report. He answered, "What else could I have said?" In a word, he had helped us a lot. He has done the spring sowing, so to speak, and we shall reap the harvest in the fall.

In any case—whether I went to high school or to the Conservatory—it was decided that we would go to Petersburg in the autumn.

The plans were as follows: Mother and I would go to Petersburg; in the autumn Father would visit us; during Christmas holidays we could go to see him in the country; in March he would again come to Petersburg; and we would all spend the summer together in Sontsovka.

Accordingly we had to rent an apartment in Petersburg and get some furniture. For the furniture, my mother went to auctions. She bought a rather pretty drawing-room suite in chartreuse, done in silk with bronze decorations (as I recall, this style was called "Second Empire Buhl"), and simpler suites in leather for the study and dining room. Since they were leaving, the people from whom we rented the apartment sold us some bedroom furniture and chinaware.

The music teacher Glazunov recommended was Mikhail Mikhailovich Chernov, a composer in his penultimate year at the Conservatory—much less of a figure then Glière. True, Glière often composed bad music. But he had a passionate love for the very process of composing, and was able to transmit that feeling to a pupil.

Chernov's talent was more modest. He had a hard time composing, and was altogether pallid and dry, personally, in the way he lived and in his work. He conceived an album of piano pieces in which each one would represent a flower. He tried, for example, to depict the trefoil in 3/4 time, in triplets, with the accompaniment in triads. Because of its dryness, his classmates called that collection an "herbarium." On the other hand, he knew counterpoint rather well and two years later he was graduated from the Conservatory with a gold medal.

Chernov had no success with my mother.

I can scarcely bear the music teacher [she wrote my father]. His lessons last forty minutes at the most. Then he plays Sergusha's little songs, or Sergusha plays them for him. Obviously he is so lacking in resourcefulness that he doesn't know what to do for a full hour. It bothers me, but I remain silent, so as not to express my opinion unreservedly. And if I did make any comments, it would be too much.[54]

As for me, I took no particular interest either in Chernov or in my impending matriculation at the Conservatory. I had no clear idea of what a conservatory was. But I was glad that it was not a high school, where the boys fought and the "newcomers" were hazed. For that matter, I wasn't very strong and didn't know how to fight. I had had no practice. "Buttery-smooth," my mother used to say of my complexion, not without tenderness.

44

During our stay in Petersburg I was taken to *The Snow Maiden, Manon,* and *Romeo and Juliet.* For *The Snow Maiden* we had seats in the seventh or eighth row, and I asked if I could sit in the front row so I could see the score being used by the conductor. There were lots of empty seats in the theater, so my mother let me. I found an empty seat in the front row.

Sometimes I would half rise, leaning on the edge of the pit, and follow the score. I still remember the pattern formed by the score: it was by following that pattern that eyes followed the music. Sometimes, after a long even stretch, the music would suddenly hit a strong accent, graphically portrayed in a vertical stack of notes.

It was as though you were looking out of the window of a railroad car, and a telegraph pole suddenly flashed by. When I had had enough of it, I would look at the stage. My mother was displeased with this.

"No more of that," she told me during intermission. "You're doing it deliberately so people will look at you and say how bright you are."

And that's what happened. A lady sitting in the next seat wondered aloud why a boy was following the score. Aunt Tanya made haste to tell her it was her nephew, and that he wrote operas himself. The lady replied that she herself was an artist and forthwith wrote a poem on the program. It began:

> My little Sergei,
> Don't be afraid
> To watch. If you're a virtuoso
> Your path will be strewn with roses.

It was a long poem, but I don't remember the rest.

The various acquaintances we visited often asked me to improvise. On one occasion, a wit suggested, "Why don't you improvise a variation of 'Siskin, Siskin, Where Have You Been'?"

Everyone was delighted. "On 'Siskin,' of course! On 'Siskin'! A waltz!"

"A mazurka!"

"A tender song!"

"A funeral march!"

So I improvised. My success was most unusual. Actually, it was no great task: I knew the tune; all I had to do was get the feel of the waltz or funeral march, and the rest came by itself. I repeated the variations at the homes of various aquaintances.

"You absolutely must write them down," my mother said. "You can see how everyone likes them."

My attitude toward this new opus was one of condescension. "Siskin!" What a theme! Nothing really interesting in it—second-rate music. But the success was pleasing, so I wrote it. Mother made herself a fair copy.[55]

The lady who had asked for a "tender song" was Maria Grigoryevna Kilschtedt, an acquaintance of the Rayevskys and herself the wife of a state councilor.

Mme. Kilschtedt, about fifty years old, was intelligent and witty. She was a poet whose verses had been printed in the newspapers, and she was preparing a volume of them for publication. They were not highly original but they were written smoothly and grammatically and were easy to read.

I wanted to undertake a new opera but didn't know what subject to use. We asked Mme. Kilschtedt's advice. She thought for a minute, and then exclaimed, *"Undine!* It's a marvelous story. And it's all right for a boy his age— everything in it is pure. I'll write the libretto myself. He can read Zhukovsky's version, but I'll work from La Motte-Fouqué's original."[56]

I had read it: not bad, but it wasn't clear how one could make an opera out of it. Mme. Kilschtedt, however, went on enthusing about the subject and suggested that I think about the story line.[57]

> From me to my father in Sontsovka.
> Petersburg, March 17 (30), 1904.

Maria Grigoryevna Kilschtedt has promised to come and see us on Friday so that she and I can plan the libretto for *Undine,* which I have decided to make into an opera. She had undertaken to write the libretto in verse. Right now I am planning it; that is, dividing it up roughly into acts and scenes.

It may turn out to be too long (five acts, ten scenes), but otherwise a lot will have to be discarded. When we were at her place, she gave me Avenarius' book, *Glinka.*[58] I have already begun to read it, and I like it.

Yesterday we went to Aunt Tanya's for dinner. While we were there I read *Glinka* and worked on the outline for *Undine.* I want to buy a pedometer. It costs seven rubles, but maybe they'll sell it for less.

On Sunday we went to a Lutheran church with Aunt Tanya. I'm very glad the dogs are in good health, and I thank them for their greetings.[59]

> From me to my father in Sontsovka.
> Petersburg, March 18 (31) 1904.

. . . Then (yesterday) we went to the Rayevskys'. While we were there I drew up a new outline for the opera, which now has the same five acts but only six scenes. This way it will be more condensed and farther from reality.[60]

So we settled on five acts and six scenes, and Mme. Kilschtedt promised to send the first act—in verse, of course—to Sontsovka in a few weeks.

During our stay in Petersburg I composed a new march,[61] since I had been told the first one was too much of a concert piece. The second one was less of a concert piece and less successful. Meantime, the prospects of having the first one played had grown dimmer, since we were moving to Petersburg.

In addition to the marches, I suddenly hit a streak of free composition. I was bored by all that harmony, counterpoint, accompaniment, and little songs with symmetrical repetition of bars, and wanted to compose something big with nobody holding onto my coattails. I began to improvise and compose, also sketching out the orchestration.

When Glière came to Petersburg, I showed this music to him, and he disapproved of it. In an attempt to straighten things out, I said this would be the development, and I would write the exposition later. Once again he disapproved, saying that you had to write the themes first and then develop them, otherwise you would end up with nothing. And so my "free composition" ground to a halt. One page of it has been preserved.[62] There you can see an attempt at harmonic innovation:

Sergusha has lost weight [my mother wrote my father] and is obviously wearing himself out, although he is not working on languages: he has no time for it. Once again our neighbors are keeping us from sleeping with their shouting, which begins at eight o'clock. We always go to bed at midnight, if not later. Or else the yard keepers start chopping wood under the windows. This evening Sergusha even wept, and I tried to calm him down.[63]

So that I wouldn't catch cold, my mother had bought me some quilted pants. When I went outside I put them on over the short pants that were part of my usual attire. Once when we were at a concert I started to take them off. Looking at me askance, a lady asked, "Are you going to take all your clothes off?"

After that I tried to take them off behind the coatrack (where I couldn't be seen so easily) because they still bothered me. But my mother was unyielding. "You mustn't take them off," she said, "or you'll catch cold."

On March 23, we left for Sontsovka, remembering to buy four-hand arrangements of Schumann's symphonies. Before we left we had seen Glazunov again at a rehearsal, and he had promised to pay another call on my mother to talk about the Conservatory. He didn't come, but he did send me the orchestral scores of Glinka's *Valse-Fantasie* and his *Kazachek*.[64] Both were signed copies.

One of the inscriptions read: "From A. Glazunov to his dear colleague, Serezha Prokofiev." When I showed it to my father at Sontsovka, he spread his hands in a gesture of puzzlement. "What do you make of that? A man with doctor's degrees from both Oxford and Cambridge universities writes 'dear colleague.' As if you were his colleague!"

My father knew that Glazunov had doctor's degrees from two of the most famous universities in Europe, and this impressed him.[65]

45

Our return to Sontsovka coincided with the appearance of the first flowers. Every day when I came back from my walk I would bring in a new flower. In most cases I would know the name in both Russian and Latin and if I didn't know, I could look it up in Rayevsky's book. My father, by way of encouraging my interest in botany, suggested I make a note of the day they first appeared.

"Very good!" I exclaimed. "And I'll make notes next year, too, and compare them." I was forgetting that next year I would be at the Conservatory.

My thirteenth birthday was marked by the appearance of a "bright-green butterfly." I recorded this in a thick (fifty-page) copybook in a cardboard binding that Mother had bought in Petersburg for fifty kopecks. When she made me a present of it, she said, "Write down everything in it. Don't miss a thing."[66]

I began writing things down immediately, while we were still in Petersburg. My first invention was a new alphabet. I wrote the vowels in a rather large flourish, joining to them, in smaller script, the consonants of that particular syllable. Each vowel and consonant had its own special shape—one that I had thought up. Taken all together, they looked a bit like Chinese writing.

I had invented the new alphabet because I wanted to encode my diary. I was thinking about resuming it and was afraid it might get into my parents' hands.

In my letters to Father from Petersburg I would report news of the Russo-Japanese War, and rumors about it. Once I sent a fable about a Flea, a Bulldog, and a Lion: the Flea was Japan, the Bulldog was England, and the Lion was of course Russia. But what caught my fancy the most was the Russian fleet: I was familiar with all the ships—their tonnage, armament, and appearance. Hence, a game: pasteboard battleships would move along the squares, firing at a certain range, and making a certain number of hits. At first the game was uninteresting, since the one who first took a hit sank first. But gradually it was improved. My favorite ships were the battleship *Retvizan* and the cruiser *Novik*. I wrote verses about them.

On my thirteenth birthday my parents gave me the complete piano works of Grieg—six fat volumes that cost fifteen rubles. My mother said, "This is a good present. Play the pieces attentively."

I played them with pleasure, although certain Scandinavian figures escaped me and left me indifferent. I liked the sonata best of all.

46

Glière kept vacillating about whether he was going to spend the summer at Sontsovka, but finally wrote saying he was not coming. It didn't matter as much as it might have, since I was going to the Conservatory in the fall. On the other hand, I had to give more time to general academic subjects.

My parents obtained the syllabi used at the Conservatory, and tutored me as for the fiercest high-school competition, not realizing that nonmusical subjects are much less rigorously taught at the Conservatory.

I didn't gain anything from this beyond sheer practical advantage, but it took a frightful amount of time.

Mme. Kilschtedt sent the first act of *Undine* with a covering letter in which she wrote (my parents read it in my presence) that "here, it seems, he can do anything." I got to work immediately.

An old fisherman (I made him a tenor) is sitting on the shore with *Undine:*

> . . . adopted, not his real daughter;
> Already eighteen years of age.

A knight, Sir Hildebrand, comes out of the woods and tells how he has been annoyed by all kinds of evil spirits as he came on his way. He had been sent into the woods by the beautiful Bertalda, who was testing him. Undine listens, sitting at his feet and at the mention of Bertalda she starts playing all kinds of pranks, first splashing water, then fleeing. When a storm breaks, she hides herself in the pelting rain and in the water of the lake.

"Just listen to the drumming of the raindrops!" exclaims the Fisherman. And he and the Knight rush off in search of Undine. Meantime the rainfall is transformed into a ballet of rivulets, marking the end of the first act (or scene).

Everything was clear to me except the transformation of a downpour into a ballet. I had my doubts about that. How could the downpour, which I perceived as a menacing phenomenon of nature that frightened the Fisherman and the Knight, become an innocent and elegant ballet?

The downpour:

But my mother liked the idea. "Ah, a ballet of rivulets!" she said. "What a marvelous thing!" And I had to go along with her. That summer I wrote the entire act and corrected it. During the same period I wrote six "ditties" for piano which became a part of the third series. The most interesting of them is March No. 3, for either piano or military band:[67]

Also, the *Vivo* dedicated to my father on his fifty-eighth birthday:[68]

I believe I also orchestrated several ditties of the preceding series during that same summer.

Back in Petersburg, before the days of *Undine,* Glière had suggested that I orchestrate some of them as an exercise. Once I had started on *Undine,* that wasn't so necessary. But I didn't begin scoring it until June or July and in the meantime I had worked on the ditties at odd moments.

I was very busy, since I was spending five hours a day preparing for exams on academic subjects. And yet in my spare moments I didn't always know what to occupy myself with.

My father would ask, "Why are you wandering around doing nothing?"

"I'm bored."

"Then read something!"

He got me into the habit of reading, and saw to it that I was supplied with books.

One day the mail arrived while we were in the orchard. The mail was usually something to enjoy: letters, newspapers, magazines. But this time, when my father opened the newspaper, his face darkened. "Chekhov is dead," he said.

I didn't know who Chekhov was but the change in my father's face astounded me and remained in my memory.

By August the first act of *Undine* had been orchestrated and I had studied the required academic subjects. Mother and I made ready to leave for Petersburg. I was not particularly unhappy about leaving Sontsovka. It was a place I didn't like very much. Only once in the past, in the carriage as we were leaving for the capital, did I have to fight back tears—trying to drive them away with pleasant thoughts about the locomotive I had saved up twelve rubles to buy. It was going to be a real one heated by alcohol and run by steam.

Yet my sorrow stayed with me—for the first ten kilometers, at any rate. But now I was leaving in good spirits: I wasn't afraid of the exams, I had a feeling that many interesting things were in store for me, and Papa had promised to come to Petersburg in a month.

PART TWO

THE CONSERVATORY

I

ON August 23, 1904, my mother and I arrived in Petersburg. I was entering the Conservatory, and this marked the beginning of a new phase of my life. We had not yet taken final leave of Sontsovka, but the center of gravity had shifted to Petersburg.

My letters were now full of news about the war with Japan, which was going badly, especially with the fleet. Concerning the assassination of Plehve, Minister of the Interior,* my mother wrote:

> The explosion was so powerful that [a female colleague of Tanya's] was whirled up in the air and then thrown to the ground . . . A huge crowd gathered. A resourceful policeman, not knowing at first what to do with such a crowd, said, "Ladies and gentlemen, there will soon be another explosion." And the whole crowd dispersed.[1]

We were using the apartment the Rayevskys had left vacant. We looked up Chernov. I was weak in elementary theory and needed some coaching. Chernov liked the *Vivo* I had written during the summer, shrugged his shoulders at *Variations on Siskin,* and had high praise for the overture to *A Feast in Time of Plague,* which he had not seen in the spring. "A full-fledged overture," he called it.

But the important thing for me was that Chernov had acquaintances in Kronstadt and gave me various details on the battleships and cruisers.

From my mother to my father in Sontsovka.
Petersburg, August 26, 1904.

Today, August 26, the day of the examination in elementary theory, I woke up at six o'clock, still worried about a number of things. I got up at 7:30 but didn't awaken Sergusha until 8:30. The fact that he was going to take the examination left him completely indifferent. To a certain extent, this is good, and is no doubt a trait of his personality. In short, Sergusha and I set out at about nine o'clock, taking a portfolio with some of his

* Vyacheslav Plehve, assassinated in July 1904. (Translator's note.)

§ 99 §

shorter pieces. There were crowds of people at the Conservatory. [My mother then describes how she went from one department to another, from the second floor to the fourth, and back again. It was finally explained to her by an official that I didn't have to take an examination in elementary theory, but that I should come back in two weeks, on September 9, for the examination in theory of composition.]

"No," I said, "on the second for the examination in general academic subjects."

"*What?* Academic subjects?" "Yes, my son is only thirteen." "Then why is he taking the composition course? Madame, do you realize [he almost asked, "Are you out of your mind?"] what the theory of composition is?" "Yes," I said with a laugh, "I realize. And I can refer you on this matter to Alexander Konstantinovich [Glazunov]." "Did he himself say that?" "Yes, and he advised it." "Most unusual! But in any case I'm very glad to hear it." And giving me a smile that was a bit too amiable, he held out his hand.

> From me to my father at Sontsovka.
> Same day.

By 11:35 we were already back home, where Aunt Tanya was waiting for us. I ran in first.

"Well, did you pass?" she asked.

"No," I said.

"What do you mean, 'no'?"

"Just that. I didn't pass."

"Really?"

"Really."

"Word of honor?"

"Word of honor."

"But why?"

"Because I didn't take the exam."

Aunt Tanya called me a swine and said we might just as well not have come until September 2.

We decided to use the extra time to look for an apartment. We were on the go until four o'clock, finally found something that was a fifteen-minute walk from the Conservatory.

Our apartment was on the third floor and consisted of five rooms. It was divided by the vestibule and a small hallway into halves: the dining room, the drawing room, and my mother's room had windows overlooking the street; my room and my aunt's room gave onto the courtyard. There were also a kitchen and bathroom. The rent, including firewood, was seventy rubles a month, of which Aunt Tanya paid twenty rubles. The apartment's shortcomings included a dingy stairway, the lack of a doorman, and the fact that the dining room was in the wrong place. My room was tiny.

2

From my mother to my father in Sontsovka.
Petersburg, September 2, 1904.

Today Sergusha underwent his baptism of fire. To the glory of our consubstantial Trinity—yours, mine, and Sergusha's work—he got good grades in the three examinations. In geography he got an "A." The teacher praised him, saying, "You are the first to get an 'A.' You know the subject very well. One would even like to try to confuse you."

In French the teacher also praised him, saying, "It is easy to see that you are well prepared." But for some reason he gave him a "B." He questioned him only a very short time, whereas he spent a longer time questioning the ones who didn't know much, and even stamped his feet if they began to conjugate *avoir* and ended up with *être*.

My impression of the Conservatory is, in general, a good one. You go there feeling that everything will be all right.[2]

My letter to my father of that same date almost amounts to a stenographic report of all the questions and answers at the examinations—not only mine, but those of my neighbors.

During the exams my mother was sitting on a chair on the hallway, waiting and worrying. A man in a green forester's jacket came up to her, bowed ceremoniously, and said, "You've brought your son, and I've brought mine. He's a violinist—an amazingly talented boy. Allow me to introduce myself: Forester Uk. I'm from the Province of Courland [or Livonia]."

When I came out after the exam, my mother whispered, "I've found you a friend—an amazingly talented boy. Let's go, and I'll introduce you."

Uk was my own age but a half a head taller, and he gave me a sour look. I didn't like him. We shook hands but didn't start up any conversation.

On the way home I told Mother, "I don't like Uk."

"You're wrong not to. You're used to your Stenyas and Serezhas. But he is a very fine boy. I'll invite him to our apartment."

The next day I took the exams in Russian and German. I got a B in both subjects.

Two days later I took the final academic exam in religion. The priest talked horribly fast. He didn't give me time to finish what I was saying, and if I hesitated he would answer for me.

"Tell me about the death of Moses. What did he leave as a heritage?"

§ 101 §

"The Pentateuch," I answered. "The Pentateuch," he confirmed (although according to historical research the Pentateuch was the work of later authors).

"Who was the leader of the Hebrews after Moses? What miracles did the prophet Elisha perform? Who was the first person Jesus Christ healed? What does the Ninth Commandment say? All right, you know it. You can leave."

From a letter to my father.

The exam was over so quickly Mama was amazed when I came out . . . He gave me a "B" and we went to the inspector to return the sheet to him, as we were supposed to. The inspector congratulated me upon my admission to the Conservatory, and shook Mama's hand. I bowed to him, and he shook my hand, too.[3]

Meantime, the "amazingly talented boy" Uk failed in two exams and had to start a grade below me. Thus contact with him was weakened automatically.

3

The main examination—on special theory—was held on September 9. As usual, we came very early—at ten, although the exam did not begin until noon.

From my mother to my father at Sontsovka.
Petersburg, September 9, 1904.

Before the examination I saw Glazunov. He came up to me, which showed that he recognized me. We greeted each other, and he immediately introduced me to Rimsky-Korsakov, saying, "She's the mother of that young composer I was talking to you about—the one you saw at the rehearsals." When we had shaken hands, I withdrew, not wanting to importune those local gods.[4]

From me to my father.
Same date.

They soon called us, and we went into the director's office. It was not really his office but his anteroom, so to speak: a long, narrow room with one window and no furniture. (It wasn't until later that they brought in chairs.) All those who were taking the exam in special theory—about twenty people—were in this room. Glazunov came out of the office. We were sitting next to the door. He shook hands with me and walked on, moving quietly. He shook hands with a few others, talked a bit with them, and then went back into the office.

Then Rimsky-Korsakov came out and simply threw up his hands in amazement. "Are you all taking the examination? All in special theory?"

"Yes," everyone answered him. He went away.

Later Glazunov and other professors passed through the room several times, talking with those taking the exam, and then went back.

They asked one of them, "Have you brought any compositions?"

"Yes, a song."

"One song?"

"Yes."

"That's not much."

"Well, you see, it *is* a song, but actually I haven't yet written an accompaniment for it."

"That's a very little indeed."

Finally they called one Burgov or Kurdov, then two others, and at last me, the fourth one. I picked up my two portfolios (one contained all the things I wrote this year, and the other the things from other years) and went into the office. There was no room in the portfolios for the bound copybook with the twenty-four "little songs," so I carried it by itself.

Rimsky-Korsakov asked me, "Are those your compositions?"

"Yes," I replied.

"And do you play the piano?"

"Yes, I do."

"I like that!" he exclaimed. And, pointing to the piano, he said, "Sit down and play!"

There was a Mozart sonata on the music rack.

It was one I had played a little a long time ago.

"This?"

"Yes."

I began to play.

"All right. Now play this." And, turning several pages, he showed me a piece that was totally unfamiliar to me. I played it, too.

There were another ten professors there besides Rimsky-Korsakov and Glazunov. They were sitting at a table across the room, drinking tea and eating rolls. As I recall, they included Lyadov, Wihtol, Solovyev, Petrov, Director Bernhard, and others.

At this point Glazunov told Rimsky-Korsakov that I was a pupil of Glière.

"What did you work on with him?" Rimsky-Korsakov asked me.

"He stayed with us last summer and the summer before, and taught me music."

"What did you do in the way of theory?"

"We went through harmony from the beginning. We used assignments from Arensky's textbook. But since I'm going to be studying harmony here, I didn't work on it at all this past summer."

"Yes," Glazunov confirmed. "I told him that he should take the harmony course."

"We should test his ear now," someone said.

"Do you have absolute pitch?" Rimsky-Korsakov asked.

"Yes."

"What is this note?" he asked when I had my back turned.

He asked me about several notes in this way.

Then someone said that I should name a whole chord. Rimsky-

Korsakov struck a bass chord. "What is that? Don't name the notes. Just tell me what kind of chord it is—what its name is."

"That's . . . a diminished seventh."

"Right. Now listen. What happens to it?"

"The upper d becomes a c-sharp."

"And what kind of chord have we got?"

"A six-five chord."

They all decided I knew enough so that it wasn't worthwhile asking any more questions.

"And now he must sing a solfeggio exercise."

"I've never sung solfeggio," I said.

"That doesn't matter," Rimsky-Korsakov said. "Here, sing me this bass part."

Since it was too low, I began to sing an octave higher, and as a result I fluffed a note. They decided that I sang on pitch but didn't really know how to sing, and said I must take solfeggio.

"In addition to harmony, of course," someone said.

"But wouldn't it be better to combine solfeggio with harmony? That way he could learn it in four weeks. The other way it would take a whole year, and he would lose a lot of time."

"Yes, it could be done that way, too."

The director said, "Have him sing in the different clefs."

"Do you know the clefs?" Rimsky-Korsakov asked.

"Of course he knows them," Glazunov said. "He writes orchestral scores."

"Orchestral scores, too?"

"Yes, and operas."

"Operas, too?"

They looked for something in alto clef, but at first couldn't find anything. Finally, however, they found something.

"But that calls for a virtuoso!" Glazunov objected.

I began to sing "o—." But Rimsky-Korsakov thought I was singing "do—." He said, "Don't sing 'do—' when it's not 'do' at all. Just sing without naming the notes."

After I had sung they asked to see my compositions. I opened the portfolio containing the things I had written this year: *Undine,* the *Vivo,* the second, third, and fourth marches, the *Variations on Siskin,* the *Song,* the *Allegro,* and the *Presto.*[5] On top of them was the list I had drawn up.

"That's a list of my compositions," I said.

Rimsky-Korsakov laughed. "A list?"

Under the list was the score of *Undine.* Rimsky-Korsakov picked it up and took it to the director's desk. Several professors gathered around him. Meantime, Glazunov said to me, "I never saw that. Did you write it this summer?"

"Yes, that portfolio contains only things I wrote this year. You haven't seen them."

Then Rimsky-Korsakov came up and told me to play *Undine.*
"And have him sing," someone said.
"But how can he sing it?" Rimsky-Korsakov asked.
"He sings his own compositions very well," said Glazunov, for whom
I had sung *A Feast in Time of Plague* last winter.
I began to play from the rough draft. Rimsky-Korsakov stood beside
me and turned the pages.

At this point I must interrupt the letter to relate an episode not covered in
it.[6] I had intended writing the overture to *Undine* later, when I had all the material ready. The first act began with three chords immediately preceding the
Fisherman's entry:

Rimsky-Korsakov said, "The voice-leading in the bass clef is not good."
And, taking out a pencil, he changed the g in the first chord to an f. The result
was:

No doubt he was equally single-minded when correcting Moussorgsky's
manuscripts. His correction did make the voice-leading more even, but it by no
means improved the quality of the music. If a correction was needed, it should
have been something like:

The letter continues as follows:

When I had played three pages—almost up to the first appearance of
the Knight—Rimsky-Korsakov said, "That's enough."
Then he asked how much of the opera I had written.
"One act."

"Why only one?"

"Because I haven't yet received the libretto for the second act."

"And who's writing your libretto?"

"A lady who is a poet."

One of the examiners said, "Let him play something for the piano."

After *Undine,* the next score in the stack was the *Vivo,* my best piano piece, which Chernov had approved. Glazunov took it and gave it to Rimsky-Korsakov. The latter put it on the music rack and told me to play it. I did.

That ended the examination. They all gathered around the examiners' table at the other side of the room and began to discuss how I could combine music study and academic courses. Nothing came of it.

Then Rimsky-Korsakov exclaimed, "Maybe he won't have to take religion. Is he Russian Orthodox?"

"Yes," he was told.

Glazunov came up to me. "Don't you know French?"

"Yes, I do."

"Do you speak it?"

"Yes."

"And German?"

"German, too."

He went over to Rimsky-Korsakov. "He knows both," he said.

Then they talked in low tones for a long time—so long that I had a chance to study the details of the room. I have drawn a floor plan, with a legend.

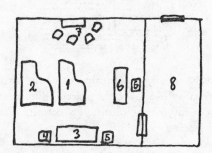

1. The grand piano I played on. 2. Another grand piano. 3. A harmonium resembling a lowboy. 4. A soft chair. 5. The chair on which I put my portfolio. 6. The director's desk and armchair. 7. The table, divan, and armchairs where the examiners sat. 8. The room in which we waited.[7]

From a letter my mother wrote my father the same day.

Rimsky-Korsakov came out and told me, "We don't know how to arrange things so that your son won't miss his academic classes, because the harmony class coincides with the classes in academic subjects."

"How many times a week will he have classes in harmony?"

"Twice."

"If he misses academic classes, he can study up on them. I can help him."

"Our inspector is very strict, and doesn't like it when someone cuts classes. If you're taking the course, you're supposed to be there. Can't you tutor him at home so that he doesn't have to attend these classes?"

"No, that would be hard for me to do."

He walked away.[8]

From my own letter.

"Where do you live?" [Rimsky-Korsakov asked me]

"In Petersburg."

"On what street?"

"On Sergiyevskaya [after the Revolution, Tchaikovsky Street], near the Tauride Park."

"What a long way off!"

"But we'll soon be moving to Sadovaya."

"What part of it? Sadovaya is a long street."

"Near the Pokrov."

"Even that is not very close."

"Well, in any case . . ." someone said.

Finally they let me leave. When I went out I found Mama talking with Glazunov and Rimsky-Korsakov.[9]

From my mother's letter.

Rimsky-Korsakov said, "We'll schedule his harmony lesson at 11:30 (that is, before the academic classes, which start at noon), and if there's no class, he can come home."

I thanked him, and he added, "That's not standard procedure—just for emergencies."

Glazunov said, "The director has agreed to admit him."

I thanked them, and asked, "Does that mean my son is accepted?"

"Yes, he's accepted."

Rimsky-Korsakov shook hands with me and Serezha, and walked away. Glazunov added, "I'm still staying at my country place. But on the fourteenth I'll move to town, and then we can see each other again."

In general it seems to me that Glazunov is kindhearted but doesn't show it because he is afraid people will take advantage of it. Therefore he holds himself back and doesn't say everything he wants to.*

I'll end this by saying one couldn't be treated any better than we were treated at the Conservatory. Everyone was attentive, and treated Serezha in a special way.[10]

* Art purchases detailed at this point. (Translator's note.)

4

Two courses in composition were taught at the Conservatory: one by Lyadov and Rimsky-Korsakov, and the other by Solovyev. The former was regarded as more prestigious. Solovyev got those student composers who had shown less promise and were as a rule preparing themselves for a teaching career. I was assigned to Lyadov's class. But he was a rather lazy man and was in no hurry to start teaching.

The first classes I attended at the Conservatory were those in academic subjects (the students taking those courses were called "scholars" at the Conservatory). Those classes made a much greater impression on me than the lessons in harmony. This was only natural, since up to that time about the only companions I had were my friends Stenya and Vasya, who were my underlings in a sense.

Then suddenly I found myself among a dozen girls and ten boys of widely varying ages. The girls and boys attended class together, the former sitting in the left rows of seats and the latter in the night. As I wrote my father, "One girl was acting up so much that she spilled her ink." She was only ten years old, and most of the time she got failing or near-failing marks. On the other side sat a student named Nikolayevsky, who was about eighteen. He wore a frock coat, a red necktie, and a heavy watch chain. He, too, got very poor grades and was terribly glad when someone else did the same.

I was indifferent to the presence of so many girls, being completely naïve in this respect. One day at home I put two rubber balls under my sweater in the position of a woman's breasts, and went to my mother in this getup.

She frowned and said, "That'll do. It's a bit early for you to get interested in such things." Then she took out the rubber balls and threw them into the next room, shouting, "Go get them!" And I ran after them.

I noticed that she had said "early," but just *what* was early and *why* it was early escaped me. On another occasion I heard someone say about a couple, "they were both so good-looking that when they went out together, all the girls looked him up and down, and all the boys did the same with her." I wondered why the boys looked at her and not at him.

The boys in the class were of the most varied nationalities: Poles, Germans, Jews, and Karaites. Their cultural level was rather mediocre. During breaks between classes I often talked with a boy named Akhron, who had a long, sharp nose. He was a grade behind me.

One day he told me, "You know, they're not going to let you go around in short pants."

"Why not? I passed the exam in composition, and Rimsky-Korsakov—"

The author at the age of seven. Taken in Ekaterinoslav.

Holograph of the polka composed at the age of seven.

The author at ten, taken in St. Petersburg. The title, "The Giant," was handwritten.

Cover of the bound score of The Giant.

Sergei Taneyev and Yury Pomerantsev in the park.

Reinhold Moritsevich Glière.

My attempt to draw up a catalogue of my works, giving the first few bars of each. (The Indian Galop *is the first entry—Editor's note.)*

Мои сочиненія.

Год		Произведение	Счетъ	Темпъ
1896г.	{лѣто}	Индійскій галопъ F-dur.	2/4	(Allegro)
		Маршъ C-dur.	C	(Andante)
1897г.	{	Вальсъ C-dur.	3/4	(Moder.)
	{лѣто	Рондо C-dur	3/8	(Alegretto)
	{январ	Маршъ h-moll (C-dur)	C	(Allegro)
1898г.	{февр.	Маршъ въ 4 руки (C-dur)	C	(Andante)
	{ноябрь	Вальсъ g-dur	3/4	(Allegto)
	{декабрь	Маршъ въ 4 руки C dur.	C	(Andte)
	{лѣто	Вальсъ C-dur (g-dur)	C (3/4)	(Allegro)
1899г.	{сентябрь	Маршъ въ 4 руки F-dur.	2/4	(Allegro)
	{ноябрь	Пьеса въ 4 руки F-dur	2/4	Allegro
1900г.	{февр-іюнь.	Опера „Великанъ"		—
1901г.	{	Пьеса въ 4 руки, d-moll	6/8	—
	{	Маршъ	C	
	{	Опера „На пустынныхъ островахъ"		
	{	Маршъ къ оперѣ	C	
1901г.	{	Багатель №1, Es-dur	2/4	Vivo
	{іюнь	1ая пѣсенка I серіи, Es-dur	C	Allegro
1902г.	{іюнь	2ая пѣсенка I серіи, A-dur	C	Andante

"My works."

"That doesn't mean anything. Rimsky-Korsakov has nothing to do with short pants. But you'll get a talking-to from Abramychev, the deputy inspector."

The next day I met Rimsky-Korsakov on the stairs and bowed to him. He looked at me absentmindedly, but then recognized me and said hoarsely, "Hello."

I was flattered that he remembered me, and couldn't restrain myself from bragging about it to Akhron.

"What's so unusual about that?" he said, quite unperturbed. "Rimsky-Korsakov is a polite man. If I bow to him tomorrow, he'll answer me, too."

Basically Akhron was right. And yet I felt that in a way he had missed the point. After all, Rimsky-Korsakov had not simply responded to my bow: he had *recognized me* and responded. But I wasn't able to explain that.

Quite different from Akhron was another boy who was very interested in the fact that I was studying theory of composition, and he kept asking me how I composed. His name was Potemkin, and he was in the sixth form, being three years older than I. He was pleasantly sociable but rather sloppy-looking. As I recall, he was studying double bass but intended to switch to voice.

I spent the breaks between classes with him and Akhron rather than with the students in my own class.

A few days after matriculation I took the exam in piano. My mother had hoped that I could take two majors: theory and piano. But I had the extra load of academic subjects. Glazunov said he was afraid that would be too much, and advised me to take only theory the first year, since *a fortiori* it involved "obligatory" piano. The theory students were given piano training, but not to the same extent as those majoring in piano.

At the examination for obligatory piano I played scales, arpeggios, scales in thirds, a Bach fugue, and a Beethoven sonata, and sight-read something. Alexander Winkler, the senior instructor, said, "All right. I can take you in my class. You read music rather well, and you don't play badly, although you need more technique."

Winkler's accepting me meant that I would be in the advanced class for obligatory piano. He was a German with a French wife; a pleasant, tactful man who composed music himself, though he had no exceptional talent. To begin with, he assigned us Beethoven's *First Sonata*.

Meantime my mother and aunt were moving to the new apartment. While our furniture was in the warehouse, rats had nibbled into the slipcovers but not into the furniture itself. During the actual moving the dining-room table fell off the van and broke into pieces.

Mother's letters to Father were full of accounts of our moving and getting settled in "Tanya's apartment." They had agreed to use that appellation for it in case the inquisitive postmaster should open a letter and perhaps spread a rumor that my father was furnishing an elegant apartment in Petersburg.

Although our apartment was only moderately handsome by Petersburg standards, it might seem very luxurious when described to someone living in the backwoods of Sontsovka.

"Serezha is very pleased with his room," Mother wrote to Father. "He holes up in it and spends all his time at his desk." This fondness for my desk was one I acquired early and have retained all my life.

What was I doing while "holed up" in my room? I studied my lessons, read, continued writing my narrative poem, *The Count,* played chess games, and drew up my catalogue of Russian naval vessels. (No longer content with just battleships and cruisers, I had added destroyers and transports, with their displacement and armament.) And I invented games, chiefly involving naval battles.

I made an attempt to resume my diary—this time without encoding it, since my desk had drawers that could be locked. There were so many events to record, and all of them so interesting. I began the diary again four days after my academic classes started, and tried first of all to bring it up to date. But I wanted to put down everything, and there was so much!

While I was chronicling those four days, a few more days had passed, and while I was covering them, even more days passed. I simply couldn't catch up, and I was unwilling to skip any days, so I gave it up.

5

One important event was the purchase of a new grand piano. Mother had learned of a big auction at which seventy-five instruments were being sold. We went for a preliminary look and chose three to bid on. Later we went to the actual auction. I followed the proceedings excitedly, particularly some of its comical aspects, such as a lady outbidding herself. On the first piano we had selected the bid-up was only five rubles, so that we got it for three hundred rubles (including customs duties and cost of delivery). The new piano had a good sound, and I liked that. "There is fretwork on the legs, pedals, and edges," I wrote Father. "In general it is very handsome and much enhances the drawing room."

Because of the auction I even missed classes at the Conservatory. On Tuesdays they issued us booklets in which our marks for the week were recorded.

I got good grades: an A for history and geography, and a B for arithmetic. "His assignments are still too easy," my mother wrote to my father. "They don't cover much, and they do it badly."

On September 22 I was told to report to the deputy inspector. Lyadov was there: short, squat, and bald, with a *soupçon* of a mustache and beard. He looked at me with his bloated eyes and said, "You see, old chap, I teach harmony from one to three, and you have academic classes at that time. So you'd better call your mother."

From the very first words—"You see, old chap"—Lyadov struck me as very different from Rimsky-Korsakov or Glazunov. He regarded teaching at the Conservatory as a burdensome duty and showed no interest in his students.

Mother showed up, and they conferred. Because of the harmony lessons I would have to miss academic classes twice a week, and the inspector would not go along with that. They gave us time to think it over.

By now it was my name day, and I celebrated it like a child, as if I were not already taking a course in theory of composition.

In the morning, while I was still in bed, Mother and Aunt Tanya brought me a box of candy and a letter and books that Father had sent. (They had arrived the day before but had been hidden from me.) Also, I was given permission to buy a letter seal, something I had been anxious to have.

I spent half the morning at the pleasant business of deciding what I should have engraved on it: "Sergei Sergeyevich Prokofiev" or simply "S. S. Prokofiev." Then we went to a toy store, where I chose a mechanical submarine and another ship with cannons you could shoot.

I had congratulations and gifts from other people, including a child's microscope that a girl cousin had sent me, with the words "To magnify your knowledge." I went to bed at eleven o'clock, so tired I slept for twelve hours.

"It has been cold and rainy here for two days," Mother wrote to Father. "Sergusha is wearing a quilted pea jacket, quilted pants, and galoshes." Those pants, which I had to put on over my short pants, were hateful to me, and I was ashamed of them, but Mother was unyielding. I dreamed of having long pants like everybody else, and secretly hoped that one fine day Akhron's prediction would be borne out and Deputy Inspector Abramychev would prohibit the wearing of short pants. As it happened, he did ask Mother to come and see him again, but it had nothing to do with pants.

"I decided to bother you, madame, because your son has fallen into undesirable company," he said. "I can see that he is a boy of good family. But he is associating with a certain Potemkin, who has a bad record with us. He is a very dissolute young man. Moreover, he is much older than your son."

When Mother came back home she was in a terrible state. "What kind of a person did you make friends with?" she shouted. "I stop keeping a close eye on you for two weeks, and you take up with God knows who. I found a friend for you—Uk, a very decent boy. But you had to take up with some good-for-nothing. And because of it, I'm called in to see the inspector."

"But Potemkin is very likable, Mamochka. As for Uk, he's as dull as dishwater."

"You will please break off that friendship immediately. If you don't, he might teach you God knows what. Has he already said bad things to you?"

"Not at all. No bad things."

And in fact I had heard nothing bad from Potemkin.

"Break it off anyway. Don't talk to him any more. If you don't like Uk, there are many other good boys at the Conservatory."

I hadn't the slightest notion why Potemkin was bad, but Mother's agitated state convinced me. Potemkin was depicted as a kind of leper who had to be avoided. The next time I met up with him I greeted him evasively and quickly walked away. During breaks between classes I tried to avoid him. For two days he waddled along behind me, saying, "I don't understand what's happened to you . . ." But I would slip away. In that way the friendship broke up.

6

The first harmony class met on September 29. These lessons were taught in "the classroom under the clock," so called because there was a clock over the door. To the left there were five students' desks, facing two windows. To the right, near the window, a grand piano, and nearer to the door a blackboard with red staves on it used for writing out music. There were five other students besides myself. The oldest, Shpis, was over thirty. "I've started on my fourth decade," he would say. "I have two children, and Prokosha, there, is only thirteen." Shpis had blond hair parted in the middle, and wore a fashionable motley-colored velvet waistcoat.

The next one was named Kobylyansky. He was rather vague, nervous, and took a dilettantish attitude toward his assignments. In addition to theory he was taking the special piano course, and he played well. The two university students were very different from each other. One of them, Grossman—very neat and foppish—did his assignments badly. The other, Asafyev—sickly-looking, stooped, and wearing a threadbare double-breasted jacket—did his work well. Shpis and Kobylyansky were rather hostile toward me: it annoyed them that a boy of thirteen should have wormed his way into such a serious class. The two university students were indifferent: I didn't bother them. Many years later I became a friend of Asafyev, who turned out to be a very good musician.

The fifth student was Kankarovich, tall and dark-haired with a pale face and a retreating forehead, as if the front part of his cranium had been lopped off.

At nineteen, Kankarovich was the youngest of the five. He sat next to me and was friendly. In addition to theory, he was studying violin. He hoped to become a conductor, and was taking the harmony course in order to get a foundation in theory.

Lyadov taught according to Rimsky-Korsakov's system and went directly into the first lesson without beating around the bush. But it probably would have been a good idea, before doing so, to tell us what harmony actually was, why it was the basis for composing music, and how those dry rules would give us greater scope in our subsequent composing. At any rate, I for one (perhaps because of my youth) never made any connection between Lyadov's lessons and my own plans for composing.

In my free time I continued to compose and enjoyed it. But I regarded the harmony assignments as a tedious chore, much less interesting, for example, than my geography lessons. I made no attempt to apply what I had learned in harmony class to my composing. On the contrary, while composing I strove to get away from all that—which was roughly the same thing I had done two years before.

Rimsky-Korsakov's system differed from the Moscow system, used by Pomerantsev and Glière, in that the Moscow teachers let the students use all of the scale degrees from the very outset, whereas Rimsky-Korsakov first taught them how to use the three basic degrees, I, IV, and V, then gradually introduced the others. This approach may have provided a more solid foundation, but it was also more boring.

The first lesson was brief: Lyadov merely explained the use of the three scale degrees. Then, beginning with the second lesson, he spent most of the time checking the students' work. He would sit down at the piano, and our little group would gather round him. He had a sharp eye and would immediately catch any mistake, which he would then proceed to mark with a pencil he took from his vest pocket: 5 for parallel fifths, 8 for parallel octaves, and 58 (this was very bad but it sometimes happened) for fifths and octaves simultaneously.

He would be very annoyed if the work was untidy—which was often the case, especially with Kobylyansky and me. I divided my attention between the music and his bald pate: it was large, very smooth, and gleaming, and it smelled like the card table we used for our games of *vingt* at Sontsovka.

7

In mid-October, Father came from Sontsovka to visit us. Mother was burning with impatience to show him our new apartment and furnishings.

However one wanted to look at it, the fact remained that Father had been left alone to work in the isolation of Sontsovka, while we had moved to Petersburg, where life was interesting.

Mother wanted to give him a hearty welcome, and make it plain that she intended the apartment not just for us but as a place where he could spend his vacations. She wrote him: "We are trying to get completely settled in before your arrival, so that everything will be both attractive and convenient. Right now we giving all our time to practical tasks. We can enjoy ourselves later."

Before he arrived, an important decision was made: I was taken out of the academic classes. When Glazunov advised my mother to send me to the Conservatory, the idea was that I would take the academic courses much as at a high school, with harmony and piano added to them. But as it turned out, the music courses took up quite a lot of time, so that there was little of it left for the courses, which suffered accordingly. Then when Lyadov's classes conflicted with the academic classes, my parents decided to have me do my academic work at home, so as to be prepared for taking the yearly finals in the spring or fall.

Father asked me, "Who is the most serious and agreeable student in the third form?"

"A fat boy named Michel Piastro."

"Then ask him to give you, every Saturday, a list of what has been covered during the week, and give him a box of chocolates from time to time as a reward."

I made such a deal with Piastro, and from then on went to the Conservatory only for the music classes. This meant fewer hours spent at the Conservatory —including the time spent walking through hallways between classes. There was less contact with those my own age, and I "returned to the bosom" of home life.

Lyadov often failed to meet with his class, and the solfeggio lessons I was supposed to take along with harmony didn't begin until November.

Little by little my mother grew dissatisfied with the Conservatory with regard to the basic matter—theory of composition. When I had been taken to Moscow, everyone had vied with one another in showing interest. And when we first came to Petersburg, Glazunov and Rimsky-Korsakov had also given me unusual attention. But when I entered the Conservatory, everything dissolved into indifference and futility.

I'm thinking of inviting Chernov to come once a week and correct Serezha's summer compositions [Mother wrote Father]. As it is, there is no action or attention on the part of anyone. No one at the Conservatory cares about talent. Mediocrity is easier to deal with, and less trouble. In a word, quite apart from the Conservatory we ourselves must not lose time. God helps those who help themselves.[11]

And two weeks later: "Chernov has been here once, and looked over a march Serezha composed. He's coming back Wednesday. At least Serezha has *somebody* to talk music with." As matter of fact, even Chernov, whom Mother had had harsh words for earlier, was good to have now.

I added a postscript to that same letter: "I have begun to orchestrate *March No. 3* for military band (dedicated to you). Mikhail Mikhailovich [Chernov] says it can be performed."

8

One Sunday, Aunt Tanya decided to go to church, and I asked to be taken along. We went to the Pokrov, an old and rather large building across the square from us. There was a large crowd of worshipers. I was observing the service closely, when I suddenly noticed that it was stifling in the church and I could hardly breathe. I got a bit frightened and wanted to tell Aunt Tanya. But before I could manage to do it I fainted and fell on the stone floor. I came to out in the street. Aunt Tanya was holding me up by one arm, while on the other side I was being supported by a parishioner I had never seen before. He kept saying, "What's the matter with you, young man? What's the matter?"

I didn't regain full consciousness until I was back home in bed. The faces of my mother and Aunt Tanya loomed up before me out of the fog.

"You're a silly boy," Mother said affectionately.

"Don't write your father anything about this, or he'll be frightened," Aunt Tanya added.

My mother's family had been very religious, and both of my aunts kept the faith they had acquired as children until the end of their days. But my mother, with her skeptical mind, began little by little to doubt the truth of Christian teachings.

In my father's family, religion was apparently of minor importance, and at the university he acquired the atheistic outlook that was dominant among the Russian intelligentsia. For him, chemistry and the decomposition of elements were much more real than the creation of the world or the doctrine of a future life. After he had married my mother, he necessarily influenced her in the direction of an even greater indifference toward religion. And when she lost first one infant daughter and then another, her indifference gave way to bitterness and even hostility.

"The worse things are, the more natural they are," she liked to say. "And the better they are, the more amazing," she would add, knowing it caused considerable distress to the pious Aunt Tanya.

When it was raining at Sontsovka, she would say, "See? Since time immemorial, not only rain has fallen from the sky but all kinds of filth."

Aunt Tanya would get angry and say, "Marie, you know I don't like it when people say things like that."

But Mother would keep at it. "Just read the Old Testament: it tells how sulfur and all kinds of filth fell on people's heads."

"Dear Lord, give us leather to put boots together," Mother used to repeat. It didn't make any sense, but it reflected her attitude toward religion.

Father was more taciturn. Although he did not give credence to the metaphysical aspect of Christianity, he respected its moral aspect and regarded Christ's teachings as the noblest manifestation of the human spirit. But what he himself believed was one thing, and the influence that religion might exert on people around him was another. He felt that science and culture were the best means of lifting the peasants out of the dark realm of ignorance in which they dwelled.

But since Sontsovka had only one pathetic elementary school, while the village was afflicted by drunkenness, bad language, and thievery, he thought that the church, too, might serve as a restraining influence. Hence he never spoke against religion, and on the important holy days he would go to church for the sake of decency.

I myself was taught religion from early childhood, chiefly because a knowledge of the Old and New Testaments and the catechism was required for admission to high school. "Later, when you're grown up, you can decide for yourself."

It was my mother who tutored me in religion. When she was away, my father took over. He was more strict, and required that, to the best of my ability, I use biblical language in summarizing the contents of a book of the Bible.

One day Mother and I were learning a prayer to be said after a meal—the one that goes: "I thank thee, Creator,[12] because Thou has filled us with Thy earthly blessings; likewise deprive us not of Thy Heavenly Kingdom." She commented ironically, "I thank Thee for the food—and, by the way, don't deprive us of the Heavenly Kingdom, either."

At this point, she thought better of it, and stopped. But I always remembered that comment.

Another time she said, "God is bored because He's alone."

And again: "Things are much better with the Eskimos. They keep a little wooden god in their pockets, and take him out and pray to him. If he doesn't do what they want, they hew him to pieces."

On one occasion, in her role of sponsor, she paid a visit to the village school and took me with her. A lesson in religion was in progress, and the teacher was explaining the omnipresence of God.

"Is God here?" she asked, knocking on the underside of a student's desk.

The little boy she was asking took it as a joke and started to giggle.

"Is God here, or isn't He?" the teacher half shouted.

The boy took fright and said nothing.

"Of course He's here! He's everywhere!" she said.

The boy shot her a sideways glance of disbelief. I felt that something absurd was going on and in my turn, I looked askance at my mother, but she just sat there unperturbed.

All these details led me to think that, when it came to God, things weren't as complicated as they seemed during lessons or church services.

At the age of eleven or twelve I began to entertain the horrible thought that perhaps my parents didn't believe in God. The idea was too outrageous. I began to clutch at religion.

"People say God doesn't exist," I thought. "But after a couple gets married in church, children are born. What more proof is needed?"

It never once occurred to me that American Indians, who believe in idols, also have children. And I never told anyone of this argument I had conceived, hence I was spared any condescending smiles.

I was generally secretive in matters close to the heart, and so I was in this case. I waged my whole struggle for religion internally, letting no one know about it and not discussing the subject with anyone. My natural proclivity was toward Aunt Tanya, whom I felt to be an ally. But I had no discussions with her and only occasionally expressed a desire to go to church—something she was glad to hear. Thus it was that we had gone to the Pokrov. But the fainting spell frightened me and my religious aspirations cooled.

At home we never talked about religion. So that gradually the question faded away and ceased to be of importance. When my father died[13]—I was nineteen at the time—my attitude toward his death was atheistic. And the same thing was true when, at the age of twenty-two, I lost a close friend who had written me a note saying "Farewell" before his death.[14] I was especially grief-stricken by the "Farewell" as coming from a human consciousness which had departed once and for all time.

9

In November 1904, I fell slightly ill. I wrote to Father:

> Both Mama and I have caught colds and are slightly ill. They took my temperature: it was 101. Just to make sure, we called Tatyana Pavlovna [an aunt of mine who was a doctor]. She listened to everything with her stethoscope, *palpated,* and *percussed,* but didn't find anything. I was given two grains of quinine for the night.[15]

A few days later I again wrote to my father:

> Today they bundled me up and hired a cab, and I went to take my harmony lesson. I couldn't very well miss another one, since I had already missed two—Wednesday and Saturday. However, I found out that Lyadov wouldn't show up on Saturday, so I really missed only one lesson, and that doesn't count as really bad. Today, for example, half of the students didn't show up.[16]

Lyadov's indifference to his course was in fact total and my mother again complained to my father about the Conservatory. "I find that it isn't giving Serezha anything. He is still isolated, and in a state of complete indifference and inactivity."

My musical life was somewhat animated when students were given permission to attend rehearsals of the concerts sponsored by the Russian Musical Society.[17] The concerts took place on Saturdays, and the dress rehearsals were held on Friday mornings. All those Conservatory students who had paid for their lessons so that their "booklets were in order" were admitted to the dress rehearsals upon presentation of the booklets. In addition, the theory students, of which I was one, were entitled to attend the Thursday rehearsals.

Besides the concerts given by the Russian Musical Society, which favored conservative programs, there were the Siloti Concerts.[18]

Siloti, who had studied with Liszt, was a good pianist but a bad conductor. He was rich and had lived abroad a great deal. The symphony concerts he promoted were very well organized, and the participants often included new works from abroad and musicians we knew little about. His concerts were more popular with the public than were those of the Russian Musical Society.

I wrote to my father:

> Today Asafyev [one of the harmony students] said that it's possible to get a pass to the dress rehearsals for the Siloti concerts, but that only Glazunov can issue them. But you can get to see Glazunov only after five o'clock, since he comes to the Conservatory only on Wednesdays and Saturdays, and teaches orchestration from one until five without a break. But you can also get a pass from Kalafati, who is deputy inspector, or something of the sort. In a word, he is always there. Today, though, he wasn't. But I'll ask tomorrow.[19]

At the first Siloti rehearsal they played Glazunov's *Third Symphony* and the finale from Borodin's *Mlada* as scored by Rimsky-Korsakov,[20] but I have retained no impression of them. On the next program there was a recitation to orchestral music, the text being from Schiller and the music by Schillings.* The composer directed, and the recitation was by the famous German tragic actor Ernst Possart. He shouted and howled.[21]

The Russian Musical Society's concert was entirely devoted to works by Anton Rubinstein, in connection with some date or other. None of it sounded very impressive, and I was bored. Chaliapin was to sing at the actual concert, but since he was going to sing to a piano accompaniment he didn't come for the rehearsal.

The rehearsal began at nine in the morning, so one had to get up early, at half-past seven, when it was still dark. One morning in the autumn when I was on my way to a rehearsal, walking along the empty sidewalk and making a loud clacking sound with my heels, a colonel emerged from a side street and began walking along behind me, his spurs jangling. Hearing my measured tread, he fell in step as is the habit among military men, and the *jing-jing* of his spurs coincided with the clack-clack of my heels. I noticed it, and at first I liked it. But then I wanted to walk at a syncopated gait. I missed one half-step, and then strode normally, my feet hitting the ground midway between two jingles of his spurs.

The resulting sound was *clack-jing, clack-jing, clack*. The colonel, who had apparently been absorbed in his own thoughts, suddenly noticed that we were out of step, and got back into step with me: The *jing* coincided with the *clack*. Two steps later I again shifted to a syncopated gait. The colonel again corrected

---

* Max Schillings (1868–1933), German composer. (Translator's note.)

his own gait, but I had got into the spirit of the game and, as he did so, I shifted to a new synocopation. The fact that he simply could not get into step apparently began to annoy him: his spurs were jingling more nervously, and as he tried to change pace I could hear him stamping his feet.

Then the jingling became fainter and was coming from off to the side. I glanced around and saw that he was crossing the street diagonally and heading up the sidewalk on the other side.

In addition to attending rehearsals of symphonic concerts, I went to the opera a number of times. I saw *Carmen, The Queen of Spades, Pan Voyevoda,* and *Boris Godunov.* As to *The Queen of Spades,* I wrote my father in a rather independent spirit: "It's a good opera, but the singing, acting, and sets were repulsive."

Pan Voyevoda was Rimsky-Korsakov's latest work, only recently produced by a private opera company. It made no particular impression on me but I did remember the symphonic nocturne played while the stage was empty so as to represent a nocturnal landscape. After this nocturne the audience called out, "*Bis!*"

I have no recollection of my reaction to *Boris Godunov*—something all the more astounding since Chaliapin was in the lead role. But several of my letters to Father during that period are lacking, and it may well be that in one of them I wrote him about *Boris.* I began every letter with a complicated system of numbering; for example, "letter no. 11 after your departure, No. 27 after our departure, and Registered Letter No. 8 after your departure." Thus it was not difficult to ascertain that five letters written in the second half of November were lacking in my collection.

The only teacher at the Conservatory who worked seriously [with me?] was Winkler, my piano teacher. During the first semester we went through four Beethoven sonatas and several Bach fugues. Lyadov was indifferent and peevish, as before, and often failed to meet his class. The solfeggio lessons he gave me (by way of exception), together with the harmony lessons, were mediocre. I read in the different clefs rather well, since I was familiar with them from orchestral scores. But I sang badly. Often I could not make my voice go where it should, and could not hit the notes I wanted to. Also, I was thrown off by the necessity of naming the notes while singing.

10

"We are still living a very isolated life," Mother wrote to Father. "You'd think we weren't in the city at all. No one comes to see us, and we don't go to see anyone."

Those words echo a very real distress. Mother had been bored in the country but was convinced that by living in the city she would automatically acquire an interesting circle of friends. Such a group of people, however, did not come into being all on its own. The people had to be found, selected, and shown special attention. This done, an interesting circle could be created little by little. But Mother made no moves in this direction and she was astounded that she saw no one but the Rayevskys and two or three of their acquaintances.

On Sundays we dined at the Rayevskys' at six. Uncle Sasha was not wealthy, but he liked to have his friends and relatives gather at his home on Sundays. On such occasions there were some fifteen people at the table.

The Rayevskys paid great attention to good manners, and this was useful to me. Cousin Katya taught me, for example, that one should not bite into a round of bread, but break off a chunk; that at home one could use a crust of bread to wipe up one's plate; that ice cream should be eaten with a fork and never with a spoon; that one could talk at the table but not so loud as to interfere with the grown-ups; that when someone was telling about something, one had to keep quiet and listen; that one had to rise when a lady entered the room; that if a lady offered one her hand, one should kiss it, but one didn't kiss a girl's hand.

The Rayevskys' governess asked me to set the following quatrain to music for her:

> Oh, no! Neither Figner nor Yuzhin [famous singers]
> Nor anyone else amazes me.
> My heart needs only you alone,
> O Leonid! O, Leonid! [Sobinov, the most melting of the tenors]

I wrote a nice, trifling little song in G-flat major[22] that gave her great pleasure.

One day at the Rayevskys' when several ladies were eating in the dining room, my Cousin Katya brought me in. I was walking behind her, not quite tall enough to come up to her shoulder. She introduced me to each of the women in turn. When she said, "Madame So-and-So," I would kiss the lady's hand. When she said, "Mademoiselle," I wouldn't. One of the guests was visibly interested in why the ladies should be introduced to such a mere lad. But then she found out it was "for the hands" and laughed heartily.

Such were my brief contacts with society. They may have been useful in that I learned a few good manners I never could have acquired in distant Sontsovka.

In mid-December we left for home, Mother had written: "Both Sergusha and I are looking forward to the trip and very glad we shall be seeing you again, because we have missed you very much." And that was true: we were glad to get back to Sontsovka.

We brought Father two pineapples—no doubt the first pineapples that had ever been seen in Sontsovka. We ate one of them the day we arrived, and saved the other for New Year's Day. Also, Father had bought caviar, smoked fish, and candy on a trip to Kharkov, so that there were lots of goods things to eat on Christmas.

I had bought a toy for each of my young friends in the country. I covered the toys with a rug and had the children guess which one was for which child. For Mother's birthday, which coincided with Christmas, I had composed *March No. 6*,[23] a rather melancholy piece, which was the last in my third series of a dozen ditties. The other things I had composed in Petersburg were: *March No. 5*,[24] a "romance" for piano,[25] not entirely uninfluenced by Tchaikovsky,

which was dedicated to Mme. Kilschtedt; and a *Grande valse*,[26] with some nice bravura passages but not much content, which was written for the name day of Aunt Katya and Cousin Katya. I also finished the second scene of *Undine*.

Dr. Reberg and his family came for New Year's Eve. Reberg had three daughters about my age, and together we had fun all evening.

But when we sat down to supper at twelve o'clock, I suddenly felt terribly tired and told Mother so in a whisper. She took me to the bedroom and put me down on the bed without taking off my clothes. I dozed off. According to our agreement, I was awakened at ten minutes of twelve, and was on hand to greet the New Year. We drank wine and clinked glasses. But to the distress of their hosts, the Rebergs wouldn't eat any pineapple: this fruit was strange to them, and its action unknown, hence it was better not to partake.

II

The year 1905 began under the sign of revolution. Young as I was, I had not noticed its approach. That is, in the fall I had no doubt heard more than once about strikes and disturbances, but I did not realize what was actually happening, and tended to see things in terms of whether or not Father would come to Petersburg.

In my letters there are no traces of what was happening and whatever thoughts I entertained must have reflected the attitudes of those around me—especially of my mother. What was her attitude toward the events of the Revoluion of 1905? Having been born into a poor family and having reached an academic high school only with difficulty, she had since early youth had her mind set on education—something that was strengthened when she met my father. She had always studied and sought out people who could teach her something. Life in Sontsovka had put her in the reverse position: instead of learning, she had to teach the peasants. And she did: she taught in the rural school and treated patients. But peasant society in those days was so benighted that all her efforts went for nothing, while her thirst for intellectual things remained. And now that the liberation movement had begun she was ready to accept it as a struggle of the liberals against the conservatives, of the have-not against the haves, but she immediately rejected it when her viewpoint changed and she saw that movement as a rebellion of the nonintellectuals against the intellectuals. In her political views she was to the left of both her sisters: Aunt Tanya, who was living with us, and Aunt Katya Rayevskaya.

It seemed perfectly natural that the family of Rayevsky, a high-ranking official, should lean toward monarchism. But Aunt Tanya was in a more ambivalent position: having been given a position in the rather prominent "Department of the Empress Maria," thanks to the protection of the Rayevskys, she felt herself to be a commoner among the nobility and while she sometimes accepted the views of those around her, at other times she protested against them. She once wrote to my mother: "Something has happened to Nikolashka," meaning Nicholas the Czar.

My father's views were less known to me. We had been separated from him by our move to Petersburg, and when we were at Sontsovka he was rather taciturn on the subject of politics. I believe that the leitmotif of education predominated with him: first teach, educate, and build schools, then grant freedom. And he did build schools in three neighboring villages, by arrangement with *zemstvo*.* Also, his thinking was along professional lines: having served as superintendent of Sontsovka for thirty years, he was no doubt giving his thought to how he might carry out his complex system of farming amid the peasant disturbances that were starting up.

On January 7, Mother and I left Sontsovka on our way back to Petersburg. En route we stopped for a couple of days in Moscow to visit relatives and re-establish contact with the Moscow musicians—which made sense, given the indifference of the musicians in Petersburg. Mother wrote from Moscow:

> The visit to Glière was very useful to Serezha. He approved of *Undine*. When he came back, Serezha said, "When Chernov was displeased with *Undine* I lost all desire to compose. But now I want to again." Glière said that everyone had been asking about Serezha: Taneyev, Goldenweiser, and Konyus. Tomorrow Serezha is paying a quick visit to Taneyev.[27]

> From me to my father at Sontsovka.
> January 12 (25), 1905.

> Here we are in Petersburg, having arrived safe and sound. Today everything is calm in the city, and the disturbances seem to have quieted

* Elective district council. (Translator's note.)

down. They say that yesterday it was a bit scary to go out on the street. But today you can move about freely, although you often run into Cossack patrols of from two to five men, and all the storefronts and shopwindows are boarded up. In general it seems more frightful from Moscow.

From Moscow we sent you a registered letter (No. 2) in which I described everything up to January 10.

On the morning of the tenth, when Uncle Peter left, we went to see Olga Yureyevna at the Boyarsky Dvor. I was amazed by the splendor of the big modern hotel in which the wealthy Smetskys were living.

It is a splendid five-story building with plate-glass windows, an elevator, and other conveniences. In a word, the best hotel in Moscow.

At about four o'clock we went to Nikoly-Yamskaya Street to see the Tikhonovs. Olga Yureyevna had asked us to come back in the evening. The only person at home at the Tikhonovs was Fanya Stepanovna. It was terribly cold in their apartment—only seven degrees on the Réaumur scale. Your breath froze in the air. They wrapped us in shawls and started a fire in an iron kerosene stove.

Colonel Tikhonov, who had apparently come home in the meantime, very much liked the March No. 1, scored for military band, and said it could be performed. At about eight o'clock we left and went back to the Smetskys', where we stayed until 9:30, since Reinhold and his wife had promised to visit us at the Hotel France. Reinhold said that on Tuesday (that is, tomorrow) Taneyev would see visitors beginning at three o'clock, and that I should go to see him and take some music.

I forgot to tell you that Mme. Smetskaya asked me to buy twenty rubles' worth of sheet music for the sanatorium (operas, etc.—she gave me a list,) taking advantage of the fact that I, as a student at the Conservatory, could get a discount of 10 per cent. The Smetskys had built, near Sukhumi, a sanatorium called "Gulripsh" for patients with respiratory diseases, and were now furnishing it. When Reinhold heard about it, he said that the "Symphony Store" gave him a discount of 20 per cent, and that he would make the purchase. So (as we had agreed on the evening of the tenth) I had to show up at his place at two o'clock in connection with getting the sheet music. But the store didn't have it in stock and promised to send it. From Reinhold's place I went to Taneyev's, arriving there at seven minutes to three. He had moved from his old place to a new one (on the corner of Maly Vlasyevsky Lane and Gagarinsky Lane). Above the electric doorbell there was a sign reading:

S. I. Taneyev
REQUESTS PERSONS WISHING TO SEE HIM
TO COME ON TUESDAYS AFTER THREE O'CLOCK

The last five words were doubly underlined.

I rang and went in. Sergei Ivanovich came out to meet me. He didn't recognize me at first, so he asked hesitantly, "Serezha?"

Then, seeing my bundle, he asked, "Are those your compositions?"

"Yes," I replied.

"And what new thing are you composing now?"

"I'm composing a new opera—*Undine*."

"*Undine?* Which one?"

"The one by Zhukovsky, from La Motte-Fouqué."

"And who wrote the libretto for you?"

"A lady poet."

"A lady poet? Ah!"

Taneyev was also being visited by a student of his about twenty-five years old.

"Well, show me your compositions," Taneyev said.

I got out my music. It included *Undine* and *March No. 1,* scored for a military band.

"I don't know anything about military bands," he said, and put the march to one side. "And what's this?"

"That's *Undine.*"

"Well, play me your *Undine.*"

When I played about half of the first scene of Act I, he stopped me.

"I'm not interested in those recitatives. Don't you have some complete number?"

"Yes, I do." And I began to play the Fisherman's aria.

"Aha! And what is that?" he asked.

"That's the downpour."

"Well, play your downpour."

I began to play it.

"What's happened?" he asked after a little while. "Has the downpour let up?"

"Yes, it has let up."

I finished the downpour.

"And you haven't written any little piano pieces?"

"Yes, I have. I have twelve new pieces."

"Well, play the one you like the best."

I played the art song dedicated to Mme. Kilschtedt.

When I had finished, Taneyev asked in amazement, "And that's the way it ends?"

"Yes, that's the way."

"Very original. And now play something fast!"

I began to play the song dedicated to *you.*

"What's that called?"

"Vivo." (Ditty No. 8, third series, which I had played before Rimsky-Korsakov the preceding autumn at the entrance examination at the Conservatory.)

"How do you happen to be in Moscow?" Taneyev asked, as he was showing me to the door.

"We went to the country for Christmas, and stopped off here on the way back (to Petersburg). We arrived yesterday, and we're leaving tomorrow."

"Well, goodbye."

"Goodbye."

"My regards to your mama."

12

We reached Petersburg exactly three days after the people, led by Gapon, had come to the square in front of the Winter Palace with a petition to the Tsar and had been fired on.[28]

The city was now externally quiet but seemed to be quaking from underground explosions, just as the ripples from a stone thrown into a pond continue to spread for a long time afterward.

> From my mother to my father at Sontsovka.
> Petersburg, January 13 (26), 1905.

It was a bit frightening to come to Petersburg: in Moscow we had heard of some terrible things. At the station Lyubov Dmitriyevna reassured us that everything had quieted down, and as a matter of fact the street riots have not recurred since then. It is dangerous to go out in the evening, and we aren't going anywhere. I won't let Serezha go out alone. Don't worry, we'll be careful.

I was very pleased with the visit to Taneyev. He inspired Serezha. We're indebted to Glière, who insisted on it. He was very warm toward Serezha and helped his morale. He promised that he would come to Petersburg and introduce Serezha to a few musicians.[29]

> From me to my father at Sontsovka.
> Petersburg, January 12, 1905.

Lyadov didn't come to class. There were only two theory students there; the others didn't come. They told me that Lyadov hadn't been there on the 7th either, and that he had also frequently missed classes before Christmas. So I missed no more than one or two lessons, and did more assignments than were necessary. For want of something to do, they [that is, my classmates] asked me to play one of my compositions. I played for them, and they liked it. They were amazed, because they thought I was composing abominations of some kind.[30]

> From me to my father at Sontsovka.
> Petersburg, January 16 (29), 1905.

We shouldn't have come to Petersburg so early. Lyadov misses both the harmony and the solfeggio classes. Please send me my wooden barrel with the figurines. [The little barrel, about twenty centimeters in diameter and painted in the Russian style, served me as a storage bin for figurines used in all kinds of games. I needed those figures to set up battles on oilcloth marked off into squares.][31]

> From my mother to my father at Sontsovka.
> Petersburg, January 16, 1905.

The papers have been coming out for only two days now, so that we couldn't try to find a student for Serezha. [It was a question of placing an ad for a tutor in academic subjects.] They say there will be disturbances today, too. All the storefronts on Nevsky Prospect are boarded over. At Eliseyev's (a big delicatessen, elegantly furnished) they stole everything in the store and broke huge, expensive panes of glass. The damage runs 15,000 rubles.

How lazy they are about classes at the Conservatory! Even the academic classes don't begin until the 14th. Lyubov Dmitriyevna is going away tomorrow.[32]

Lyubov Dmitriyevna was a country acquaintance of my father's. She had held some kind of position in one of the villages near Sontsovka. After saving up a little money, she had come to Petersburg to have a look at the capital and, at Mother's invitation, was living in our apartment. She wanted very badly to gain entree into General* Rayevsky's home, which put Mother in a difficult position, since it was not clear whether a profoundly provincial woman would be in her place among the starched-shirt types who gathered at the Rayevskys'. But Lyubov Dmitriyevna insisted, so Mother had to ask Aunt Katya.

"The thing is, Marie," Aunt Katya said, "I'm afraid she'll feel awkward at our home. But if she wants it so badly, why, bring her, of course."

Mother conferred for a long time with Aunt Katya and finally the two of them tried to explain diplomatically to Lyubov Dmitriyevna that it would be better if she didn't go to the Rayevskys'. She was mortally offended and left Petersburg the next day. This stupid incident left us with an unpleasant memory for a long time to come.

* Prokofiev's Uncle "Sasha" Rayevsky had a rank in the civil service equivalent to that of a general in the Army, and was so addressed. (Translator's note.)

13

My father came from Sontsovka for Mother's name day, which fell on January 26. I don't recall the details of his visit, but a student tutor was found for me, and Father gave him detailed instructions on how to instruct me.

For Mother's name day I composed a "romance" for piano in serious style. It was the song ditty in the fourth series:[33]

At about the same time I composed the third ditty of the fourth series.[34] It was pensive, lyrical, and not especially long, with the result that formally it held up better than the others of that period.

Looking at my ditties of that period in a general way, I could say that from time to time I composed big pieces conceived on a broad scale, and they always turned out a bit rough and unfinished. But along with them were pieces that were short and more intimate, and these were more finished and formally superior.

Among the operas I heard at that time was Tchaikovsky's *Oprichnik*. Siloti's concerts had been suspended before the end of the season, probably because of the revolutionary events. Port Arthur fell, and our Port Arthur squadron perished with it. No longer did the newsboys run along the street under our window, waving extras and shouting, "Ballbardment of Port Arthur!"

When I went to concerts in the Great Hall of the Conservatory—a long, narrow hall framed with a single balcony—I imagined it to be a drydock in which a cruiser would soon be laid up for repairs—such was my love for the Navy.

From me to my father at Sontsovka.
Petersburg, February 5, 1905.

Just imagine! They started a strike at the Conservatory. Today when I went for my harmony lesson I saw that little knots of people had gathered everywhere, students of sixteen and seventeen, shouting and making a lot of noise. The class met anyway, but not even half of the students were there. One of them, Kankarovich, didn't come until after two o'clock instead of at one. He had been at a meeting in the Little Auditorium, where more than forty people had gathered. They all argued, and made noise, and finally signed their names. The main thing was that they didn't have any aim. [This shows the influence of the talk I heard at home, which I of course repeated. My mother's viewpoint was as follows: since we had left my father in Sontsovka and come to Petersburg so that I could study, the thing to do was study and not become involved in unfathomable matters.] In general, the students are protesting, for example, the fact that one of their number in a certain class is a soldier who shot at the workers during the disturbances, and that they do not want to have a "murderer" as a fellow-student. Second that Auer, the professor of violin, is very irritable and is always cursing out the students; that, in their opinion, he dropped one student for no reason at all [he dropped him because he had missed a lot of classes]; that at every lesson he spends ten minutes more with one girl student he knows than with the others. [Auer was very famous and did what he wanted.] Finally, that today one of the attendants behaved rudely, saying they were nothing but "kikes," that they had killed the grand duke,* etc.

My assignments were rather well done, although two unusual mistakes were found: cross-relations.

After the lesson Kankarovich began to make a speech, explaining to Lyadov why they called a meeting. In general he talked nonsense. As Lyadov put it, these things are family matters that could be settled without a lot of fuss simply by going to the director. And our whole class disagreed with Kankarovich, saying that they were always protesting over trifles, and that we might suffer if the Conservatory were closed: we would lose a year, and we would lose the tuition money we had paid.[35]

Four days later my mother wrote: "The railroad strikes have begun. For all I know, they may prevent us from seeing each other." And later; "On Monday we went to see Marya Grigoryevna (Kilschtedt). Sergusha had written a very pretty accompaniment to the ballad sung by Undine at the beginning of the second act. He recopied four pages of it, and we took them to her. She liked them very much." In general Mme. Kilschtedt treated me affectionately, though this did not prevent her from making a barbed remark from time to time. When we were standing in the vestibule taking leave of Mme. Kilschtedt,

* Grand Duke Sergei Alexandrovich, uncle of Nicholas II, and husband of the Czarina's sister, was assassinated on February 4, 1905. (Editor's note.)

Mother leaned on my shoulder and said the familiar French words, *"C'est le baton de ma vieillesse."* Mme. Kilschtedt quickly commented, "That translates into Russian as 'the cudgel of my old age.' "

14

From me to my father at Sontsovka.
Petersburg, February 9 (22), 1905.

Today I had harmony and solfeggio. The solfeggio went off really quite well. My harmony exercises were probably the best ones turned in today. I have begun to keep statistics on the mistakes made in harmony class. It's too bad I didn't think of it before. But first, I didn't know all the other students then; and, second, it never occurred to me. In any case, next year I'll keep account of all the mistakes in counterpoint from the very beginning.[36]

I kept those statistics for eleven lessons. Lyadov would sit down at the piano, put a copybook containing exercises on the music rack, and play the exercises, marking the mistakes in pencil and from time to time making acid remarks.

I would stand behind Lyadov holding a notebook and eagerly jot down each mistake and what it was called. These included parallel and hidden octaves and fifths, cross-relations, bad suspensions, bad passing tones, bad harmonies, bad sequences, incorrect resolutions, etc., totaling nineteen types of mistakes in all. Back at home I arranged them in nineteen columns, showing the total number of exercises turned in by each student, the total number of mistakes, and the number of mistakes per exercise for each student (in the form of a decimal fraction with an accuracy of one hundredth). In a word, I had an entire bookkeeping project at home, not to mention keeping account of the mistakes I myself had made that Lyadov had marked in my copybook, since in class I didn't have time to jot down my own mistakes. My classmates at first regarded this project of mine with astonishment, then with hostility. But I never noticed it, having been carried away by the sporting interest of the whole thing, and fearing more than anything else that I would miss a mistake.

At the second lesson Kobylyansky was scathingly criticized by Lyadov, who crossed out all manner of things in the pages of his copybook. When he came back from the piano, all red in the face, he asked me in a half whisper, "What are you jotting down there?"

"I'm keeping statistics on mistakes."

"What business is it yours how many mistakes a person makes" he exploded.

Our talk was interfering with Lyadov's teaching. "Quiet down, gentlemen!"

he muttered. And we did. But after class, when Lyadov had left, Kobylyansky again went after me.

"I came here to study the theory of composition, and it's nobody's business what kind of mistakes I make in my exercises, or how many I make. I can assure you that it's of no interest to anybody."

"To the contrary, it's highly interesting! For example, today you brought in [at this point I consulted my notebook] one exercise, and it had eleven mistakes in it. Asafyev brought in six exercises, and there were only eleven mistakes in all six. From this it is quite obvious that your work is six times worse than Asafyev's. In the near future I intend to plot a curve—"

"That's childish and unbearable!" he raged. "I completely fail to understand how you got into this class, which is intended for adults and not for the adolescent generation."

"If you would shout less and pay closer attention to your work," I said didactically, "both your progresss and my statistics would—"

I never finished the sentence. Kobylyansky jumped on me, threw me to the floor, and pulled my ears. But he did it with no great force, rather to humiliate me than hurt me.

I jumped up and tried to throw myself on my attacker, but he was protected by the solid frame of Shpis. The latter waved his rolled-up copybook under my nose and said in a conciliatory tone, "Come now, Prokosha, don't fume. We came here to study music. But because you're so young, you've created an atmosphere that is all wrong for us."

With that, the incident was over. Kobylyansky did not come to the next two lessons, and I was able to jot down mistakes quite undisturbed: my other classmates didn't interfere.

An announcement has been posted at the Conservatory (I wrote to my father) stating that Rimsky-Korsakov, Glazunov, Solovyev, the director, and certain other important persons have proposed that all adult students assemble on February 10 in the Little Auditorium to talk things over and explain their demands.[37]

From me to my father at Sontsovka.
Petersburg, February 13, 1905.

Some people are saying that the Conservatory will be closed until September. But others are saying that it won't be closed; first, since there are many against the strike; second, because there are many adolescents there. In our class, two students—that is, one third of Lyadov's theory students— went on strike: Kankarovich and Kobylyansky. The former is one of the chief strikers and throughout his life was a rebel. He takes part in everything—in all the meetings. Yesterday he asked me, "What? Are you going to continue attending harmony class?" "Of course I am," I said. "In that case," he said, "farewell." And he turned and walked off. Just why

Kobylyansky is striking, I don't know. In the first place, he is a tuition-free student. And in the second place, as a tuition-free student, he has two majors: piano and theory of composition.[38]

Unfortunately, both of our "revolutionaries" turned out to be the loudest protesters and the least accomplished musicians—something that could only compromise them in my eyes.

15

My mother kept a close eye on everything that was happening at the Conservatory, and she wrote my father:

> Some of the students' demands are very sensible. For example, they want monthly opera productions with students participating: singers, conductors, and a full orchestra, with students playing on the instruments they are studying. That was Rubinstein's idea when he built the theater in the Conservatory building, but now it is always being rented out. Also, they want a library, a higher level in academic studies, and polite treatment from the attendants and the professors. For example, they say that Auer hits students over the head with his bow. The situation right now can be compared to an impending storm when the air is heavy and it is hard to breathe.[39]

Mother was also having a hard time breathing because of worrying about my father, left alone in Sontsovka to untangle the complex relations that had arisen between the landowner and the peasants.

Then a new worry loomed. "According to the papers, cholera is spreading everywhere," she wrote in her next letter. "My advice to you is to start cleaning out the barnyard as soon as the thaw begins, since it has always been foul-smelling anyway. Drive all the livestock and calves out of the barnyard. Clean the hen houses and wash them with carbolic acid."

From me to my father at Sontsovka.
Petersburg, February 16 (March 1), 1905.

I had a harmony lesson today. My exercises were among the best. Kobylyansky, who has been on strike, is back in class, but Kankarovich doesn't come at all. Fiveisky—the student from Moscow—showed up today after an absence of almost three months. But he had done his exercises quite well. Several times Lyadov said, "Very musical!"

From me to my father at Sontsovka.
Petersburg, February 20, 1905.

The concert was amazingly uninteresting: they played something very long and boring by Mozart. [Then, and for a long time afterward, I didn't like Mozart, probably because I didn't find in him those interesting harmonies and that dramatic content which especially interested me in music. My antipathy was so well defined that when someone began to praise him I would exclaim, "How can you like Mozart!"] Berlioz's *Flight into Egypt* was also rather boring. The most interesting item was Glazunov's *Concerto for Violin and Orchestra.* The composer conducted, and Auer played the violin. The former was much applauded, but the latter was hissed for political reasons.[40]

Today was the Rayevskys' wedding anniversary. We went to see them. I had composed Ditty No. 40 for them (and dedicated it to them). [41]

There were many guests at the Rayevskys', but their spirits were not gay. Their daughter, Katya, had been seriously ill with something like typhus. The complications had affected her ear, and she had not yet recovered her hearing.

One of the guests was Nadezhda Vladimirovna Pavskaya, whom we had known for a long time, first as a poor girl called Nadya, then as the wife of an officer. By now her husband had been appointed to the general staff with the rank of colonel. In inviting Mama to visit her, Nadezhda Vladimirovna said I should come along too, since she also had a son.

I was a bit disappointed when I found out that Vanya Pavsky was four and a half years younger than I: I was almost fourteen, and he was only nine. But he turned out to be a lively boy, plump, vivacious, with charming dimples in his cheeks—and he, too, was interested in the Navy. He was astounded by my knowledge of the subject and delightedly adopted all the games I had invented for naval battles, wherein cardboard battleships were moved from one square to another. In a word, after adults like Shpis, I had found a youngster to whom I could give orders—but a youngster who was very nice and keen-witted. So we became friends.

16

From me to my father at Sontsovka.
Petersburg, February 23, 1905.

On Monday, February 21st, when I went to the Conservatory with a fugue I was taking to Winkler, I saw that the door was closed. There was a notice posted on it saying that the Conservatory would be closed on February 21, 22, and 23. There was a group of about ten students near the door. One theory student said that the strikers had begun to use force, and that if anyone tried to attend class they would evict both the students and professors from the classrooms. It was because of this that the Conservatory was closed for half a week. It was very distressing. We had already missed two classes with Lyadov and for Saturday before Ash Wednesday the question arose: would there be a class or not? Besides, later on Lyadov will drive us terribly hard to catch up.[42]

In early March my father came to Petersburg for two weeks. He said that in the summer he would buy me a bicycle—a regular one of the kind adults use —and suggested I study the problem as to the best kind to buy: a new one or a used one of good make.

"But," he said, "just make sure you don't buy one with low handlebars. You should sit upright and not bent double."

From me to my father in Moscow.
Petersburg, March 19 (April 1), 1905.

I did one chorale for him [Lyadov] and one exercise. I made very few mistakes. Almost all the students were there, except for Grossman and Kankarovich. Even Fiveisky was there.

During class Lyadov got a letter from the Conservatory inviting him to a meeting to consider the question of expelling all those who had broken glass and were taken to the police station.[43]

Rimsky-Korsakov has published an interesting letter about the St. Petersburg Conservatory in a Moscow newspaper.

[Apparently this refers to the composer's famous letter of March 16, published in the newspaper *Rus.*] He writes that he has already advised, several times, that the Conservatory be closed until September 1st.[44]

Lyadov says he doesn't know whether there will be any exams in music or not. It may be that they'll be held in the fall, and maybe they'll move us into the next class without examinations. Then next year, in the spring, when we go from counterpoint to fugue, we'll be examined in counterpoint and harmony at the same time. This isn't very likely, since we have students who could hardly pass the exam between harmony and counter-point: Grossman, for example, and maybe Kobylyansky.[45]

> From me to my father at Sontsovka.
> Petersburg, March 20, 1905.

I turned in two exercises and had five mistakes. As for the others, Asafyev made eighteen mistakes in five exercises, and Kobylyansky made eleven mistakes in one exercise. Fiveisky's exercises were done neither badly nor well. . . .

Yesterday I composed a "little song" for piano, No. 41 (the fifth in the fourth series.)[46]

My new suit is a success: everyone likes it very much.[47]

> From me to my father at Sontsovka.
> Petersburg, March 23, 1905.

Today I went to Lyadov's class. I had done seven exercises for him. He said, "Yes, today you have done the chorales much better." And he repeated it twice.

I wrote you that during the last class Lyadov received an invitation to a meeting in the Conservatory. Here is the way that session ended. Rimsky-Korsakov began to make a speech in which he condemned the actions of the board of directors. At this Bernhard, the director, who was chairman, rang the bell (broke off the speech), got up, and left the session.

The board of directors of the Musical Society (under the chairmanship of Grand Duke Konstantin Konstantinovich) informed Rimsky-Korsakov that he was dismissed from his position as professor because of his letter (the one I wrote you about when you were in Moscow.)

Meantime, Bernhard has resigned. The position of director was offered to Glazunov, but he said that if Rimsky-Korsakov is dismissed from the faculty, he not only has no desire to be director of the Conservatory but will also resign from the faculty. And if Glazunov and Rimsky-Korsakov leave, they will be followed by Lyadov, Esipova,* Benois,* Verzhbilovich,* and many others. Probably Rimsky-Korsakov will be asked to stay on.[48]

On Monday I went to see Winkler at his home. He lives in a fine ground-floor apartment in a building (No. 43) on the corner of the Fontanka and the Kryukov Canal with a handsome flight of front steps. His study (where he has his piano) rather reminds one of a greenhouse: a square room with lots of daylight coming in, and full of palms. He worked with me for an hour, but we didn't manage to get through everything. He said I had learned the pieces "rather well."

Yesterday I went to the Belyayev Music Library and got all the orchestral scores I could for the next concert (three pieces), so now all the theory students are very put out with me.[49]

---

* Anna Esipova (1851–1914), concert pianist and teacher; Alexander Benois (1870–1960), artist and stage designer; Alexander Verzhbilovich (1850–1911), cellist. (Translator's note.)

17

The Belyayev Music Publishing House, headed by Rimsky-Korsakov, Glazunov, and Lyadov, had set up a special library of the works they published for the use of those students at the Conservatory taking theory of composition. This served two purposes: first, the theory students could become familiar with well-printed orchestral and piano scores; second, the works published by Belyayev were promoted among young people. When, on a stopover in Moscow, I asked Glière about that library, he said, "That's very good. You can check in advance on what pieces are going to be performed at concerts, get the scores for them, and study them at home. Then go to a rehearsal or two, taking the scores with you. But when you go to the concert, leave the scores behind so you won't be distracted from listening to the music. In that way you can study any given piece thoroughly, and it will be very useful to you."

I decided to follow Glière's advice, and when I noticed that a certain piece published by Belyayev was going to be performed at the next concert, I went to get the score. But it turned out there weren't any available. I noticed another piece that was to be played at the following concert, and again went to the library. Once again there were no scores on hand.

"What's going on," I asked the librarian. "Why do you never have the particular scores a person needs?"

"Very simple," he said with a laugh. "The theory students take out those scores so they can follow them during the performance."

"But I came a whole week before the concert."

"Yes, but some people come two weeks before."

I looked over the programs three weeks in advance and got the scores of all the works that were going to be performed. They included Zolotarev's* *First Symphony,* Wihtol's *Das Fest der Ligo,* and some others. Since for most of these works the library had only one copy of the score, it is understandable why the other theory students were "very put out with me," as I wrote my father.

But when I came to the first rehearsal, my popularity was great. One of the older theory students, Malko, asked permission to sit next to me. (Before that he had never wanted to talk to me.) Another theory student sat on the other side, and three more took seats behind me, peering over my shoulders at the score. After intermission I purposely took another seat. But they located me right away and again took seats around me.

I was beaming with pride. But my excellent spirits were soon spoiled by a small unpleasantness. At one point, when the tempo of the music was rapid, I lost my place and didn't turn the page in time. After that, whenever it was time to turn the page, the person sitting behind me (apparently a band leader) would

* Vasily Zolotarev (1873–1964), Soviet composer, professor at the Minsky Conservatory since 1933. (Translator's note.)

reach over my shoulder and wave his hand. This exasperated me terribly, since I could read scores as well as any of the other theory students, but I couldn't tell him that.

As for the pieces themselves, the Zolotarev symphony was rather dull, while *Das Fest der Ligo,* based on Latvian national themes, was more lively.

18

From me to my father at Sontsovka.
Petersburg, March 27, 1905.

As was to be expected, after Rimsky-Korsakov was dismissed from the Conservatory, Glazunov, Lyadov, Auer, Esipova, Benois, Verzhbilovich, and others resigned from the faculty.

Everyone is expressing sympathy for Rimsky-Korsakov. One hundred and thirty-one professors sent him a message of solidarity, and the Moscow musicians have protested his dismissal. Even high school students have sent him a message of solidarity.

For next year there exists [a plan that] all we students (six of us) will take group private lessons in counterpoint from Lyadov. From Lyadov and not Rimsky-Korsakov, since Rimsky-Korsakov either charges a terribly high fee for a private lesson or else he gives it gratis, and either way is awkward. Lyadov charges from six to ten rubles per lesson. Therefore each of us six will have to pay anywhere from one ruble to one ruble and seventy kopecks.[50]

From me to my father at Sontsovka.
Petersburg, March 30, 1905.

During the past three days they have held rehearsals for the third Belyayev concert. I was at all three. It was very pleasant, as the pieces they were playing began gradually to be more and more to my liking—especially since I had the score.

The theory students are sending a statement to the board of directors of the Conservatory saying that since Rimsky-Korsakov, Glazunov, and Lyadov have left they no longer want to remain at the Conservatory, and asking that their papers be returned to them. They asked me to sign it, and with Mama's permission I did. [Very important: the first time I made a political protest.]

You simply can't imagine who is going to replace Korsakov. It turns out that Bernhard, the former director, is going to teach harmony and counterpoint in place of him and Lyadov, while Solovyev will be director. It is easy to see why the students are leaving and will take private lessons with Rimsky-Korsakov next year. Many of them say he will teach them free or, if not, will charge ten rubles a lesson.

I went to Winkler's home twice this week. At the last lesson he asked, "are you going to stay on at the Conservatory?"

"No," I said, "I'm leaving."

"Of course. It's not worthwhile staying on."

Chernov said the same thing: that Bernhard won't teach anyone anything new.

It turns out that the letter for which Rimsky-Korsakov was dismissed was published in *Russkiye vedomosti,* No. 2. Please clip it and save it.[51]

Bernhard, the director, a man with a sleek face and splendid side-whiskers, was an organist by profession. In this field he was even credited with a kind of heroic feat performed when he was playing the organ part in a work for orchestra and chorus being conducted by Rimsky-Korsakov. During one passage where the chorus sang without accompaniment, it began gradually (and unmercifully) to lower the pitch—so much so that later on, when it was time for the organ to enter, the chorus turned out—to the horror of Rimsky-Korsakov—to be a full tone lower than it should have been. But Bernhard kept his presence of mind and entered in the same key, transposing his own part accordingly. In this way, they finished that section in good order and began the next section in the correct key. This feat enhanced Bernhard's reputation. Hence it was all the more surprising that he should now come into official conflict with Rimsky-Korsakov.

> From my mother to my father in Sontsovka.
> Petersburg, March 31, 1905.

Our country is now passing through such an unprecedented period that every day brings new things, like another year. Last autumn we sent our son to the Conservatory, and now in the spring we are taking him back. Could one have imagined that?

We have had to find out, to our own cost, that one cannot swim against the current.

All the theory students are leaving and will be going to the office at the same time to get their papers back. Personally, I am convinced that everything will be straightened out; that Rimsky-Korsakov will be the director; that the other professors will come back; and that the students will be admitted again. In the extreme case, Serezha will have to club together with the other students and take private lessons from one of the professors, thus doing a year's work outside the Conservatory.

But what else can be done? When we see you again, we can discuss it together.[52]

> From me to my father at Sontsovka.
> Petersburg, April 3, 1905.

Lyadov said that in all likelihood Rimsky-Korsakov would not come back to the Conservatory. For two years he has been saying he would leave it: he wants to lead a quieter life and compose. But if the board of directors asks his forgiveness and gives him satisfaction in general, Glazunov and Lyadov will come back to the Conservatory. Glazunov will teach free composition and fugue in addition to orchestration, and Lyadov will teach harmony and counterpoint.

Tomorrow I am taking Winkler the last movement of Beethoven's *Sonata No. 7* (it is the eighth sonata I have worked on with him) and [Bach's] *Fugue No. 13.* (This is the thirteenth fugue I have studied with him.)[53]

Mother wrote the following about the Conservatory:

These days it seems that everything has quieted down. They say that about forty persons are due to be expelled—probably the ones responsible for the "stinking obstruction." (i.e., they used a strong-smelling chemical compound to make it impossible to hold classes.)[54]

And a few days later: "Now they are again tightening up on everything and everybody. For example, there is a ban against performing anything of Rimsky-Korsakov's, whether operas or other compositions. The contradictions have been transformed into a system."

The crackdown on Rimsky-Korsakov's works began in earnest after the premiere of his opera *Kashchei the Immortal,* which turned into a huge political demonstration during which he was loudly hailed by young people of revolutionary learnings. I myself did not go the premiere. But I was at several rehearsals, and I very much liked *Kashchei*—especially the part of Kashcheyevna.

19

One night scarcely a week after we had written Father of my intention to get my papers back from the Conservatory, we got a telegram from him. He was full of anxiety. To him, far away in the country, everything seemed more frightful than it actually was. Also, he remembered what he himself had gone through in his student years, when he had refused to betray his classmates of revolutionary bent, and it had cost him his diploma. Now he was entertaining all kinds of frightening ideas; that his son, having at age *thirteen* taken back his papers from the Imperial Conservatory, would in the future lose his right to continue his education. Given my father's reverence for learning and culture, what could be more frightening than that?

In order to understand his reluctance to sacrifice his son's career to the nebulous turmoil at the Conservatory, one would have to know my father and be familiar with his conviction that the first thing to do was to educate the people, then go on via such education to political freedoms.

> From me to my father at Sontsovka.
> Petersburg, April 6 (19), 1905.

Last night we got your telegram saying you were worried about taking back my papers from the Conservatory. It turns out (I learned this only today) that there was no need for alarm, since the papers were never filed at the director's office—for reasons I have not yet ascertained. In any case, even if the papers had been filed with the director, we would be free to take them back in the fall.

But if Rimsky-Korsakov and the others return to the Conservatory before fall, we may not take the papers back at all, since on the statement we signed we said that "after the dismissal of Rimsky-Korsakov we find it impossible to remain at the Conservatory," or something of that kind. But since that document never reached the director, there is no question of taking back my papers.[55]

> From my mother to my father at Sontsovka.
> Petersburg, April 7 (20), 1905.

Dear Musenka!

I was very saddened that you were so worried by our news. From far off, everything looks different, but when you're close to things, you are guided by the most realistic considerations. *I shall not take the papers back from the Conservatory.* Right now it is altogether deserted; only the doormen have remained loyal. Joining forces with them is not really a brilliant idea. Both Lyadov and Winkler know Serezha's intention: to leave the Conservatory if the best professors leave. I should have made that clear.[56]

(The reason our protest never reached the director was that the students in charge of drawing it up had decided not to deliver it to him.)

On April 5, Lyadov's students were photographed with him at the same studio where Rimsky-Korsakov had been photographed the day before with those who took part in the production of *Kashchei.* That photograph was preserved and has since appeared quite often in newspapers and magazines.

In it one can see what a little puppy I was, and it becomes understandable why my presence annoyed some of my classmates who were convinced that a class in the theory of composition is something for adults. Since it was only two weeks before Easter and we were planning to go to Sontsovka for Easter, in the photograph I am asking Lyadov whether it would be worthwhile to come back to Petersburg after the holidays.

Lyadov, lazy by nature and rather indifferent toward his teaching, thought for a while and then said that perhaps it would not be worthwhile. Then a day later he added that he would bring the whole course to a conclusion, in a rough way, before Easter. At the same time he explained that in the spring there would be no examinations in academic subjects at the Conservatory. I felt a kind of relief when I found out that the business would be postponed until fall. Actually, however, those feelings of relief proved to be premature, because all that summer my parents nagged me into working three or four hours a day on academic subjects. Of course, thanks to that I got a much better foundation in all the subjects. But Lord, what a pleasant thing a free summer would have been.

"Kankarovich and Shpis have promised to write me in August about the state of affairs at the Conservatory," I wrote my father. And in that same letter I reported to him the results of my keeping statistics on mistakes. After eleven classes I came out first with 2.42 mistakes per exercise. Asafyev was second with 2.57, and Kankarovich third with 2.66. Kobylyansky was at the bottom of the list with 6.06. At this point, however, I must throw doubt on the accuracy of my statistics, since objectively speaking I was by no means the best student, and Asafyev of course did his exercises better than I did mine. The inaccuracy of my statistics was a result not of my unscrupulousness but of the fallibility of the method itself. Lyadov marked most of the mistakes in the copybooks with his pencil. But some he merely mentioned without taking his hands from the keyboard. These, too, I jotted down in my record. But I had to record my own mistakes after I got back home, since during that part of the lesson while Lyadov was working with me I was busy following the exercises with my eye and listening to what Lyadov was saying. At home, therefore, the only mistakes I had in front of me were those Lyadov had marked in pencil, and though I tried conscientiously to remember all those he had pointed out verbally, there was willy-nilly a certain "leakage." If we now assume that for each lesson the count of my own mistakes fell short by two, it means that for eleven lessons the total was twenty-two—a sufficient number to give me odds over the other students.

20

Spring was in full bloom when we reached Sontsovka. The irises, bird cherries, and pear trees had just blossomed. They were followed first by the cherries, plums, and apples, then by the chestnuts and lilacs.

I recorded all this in my table for the flowering of plants.

I gave my friends the gifts I had brought them from the city, and then ran to inspect my summerhouse and all the child's junk I had stored there for the winter. In the summerhouse, the other children and I recalled the death of poor Amishka, the cat. One winter night she crawled into the empty furnace (it was warm there, and the ashes were soft). Gavrila came and shoveled in coal, then lighted the furnace. A terrible yowling and squealing came from the furnace, and a few seconds later Amishka leaped through the flames and out of the furnace. She died a few weeks later.

A bicycle I had bought in Petersburg arrived at Sontsovka ten days after us. Surrounded by Stenya, Serezha, and others, I set off for the big orchard, where there was a long, straight path, to learn to ride it. I learned rather easily, and then began to ride at a speed from which nothing good could come. Nor did it. One fine day I flew off the seat and fell on the bike beneath me. It was not a graceful fall, and I got a gash in a place that modesty will not allow me to name. My parents sent the carriage for Dr. Reberg, and then began poring over medical books, looking for the Latin name so it would sound more proper. When Reberg arrived he disinfected the gash and sewed it up with some pretty needles. It didn't hurt, and in a few days it had all healed over. But from that time on I rode the bike more cautiously.

21

Meantime, things were going badly in the war with Japan. Everyone expected a lot from our huge fleet under Admiral Rozhestvensky, which had sailed around Africa and Asia to Vladivostok and was now somewhere near Japan. I knew every battleship and cruiser in that fleet by heart: all the details of how they were armed and armored. An engineer who had come to Sontsovka on business—one of those people who talk about themselves loudly, at length, and with great satisfaction—was telling us that he had made a bet with someone that we would lose the war: if Japan won, he would whip his opponent publicly, and vice versa. I looked at him with a kind of horror. The idea that we could lose had never entered my head, and I looked with amazement at this man who had agreed to be flogged—and publicly, at that.

But the engineer left, and one fine May day, in a newspaper that had come in the mail, we read an incredible telegram from either Shanghai or Hong Kong that said more or less the following: "Fishermen believe that the capsized vessel was the Russian battleship *Borodino*." I felt dizzy. I was so familiar with all Admiral Rozhestvensky's ships; I knew all the characteristics of each one so well that I regarded each ship as a personal acquaintance. And now the *Borodino* had capsized! I had known that the fleet was going to fight the Japanese to the death, but I hadn't realized that some ships might perish in the battle.

At Sontsovka we got the mail only twice a week, so we had to wait another three days before getting more news. Finally the papers came, with news of a total defeat: in the battle in the Tsushima Strait all my favorite ships had been sunk. A few others had surrendered, and only a couple of smaller vessels had gotten away to Vladivostok. As I sat there in an armchair in the drawing room, I was completely downcast, like a man who has suddenly lost his whole family. My father, probably no less distressed by our defeat than I was, felt sorry for me.

And as he passed through the drawing room near my chair, he said very gently, "What's the matter? Feeling bad about your battleships?"

I waved him away, mainly because I didn't want to burst out wailing.

22

During May, June, and July I wrote half of the second act of *Undine*. Like the rest of *Undine,* this music has not been preserved, and I don't remember it well. But in any case the second act was less naïve than the first: it has more harmonic ideas, and even inventions. I couldn't give much time to composing, since my parents were giving me thorough tutoring in academic subjects, having increased the lessons to five hours a day—in addition to which I had one hour of piano. As before, my mother taught me French, German, and religion, while my father was in charge of the other lessons, for which he had set up a precise schedule. He was systematic, sometimes even to the point of being a bit boring, but he was lenient with me, giving me pieces of chocolate and even letting me lie on the sofa during lessons, for which he called me a "lazybones."

In the summer my father wore a cream-colored tussore suit and a silk string tie with pompons. His light-colored trousers were easily soiled by the dust, so he often changed into dark ones. It was customary in the summer for men to wear a dark jacket and light-colored trousers, but my father wore just the opposite: a light jacket and dark trousers. His fingernails were always impeccably clean: he once called my attention to this and emphatically demanded that I keep mine in the same condition. In the morning he would drink one cup of coffee with four lumps of sugar, and two glasses of tea with three lumps. Later in the day he would eat clotted sour cream, presumably as recommended by Mechnikov.* His idea was that clotted sour cream promoted longevity; that, for example, the fact that everybody in Bulgaria ate clotted sour cream accounted for the large number of very old men there.

In France, on the other hand, there were many cases of cancer because the French ate a lot of lettuce. I simply couldn't understand those strange Frenchmen: they of course knew that lettuce caused cancer, and yet they went on eating it—and in large quantities at that.

A few years later my father had a case of typhus, after which he stopped smoking—something that demanded quite a bit of willpower. But sometimes he still dreamed at night that he was lighting up a cigarette. When he woke up he would be feeling out of sorts and distraught because his willpower hadn't held out, and he would be overjoyed when he realized it was only a dream.

Toward the end of the summer even longer hours were devoted to the les-

---

* Ilya Mechnikov (1845–1916), the famous Russian biologist, did a good deal of research in the field of geriatrics. (Translator's note.)

sons with my parents, in view of the approaching exams, and I stopped composing altogether.

But in July, for my father's birthday, I had written a rather long "romance" for piano (it was my fourth, and the seventh ditty in the fourth series).[57] It had a long introduction in an elevated mood, and some stormy Schumannesque passages in the middle section. I liked it and regarded it as a successful work.

23

Because of the war with Japan our local veterinarian, Klenov, had been called up for military service in the Far East. One evening his successor appeared, to give vaccinations and treat our prize stallion, Tormentor, who had some kind of disease.

The veterinarian was provided with a pitcher of water and a basin so that he could wash up (in the summer the dust is thick in the black earth region), and a half hour later he was sitting at the dinner table praising the "beautifully fertilized" fields of Sontsovka that he had noticed in his way to the estate.

"Pardon me," my mother said, "but we don't even know your name."

"Vasily Mitrofanovich Morolev," he replied. "Just imagine! Recently I had to write to a certain individual, pointing out several blunders he had made, and he answered: Don't try to teach me morals, even if your name is Morolev. I got fearfully angry. It's such bad manners to pun on a person's name!"

He said this, however, in a humorous tone of voice. In general, humor was a basic part of his nature. His talk was larded with witticisms, and for this I liked him right away. He had a mustache like Maupassant's, blue-tinted eyeglasses worn as a pince-nez, and a bass voice. He became interested in me as soon as he learned I was studying at the Conservatory, since he had a passion for music and played the piano rather well. After dinner he dragged me to the piano and wouldn't let me get up from it until late at night. He had me play all the Beethoven sonatas I had worked on with Winkler during the winter. But he was especially interested in the ten mazurkas or Scriabin's Opus 3, which he saw on the music rack. (I had bought them in Petersburg, just before we left, as something new and *pungent*.) I played through them, trying to grasp something of the new composer's unusual style. Morolev found them both irritating and pleasurable, but he was completely delighted that he had come across something new.

The next day, when he went to treat Tormentor, I was constantly at his side, talking music without letup.

In the stallion's stall, he asked me, "You mean you really don't know Rimsky-Korsakov's opera *Sadko?* It's a fine piece of work. When you go back to Petersburg in the fall, be sure to go and hear it, and buy a piano score of it. In the first act there is a chorus in 11/8 time so exciting that you simply can't sit still in your seat."

I gave a start. "In 11/8? I know that in *The Snow Maiden* Rimsky-Korsakov had a chorus in 11/8, and I even heard that one conductor, who simply couldn't manage to conduct that chorus, kept muttering all during the singing of it: 'Rimsky-Korsakov has gone completely mad!' But when I tried it, it turned out that that phrase doesn't fit the chorus from *The Snow Maiden,* because it comes out 'completely mad.' "*

"Wait a minute!" Morolev exclaimed excitedly. "Maybe that phrase fits *Sadko!*" And he began to sing, in turn, "Hail, Sadko, handsome lad!" and "Rimsky-Korsakov has gone completely mad."

"It fits! It fits!" we shouted at the same time. And we began to sing the theme of the chorus, first with one text and then with the other:

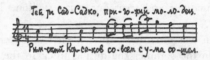

Morolev glanced at his watch, lifted up the horse's tail, and pulled out the thermometer. "Yes," he told the stableman, "it's a little high. We'll have to give him a laxative."

Then he turned back to me and continued: "And in that scene where Sadko is sailing off on the ship, what a wonderful chorus: 'The heights, the heavenly heights!' It's sung by a small male chorus in A major. Then without any transition the entire chorus and the orchestra come in with the same music in F major. . . .

"The entire chorus and the orchestra, you understand, but pianissimo and without any transition! I had to hold onto my seat with both hands so I wouldn't jump out of it."

When we got back to the house after he had treated and given the vaccinations (the sheep took the injections rather meekly, but the hogs squealed to the high heavens), Morolev persuaded my father as a special favor to cancel my lessons for the next day, and he literally tormented me, making me play all Bach's preludes and fugues, repeat the Scriabin mazurkas, and introduce him to my latest ditties.

We parted friends. But he lived a long way off—thirty kilometers, which meant a round trip of sixty kilometers—and it wasn't until the next month that he was able to get back to Sontsovka.

---

* A rough equivalent of the Russian phrase in question, *s úma sóshel,* where the stress has been displaced in both of the last two words, i.e., from the regular pronunciation: *s umá soshél* (Translator's note.)

24

In his brief reminiscences, written forty years after that meeting, Morolev describes the visit as follows:

. . . In the summer of 1905 I paid a visit to Sontsovka. As my tarantass drew up to the house where Prokofiev lived, it was surrounded by about ten boys of various ages, all on stilts. My driver growled, "Hey, you boys! You've scared the horses! Look, the black has laid back his ears!"

But of course the boys only laughed and continued to crowd around the tarantass. Then one of them turned to me: "Did you come to see us?"

"And would you be Serezha?" [That past winter Morolev had visited Sontsovka and learned of my existence from my father, who also told him that I was studying at the Conservatory.]

"Yes. Come on in. Hey, boys! You can get off your stilts now. The game is over."

"Are you the commander of this platoon, Serezha?"

"Oh yes. They're all my friends."

As his father told me later, Serezha was very popular with the other children because he always thought up the most interesting games of cops and robbers, travelers, etc. When he went off to Petersburg to study, the others missed him, since without him they didn't have anything to do. They often came to the house to ask if he was coming back soon. When summer vacation drew near, they were especially excited, and they would greet him with unfeigned delight.

So we went into the house. After I had exchanged greetings with Serezha's father and he had introduced me to his wife, whom I had never seen before, he said, "Well, it looks like you and Serezha have already become acquainted."

We talked about the business I had come on, and made arrangements for the work I would have to do the next day: vaccinating livestock against a local epizootic. After dinner we went into the drawing room, where the grand piano was. When Serezha sat down at the piano, he asked me slyly, "What shall I play for you? I don't know what you like best."

I told him that I'd like to hear what he played at the Conservatory.

"Do you want to hear a Beethoven sonata?"

"With pleasure. Which one?"

"Which ones do you know? Would you like to hear the 'Pathétique'?"

I said yes, and he began to play. And what playing! Clarity, purity, expressiveness—and at the same time you felt that no passages gave him trouble; that he was playing with ease and fluency. Then he played several pieces by Schumann and the Scriabin mazurkas. After each piece he would ask me, "Did you like that?" And he was very satisfied to get an affirmative answer.

In general, those reminiscences correspond to my own. They describe the same landscape, but from a different aspect. So much the better. But I must make one correction. With respect to my playing, Morolev wrote: "Clarity, purity, expressiveness—and at the same time you felt that no passages gave him trouble." That is greatly exaggerated.

I did, of course, play expressively. But there was no purity, and the clarity was only illusory. Or rather, I did have the skill to emphasize things where necessary, which in an extreme case could pass for a certain kind of clarity. As for the scale passages, I missed notes in at least half of them, although I often did it rather adroitly.

One of two things was true. Either Morolev had become starved for music in his backwoods environment and took my "surprise attack" for purity of execution, or when he was writing his reminiscences forty years later, my not very precise playing of 1905 was overshadowed for him by my subsequent style (about 1910, when I had overcome many bad habits).

In any case, at the time I had the impression that he was listening to me not so much for the way I played as for the new things I was playing.

So much for Morolev's reminiscences right now; I shall come back to them later.

25

That summer my father began to give me adult books to read. Up until then I had read literature for children and adolescents, and had gone through a good deal of Jules Verne. Now I was given Gogol, Turgenev, Danilevsky,* and Sienkiewicz. But I still read Jules Verne with pleasure. I had learned somewhere that he was so prolific he dictated three novels at once. And I imagined him pacing about a room with three desks behind which sat three secretaries, simultaneously dictating three different novels to them. The first book by Turgenev that I read was *A Nest of Gentlefolk*. When my father asked me how I liked it, I blushed violently and said something unintelligible. It was the first book about love that I had ever read, and I was so inexperienced in such matters that I didn't even know one could write about them.

The transition to "adult" literature struck me as important, and I began jotting down the titles of the things I had read, giving them grades. *A Nest of Gentlefolk* got an A, *Dead Souls* an A minus, *Taras Bulba* and "Viy" a B, and "Old World Landowners" a C. Among the books by Danilevsky that Father gave me were *Fugitives in Novorossiya* and *The Return of the Fugitives*—proba-

* Grigory Petrovich Danilevsky (1829–90), a popular novelist. (Translator's note.)

§ 146 §

bly because they described the gradual settlement of the wide-open spaces in our own region. These two novels got an A and a B plus respectively, but Danilevsky's later works got C's. I did, however, very much like Sienkiewicz's novels *With Fire and Sword, The Deluge,* and *Quo Vadis?*. (They all got A's.)

In one book that was a kind of cross between children's literature and popular science, I read about spiritualism and was entranced by the subject. I wanted to find out this phenomenon in greater detail. But when I tried to start up a conversation about it, my parents would not continue the discussion and they gave me no more literature on that subject.

I eventually lost interest and started on another project: drawing up a catalogue of dogs' names. I would pester everyone I met with questions about what dogs' names they knew ("And besides that . . . and besides that,") and then enter them in my catalogue in alphabetical order.

Once when I was wandering in the depths of the big orchard, I came to the creek that ran along the bottom of the hill.

For the most part it was small and shallow, especially in the summer but at this particular spot there was a deep pool—if you went in, the water was up to your head. From the pool came shouts and the sound of splashing. When I had gone through the underbrush and reached the high bank, I saw five naked bodies wallowing in the pool: two boys and three girls. The boys were trying to catch the girls by the legs, and the girls were screeching and trying to get away.

"Hey! What are you doing there?" I shouted, not really having any clear idea of what was going on.

The bathers yelped and scrambled up the opposite bank, then grabbed their clothes and ran into the underbrush, trying all the time to keep their backs turned to me. I went on my way, somewhat roused by the encounter, although I had no notion what had prompted them to indulge in such a pleasurable pastime.

This time when Aunt Tanya came from Petersburg to visit us, she brought me a real camera instead of the usual toy carriage. True, it was small (four and one-half by six,) but it could be loaded with six plates and could be used either for a snapshot or for taking a picture with time exposure. It came with all the equipment needed for developing and printing.

In the evening Aunt Tanya and I would lock ourselves in my room with the door and windows carefully curtained. There, under a red light, we would watch tensely as the image of the negative gradually formed on the pale pink plates immersed in the developer.

In June a distant girl cousin of mine came to Sontsovka. She was a rather meek-looking girl of sixteen, and I remember that she used to play croquet with Aunt Tanya and me. Late one evening Egorka—one of the actors in my *Giant* who was by now seventeen and had recently returned from the city—was seen standing under her window. My parents grew alarmed and told Marfusha to find out what was going on. Two days later, she caught the young Romeo and

Juliet red-handed at the same window. This sent Mother and Aunt Tanya into a rage. They isolated my cousin so I wouldn't come under her *baneful* influence and my father, in his anger, locked himself in his study.

I was too young to understand much of what was going on, or why—a few days later—"Juliet" was sent away from Sontsovka. No doubt her meek exterior concealed a passionate heart: three years later she killed herself, for what reasons I never learned.

26

Meantime the revolutionary spirit was gradually making itself felt even in the backwoods of Sontsovka.

On June 29, while the dedication day of the Sontsovka church was being celebrated, an anonymous letter was nailed to the fence of the big orchard. It was addressed to my father and among other threats stated that it was high time for the landowners and their managers to get out of Sontsovka before they were dealt with in the appropriate manner.

My father was alarmed and called a small meeting of peasants. I don't know what was discussed there but I believe it was all rather peaceable, since the letter was apparently of outside origin and indifference still prevailed in the age-old core of the Sontsovka peasantry.

My father was still building schools under instructions from the *zemstvo,* or elective district council: he had finished one in Alekseyevka, was building one at Andreyevka, and had begun one at Sontsovka. But in August, when the mown hay had been piled into high stacks which were often several kilometers distant from Sontsovka, fires began to break out. The peasants were burning out the landowners. Usually this happened around midnight, when I was asleep. I would be awakened by the sounding of the alarm, and in the dark southern night the bright flow of flames could be seen on the horizon. I would feel uneasy and anxious and my parents would send me back to bed, where for a long time I would toss from side to side, unable to go to sleep.

I didn't compose much that summer. I wrote only one ditty for piano, although I began two others, which were completed in Petersburg.

At that time the style of these ditties was following two separate lines of development: some of them were broadly conceived but executed rather roughly owing to a lack of technique; others were more modest in conception but more *serrés*. The three ditties dating from that summer belonged to the first category. The seventh ditty of the fourth series was called *Romance No. 4* and was composed in July for my father's birthday.[59] It was the longest of my four piano "romances," with a sizable introductory section and a developed exposition. I took a serious attitude toward it and regarded it as a considerable opus.

I completed the eighth ditty of the fourth series in September in Petersburg, and dedicated it to my father on his name day.[60] In terms of form, it was more successful than the others.

With the coming of August, the situation at the Conservatory was still up in the air; that is, it was not known whether Rimsky-Korsakov and Lyadov would return to the faculty. In order that I should continue courses at the Conservatory even if they did not return, my parents decided I should take a second major, piano, and go on studying with Winkler in that connection, since he was conscientious and attentive to his students' needs.

Actually, Mother had always cherished the idea of my being a pianist and although the influences I had come under in both Moscow and Petersburg had favored my studying theory of composition, she was now glad that she could get me back on the course she loved best of all.

With regard to academic subjects, I was to take the exam for graduation from the third form to the fourth (fourth form of prerevolutionary times equaled the sixth or seventh of today). Since the time was drawing near for these exams, and for the entrance exam for piano class, we left Sontsovka for Petersburg on August 20.

In accordance with our habit, we stopped over in Moscow for two days so as not to lose contact with the Moscow musicians we knew. But neither Glière nor Taneyev had yet returned to the city, so that our stopover was fruitless.

27

We reached Petersburg on August 25 and were met at the station by Marfusha. The apartment was being refurbished, and everything was topsy-turvy. They had whitewashed the ceilings, ". . . and Mama and Aunt Tanya have pretty wallpaper in their rooms," I wrote to Father. The floors in my mother's room and the vestibule had been newly painted, so that we had to use the back entrance. But my room was accessible only through the vestibule, so that I had to spend the first night on the sofa in the dining room.

> From me to my father in Sontsovka.
> Petersburg, August 28, 1905.

On Thursday, August 25, I went to see Shpis. He was not at home, but was to come back from the country on the twenty-seventh. I went to Glazunov's, but he too was still in the country, and no one knew when he would return. I came back home, and then went to call on Chernov. He was on military duty and was stationed at Kronstadt. Then I went to see Kankarovich. He had moved to another apartment. I got the address and went there: he was playing violin at a soiree in Oranienbaum. On the way home I stopped by Winkler's and asked if he was back from the country yet. I was told he would be back that day.

The next day (the twenty-sixth) I went back to Winkler's place and rang the doorbell. I was told that he had just stepped out to the store and was expected back any minute. Sure enough, he showed up in a few minutes. First he acknowledged my greeting with a rather cold "Hello." But when he recognized me, he exclaimed, "Ah! So it's you!" and, by now very gracious, showed me into the drawing room and offered me an armchair.

When I had begged his pardon for disturbing him, I said I had come to ask his advice: since Rimsky-Korsakov, Lyadov, and Glazunov had left the Conservatory, I was going to study with them along with other students on a private basis, or perhaps they would open a music school; but at the Conservatory I wanted to switch from obligatory to special piano.

Winkler said that special piano required a lot more work, etc. I told him that last year I had wanted to take two majors but was afraid it would be hard and so took only harmony, but that that had turned out to be rather easy, and now I wanted to take special piano. Then I said that, if possible, I wanted to continue working with him.

"Well, all right," Winkler said. "I'll be glad to take you. But if you're going to be my student, I'll want to hear how you play at the examination. It may be that you have done some very good work, but there are still certain nuances to be corrected. [Winkler was untalented but extremely conscientious.] And in special piano we have to work somewhat differently and much harder. What have you prepared for the exam?"

"The *Sonata No. 11* in B-flat major (Beethoven) and the First Fugue (Bach). I know them by heart."

"Well, that's a good sonata. And the fugue—it's in C major?"

"Yes."

"Then you'll have to learn one more fugue, so that there'll be a choice at the examination. You don't have to memorize it. Pick the one you know best."

"No. 5, in D major?"

"That would be all right. By the way, did you know there is still hope that Lyadov and Glazunov will come back to the Conservatory?"

"Really?"

"Yes. Safonoff has been appointed and confirmed as director of the Petersburg Conservatory. But he is very sick right now, and it is hard for him to direct both conservatories, so Gabel is filling in for him temporarily."

"And Rimsky-Korsakov isn't coming back to the Conservatory?"

"No."

"Does that mean Lyadov will teach counterpoint?"

"Probably. And Glazunov will teach free composition. Have you been to see Lyadov?"

"No. Is he in Petersburg?"

"Yes. Go to see him. He'll tell you the whole story."

"I'll be sure to go."

"And come and play that sonata for me sometime in the next few days."

"But the exam is tomorrow."

"Oh yes. So it is. But don't go to it. There are always two or three make-up exams. Tell them you can't take the exam on the twenty-seventh for some reason or other: either you haven't prepared pieces to play at the exam or you still don't have a piano. You don't, do you?"

"Yes, I do have one."

"Well, it doesn't make any difference. So come and play the sonata on Monday at ten or eleven o'clock. Can you do that?"

"Yes. Much obliged."

Winkler went with me as far as the front flight of steps.

That same day I went to see Lyadov. At first he didn't recognize me. Then he exclaimed, "Ah! So it's you!" and showed me into the drawing room.

I asked him, "Anatoly Konstantinovich, are you staying at the Conservatory?"

"As before."

"Does that mean you're staying?"

"No, I mean things are as they were last spring. I'm leaving."

"They say you're opening a music school?"

"No, it didn't work out. Well, were you in the country for the summer?"

"Yes."

"Did you compose anything?"

"Yes, I did."

"You must have come to town just recently."

"Yes, yesterday."

"With your mama?"

"Yes. Now I'm going to take special piano at the Conservatory."

"Aha!"

"Do I have to submit an application?"

"I don't know about that."

"Please forgive me for having disturbed you. Goodbye, Anatoly Konstantinovich."

"Goodbye."[61]

There are two reasons for my having dwelled in detail on these two dialogues: first, they were recorded the next day and hence are accurate; second, there is something very curious about the contrast between Winkler, always concerned and attentive, and Lyadov, absolutely indifferent to his students. I can still see him—the corpulent figure, the swollen eyelids, the bloated face, the short arms with the hands stuffed deep into his trousers pockets—as he swayed on the tips of his high shoes with prunella uppers, waiting for his student to go away and leave him in peace.

28

From my mother to my father in Sontsovka.
Petersburg, August 29 (September 11), 1905.

Yesterday Serezha went to see Shpis. According to him, only three of them—Shpis, Serezha, and Asafyev—will be taking lessons with Lyadov. As for the others, well, the person who doesn't pay on time gets left behind. Within the next few days Shpis is going to see Lyadov to talk things over. Perhaps he'll see Glazunov, too.[62]

From me to my father at Sontsovka.
Petersburg, August 31, 1905.

Today I took the exam for special piano and was accepted for the introductory class with Winkler. It was one of those make-up exams that Winkler had mentioned. They didn't spend much time examining me, partly because I had already studied with Winkler and partly because a great many people were taking the exams (about eighty, most of them girls). The examiners (there were eight or nine of them) sat at a big table except for one of them, who stood by the piano and told the student what to play, asked him questions, etc.

I was asked, "How old are you?"

"Fourteen and a half."

"Where have you studied piano?"

"Last winter I took obligatory piano with Winkler."

Winkler confirmed that he had agreed I should study with him, and that I was a former pupil of Rimsky-Korsakov.

"Ah, Rimsky-Korsakov!" the examiner exclaimed.

"That's interesting!" My mother wrote to my father: "Winkler, who wanted to support Serezha at the exam, said, 'He is a pupil of Nikolai

Andreyevich.'* It was not a deliberate lie, since for some reason he has always had the impression that Serezha was a pupil of Rimsky-Korsakov. Several times last winter he asked Serezha, 'Are you with Nikolai Andreyevich?' 'No, I'm with Anatoly Konstantinovich.' But a short time later he would ask the same question. That mistake couldn't have hurt anything, since Rimsky-Korsakov still fascinates the former faculty."

The examiner had me play two scales, then a few bars of the Beethoven sonata, then asked me to play something I had composed myself. I wasn't ready for that, but I began to play my most recent piece—the one dedicated to you, *Romance No. 4*—which in my opinion is the best. But to my great disappointment they let me play only the introductory section, which didn't represent anything special except perhaps a knowledge of harmony.[63]

On this point Mother wrote Father:

After the examination [Winkler] met Serezha in the hallway and asked. "Why didn't you play that composition of yours you played for me last year?" [He meant the *Vivo*, written a year earlier.] That showed he regretted that Serezha had chosen something unsuccessful from among his pieces. They didn't let him play the whole thing—only that unattractive introductory section. I found it unattractive and awkward back in Sontsovka. But Serezha thinks it has some pretty harmonies.[64]

This incident left me with injured feelings like those I had gotten from the encounter with the girl who had studied with Safonoff when we each played the Beethoven sonata.

For in fact, despite my mother's opinion and despite what I had written to my father when I said the introductory section did not represent anything special, I was deeply convinced that that romance was my most successful composition. But when I was playing it before those conservative judges and was just coming to the best part, I was suddenly seized by the shoulder, and someone said, "That's enough. Now play us a modulation, for example . . ." For that matter, they hadn't let me finish the modulation: they just announced that the examination was over.

The introduction to *Romance No. 4:*

* Nikolai Andreyevich is Rimsky-Korsakov, and Anatoly Konstantinovich (mentioned later) is Lyadov. This form of address, first name plus patronymic, has not always been strictly followed in the translation elsewhere, but in this case it was felt to be indispensable in preserving the tone of the dialogue. (Translator's note.)

I wandered around the hallways for about two hours before Winkler came out of the room where the examinations were being held.

"Your lessons will be on Wednesdays and Saturdays at ten in the morning," he said. "Don't bring any pieces to the next lesson. To start with we'll work on techniques to strengthen your fingers. It'll be a bit boring a first, but there's nothing we can do about it."

29

The exams in academic subjects began a few days later. The arithemetic teacher recognized me and began to ask me about fractions, sometimes putting questions that were rather unpleasant. For example, he asked me what would become of a proper fraction—and likewise an improper fraction—if the numerator and denominator were increased by a certain number. I thought of the simplest proper fraction, $\frac{1}{2}$, and added one to both the numerator and denominator. It came out $\frac{2}{3}$. So it had increased, where an improper fraction would decrease.

"Right," the teacher said. "And in both cases they would approach unity."

When he had asked me a few more questions, he said, "I don't see any reason for continuing your ordeal. It's plain that you know your arithmetic." And after giving me an A, he dismissed me.

The geography teacher also recognized me. After waiting a whole hour (while he examined five students in line ahead of me) I answered some questions about Scandinavia and France and got another A.

The French teacher asked me (in French), "As I recall, you got a decent grade from me last year."

"Yes, a B."

He had me read and translate a little excerpt, then he dictated a half-dozen lines. After correcting *officier,* which I wrote with two c's, he gave me an A.

The German teacher asked me (in German), "Whom did you study with this summer?"

"With Mama."

"Is she German?"

"No, she's Russian."

He asked what textbook I had used and how far I had gotten through it, dictated a half page (I made three mistakes), had me decline a noun with an adjective and then gave me an A minus.

The Russian language teacher put me through quite a few paces on syntax, and gave me a B for written work, another B for oral work, and still another for general work.

But in a letter to my father I disputed the teacher's own syntactical analysis, finding that he had made three mistakes.

"Ah, Prokofiev!" the history teacher greeted me. "We're old acquaintances. Sit down."

I was rather cocky in answering questions about Alexander the Great and the Peloponnesian War, but I didn't know what the Edict of Milan was.

"You never heard of it?"

"No."

"That was an edict promulgated by Constantine the Great, granting freedom of worship to Christians."

I remembered and said I had known. He was satisfied and gave me an A.

The last examination was in religion. The priest went through all the services. I later wrote to my father: "I'll tell you only what I didn't know: how many passages of scripture are read at Vesper, whether the Czar's family is mentioned in the Great Liturgy, and a few other trifles. But since he never gives anyone an A, I got a B."

30

Father had been making ready to come to Petersburg in mid-September, but as usual he couldn't get his affairs in order. Mother counseled Father: "Please come. For once in your life, forget your interminable business matters. If we have good September weather we'll take a trip outside the city. Last Sunday we went to Pavlovsk. That wonderful northern landscape! Everything green: plush-green meadows full of clover in bloom; lakes, and foothills." In the same letter she recounted what had been happening in the musical life of Moscow (as she had heard it from Tatyana Pavlovna, the lady doctor):

Taneyev has left the Moscow Conservatory because of Safonoff's impudence and tyranny. In taking a year's leave of absence, Taneyev named Ippolitov-Ivanov as his successor. Taneyev has shown that under conditions of autonomy, the professors should choose the director. Safonoff said some crude things to Taneyev, and the latter replied that he had already heard all that from cabdrivers. Things out of joint everywhere! What a time this is!

With respect to herself, Mother wrote: "Everyone who has seen me thinks I have come back in worse condition than when I left. I have turned sallow and pallid and grown old. We are drinking white wine to help our morale. Sergusha is looking good."[65]

From me to my father at Sontsovka.
Petersburg, September 11, 1905.

Yesterday I went for my first piano lesson with Winkler. He said that for a couple of weeks I'll be doing nothing but exercises to strengthen my fingers and develop my hands, and he showed me the exercises. In general, they are boring, but for me they are still interesting as a novelty. [Someone had finally bridled me. Up to that time I had played anything I wanted, but always rather carelessly, and I kept my fingers straight as sticks. Winkler demanded that I play more precisely, that I bend my fingers and place them accurately.]

On September 8, I went to Shpis's place to find out how things stood. He told me that he would never make a deal with Asafyev, since he is still a student at lecture courses, while he himself gives lessons. But on Sunday we decided to go to Lyadov to make an arrangement for private lessons. Today I went to see Shpis so that we could go to Lyadov's together, and right out of the blue he told me that they [Asafyev and Shpis] had already been to see Lyadov, and he told them to wait because it was possible that he, Glazunov, and even Rimsky-Korsakov still might come back to the Conservatory. He said that in any case they would know in ten days or so.[66]

But things dragged on—not for ten days but a whole month. On October 10 I wrote to Father:

> I went to see Shpis. He has obviously cooled toward the idea of taking private lessons from Lyadov together with Asafyev. He says he is very busy, and in general he was rather boring. (Of course! He wanted to get rid of a mere boy like me.) But finally he said that on Saturday he would have a talk with Asafyev, and that today I would get their final answer in a letter.[67]

And so the final answer came at last.

> I really don't know what to advise you [Shpis wrote]. The thing is that if we—that is, Asafyev, Fiveisky, and I—take strictly private lessons from Lyadov, and if he comes back to the Conservatory, we'll continue to take lessons from him at home. If you want to take lessons from him, I suggest you talk to him directly. He won't be in Petersburg until Thursday.
>
> VASILY SHPIS.

In a letter to my father I commented:

> That was a terribly swinish thing to do. Mama drew up a rough draft of a letter scolding him [that is, a letter for me to send to Shpis], and I went to see Lyadov to ask when he could receive Mama to talk about giving me private lessons alone. Despite the last line in Shpis's letter, I found Lyadov at home.
>
> "As it happens," Lyadov told me, "I'm giving a private lesson to some other students tomorrow—Wednesday. You come too."[68]

When Shpis came to Lyadov's on Wednesday for the lesson, he was amazed to find me there, since he had written me that Lyadov would not be in Petersburg until Thursday. I asked Asafyev about arrangements for paying for the les-

S. A. and M. G. Prokofiev.

Holograph (at age twelve).

Artur Nikisch. (Nikisch was conductor of the Boston Symphony Orchestra,
1889–93—Editors' note.)

"Twig from Palestine"—my first art song.

A. B. Goldenweiser.

Maria Grigoryevna Prokofieva.

Alexander Glazunov, "...with Doctor's Degrees from both Oxford and Cambridge Universities."

Panorama of Moscow.

The Bolshoi Theater.

Moscow: A horse-drawn streetcar near the Church of Christ the Savior.

Moscow: Kuznetsky Bridge Street.

слъ включаетъ 2 или нѣсколько согласныхъ, то всѣ[2] онъ изображаются на одной линейкой.

Чтобъ отдѣлить слово отъ слова ставится знакъ ⌣. Вотъ письмо на этомъ языкѣ:

"Войны съ 1800 года"

[constructed alphabet text]

Переводъ: Самая послѣдняя война была между Россіей и Японіей, а до нея Китай воевалъ съ Европой и былъ побѣжденъ, но воевалъ и съ Японіей, но она его побѣдила. Америка воевала съ Испаніей и ослабила ее. Еще въ семьдесятъ пятомъ году мы побили Турокъ на четыре года раньше нѣмцы разбили Наполеона Третьяго и взяли у французовъ двѣ провинціи.

"My first invention was a new alphabet."

sons, Asafyev said Lyadov had deferred that question, and for the time being they were reviewing harmony, taking a lesson once a week.

And so the lessons got under way. They were neither good nor bad, and progressed at a kind of jog trot. Lyadov apparently regarded it as his principal duty to work with us, even gratis. But because he was so profoundly lazy, he did it in an indifferent, boring manner that aroused little interest on our part.

Winkler was of a totally different breed. He was a good musician, and a composer whose works were published by the Belyayev firm. He was not talented but he was conscientious and a man of good will. But now another obstacle arose. The Conservatory would open one day and close the next, so that my lessons with Winkler had no continuity. Finally one day in late October, Winkler told me that I should come to his home and take private lessons on those days when the Conservatory was closed.

I wrote to my father:

> Today I went to Winkler's and took him an étude. He said that I didn't know how to keep hold of myself while playing: that one bar would be good and the next one bad; that in general the first part of the étude was not bad, but the middle part was not especially good.[69]

It was at this time that the carelessness I have mentioned earlier began to tell. It was because I had played many pieces of all kinds without ever learning anything really perfectly.

31

Politically, the autumn of 1905 was a rather restless time. The railroad strikes began in October, cutting off the mail service. Mother wrote to Father: "I wonder if this letter will reach you, and whether you, poor soul, will get these lines. In the country they are like the dove from Noah's Ark."

The manifesto on the founding of the State Duma and the granting of freedoms was promulgated on October 17. My mother welcomed the Constitution, but within ten days she had begun to have doubts. She wrote to Father:

> Everyone is saying that the manifesto of October 17 is not authorized, that there are only words people no longer believe, and that there is neither freedom of speech nor personal freedom. They drove everyone away from some meeting that was being held in an authorized place in Petersburg.[70]

And once again the concern for my father:

> It makes me very sad that we are not together in this time of troubles. My heart aches for you, for everything, and for everyone. Things are relatively better for us on Pokrovskaya Square, as if in some province. The

market is open every day, although you see the mounted police going past from time to time. There is no more electric current in our apartment. . . . We have been lighting miserable lamps, and going around like blind people without glasses. The water is still running.[71]

From another letter: "The streetcars have not been running for a week. Without them it's simply a catastrophe."

And from another: "Tomorrow the bakery shops will be closed, along with many other places, no doubt."

Mme. Kilschtedt, my former librettist for *Undine,* paid a call on Mama. She was full of anxiety, weeping and shouting. She had grown old and gray and was taking her leave of the world, ready to die with the dying social order.

Mother wrote to Father: "Nobody knows and nobody can say whether this is the end of the world, or whether it has been postponed, because nothing like this has ever happened in Russia."

And in another letter: "The question, of course, is whether the bank will be robbed, or whether they can defend it adequately."

At that time my father was nearing sixty. He was in private employment— well paid, but with no illusions about a pension. Therefore, instead of spending everything he made, he put some away for his old age. My parents favored everything progressive but they were worried about what might happen to the savings they had put into the bank.

From another letter: "We are living quietly and peacefully in our monastery [we constantly heard the bells from the Church of the Intercession] but somehow my heart is heavy."

But then the mail and telegraph services began to "destrike," as I wrote in a letter to my father, and we started getting news from him. "We are yearning to see you," Mother wrote him, "but we are apprehensive about your traveling, since feelings are at fever-pitch everywhere, and all kinds of unforeseen things are happening." Then comes a rather amusing show of concern for his health: "I suggest you stop using a syringe on your nose—all the more so since your hearing is no good and you make a terribly loud noise when you blow your nose."

That fall Father visited us twice: in late September and early November. While he was there he brought me up to date in my academic subjects, and drew up a detailed schedule for me to follow in his absence. I was to send him my assignments, compositions, etc., via parcel post.

I registered with a library where I got the books on a list my father had drawn up. That fall I read Tolstoy's *War and Peace,* Thackeray's *Vanity Fair,* Goncharov's *The Frigate Pallas,* and a selection of Ostrovsky's plays.

I was enthralled by *War and Peace,* although of course I was bored by the endless discussions at the end of the novel. But even apart from those discussions, it was plain to me that, if Tolstoy had managed to cut the novel in half, from four volumes to two, it would only have gained by it. And this opinion was strengthened at the various times later on when I came back to *War and Peace*. As for the female characters in the book, I did not sympathize so much with Natasha as with Sonya, whose fate made me very sad.

I was still giving grades to the books I read. *War and Peace* and *Vanity Fair* got A's, but Ostrovsky's comedies got D's and C's.

I continued to take an interest in theatrical form, and even wrote a long comedy of my own. It was a kind of detective story, and I never thought up a title for it. The story was borrowed from one of the plays we had dreamed up and performed at Sontsovka—but this time I had complicated it with all kinds of legal conflicts—occasionally amusing, but for the most part awkward. I spent two and a half months writing the comedy, and it took up sixty-two pages in my "second volume."

32

At that time it was difficult to go to the opera in Petersburg, because the Maryinsky (Opera) Theater had a great many subscriptions and tickets were sold to the general public only on Fridays. (Aunt Tanya had an acquaintance—a colleague by the name of Nebolsin—who together with a few other people had subscribed to a box in the Maryinsky Theater. These subscriptions, renewed every autumn, were prized treasures. They were even bequeathed in wills and given as dowries. But as it happened, Nebolsin did not use his box seat, and from time to time he would let us use it. Therefore, Mama and Aunt Tanya went so far as to invite him to partake of a turkey sent from Sontsovka.

This box wasn't a very good one, being in the third tier on the side, but that fall I heard several operas, including *Tannhäuser* and *The Snow Maiden*. *Tannhäuser* struck me as rather boring, but I liked the chorus of pilgrims coming from far off.

About *The Snow Maiden,* which I had heard for the second time, I wrote my father as follows: "Tonight we are going to *The Snow Maiden,* one of Rimsky-Korsakov's best operas. The production at the Maryinsky Theater was premiered recently, and it has been highly praised. I have a score that I am taking with me." Dr. Reberg had given me the piano score of *The Snow Maiden* at Sontsovka. At first it left me cold. But I gradually acquired a taste for that opera, and ever since I have been very fond of it.

Aunt Tanya told me there was a liturgy composed by Tchaikovsky that was very interesting and not at all like choral music for the church. When you heard it, she said, it was "just as though they were all singing operatic arias," for which reason it was not allowed to be performed in churches.

Only once a year, in the autumn, on the anniversary of Tchaikovsky's death, this liturgy is sung in one of the churches of the Alexander Nevsky Monastery.

"Oh, how interesting!" I exclaimed. "Let's go and hear it on that day."

"We really should," she said thoughtfully. "But on that day the crowd is so big you can hardly elbow your way through the church. All the famous artists come, and in general all the important people in Petersburg."

So we never made plans to go and hear Tchaikovsky's liturgy. But I remembered it as something very interesting that one should definitely hear. And the fact that it was sung only once a year on the anniversary of the composer's death endowed it with a special poetic quality.

Nebolsin introduced us to a relative of his, also named Nebolsin, a lawyer with a black mustache, a plump face, and a pince-nez that he wore on a black ribbon. He held progressive views that, however, he expressed in a didactic manner—something that often irritated the person he was talking to. His son was a high school student about my age who went around in a crimson shirt. He played chess with me and lost. He told me that he published a monthly journal printed on a typewriter, and suggested I take over the chess column and publish our game with comments in the next issue. He himself wrote the lead editorials, in which he rather venomously insulted the Cossacks who had taken part in putting down the workers.

I accepted his suggestion with pleasure, although I could not understand why such a poor game as ours should be published. When my parents came into a room he didn't rise to greet them, but merely lifted himself up from his chair a little.

For some reason this acquaintanceship didn't develop. I suspect that my parents were unenthusiastic about the news that I was going to write for a revolutionary journal, even though it was only in the innocent role of a chess columnist. What if something should happen? Thus the Nebolsins imperceptibly faded from my horizon.

33

Journals with a political slant were still beyond my sphere of interest, and I much more willingly made friends with the likes of Vanya Pavsky, despite his being so young. He was a very cheerful, lively youngster. When I beat him at chess, he would say, "But there is still Uncle Kolya. He plays very well."

I played a game with Vanya *à l'aveugle,* with him sitting at the board and calling out moves to me while I sat with my back turned and followed the game in my head. I won again. And again he said, "Uncle Kolya plays chess very well. He can beat anybody."

I was very interested in that Uncle Kolya, because I was eager for a worthwhile opponent. By way of amusing myself I even made up chess games in my head, without a board, and then played them on the board.

At the Pavskys' my mother met the family of the surgeon Pototsky, the chief medical officer of the Obukhovskaya Hospital. They had a government-owned apartment with a rather large drawing room that the ladies decided to use for purposes of teaching their children to dance. They got a teacher from the ballet and fixed the time for the gatherings at three on Sundays. I hadn't the slightest notion why I should learn to dance, but Mother was inflexible and said I had to. I was the oldest in the group. All the other children were very young. I had absolutely no interest in dancing with girls of seven, so for me they invited the seventeen-year-old daughter of their neighbor. She condescendingly did a few turns with me, but likewise proved to be outside my orbit.

One day I was told that Lelya Skalon would come to the lessons, and I pricked up my ears. I had met Lieutenant Colonel Skalon's family at the Pavskys', and I very much liked Lelya, a girl of thirteen. She was rather timid and rather pretty, these being the only qualities she displayed. But she was the first girl I liked and with whom (in the children's rooms at Vanya Pavsky's) I tried to flirt—unsuccessfully, as it happened. But she did not show up for the dancing lessons, and I totally lost interest in them. In the final analysis, those lessons gratified my mother much more than me. "Serezha danced rather well," she wrote to my father, "and discovered it was more fun than he had thought it would be. Eight mamas came with their children. We drank tea, looked on, and chatted."

While chatting pleasantly with the other ladies, my mother never noticed that I did not understand the nature of the dance steps, did not like them, and learned almost nothing.

34

On October 26, Lyadov began to teach us counterpoint, while still giving us assignments in harmony. We had the illusion that the year would not be wasted, since we were already doing counterpoint.

Actually, since Lyadov had started teaching us counterpoint only in late October, and we had only one lesson a week, he naturally could not get us through the whole course. The year was not wasted, since we profited from the lessons, but graduation from the Conservatory was a year further off.

When the lessons in counterpoint began I resumed my record of mistakes, and kept it through nine lessons, until mid-January. According to my statistics, I had an average of 0.56 mistakes per assignment, and was in second place. Asafyev was in first place with 0.46, Kankarovich in third place, and Shpis in fourth place. Shpis dropped out of the class in early December, and Fiveisky didn't turn in a single assignment during all that time. "He was my laziest pupil," Taneyev used to say of him.

One day in November I asked Lyadov, "Anatoly Konstantinovich, will we soon be writing little songs?"

"What little songs?"

"Minuets and the like."

"Ah! All right, gentlemen. For next time, write a minuet apiece. No, wait. Next time I'll explain the form, and then you can write them."

At the next lesson he demonstrated the binary form. "With this, you have to write such small pieces," I explained to my father, "that the entire piece takes up only one staff across the page—which is of course very hard to write. On Wednesday the thirtieth I'll bring in my first one. Interesting."

As soon as we went from assignments to actual composing, I became animated and things got "interesting." But Lyadov wasted no time in deadening all animation. After the next lesson I wrote my father:

> It turned out that none of the students' little pieces were written the way he wanted them to be. Lyadov had told us that in this binary form we should write as if for the piano, and he said nothing about voices. But when we brought in our pieces, he said our voice-leading was miserable—that we wrote like Cui and other dilettantes. For example, it was not permissible that there should be six voices to start with, that two bars later three of them should disappear, and then eight voices come in in the next chord.[72]

Lyadov may not have noticed it, but with his grumbling and scoffing he poisoned all desire to work. His demands for purity in voice-leading were useful, but his hostile tone ruined everything. And he had harsh words not only for us but for some of the great composers as well. Mozart and Chopin were the only ones whose voice-leading he considered irreproachable. As for Beethoven and Schubert, he often insulted them.

That fall I began to jot down the titles of works I had heard performed by orchestras, giving them grades just as I had done with the books I had read.

The list began with the overture to Borodin's *Prince Igor,* to which I gave a D. This is amazing, but I still remember how much I disliked that overture. I also disliked Beethoven's *Egmont Overture,* even though I had heard it twice, and gave it a C. The pieces I liked were the suite from Rimsky-Korsakov's *Mlada,* Glazunov's *Poème lyrique,* Tchaikovsky's *Variations on a Rococo Theme,* Lyadov's *Russian Songs for Orchestra,* and Taneyev's symphony— perhaps out of respect for the composer.

From my mother to my father in Sontsovka.
Petersburg, October 23, 1905.

> Yesterday the three of us went to Siloti's concert. We saw all the luminaries: Rimsky-Korsakov, Glazunov, Lyadov, and Winkler—naturally, only when they were at a distance or on the stage. Rimsky-Korsakov received a big ovation: the whole hall resounded, and he was called back three times. He was deeply moved, and he even swayed on his feet.[73]

At the next Siloti concert they played Taneyev's symphony, to which I listened very closely. This explains the high mark I gave it, since it is easily possible to dislike such a complex piece at first hearing. At that same concert I was greatly impressed by Borodin's setting of "For the Shores of Thy Distant Homeland"* as orchestrated by Glazunov. That art song has been one of my favorites ever since.

At a rehearsal, one theory student asked another, "Why did they ask that soprano to perform?"

The other theory student (well on in years, and balding) replied, "Because So-and-So did his bit for her." And he named one of the promoters of the concert.

"But why did he do his bit for her?"

"Probably because she did her bit for him," was the answer. And they both laughed.

I was following the conversation with an attention evident to them, but didn't understand what it meant.

The bald student waved a hand in my direction. "Prokosha is a good lad, but he doesn't know about such things," he said. Then they went off a few paces and continued the conversation.

As a matter of fact, my innocence in those days was almost total. For example, I thought roosters' eggs were bigger than hens' eggs.

35

By way of honoring the name day of "both Katyas" (as my mother called Aunt Katya and Cousin Katya), I decided to finish Ditty No. 42,[74] which I had started on that summer. It was a rather long piece, serious in tone, and not very shapely. It was more like the piano score of an orchestral piece than a piece conceived for piano. In a word, it was not suitable for a gala performance on a name day, and it passed unnoticed.

From me to my father at Sontsovka.
Petersburg, December 1 (14), 1905.

On Saturday the third [of December] there will be a big Siloti concert with Chaliapin and, on the same day, a symphony concert at the Conservatory. There is a controversy as to which concert will be better: on the one hand, Chaliapin; on the other, an interesting program: Beethoven's *Symphony No. 3*, the "Eroica," Grieg's *Piano Concerto*, and Rimsky-Korsakov's *Capriccio espagnol*, plus a famous Italian singer. Today I was at the rehearsal for the Siloti concert, and tomorrow I shall kill two birds with one stone: since I figure that the first thing to be played at the rehearsal at the

* One of Pushkin's anthology pieces. (Translator's note.)

Conservatory will be the symphony, while Chaliapin will not sing early in
the other rehearsal, I'm going first to the Conservatory to follow the Beethoven score, then I'll go to the Siloti rehearsal. Aunt Tanya is going to
the Chaliapin concert, but Mama and I are going to the Conservatory. The
Rayevskys got tickets for Chaliapin.[75]

I really was very much caught up in all the fuss about the concerts, but, as
has been seen, it was the interesting program that won me over, not the famous
Italian singer. Unfortunately, I did not record my impressions. But I had heard
Chaliapin before.

On his way back to Sontsovka after visiting us in Petersburg, Father
stopped off to see his employer Sontsov at his Kursk estate to talk with him
about the future disposition of Sontsovka.

Sontsov told him that he had divided the estate into three equal parts, one
for himself and one for each of his two grown sons (the older was thirty). The
advantage for the sons was that they could come into their shares before their father died. But he had kept one third for himself, since he had had at first one illegitimate family and then another, and he wanted to provide for both of them.

The older son was interested in Sontsovka and had even talked to my father about buying a plow with steam traction to increase the yield. But the
younger son, who was serving as vice-governor of a western province, asked my
father to arrange for the sale of his share.

Father thought the peasants might be interested in buying it, and that in
this way their revolutionary ardor might be cooled a bit. But he was mistaken,
because only the well-to-do peasants could have any interest in buying land, and
it was the poor peasants who were revolutionaries.

While visiting Sontsov, my father asked him if he had any objections to his
(my father's) absences from Sontsovka when he was visiting in Petersburg. Sontsov was very much the gentleman and exclaimed, "By no means, Sergei Alex-
eyevich! As much as you like!"

From Sontsovka, Father wrote that although things there were quiet
enough on the surface there was latent trouble. It was therefore decided that we
would not go to Sontsovka for Christmas that year: instead, Father would come
to Petersburg.

We saw the New Year 1906 in at the Rayevskys'. At their home this event
was celebrated with considerable fanfare, and patriarchal traditions were observed. At 11:30 we all sat down at the table. We sat by families—husbands with
their wives, brothers with their sisters. At five minutes to midnight the hosts
made sure that all their guests had food on their plates and wine in their goblets
—meaning they would live in plenty for the entire year.

At midnight, when the clock slowly struck twelve, all the guests raised their
goblets, while Aunt Katya and Uncle Sasha got on their knees to pray. At the
last stroke Uncle Sasha rose to his feet and congratulated Aunt Katya. At this,

there were much shouting and noisemaking as people clinked glasses. Then the Rayevskys went into the kitchen to congratulate the servants.

That season I did not compose much music. *Undine* had gotten bogged down completely. But I did finish the fourth series of ditties; that is, I wrote twelve of them, as I had done for the preceding three years, so that I had a total of forty-eight. The fillip that Glière had given me in Sontsovka induced an even motion of long duration and got the upper hand over Lyadov, who with his binary form stimulated no desire to compose.

In November and December I wrote four ditties: the ninth, tenth, eleventh, and twelfth of the fourth series.[76] Two of them, an elegy and a minuet, were short. But the tenth took up thirteen pages and was broadly conceived with dramatic shifts in mood, harmonic inventions, and even a combination of two themes:

The main theme is in the right hand, and fragments of the second theme are in the left. Like the ditty written for the name day of the two Katyas, this piece was not shapely, not very pianistic, and rather resembled a piano arrangement of a piece written for orchestra. I probably would have written it for orchestra if I had been better able to handle orchestration.

By contrast, the twelfth piece was done simply, a clear, warm Mendelssohnian style. I would say it was successful:

36

From me to my father in Moscow.
Petersburg, January 18, 1906.

There have been reports in the newspapers that in Moscow the Conservatory has reopened, and that students who do not pay their fees before the twenty-first will not be considered as such. When I asked Winkler whether the same thing would happen with us, he said that in any case it would not be amiss to pay the fees, that one should not lose hope that the Conservatory will reopen, and that they were having a general session of the faculty today. So my conclusion is that there will be no class at Lyadov's. But of course I'm going anyway.[77] [What follows is a postscript written in pencil.] I have just come from a lesson with Lyadov. I am writing this at the Nikolayevsky Station, and will put the letter in the mail car. The lesson lasted only a half hour or forty-five minutes, since Lyadov, as I had thought, was in a hurry to get to the session. He managed only to look over the pieces and the chorales, and of course criticized everything. He did not look at the counterpoint, which is very annoying, because I'll have to do the same thing over again.[78]

Two days later I was at Winkler's home for a lesson. (I was still taking them there.) He approved of the étude I had brought him.

"Is it true," I asked him, "that there will be a big students' meeting on the twenty-third?"

"That's right. Were you invited to it?"

"No."

"If you get an invitation, you'd better go, because at the end of the meeting they're going to vote whether the Conservatory should be reopened, and it would be well to have as many votes in favor of it as possible. If there are only a few votes against it, the Conservatory will reopen."

The meeting was held and led to the closing of the Conservatory. Glazunov had already been named director. He agreed with the decision but warned that there would be examinations in the spring.

37

[This chapter opens with two letters from Prokofiev's mother to his father, one of which mentions a *Scherzo* that Sergei wrote for her name day and performed for her guests on that day—January 26, 1906.]*

Obviously, that *Scherzo* (Ditty No. 50, otherwise the second ditty in the

* Translator's note.

fifth series)[79] didn't come across very well to the audience, since there are no comments on its qualities in the letters. From the viewpoint of piano technique; it is written in double thirds in the right hand, and in this respect one feels the influence of certain technical pieces I learned or heard at the Conservatory. Schumann's *Toccata* made a special impression on me.

The first ditty in the fifth series was composed in a more dramatic style.[80] Somewhere along the way the upper voice of the melody is suddenly joined by a voice in the bass, which for a time moves in parallel octaves with it, as if emphasizing it, then leaves it and become independent. It seemed to me that this doubling in the bass emphasized and enhanced the expressiveness of the melody:

The parallel octaves in the third and fourth bars were at first conceived as follows:

But then I "grew fearful" and wrote them as shown in the first example. And yet this motion of the upper and lower voices in parallel octaves turned out to be a device I often used subsequently.

My aunt, Katya Rayevskaya, had taken her daughter Katya to Vienna. Cousin Katya was twenty-one, a pretty and even delicate girl who had been graduated from the exclusive Smolny Institute. The year before, she had contracted typhus, with complications in the ear. After taking her to numerous Petersburg doctors with no particular success, her parents decided to take her to Vienna. Uncle Sasha sighed and groaned that they didn't have the money, but he was told that it was better to provide a daughter with a dowry smaller by a thousand rubles than to give away a deaf bride at the altar.

My mother wrote to my father:

> Many acquaintances saw them off with flowers, fruit and candy. Alexander Dmitriyevich [Uncle Sasha] had been trying to get a special compartment, but instead they gave them a special car, saying they couldn't assign a special compartment. They were apprehensive about going in a separate car, although they had been assigned a special conductor, but there was nothing to be done about it.
>
> In a day and a half they'll be in a foreign realm. No doubt they'll be amazed.[81]

My mother had yearned all her life to go abroad, and at Sontsovka she had even subscribed to a magazine that gave information on foreign travel. Hence she was especially interested in her sister's departure.

38

In February 1906 an important change took place in my study of the theory of composition. My parents were not satisfied with Lyadov's apathetic teaching. True, the lessons were free, but they were conducted listlessly. Having already spent so much money on the move to Petersburg, they felt it was better to pay Lyadov something, if only he would really get to work.

> From my mother to my father in Sontsovka.
> Petersburg, February 3 (16), 1906.

> Yesterday Serezha began taking private lessons from Lyadov, twice a week at five rubles per lesson. It came about as follows. At the lesson of January 25, Lyadov said, "There will be an examination in the spring, and you will all fail." Kankarovich asked, "In harmony or counterpoint?" "Harmony, of course. I'm giving you counterpoint so as not to waste time." I decided to go to see Lyadov and have a talk. When I got there, I offered to pay him for the past six months, but he declined. Then I asked him if he would please give Serezha private lessons so the year would not be lost, since it was for the sake of his lessons that we were living in Petersburg. He agreed. I asked him to point out my son's shortcomings. He said that Serezha has a very frivolous attitude toward everything, and must work more seriously. He knows the rules, but makes mistakes and does not keep a critical eye on his work. "I will overwhelm both you and him when I say that he must work on harmony. First the ABC's, then the symphonies—otherwise he won't amount to anything.
>
> After hearing that, Serezha promised to pay closer attention to his work to correct his shortcomings in harmony in three lessons so he could move on to counterpoint. He had his first lesson at six o'clock yesterday, February 2. They worked for one hour and six minutes [I had given my

mother the exact time]. The lesson was thorough, meaningful, and much more interesting than the ones with the other students. Serezha is not going to attend the group class, and he is not going to tell the other students he is taking private lessons. My feeling is that Serezha will catch up by spring. It's too bad that Lyadov declined to give him private lessons last fall. No doubt he figured that the Conservatory would reopen, but it is now obvious that it will hibernate until next fall.

Yesterday Glière and his wife had lunch with us. They have come to town for three days. The statue of Glinka [the "statue of Gnilka," as our cook said] was dedicated at the Conservatory today.

The unveiling took place in the morning, and the formal dedication during the day. Tonight they are performing his opera, *Ruslan and Lyudmila* at the Maryinsky Theater, and are giving out free tickets. We won't be able to get in: all the tickets have been handed out selectively and on a basis of who knows whom. Glière wanted to stop by and look at Serezha's compositions, but he is only here for a very short time and is very busy. They are getting ready to go to Berlin with their daughters (Liya and Nina) and their nursemaid—an entire Noah's Ark—to study music and listen to music.

Keep healthy and take care of Elena [the mother of Stenya and Serezha], I'm very sorry for her.[82]

From me to my father at Sontsovka.
Petersburg, February 3 (16), 1906.

As Mama has written you, I have now started taking private lessons with Lyadov, and I had my first one yesterday. He looked over the assignments more closely than when other students are there, and said that this time my chorales—and my harmony in general—were better. Since I am now taking lessons from Lyadov twice as often, and am working more on them, I couldn't spend much time on my academic subjects this week. I didn't work at all on the ones Mama is in charge of, and only an hour or two on yours.

I thank you very much for the list of books. The trouble is, I can scarcely manage to read them now. Some of them I have already read; for example, the trilogy about Gogol,[83] *Pushkin's Childhood Years,* by Avenarius,[84] and Verne's *Floating City, Eighty Thousand Leagues Under the Sea,** and *Voyage to the Moon* (the first and third in French).[85]

From me to my father at Sontsovka.
Petersburg, February 9 (22), 1906.

In an hour I'm going to take a lesson with Lyadov. Usually I go there at six o'clock, but today he said I should come at one. I'm taking him a chorale and twelve variations on a theme he gave me. These are not like

* The last two titles in this sentence should read *Twenty Thousand Leagues Under the Sea* and *From the Earth to the Moon.* (Editor's note.)

those variations on Handel that I play for Winkler: I simply have to use the means allowed by harmony, although I have a waltz and a mazurka.[86]

> From me to my father at Sontsovka.
> Petersburg, February 12 (25), 1906.

On Thursday I went for a lesson with Lyadov, and took him a chorale and variations on a theme he had given me. Many of the variations were good, and the chorale was not bad. He showed me another way of writing chorales, and told me to write a waltz and two chorales with this new method.

I asked him whether I would be taking fugue or counterpoint in the fall. He said counterpoint. [I recall that I didn't like writing that: it meant I had lost a year.] When I said we had three months, and that perhaps I could cover it roughly and continue with correspondence lessons in the summer—I would do the assignments and send them to him, and he would correct them—he replied that, first, he regarded correspondence lessons as completely useless and, second, that the most important part of the theory of composition was harmony. Hence we would cover all aspects of harmony (even at the Conservatory they don't teach it that way). And the next in importance was counterpoint, hence it could not be condensed but should likewise be covered thoroughly. As for orchestration, he said that although it was taught parallel with fugue I could take it at the same time as counterpoint.

He told me that I didn't know how to savor each note in a chorale, that I was working diligently and was contributing a lot, but that I didn't have "it."

He asked me who my favorite composer was. I said Tchaikovsky, Wagner, and Grieg. He replied, "The first two are good, but the third is a harmful influence."[87]

I had spoken sincerely about Tchaikovsky, although I was far from knowing all his works. Of his symphonies I knew only the *Second,* and I didn't know his chamber music at all. I had named Wagner for snobbish reasons. I had heard that his music was good, and that he was much discussed in musical circles, but I had never heard either the *Ring* or *Tristan,* and my understanding of *Die Meistersinger* was limited. As for Grieg, I knew his works for piano rather well. Even before I entered the Conservatory, my parents had given me a complete set of them in six volumes, and I played them over and over, always enjoying them. But Lyadov had no particular fondness for Grieg. He felt that his voice-leading was rather poor, that he lacked technique, and that in general he was a dilettante.

39

From me to my father at Sontsovka.
Petersburg, February 16 (March 1), 1906.

Today we had your letter saying you were postponing your departure until Tuesday. That is bad news, because we have missed you, and it's too bad you won't catch the first Belyayev concert. Among other things, they're going to play Rimsky-Korsakov's symphonic sketch based on a theme from Pushkin's "There's a Green Oak on the Curved Seashore."* It is a very interesting piece. Probably they will also perform Scriabin's *Third Symphony*. [Thus my predilections were not limited to Tchaikovsky, Grieg, and the mythical Wagner!]

On Saturday I went to Winkler's and took him an étude. He said "not bad at all" and never once stopped me while I was playing, which showed it was good. He assigned me another one. I conveyed Lyadov's greetings, and he beamed.

Today I had a lesson with Lyadov. At the last lesson he had told me to write a waltz for strings. I did it and brought it to him today. The chorales were not bad in certain places [!]. He showed me a new way of writing chorales—imitation in triplets. Then he told me to study certain works with good counterpoint and gave me Tchaikovsky's ballet *The Sleeping Beauty*, which was inscribed: "To my dear friend, Anatoly Konstantinovich Lyadov —P. Tchaikovsky." [It is curious that Lyadov chose that particular work. Seemingly, he might have chosen something else for counterpoint. I played through *Sleeping Beauty* but didn't like all those ballet numbers, so the piano score was left lying on the shelf.] The period of concerts begins in the second week of Lent. It lasts ten days, and in that time I'll have to attend five rehearsals and three concerts. But then I'll have to fast until autumn.

The composer Arensky died a few days ago. His case had been hopeless since last fall. He wrote two operas and many other things, lots of them beautiful. (When Asafyev, Kankarovich, and I saw Lyadov at a concert, he reprimanded us rather sharply for not having gone to Arensky's funeral.)

Papa, I'm sure that right now you're sitting in your study figuring out how many hours a day you'll be teaching me in the summer: seven or seven and a half![88]

At this high point, the correspondence between me and my father shows a gap of two months. As I recall, he came to Petersburg about then, and several of the letters written after he left have been lost.

I do have, however, a good recollection of the performance of Scriabin's *Third Symphony* (*The Divine Poem*), of which I had given my father advance

* This is another of Pushkin's anthology pieces: the introduction to his narrative poem *Ruslan and Lyudmila*. (Translator's note.)

notice in my last letter. I went to all the rehearsals, being very interested in this new symphony by Scriabin, whose mazurkas had so much intrigued me the summer before. A good many things in the symphony struck me as remarkable, but there was also a lot I didn't completely understand. The most interesting thing, however, was the figure cut by Rimsky-Korsakov at those rehearsals in the Hall of Columns. He sat right in front of me, next to the German conductor Beidler, who had come to Petersburg to conduct at some other concert and was coming to the rehearsals to familiarize himself with this new Russian symphony. A music stand was placed in front of them, and on it Rimsky-Korsakov put the score of *The Divine Poem* that he had brought with him. In his own compositions, Rimsky-Korsakov was always interested in new harmonies; in *The Golden Cockerel,* for example, he invented quite a few of them. But Scriabin's inventions and all his *écroulements formidables* (an indication in the score) affected him as if an electric current had been sent through his seat. He kept jumping up and waving his hands, or shrugging his shoulders, or jabbing his finger at the score and saying something excitedly to Beidler, who just sat there settled back in his seat looking ruddy and healthy and smiling faintly. Yet there was good reason for Rimsky-Korsakov's strange behavior. He himself had published the score. But now, if you please, what impossible sounds were pouring forth! Yet there was no way he could have avoided publishing the score: Belyayev, in making testamentary disposition of his publishing house and putting Rimsky-Korsakov in charge of it, had stipulated that it publish everything that Scriabin wrote.

In March, I wrote Ditty No. 51, a long one in the style of a romantic ballade.[89] Unlike most of the others, it was not dedicated to anyone: I wrote it for myself, so to speak. It had some interesting harmonic ideas and began:

These last two measures were developed at the end of the piece as follows:

In another place we find this sequence:

That sequence struck me as very expressive, and I also used it in *Undine,*
on which I was still doing a little work between assignments.

40

I had my fifteenth birthday in April. Aunt Tanya took me to see her friend
Mme. Akatyeva. The latter had a son eighteen months younger than I who had
recently entered the Cadet Corps. He was a boy with bad morals—green but already ripe, as they say—but he drew very well and showed me a whole pile of
sketches of a war between lapdogs and monkeys. I liked the idea, and during an
entire year I did sketches of a war between lapdogs and monkeys, laying out the
battles and individual scenes from them. But while Kolya had sketched his
scenes beautifully, mine were clumsy and childish.

"Are you carrying on flirtations with any girls?" he suddenly asked me one
day, looking up at me over his sketches with a piercing glance.

"F-f-flirtations?" I asked in embarrassment. "No, I'm not."

"Why not?"

"Just because it's not very interesting."

"Not *interesting!*" he mimicked me, and then went on with his sketching,
not deigning to continue the conversation.

Mother was not very pleased with this acquaintanceship, and I heard her
tell Aunt Tanya that it wasn't a good idea to take me to the Akatyev's any more.
But for a long time I had the notion that flirtations were something not particularly nice and it was better to do without them.

My lessons with Lyadov ended on April 24 (Old Style) and those with
Winkler on the twenty-ninth. The conscientious Winkler made it a point to go
over with me, in a kind of preview, all the pieces he had assigned to me for
study during the coming summer.

At the last lesson with Lyadov I gave him a heavy sealed envelope.

"What's that?" he asked.

"Mama told me to give it to you."

He opened the envelope, and a lot of gold coins spilled out on the desk.

"Ah," he said. Then he pushed the coins aside disdainfully and covered them with a pile of sheet music.

> From me to my father at Sontsovka.
> Petersburg, April 27 (May 10), 1906.

Don't be surprised if you read [in our telegram]: "Arriving at such-and-such a time at Zhelannaya Station." This is because I have discovered a new through train whose route is Moscow–Lozovaya–Konstan-tinovka–Yasinovataya–Mariupol. In this way we won't have to change trains and will arrive at Yasinovataya three hours earlier. I don't yet know which route we'll take, since Mama doesn't trust my new discovery entirely. In any case, if the telegram says we're arriving at Zhelannaya, that will be why. If not, we'll be arriving at Grishino.[90]

This last letter from the correspondence with my father is apparently the latest in date of those preserved from that correspondence. I collected and even bound the letters from the first two years when we corresponded, 1904 through 1906.[91] Those from the next three years were collected but not bound. They were lost during the Revolution, in 1918.

41

In early May of 1906 (Old Style) we returned from Petersburg to Sont-sovka. The train I had "discovered" proved to be the right one and got us there conveniently, reducing the changes of trains from three to two. So began another summer at Sontsovka—which, like the preceding one, alas, was no real vacation.

A few days after we got there my mother and father began giving me regular lessons in academic subjects in accordance with a schedule my father had drawn up. But I managed to compose anyway, and between May and September I wrote eight ditties, thus completing the fifth series by September instead of December. Yet "completed" is not an entirely accurate word, since three of those ditties were never really finished.

At this point I take the liberty of quoting in its entirety a little waltz I wrote shortly after coming back to Sontsovka (Ditty No. 5 of the fifth series). It has a certain unity, and Asafyev later said of it: "Compact (forty-one bars) but with harmonic whimsicality; elegant but not mincing."[92]

It may be that in the summer of 1906 I also worked on *Undine*—that is, on the last act, to which I had skipped from the unfinished second act.

Morolev, the musical veterinarian, showed up, and two of us immediately had an intoxicating bout of music-making. He made me play everything I had studied with Winkler during the winter; then everything new I had composed; then the Beethoven sonatas I had played for him the summer before. From all this he chose what he especially liked and had me play it for him again. He was particularly fond of Saint-Saëns' arrangement of a Bach B minor gavotte. I, too, was fond of that gavotte. Who knows? Perhaps it was because of that piece that in later years I liked composing gavottes so much.

When I was exhausted from playing and tried to get up from the piano, Morolev would say, "What does it cost you? You may not care, but for me it's a great pleasure."

42

The following is from those reminiscences of Morolev's I quoted earlier:

The next day after work we heard still more of Serezha's music. He played the rivulet ballet music from *Undine,* and various other things: a barcarole and an art song.

I left for home, enchanted with my new acquaintanceship. When I got there I told my wife what a talented musician I had seen at Sontsovka. And I proved to be a prophet, since even at that time I predicted that Serezha would become a celebrity, that he was not just another *Wunderkind* but a genuine talent, both as virtuoso performer and as composer.

The Prokofievs were very hospitable, and it was always a great pleasure to make a side trip up the road (and sometimes not up the road) to their house. It was a delight, after work, to hear Serezha play and to play chess with him. At home they even teased me: "You're going somewhere else, but you'll probably come back from Sontsovka: it'll turn out to be on your way." (This was said when Sontsovka was in the opposite direction.)

In the summer of 1906, Serezha returned to Sontsovka a still more accomplished pianist. He introduced me to concertos by Saint-Saëns and Rimsky-Korsakov written for two pianos, Medtner's *Fairy Tales,* and Scriabin's *Preludes*. He was very fond of those two composers.[93]

At this point I must repeat the remark I made apropos of the year before. At that time, everything I hadn't learned well I played sloppily, so of course any comment about "accomplished pianism" was out of place.

Morolev's wife, Mariya Ksenofontovna Moroleva, who had come to Sontsovka and met my mother, wrote of her as follows:

. . . She had a genuine and selfless love for [music] and played very well. It is no wonder that her son, from his first moments of consciousness, had music in his soul. It wasn't necessary to "teach music" to Serezha. All he had to learn was the technique of playing. From earliest childhood, the world of sounds was his own world—one that he understood as a person understands his native tongue—the language his mother speaks. His mother was much concerned with his physical development and made sure it was well rounded. In her own words, he was impulsive, impressive, and easily carried away. And it was essential, while not hampering his will or weakening his character, to safeguard the uniqueness of his development, at the same time guiding it and providing a framework for it—but to do this in such a way that he never noticed it.

"One example of this," his mother told me, "is his regular pastime of walking on stilts. The best student at the Conservatory, who is majoring in piano, who should protect his hands more carefully than anything else, and every day he chooses the highest stilts for himself and goes off on them, along with a gang of other children, for several hours of walking on stilts through the fields and meadows. And I sit there and wait, wondering whether he will return safe and sound, or whether perhaps they'll bring him back with a broken arm. If they did, what would be left in life for either me or him?"

And yet she did not forbid Serezha to use his stilts, but merely tried to get him interested in other games that were safer. And this was her approach to everything.

The same thing was true with regard to music. She had been brought up on models of strict classical music and loved it. But Serezha had been an innovator since childhood, and at age fourteen he would say harshly, "Chopin is a mulberry tree!"

It is difficult to explain this expression to northerners who are unfamiliar with mulberry trees and haven't eaten their fruit to surfeit, as most southerners have. In any case, Serezha's mother would only smile indulgently. She took the same attitude toward his innovations in music as toward his usual pastime, carefully and lovingly safeguarding his originality and waiting patiently.[94]

We had an abundance of mulberry trees in our orchard at Sontsovka. In midsummer it was covered with berries of a bluish-violet or whitish-yellow color that looked something like raspberries or blackberries. Their taste was sweet and somewhat cloying, which provoked the comparison with Chopin: I knew only his waltzes and nocturnes and was annoyed by their effete pleasantness. At the time I scarcely knew his more virile sonatas and études.

By the time Morolev visited us again I had composed a march in F minor (the sixth ditty of the fifth series).[95] Morolev liked it very much. He made me play it over and over; he himself sat down at the piano and played it several times; and he asked me to copy it out for him. I did so, and since he liked it so much, I dedicated it to him. From then on it was known as "Morolev's March."

Later I used it in Opus 12 in altered form. The first version did not have the shocking harmonies I devised for the second: it was simpler and more naïve. Also, I wrote a new trio that was less ponderous. But Morolev remained loyal to the first version, which he preferred "to any and all novelties."

43

When Morolev left, calm returned to Sontsovka, and along with it lessons in many academic subjects.

That summer I decided to write a long piano sonata. I was determined that the music would be more beautiful, the sonata interesting technically, and the content not superficial. I had already sketched out some of the thematic material. In this way I began to work on the F minor *Sonata No. 2,* in three movements, and wrote a good deal of it in a very short time. It proved to be a more mature work than my other compositions of that period, and for several years it towered above them as a solid opus. Later I discarded the second and third movements, then reworked the first and made it into *Sonata No. 1, Opus 1.* But alongside my serious numbered works, that sonata seemed too youthful, somehow. It turned out that, although it was a solid opus when I was fifteen, it could not hold its own among my more mature compositions.[96]

I spent quite a bit of time on photography. I went walking on stilts less than I had the year before, but on the other hand, I arranged several chess tournaments with anybody who could do so taking part.

44

Life at Sontsovka went on in its own quiet way. One day Father proudly brought in from the garden a narrow squash—a vegetable unknown to Sontsovka up until that time. When cooked by Katerishenka in thick sour cream it was very tasty. Katerishenka was an excellent cook. When she had prepared some dish especially well, my mother would tell Marfusha, "Give Katerishenka a big glass of cordial."

From the kitchen would come Katerishenka's voice saying, "Ah, Mistress. A glass of the white would be better!"

After dinner Mother usually went to sit down on the sofa, and the cook would come in and stand in front of her with her chin cupped in her hand, waiting for orders for the next day. Everybody would be stuffed, and although the choice of entrees was limited, this business of the next day's menu was always difficult.

"Well, Katerishenka," Mother would ask, "what shall we slaughter for tomorrow?"

"There's a good turkey," Katerishenka would improvise.

For that matter, life at Sontsovka was far from idyllic. Politically, for instance, there was a good deal of unrest. By way of protecting his property, Sontsov had sent five uniformed guards with guns who were supposed to patrol the estate. This was a tactical error: the presence of the guards irritated the peasants, and we started having fires again: first the pigsty was burned, then a haystack far from the house. On dark nights the alarm would sound, and flames would light up the horizon. I found it very upsetting to be awakened in the middle of the night by the leaden clanging of the bell. I got nervous, and for a time couldn't sleep if I didn't take Sulfonal.

Father was afraid to go alone on his trips to Andreyevka to take money to the post office, or to Bakhmut on business. The man he took along with him on these trips was Fedor Kislitsyn, an overseer at Sontsovka who was in charge of all the flocks of sheep. Kislitsyn himself had a rather good little farm. He was tall, heavy-set (a bit reminiscent of Glazunov), and physically strong. When he rode with Father in the carriage he took up more than half the seat. His great weakness was vodka. Two years later, in a state of total drunkenness, he shot himself. He had been sitting on a bench, and aimed at his mouth. The shot tore off his jaw, and he died in agony.

45

In early September, Mother and I went to Petersburg. I did well on the academic exams for the fifth form, getting mostly A's and only two or three B's. But, as I said earlier, none of my letters to Father from this period have been preserved, and I don't remember any details about the examinations. For that matter, it is quite possible that I wrote no letters about the exams, since while I was taking them we learned that Lyadov and Winkler would not meet their classes until about October 1, which left us three weeks of free time, and Mother promptly decided we should go back to Sontsovka for all of September—a fine, sunny month in that part of the country.

I don't recall whether my *Grande Sonata*[97] in F minor was completed by then or whether I finished it in Petersburg later. But in any case most of it was in quite decent shape, and Morolev liked it. He listened to it and then played it himself, trying to perform the first movement with some brilliance (he especially liked the subordinate theme, which he played with evident pleasure, swaying a bit), the second seriously and dramatically, and the third gaily and in a light vein.

At his request I wrote out all the main themes, and I am now quoting from his copy of the sonata, since my own manuscript has been lost.

I shall not quote the first movement, since the themes remained basically the same in my published Opus 1.

Second movement, first theme:

Second theme:

Third theme:

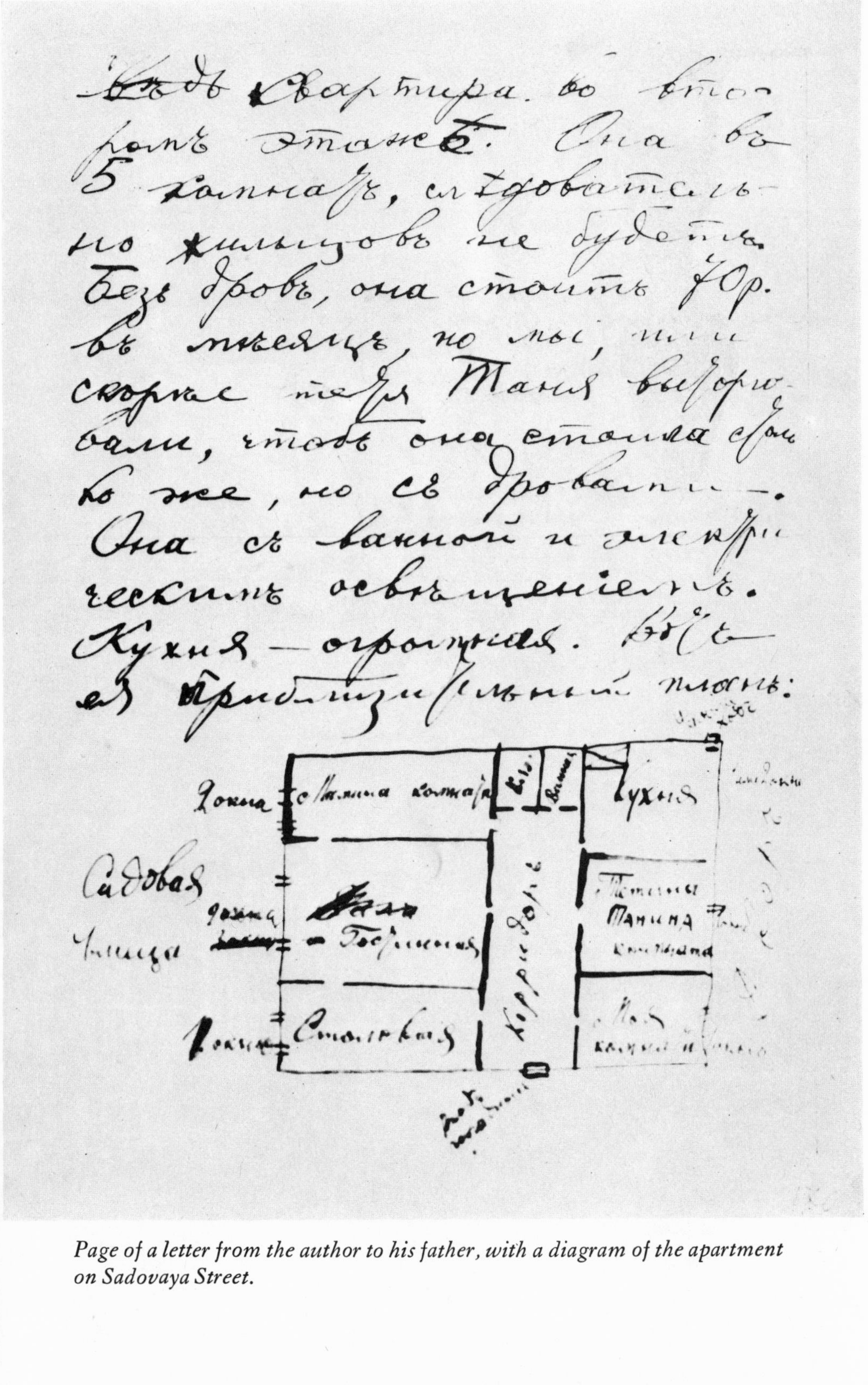

...дъ Квартира. во вто-
ромъ этажѣ. Она въ
5 комнатахъ, слѣдователь-
но жильцовъ не будетъ.
Безъ дровъ, она стоитъ 40 р.
въ мѣсяцъ, но мы, или
скорѣе теперь Таня выбира-
вали, чтобъ она стоила столь-
ко же, но съ дровами. —
Она съ ванной и электри-
ческимъ освѣщеніемъ.
Кухня — огромная. Вотъ
ея приблизительный планъ:

Садовая
Улица

Page of a letter from the author to his father, with a diagram of the apartment on Sadovaya Street.

Sketch of a naval battle, from the author's notebook.

St. Petersburg: Nevsky Prospect.

St. Petersburg: Sadovaya Street and Sennaya Square.

The St. Petersburg Conservatory.

Nikolai Rimsky-Korsakov.

Anatoly Lyadov.

N. F. Solovyev.

Boris Asafyev.

Joseph Wihtol.

Alexander Siloti in his studio.

Fyodor Chaliapin as Boris Godunov.

St. Petersburg: the Maryinsky Theater.

Sergei Prokofiev and M. G. Prokofieva (second from left) at the Rayevskys'.
Cousin Katya is in the middle.

Cousin Katya and her father, Alexander Dmitriyevitch Rayevsky.

Finale, first theme:

46

By October 1, Mother and I were back in Petersburg. The Conservatory was functioning normally: Glazunov was director, and both Rimsky-Korsakov and Lyadov had rejoined the faculty. But Rimsky-Korsakov was no longer teaching counterpoint and fugue: he had turned them over to Lyadov, keeping orchestration for himself. We were advanced to counterpoint class without having to take an exam, but instead of Rimsky-Korsakov we had Lyadov again as our professor.

Of the seven students who had started in the harmony class two years before, there were now three of us left: Asafyev, Kankarovich, and I. Grossman and Fiveisky had vanished altogether, while Shpis and Kobylyansky dropped out gradually. Shpis had begun to compose an operetta and faded from the horizon little by little. Kobylyansky was majoring in piano and was soon lagging a year behind us in theory of composition.

On the other hand, four new students had joined the class: Miaskovsky, Saminsky, Elkan, and Chefranov. Although all four of them were mainly interested in counterpoint and already knew harmony, Lyadov and Glazunov took the same position with regard to them that they had taken with regard to me: that harmony is the basis of the theory of composition, and that one's work in harmony must be done at the Conservatory.

I had been treated rather drastically in that respect, but the four new students were much older than I, and besides, all four of them protested that they had wanted to enter the Conservatory the year before and had lost a year because it was closed. It was necessary to make an exception and admit them to classes in harmony and counterpoint at the same time. This meant very intensive work because of doubled assignments, but they promised to work hard.

Miaskovsky showed up at the Conservatory in the uniform of a lieutenant in a battalion of engineers, with a big yellow portfolio under his arm. He had a mustache and beard and was very reserved, polite, and taciturn. His reserve attracted people to him and at the same time kept them at a distance. He was twenty-five years old.

Saminsky was the exact opposite: his behavior was unrestrained and his manners bad. His rather short torso was topped by a big, round head, and his lips were thick. The roundness of his head was emphasized by a short haircut. To me, he resembled a chess pawn, and with the straightforwardness of a boy of fifteen I immediately disliked him.

The other two were less interesting. Elkan was a meticulous, well-groomed Estonian who spoke Russian with an accent; and Chefranov was a strange, neurotic character from the same distant Russian town.

Although Asafyev, Kankarovich, and I had had more than six months of counterpoint the year before, it cannot be said that we now did our assignments any better than the four new students. Hence I conclude that Lyadov was correct in deciding to leave us in counterpoint, regarding the lessons we had had the year before as preparatory exercises.

Miaskovsky wrote out his assignments neatly and meticulously, making relatively few mistakes. But Saminsky's and Chefranov's work was dirty and sloppy.

47

The orchestration class, which Rimsky-Korsakov taught in tandem with counterpoint and fugue, began soon after the counterpoint class had first met. There were quite a lot of students, and it was supposed that Rimsky-Korsakov would teach the class in two sections. But he changed his mind, combined the two sections into one class, and doubled the time; that is, he taught for three or four hours in one session. No doubt he saw two advantages in this: one for himself, since he would have to come to the Conservatory one time less; and one for the students, because of the large number of assignments brought in and corrected—since a student could profit not only from the comments on his own work but from those on the work of his classmates. But it didn't turn out that way at all. The class met in the "room under the clock," where we had had harmony class two years before and where our counterpoint class was meeting this year. But there were so many students that they were sitting not only at the desks but on the window ledges as well.

When Rimsky-Korsakov sat down at the piano to go over the assignments, so many people crowded around him that the score on the music rack could be seen only by those in the first two rows.

The long class period was exhausting, and it was difficult to pay attention all the time. To put it briefly, the serious students, realizing how much they could learn about orchestration from lessons with a man like Rimsky-Korsakov, concentrated and did in fact profit from them. But I was only fifteen. Although I found Rimsky-Korsakov interesting, and tried to do my assignments correctly, I didn't bother to pay attention when the other students' work was being discussed. As a result, I didn't get much out of those lessons.

Before class I liked to go down to the cloakroom, which had a window looking out on the square, and watch as the figure of Rimsky-Korsakov, on his way to the Conservatory, emerged from Glinka Street at the end of the square. When the weather began to get cold, he would wear a raccoon coat—very short and not at all right for his tall figure—belted in tightly, and his beard would stick out over the high, turned-up collar of the coat.

Many of the students were affectionate toward Rimsky-Korsakov, and more than once I heard Miaskovsky call him "Korsanka." In class he would draw diagrams of instruments showing the arrangement of the finger holes, and explain why the covering or opening of certain finger holes on the flute produced such-and-such a tone. While doing this he would sometimes turn toward the students and ask, *"Ponimayete?"** He pronounced the word as though it ended in *"aite"* or *"aint."*

When he was correcting work he would first write the note and then put a sharp or flat in front of it. (I was used to writing the sharp or flat first, then the note.)

After he had explained the stringed instruments to us, he suggested that we orchestrate a Beethoven sonata for string quartet. To begin with I chose the first movement of the *Third Sonata,* in C major, but it wasn't especially interesting, since I felt the urge to score it for a full orchestra. A string quartet seemed lacking in tone color—possibly because we weren't able to get the maximum out of it. Then, when he had explained the full orchestra to us, he gave us some Schubert four-hand marches to score. This choice was unexpected. No doubt he chose them because they had many even tuttis, and he wanted to teach us to orchestrate those tuttis. But that was so monotonous and boring that I did my assignments with distaste.

When Rimsky-Korsakov was seated at the piano going over an assignment or playing an example from a score someone had brought him, he would sometimes ask the nearest student to play one of the voices for him. They say that he once told a student, "Sing me that bass part."

The student tried, but then muttered in embarrassment, "I can't. It's too low."

"A composer must have a seven-octave voice," Rimsky-Korsakov said didactically, and then sang the theme himself in a hoarse bass voice.

* "Do you understand?" (Translator's note.)

48

In Lyadov's class, along with our exercises in counterpoint, we began once again to write short eight-bar pieces in which the first four bars were called the main phrase and the second four bars the subordinate phrase.

It cannot be said that the things I wrote were to Lyadov's liking. But I wrote quite a few of them, and later some of these specimens found their way into more serious works. Thus it was probably in the autumn of 1906 that I made the first sketches of the G minor gavotte that found its way, after many re-workings, into Opus 12.[98] But it wasn't only my pieces that Lyadov grumbled about: the same thing happened to Kankarovich and Saminsky and others.

"Your right hand doesn't know what your left hand is doing," Lyadov used to say. This expression was not one that he just chanced to utter: it was one of his favorites. Later I often heard him apply it to the music of the "modernists," whom Lyadov could not abide. "They are real Christians," he would say. "Their right hand doesn't know what their left hand is doing."

On another occasion after a lesson, as he stood in the middle of the class-room surrounded by a half-dozen students, Lyadov said, "If I had money, do you really think I would be teaching you? Except for maybe two or three of you, you won't become composers in any case." (In later years Asafyev said he had heard somewhere that Lyadov named Miaskovsky and me among those two or three.)

"You do your assignments badly, with sloppy part-writing and a complete lack of style." Then, jabbing a finger at someone's ill-starred copybook: "What is that? Some kind of bridge with arches!"

As a matter of fact, the notes in the copybook were connected by very prominent slurs that from a distance resembled the arches of a bridge. Lyadov demanded that from the viewpoint of calligraphy our assignments be written neatly and meticulously, and of course he was right. But we remembered that Beethoven had written sloppily, and it never occurred to us that we should proceed otherwise.

Tchaikovsky used to say that there are three phases in the life of a composer: the first, when he writes untidily, because he can't do any better; the second, when he tries to write as neatly as possible, because his works are beginning to be performed, and conductors are more willing to learn a neatly written score than a sloppy one; and the third, when he again begins to write haphazardly, since he is so famous that his manuscripts will immediately go to the publisher, and the engravers will manage to decipher them regardless and will engrave them neatly.

49

The miasmal climate of Petersburg had affected my nose, which was constantly dripping as a result of a chronic cold.

"Oh yes," my mother said. "I'm very fond of Petersburg. But they're right when they say that Moscow was built on seven hills and Petersburg on seven swamps."

After several visits to Tatyana Pavlovna (my doctor-aunt) I was finally taken to a famous doctor who had treated Katya Rayevskaya's ears. He took a little stick with menthol on it and stuck it up my nose, relieving the congestion in a pleasant manner. He also prescribed some medicine to be taken at home. After this, my cold seemed to get better.

My father came for Christmas, and we saw the New Year in at the Rayevskys', as we had the year before. My parents said that as a holiday gift they were giving me the piano score of an opera. When I asked which one, they said whichever one I chose. I chose Wagner's *Die Walküre*. I scarcely knew the opera, but I felt—perhaps because of talk I had heard at the Conservatory—that I should get to know it. I found it interesting to play, and I liked much of it, although there was also much that was hard to master.

The most important musical event in January (1907) was a jubilee concert celebrating the twenty-fifth anniversary of Glazunov's activity as a composer. He had composed his *First Symphony* in 1881, and his *Eighth* in 1906. Both symphonies were performed at the jubilee concert on January 27 (February 9). In between them came Lyadov's *Welcome to Glazunov* and Rimsky-Korsakov's *Hail to Glazunov*, along with greetings and congratulations. The Hall of Columns had a festive appearance. The *First Symphony* was conducted by Rimsky-Korsakov, whom I saw at the podium for the first and only time. I was astounded to notice that before going onstage to begin the concert, he was standing off to one side near a column, talking to someone. At concerts, I was used to seeing the conductor appear from out of nowhere and then start things off. But there was Rimsky-Korsakov in his frock coat, standing next to a column in full view of everyone.

I didn't like the *First Symphony* as well as the other Glazunov symphonies I had heard, and Rimsky-Korsakov's conducting made no special impression on me. There were a great many delegations there to congratulate Glazunov, and they all brought wreaths or big baskets of flowers. Glazunov received them on the stage. They slowly filed up to him, passing behind the white columns and making a long queue that extended the entire length of the hall. It was a very festive procession. Glazunov was at the height of his fame—a height from which he declined during his remaining years. His fiftieth jubilee, celebrated twenty-five years later in Paris, was incomparably more modest—I would even say vexingly modest.

The concert concluded with a performance of his *Eighth Symphony,* which I was hearing for the second time. I liked it much better than the *First.*

At the Conservatory, Glazunov always wore a frock coat (no doubt in order better to look the part of director). It sat amply on his bulky torso, and in one of its deep pockets he carried a big cigar case with ten big cigars in it. Glazunov would smoke one cigar after another, and when he walked through the hallways of the Conservatory he would leave the light aroma of a fine cigar behind him. We would sniff and say, "The director has just passed this way."

His eyes were like two dark cherries. But later on those cherries went bad, and something unpleasant appeared in them.

On New Year's Day, Cousin Katya read me these lines from Apukhtin:*

> Dawn was just breaking: the boat left the dock.
> Words of greeting—the last still rang in one's ears.

She called my attention to the lyricism of the poem and said it would be good to set it to music, and even better to write an art song for voice, violin, and piano. I liked the text and the idea of such a combination and set to work. I should point out, however, that I was not entirely taken by the idea of combining the violin and voice, or the role that the violin would have to play in the art song. And of course I did not fully exploit the possibilities of the violin's participation in the ensemble. Probably in suggesting the violin my cousin saw more in her dilettante's imagination than I saw. But by way of compensation I put into the song some harmonic ideas by which I tried to represent the phantasmal dawn, and in general I strove toward a further development of the harmonic idiom.

* Alexei Apukhtin (1841–93), author of graceful, sentimental verses (ridiculed by Mayakovsky in *The Bedbug*). Some of them were set to music by Apukhtin's childhood friend, Tchaikovsky. (Translator's note.)

Here is a fragment from the middle of the song (a bright moment following the gloom of the first part):

The song was never performed by the ensemble for which it was intended; that is, for voice, violin, and piano. I played it on the piano for Cousin Katya, but it obviously didn't come across to her. Later I rewrote it and dedicated it to Morolev, but he too was cool toward it. So it fell into oblivion for a time. But the poem helped me: a few years later I came back to it and wrote a completely new art song, this time with no violin. It was published as Opus 9.[99]

50

That same January, I began to compose some short piano pieces that I jotted down in a thin music book with a bright green cover.[100] The first piece, in a lyrical, intimate vein, was called *Reproach:*

It begins:

Reproach was well received whenever I played it, probably because I wrote very few lyrical things, so that it was a pleasant surprise for a good many people. *Reproach* was followed by others—*Rondo, Eastern Song*—and by March I had written five or six of them. Although *Eastern Song* was a "ditty," with the writing of *Reproach* in the new notebook I stopped using the official name of "ditty" that I had given to my piano pieces over a period of five years dating from the first of them—the one I wrote with Glière in song form.

I wrote exactly twelve of them per year, and between the ages of eleven and fifteen I wrote five series of them, or sixty in all.

As things worked out, I would write a ditty for the birthday or name day of my father or mother, or sometimes one of the Rayevskys or Aunt Tanya, and would dedicate it "To Dear Whomever." This first became a tradition, then a duty against which I finally rebelled.

"I want to compose when I feel like it, and not for somebody's name day," I told my mother.

Thus did the practice of punctual dedications on family holidays come to an end in 1907.

Meantime Miaskovsky and I began to form a relationship of sorts. My compositions had been of help in this respect. I had the feeling that Miaskovsky was getting used to me, and that in any case he no longer regarded me as a mere boy.

One day he remarked, "No matter how often I've tried to play a four-hand arrangement of Beethoven's *Ninth Symphony* with somebody, I've never played it all the way through."

"Let's try it together," I said. "I'm sure we'll play it through."

"All right, let's try."

Since he lived far from the Conservatory, I promptly suggested that he come to my place that same day, after the counterpoint lesson. He agreed. I was proud that a full-grown man—and an officer at that—was going to be my guest.

As I showed Miaskovsky into the apartment, I shouted, "Mamochka! Just guess who's come to visit us. It's Nikolai Yakovlevich!"

"No! What brings you here?" she called back from the other room, hurrying out to meet her guest. Miaskovsky was taken aback by such a hearty reception. But when Mother saw him, it was her turn to be surprised.

"You must forgive me," she said. "We have a friend in the country named Nikolai Yakovlevich Klenov, and when Serezha said Nikolai Yakovlevich had come, I thought—"

"This is Nikolai Yakovlevich Miaskovsky," I explained. "We want to play four hands—the Beethoven *Ninth*."

And we did in fact play through the symphony. We played the first and second movements with enthusiasm, we found the third difficult and uninteresting, but our enthusiasm returned with the fourth.

After that, we would meet periodically to play four hands. Miaskovsky always took the left-hand part, stubbornly refusing to play the right. "I have no business playing the right-hand part," he would say. "My fingers aren't fast enough."

The next time I went to his home, and we played Glazunov's *Fifth Symphony,* then his *Seventh,* followed by Beethoven's *Seventh* and Rimsky-

Korsakov's *Scheherazade*. Then we played Reger's *Serenade* several times, etc. In short, we had a binge.

51

In tandem with the orchestration class, a class in score-reading was organized. It was taught by Nikolai Tcherepnin, then a young instructor. The work for that class was done in two different ways. In the classroom itself, the student would sit at the piano and sight-read—or try to sight-read—the score. Tcherepnin, sitting beside him, would explain the best way to do it, pointing out where he should play a certain part an octave lower, where he should use the first finger of the left hand to hit a note that the right hand could not play, etc. Then, for homework, he would give the students scores to learn so that they could play them more or less smoothly in class on the basis of procedures he had taught them.

I read scores rather fast, but I didn't study them thoroughly, since I didn't regard that class as especially important. Meantime Tcherepnin was getting to know his students, lining up candidates for a future class in conducting.

At that time the Conservatory had a student orchestra that was under the direction of Tcherepnin and was conducted either by him or by one of two or three students already taking the course in conducting.

Tcherepnin organized a student orchestra—the "junior orchestra," he called it—consisting of student musicians who were as yet unskilled. The idea was that they should serve as understudies so that they could replace graduating students who were leaving the "senior orchestra." It was Tcherepnin's intention to let inexperienced conductors work with the junior orchestra at first. Then, when they had improved and acquired skill, they could switch to the senior orchestra.

One day I went into the Little Auditorium, where the student orchestras rehearsed twice a week. Tcherepnin encouraged such visits, since at these sessions we could hear some of the scores we had gone through in class. Also, we could listen closely to the sound of individual instruments and in general become familiar with the orchestra. The first sight that greeted my eyes was Uk—that same Uk with whom my mother had unsuccessfully tried to get me to make friends when I first entered the Conservatory. He was with the second violins.

During the break I asked him, "Uk, why are you with the second violins and not the first?"

It was the stupidest kind of question, since the fact that some violinists were playing in Violins I and other in Violins II by no means meant that the former were good violinists and the latter not so good. But the effect on Uk was as if I had hit him in the face. He blushed and stammered out something unintelligible. But he concluded quite correctly, "I'm there because somebody has to play in the second section."

I was pleased that he was so angry: he was so boring that I had no kind feelings toward him. During intermission I decided to continue my charming game. I purposely placed myself behind Uk, and then said to someone, loud enough for him to hear, "It's a funny thing about Uk. Why is he playing in the second violins?"

Uk blushed again and turned away.

The unpleasant conversation that might have taken place was cut off by Tcherepnin, who came up to me with quite other ideas in mind.

Putting a hand on my shoulder, he asked, "Would you like to be a conductor?"

"I really never thought about it."

"Would you like to join the conducting class?"

"I really don't know."

"Well, as you like," he said in a disappointed tone, and walked away.

The course in conducting opened up unusual prospects for a student, since he would be earmarked for an important role in the future as conductor of a symphony or opera orchestra.

Students virtually broke in the door trying to get into Tcherepnin's class, but he rejected the majority of them: one would lack development as a musician, another would be a poor score reader, and another would be good at the actual reading but not able to play well enough. Tcherepnin saw me as an individual meeting all his requirements. (True, it was not good that I was so young, but that would take care of itself in a few years.) He had made me the proposal, and I had answered neither yes nor no. How stupid! It really was stupid, of course, but at the time I didn't realize it.

Yet the contact with Tcherepnin and his orchestra produced another effect. That orchestra was used for the occasional opera productions at the Conservatory, in which the voice students took part. They learned the operas of the classical repertory. But from time to time there would be a production of an opera by a graduating theory student, if he was talented. I began thinking about *Undine*. What if I should finish it and get it performed as a student production? The first two acts were almost finished. But during the three years since I had written them, my idiom as a composer had changed, and I recognized the childishness of the first act.

I decided to get to work on the second half of *Undine*, then go back and rework the second act, and do the first act over completely. Of course there was something fallacious about that project: one should not continue, at sixteen, with an opera begun when one was thirteen. If I had had ready at hand a workable libretto with a different subject, I probably would have used it. But I had no such libretto, and I was used to *Undine:* hence the rekindling of an old flame. I wrote only a little at a time but steadily, and the opera progressed.

52

One day after orchestration class, Rimsky-Korsakov asked a student of his, Shakhovskaya, if it was true that she was giving lessons to a young girl-composer named Irena Eneri.

"Yes, it's quite true. She is taking private lessons with me."

"Is she a talented girl?"

"In my opinion, she is."

"And what about those variations on a theme by Rimsky-Korsakov she has composed?"

"I haven't heard of them. But I'll try to find out and bring them next time."

"Yes, do bring them."

I had already heard of Irena Eneri as a very capable and nervous girl of about ten who had written a lot of compositions that were immediately published. Either some publisher was interested in her or her parents had money and were publishing the music at their own expense. "Eneri" was a pseudonym: her name in French, Irène, spelled backwards.

Shakhovskaya did in fact bring Eneri's variations on a theme by Rimsky-Korsakov to the next class, but they were disappointing.

"Uh-huh," Rimsky-Korsakov said, tugging at his beard. "She took a theme from my harmony textbook. Well, play it anyway."

Shakhovskaya played the piece, but the music was very naïve.

53

I had no acquaintances among the girls at the Conservatory, although there was no lack of them: there were lots of them walking through the corridors or sitting on window ledges. But no opportunity to strike up an acquaintance had presented itself, and for some reason I wasn't able to bring it off by myself.

The girls in Winkler's class were much older than I, and not very interesting anyway. And I had no classmates my own age through whom I might have met some girls. In counterpoint class I had established good relations with Miaskovsky, Zakharov, and Kankarovich, but we talked only about music: they never talked to me about "it."

For that matter, I noticed several girls my own age and watched them during breaks between the academic classes. One of them had a rather strange last name: Eshe. When I wrote her name in French, "Eche," I noticed that each letter stood for a note.* Remembering that music had been written on themes derived from names (for example, the variations on the theme B-a-c-h), I tried to write a theme based on E-c-h-e. And since it struck me as successful, I used it—with imitations, at that—as the subordinate theme in my *Third Sonata,* which I was just starting to compose. The *Third Sonata* proved to be very dynamic and much more angular than my "decorous" *Second Sonata.* In later years, after much reworking, it remained my *Sonata No. 3,* keeping its number in the new opus listing quite by chance.[101]

In the meantime I learned that in German "Eshe" means "ash tree," and that it should be written "e-s-c-h-e" rather than "e-c-h-e." In this combination, too, all the letters designated notes, but the theme came out somewhat differently. By twisting it around this way and that, I soon composed a short piano piece based on it—a piece that, for that matter, I never showed to anyone, since I considered it a mere trifle. But three years later I reworked it. I quote the 1910 version,[102] since that of 1907 has been lost:

At about that same time I began to jot down those themes and melodies I especially liked. I wanted to have a notebook with the very best melodies from various composers. Into it went "Walther's Prize Song" from *Die Meistersinger,* the pastoral melody from Tchaikovsky's *Manfred Symphony,* the theme from the introduction to his concerto in B-flat minor, and so on. I made my selections with unhurried discrimination, jotting down only those themes which really amazed me with their beauty.

At my request, Miaskovsky showed me a piano sonata he had recently com-

* The reference is to the German system of naming notes, in which "h" stands for "b" ("b-flat" being designated by "b"). (Translator's note.)

pleted. There were many things in it that I liked and some that I didn't like, but I could feel immediately that it was a serious work by a serious musician, and for me it was important to see how fledgling composers work when they are beginning to compose seriously. This was Miaskovsky's second piano sonata; he had already written his first when he entered the Conservatory. One movement was in C minor, and I remembered the meter as 12/8. But recently, in the course of working on this autobiography, I asked Miaskovsky, and he said the sonata was not in 12/8 but in 6/8. We couldn't check, because the manuscript had been lost and only one theme of it had been used elsewhere: in his *Sonata No. 4,* Opus 27, constituting the first two measures.

54

In the spring of 1907, I showed Miaskovsky the exposition of my third piano sonata—the one in which I had used Eshe's theme. He laughed at the meticulous way in which I assigned numbers to my sonatas, and said, "The time will come when you will cross out all that and designate the first sonata you publish as *Sonata No. 1.*"

Looking ahead from that time, I can say that he was right. After writing a half-dozen sonatas, I waited for the happy moment when my things would begin to appear in print. When that happened, the second sonata (dedicated to Morolev) became *Sonata No. 1,* but only after a rather thorough reworking. *Sonata No. 2* in the new numbering was an entirely new one. And *Sonata No. 3* was the one I first mentioned in this chapter: it too had been reworked before being published, but its number was not changed.

This sonata was in A minor and was "dryer" and more impetuous than the one written just before it and dedicated to Morolev. On the other hand, it was much more mature and after reworking took its place with my other opuses on equal terms; whereas the "Morolev" sonata remained rather childish even after revision, and many people have reproached me—not without good grounds—for having published it. By the time I composed *Sonata No. 3* I had mastered the form, and I even thought up some digressions to give it variety. In the recapitulation* I employ for the first time a device I always used later when writing in sonata form: the restatement is set forth somewhat differently from the first statement and is shorter.

The students in all the classes in theory of composition were excited when they heard the rumor that within the next few days there would be a dress rehearsal, at the Maryinsky Theater, of a new opera by Rimsky-Korsakov with an infinitely long and improbable title. This was for the first production of *The*

---

* This sonata has only one movement. (Translator's note.)

Legend of the Invisible City of Kitezh and of the Girl Fevronia. The older theory students, who had already been at some of the private rehearsals, said the opera was extremely interesting and had all kinds of new things in it, I was one of the first at the theater door, having arrived there an hour before the rehearsal was to begin. I was concerned whether they would let the theory students in. Gradually a whole crowd of us assembled, and they finally let us in, giving us two box seats in the second tier on the right. I had a seat next to an advanced theory student, Malko, who was holding the piano score of the opera. He was not without a sense of humor, and as he leafed through the score, he said, "At the Conservatory they teach us good voice-leading. But what does Nikolai Andreyevich [Rimsky-Korsakov] himself write? Look how the voices pile up. And he pointed to:

I was immediately taken with *Kitezh.* "Show us, Mikhailushka," was sung against whirling music from the orchestra; the chorus, "O people, woe will befall us," was written in an incredible meter. The frightening horns of the Tatars offstage (muted tuba), the entire part of Grishka Kuterma, performed by Ershov with great brilliance and dramatic feeling, the marvelous flowers growing in the deep forest—all this was new and stunning. But what I liked best of all was "The Battle Near Kerzhenets," which at the time struck me as the best thing Rimsky-Korsakov had written.

I talked so much about this opera at home that my mother told me to get three tickets (for her, Aunt Tanya, and me) for the first performance. I did this with no trouble, and then asked if I could go to the second or third perform- ance. During one of these performances, at the most festive moment in the sec- ond act, when the glockenspiel and balalaikas were ringing out and the chorus was singing a paean to the Prince's bride, the horse hitched to Fevronia's cart had a little accident. A member of the chorus who was standing next to the horse shifted position so as to screen the horse's naughty behavior from the audi- ence as much as possible. But a thick stream flowed clear across the stage and over the footlights and drizzled into the pit. Two musicians leaped from their seats. But they got control of themselves and went on playing, having merely moved a little apart. (When I went to the next performance, I was astounded to see that the stain had not been washed away: I could still see it from my seat high in the gallery.)

All in all, I saw *Kitezh* four times: Yet when my father came from Sontsovka, I dragged him to it too. I remember that he came on the express train that spring, arriving toward evening. When I met him at the station it was still light, although it was already evening. Two evenings later, when he and I went to the Maryinsky to see *Kitezh,* it was light as day.

Father had told me to get the best seats I could, so I was able to relish the opera to the fullest and at the same time oblige my father by telling him in advance of those bits that merited special attention.

55

Spring exams had begun at the Conservatory. I was to take exams in both Lyadov's course and Winkler's course. Students taking theory of composition were supposed to take one exam every year: when going from harmony to counterpoint, counterpoint to fugue, and fugue to form. We had been moved up from harmony to counterpoint without being examined, since we had spent two years on harmony, and when we said we knew it, they believed us. But now I was afraid of the exam. Although I had worked on counterpoint both the year before and during the current year, I did not feel at home in it, and the mark required to move on to fugue was rather high—a B.

The examination itself lasted three days. On the first day I wrote an ornamented five-voice contrapuntal piece based on a *cantus firmus.* On the second day I wrote a three-voice imitation in the strict style—a kind of fughetta. On the third day we had an oral exam that involved sight-reading in clefs; that is, from several staves, each in a different clef. On the first day's problem I wrote tolerably well but not brilliantly. On the second I did rather poorly. On each of these I got a C plus. But my sight-reading in the different clefs was rather good, and I got a B plus, so that I came out with an average grade of B, or passing. And yet this average was not correct, since the two written problems in counterpoint were much more important than the reading in various clefs, hence the average mark should have been lower than a B—that is, lower than what was required to go on to fugue. In any case, I got a B and was very glad to be moved up to the next course. Asafyev did well, Miaskovsky fairly well, and a few others just slipped by the way I did. In general, no one distinguished himself in the exams.

I did not take an exam in solfeggio, since it was somehow overlooked. I must admit that although I had learned how to do solfeggio in general—that is, how to sing in the various clefs and name the notes—I did it rather poorly, frequently confusing the names of the notes and not always getting the pitch right, since my voice wouldn't do what I wanted it to. This defect cost me dearly later when I began conducting orchestras and at rehearsals sometimes had to sing a note or theme. It's very unpleasant when you try to sing and nothing comes out.

The program of piano study was divided into two sections: the first course and the advanced course. A student could spend as much as five years in the first course, then, when he was technically ready, he would take a rather strict exam for promotion to the advanced course. Among other requirements, one had to learn scales in double thirds, major and minor, in parallel and contrary motion. In order to do that you had not only to memorize complex fingering (a whole branch of mathematics!) but to teach your fingers how to follow the patterns.

Once in the advanced class, the student might put in another five years before he himself felt—or his teacher felt—he was ready to take the exam for graduation from the Conservatory. During the intervening years there were checkup exams of no great importance. Since, however, they were held onstage in the Little Auditorium, they served as a useful kind of shock treatment for those planning to become concert artists. But they were so burdensome to the professors, and especially to the director (imagine having to listen to all the students at the Conservatory!), that a few years later they were abolished.

I was in the first course and not yet ready to move up to the advanced course, so I had merely a quiet little checkup exam. I played the Grieg sonata for it. I loved that piece and had asked Winkler if I could study it with him in class. It came out well, no doubt because I so much enjoyed playing it, and Winkler scheduled it for the exam—though only the first movement. At the exam I got a B plus and many congratulations. And I was advanced to one of the places in Winkler's class—which, however, could not be said to consist of brilliant students.

56

That spring we went back to Sontsovka later than usual—about mid-May, as I recall. After the long winter he had spent alone, Father was glad to see us. True, he had come to Petersburg several times, but they were relatively short visits. Most of the autumn, winter, and spring he had spent in complete solitude at Sontsovka, in the howling blizzards of winter and the thick, axle-deep mud of late autumn and early spring. The long evenings of autumn and spring were especially tedious. But Father did not want to give up his job: he would have to economize drastically, even though he had put something aside for old age. As it was, with his 20 per cent commission on the income from Sontsovka, which had risen a great deal in recent years, he was reaping the results of his twenty years' work at Sontsovka.

During that winter I had matured quite a bit in my appearance, and had begun to part my hair instead of wearing bangs—something that is all right for a boy but hardly suitable for a young man of sixteen.

One Sunday when we went to the Rayevskys', they received a visit from a rather refined lady with a son younger than I. He was wearing the handsome uniform of the aristocratic Corps de Pages, and bowing courteously to everyone. But what amazed me was the way his hair was done: parted, very carefully combed, slicked down, and even waved so that in one place the curls rose up a bit and then bent elegantly backward. I still remember that hair-do, although I don't remember the boy.

When we got home, I declared to my mother, "Mama, I want to wear my hair in a part."

"Why, Serezhenka! What on earth for?" she objected. "You look so nice in bangs. But if you combed it back in a part you'd always be having trouble with tufts and wisps sticking up."

So while in Petersburg I didn't manage to change my hair style to a part. But back at Sontsovka, before getting a haircut (I was always given a close hair-cut for the summer), I gave myself a shampoo and combed my hair back on both sides. It was unruly and stood up everywhere in tufts and wisps, but I went in to breakfast like that anyway.

"Do you think *that* looks good?" my mother asked Morolev.

"Not at all. When it gets disheveled, it'll look better. But when it's wetted and sleeked down, it looks quite unbecoming."

During the first part of the summer I saw Morolev only rarely. He had been promoted and transferred from the village of Grishino to the town of Nikopol, on the Dnieper, and by July 1 he had left, much to my regret. Commenting on the piano pieces in the notebook with the bright green cover that I had sent him in February, he said that with the exception of the tender *Reproach* they were all rather vicious puppies that nipped painfully. This sobriquet, "puppies," caught on—replacing the equally absurd label of "ditties" that had been given to my earlier pieces. When I got the notebook back, I copied out *Reproach* for Morolev, at his request. A penciled note on the margin read: "Play very *piano,* tenderly, and rather serenely."

Among the other works I played for Morolev was the end of Act V of *Undine.* The fact that I had written the fifth act did not mean that I had finished the opera: there were unfinished bits in some of the earlier acts, and Act I, composed at the age of thirteen, was in a more childish vein than the others, differing from them so much that I planned to compose it again from scratch. Act V (and hence the whole opera) ended as follows: a room in Hildebrand's castle, to which he has withdrawn alone after the celebration of his and Bertalda's wedding. Hildebrand is dissatisfied and feels no joy. At this point Undine emerges from the underwater kingdom through an artesian well left unguarded by the servants. She embraces him, consoles him, and lulls him to death. The priest enters, and exclaims in amazement, "Undine? Is that you?" To which she replies:

During the last two bars the curtain falls. I liked the idea of ending a long five-act opera with only a simple lyrical phrase and no embellishments. But Morolev did not think much of my idea.

"It's rather weak," he decided. "And besides, how can you possibly end a long five-act opera with two quiet chords that don't even involve a real cadence?"

I sulked. It wasn't possible to demonstrate in words that, contrary to his opinion, ending an opera in that way was very interesting and even touching. So I just sulked. I had been criticized all too often for my lack of lyricism. And now, when I had devised a lyrical ending for an opera, no one appreciated or accepted it. I was put out.

But Morolev was so likable and amusing, and he loved music so much, that one could not remain angry with him for long. Moreover, these were his last days in our district. When we said goodbye we agreed that, first, we would play four games of chess by mail, and, second, that I would soon come to visit him in Nikopol.

57

When Morolev had left, I again began thinking of my Conservatory friends. I had made agreements with both Miaskovsky and Zakharov that we would write each other during the summer and send each other our latest compositions. I had reached that age when correspondence becomes an important part of life— almost a holy rite. And so I wrote my first letter to Miaskovsky, not suspecting that it would lay the foundation for a long correspondence we would carry on all our lives. Miaskovsky's lively responses, and our mutual analysis of the works we sent each other, were such that that correspondence undoubtedly contributed more to my development than Lyadov's dry, peevish teaching.

> From me to Maiskovsky in Oranienbaum.
> Sontsovka, June 26 (July 9), 1907.

Esteemed Nikolai Yakovlevich (Dear Kolechka):

I am sending you together with this letter two piano puppies.[103] [The two piano pieces had been sent in a registered parcel at the same time as the letter. I wrote "together with" because I wanted to express myself with style.] When you analyze them, pay special attention to the themes, which play an important role. Then think about what they should be called. [During later years I often asked Maiskovsky to think up names for my pieces, and in most cases he did very well at this. It is curious that I should have made such a request in my first letter to him.] Especially the second: I would say the idea in it is clearly expressed, but you'll never think up a name for it. [The pieces I sent him on this occasion have not been preserved, but I remember that the first one was tentatively called *Carnival,* and that it contained a theme I later used in my *First Piano Concerto.*]

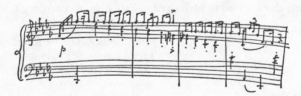

You will of course give me the most precise suggestions on those various fine points. How are things going with your symphonic poem on a "very good" subject? [Apparently I was referring to *Silence,* which Maiskovsky was already planning at that time.] I have completed the first movement of the sonata I showed you at the exam. Probably there will not be any second, third, or fourth movement, and it will remain *à la Maiskovsky,* in one movement: pretty, interesting, and practical.

I recently chanced to write a sonatina in two movements. Writing it was very interesting: I did it as simply as possible, and it came out happily. [The sonatina was later lost. All I remember of it is the following fragment from the subordinate theme of the first movement:]

I am still writing the last part of Act IV of *Undine,* which I gave you in May.

Your fifths were indeed beautiful. The others didn't make any gross mistakes—just some roughness here and there, and hidden octaves in Zakharov's case. The others who were going into fugue wrote their five-voice counterpoint smoothly.

My three-voice composition came out less well, although there wasn't a single bad mistake, and even the stretto was good. But when all is said and done, only Asafyev passed legitimately, since a B was required, and nobody else got it.

Well, so long for the time being. I expect some puppies in return. You have of course forgotten my address. [This wasn't very polite, but someone had once written that to me, and I found it rather elegant.] It is: Andreyevka Post Office, Bakhmutsky District, Ekaterinoslav Province.

Best regards,
S. Prokofiev.[104]

58

The same day I wrote to Miaskovsky, Zakharov was writing to me.

From Boris Zakharov to me at Sontsovka.
Terioki, June 26, 1907.
(Received July 2, 1907.)

Dear Colleague:

Why don't you keep your promises? You said you'd write as soon as you got to the country, but I haven't had a word yet. That's not good, young man! But since I'm not vindictive, I'm writing first. I'd be terribly interested to hear about your exam in piano. [Zakharov's interest in piano was beginning to get the upper hand over his interest in composing.] Also, how things stood when you took leave of Lyadov, and what you are doing now. I imagine you've already managed to knock out (forgive the crude expression) a whole batch of so-called puppies. Isn't that so? How is your *Undine?* Last week I was at Asafyev's place in Pargolovo. He is planning to write another children's opera but hasn't chosen the subject yet. I'm now working on studying forms, and as a result, new horizons of which I formerly had no notion are opening up before me. I can't say I'm composing much—mostly rubbish. For a time I was in a so-called religious mood and wrote several motifs. [Zakharov never talked to me about his religious feelings—neither then nor later. I don't think he was very religious. But the Orthodox tradition was strong in that merchant-class family, and he yielded to it—perhaps only so as not to go against the wishes of his father and other adults.] One of them, a *Paternoster,* was performed last Sunday at the local church. It was pleasant to hear my own composition—all the more so, since I am satisfied with it, and it sounds rather good. In one place Lyadov (i.e., his lessons) helped me, since I put in a bit of counterpoint.

When I think of the fugue course that is coming up, I get the shivers: more of Lyadov's sneers and his lack of style—in a word, all those charms you already know about.

Yours,
B. Zakharov

P.S. Perhaps you have lost my address. It is: The Zakharov Dacha, Terioki.[105]

I immediately answered Zakharov's letter. This reply of mine has not been preserved. I received no answer. Thus my correspondence with Zakharov did not develop. At that time I did not yet know that it was typical of him to put on an enchanting smile and cast a hook, then, when someone had taken the hook, to vanish into thin air with his beautiful smile. As a wealthy young man, he lived in a huge and very handsome dacha among a large family with quite a few young people. One gathers that he switched his interest from correspondence to local matters, which he apparently found more attractive.

59

By contrast, Miaskovsky was very punctual. He took my lettter seriously, and I soon received a detailed reply. It was couched, however, in a terribly illegible scrawl. And since I wasn't used to it, I labored hard over it—from time to time shouting with delight at one of Miaskovsky's unusual expressions. Afterward I even read the letter to my father. He shook his head and said, "Just look at the kind of letters people are writing now!"

From Maiskovsky to me at Sontsovka.
Oranienbaum, July 12, 1907.
Received July 18, 1907.

Most Beloved Sergei Sergeyevich:

I have been waiting—but in vain, until just now—for an opportunity to respond in worthy fashion both to your letter and (especially, of course) to the puppies you sent me. From the totality of what I have "created" during this time, I could find nothing that had the slightest little chance of pleasing you [from this it follows that in the spring I was rather critical of the music he had written], so I have decided simply to send you an "empty" letter without any enclosures—in doing which I am of course showing you the blackest kind of ingratitude. But there it is. . . .

Your music gladdened me to the point of clouding my mind. [It was when my father read this that he exclaimed, "Just look at the kind of letters people are writing now!"] Along with your repulsive (not for me of course) scribbling of the most frightful combinations (especially in the second piece) there are rather convincing moments. And the over-all tone, the overwhelming ardor, and that causticity which I am so extremely fond of in you, if one may so express it [Father: "Come on! Read that again!"], are so vivid that they unquestionably make up for their defects. At the outset I was of course annoyed that I could play only one note with each hand, and at the opposite ends of the keyboard at that. But when I played the pieces at a tempo (half as fast as yours, of course) that enabled me to understand the general tone, I was fully satisfied—especially with the first piece. The second has more mud in it [My father: "But what strange expressions he uses!"] and is somehow more vulnerable.

So far as the title of the second piece is concerned, I have nothing to say. In general I am not fond of titles, and so I immediately liked the second piece as it was, without any name. *Carnival* is fitting for the first piece: it has a lot of recklessness in it. Perhaps some carnival character would be suitable for the second piece, too: its beginning reminds me of Mime and his sobbing. [Obviously Wagner's *Ring* tetralogy was fashionable among us.] Incidentally, my opinion is that the last *più mosso* in the first piece would be improved if you wrote it as follows: octaves in the left hand instead of the four eighth notes, sixteenths in the right hand to correspond to the broken chords, and the tempo left unchanged. The way you have written it, one doesn't immediately grasp the change in tempo, since your indications do not explain that the actual speed is doubled. I concluded from the notations on the "things" that they were my property, and hence I shall not return them. If, of course, you do not agree with my conclusion, I shall proceed as you direct me by letter.

All my plans for orchestral diversions have foundered on my profound laziness and sluggishness. I can't get beyond the confines of the piano—and occasionally piano and voice. I constantly muddle along with such trifles as my *Third Piano Sonata* (in two movements, the first being a small three-voice fugue, *Lento*). [He later added two more movements, and the piece became his *First Piano Sonata,* in D minor.] Also, out of sheer idleness I have thrown together a dozen fragments for piano, some of which are indecently brief (eight bars) and risky. I really can't bring myself to send them along. Last week I set seven poems by Baratinsky* to music, but the songs are very ordinary and would be of no interest to you. [They were later published as his Opus 1.]

One of my most piquant amusements this summer has been the study of harmony with Monsieur Kobylyansky, whom Lyadov sent me—no doubt in order to exasperate me completely. Every Tuesday he comes to fish out fifths and octaves, play totally nonsensical modulations, and in between listen to heartrending love songs and frivolous things from operettas. There's pleasure for you! In a few days I'm going to Asafyev's to recover. I'll be expecting your sonata and the sonatina.

Goodbye for now.
Yours,
N. Miaskovsky.[106]

From me to Miaskovsky in Oranienbaum.
Sontsovka, July 22 (August 4), 1907.

Infinitely Beautiful Nikolai Yakovlevich:

Very nice! Frightfully nice! . . . "I am showing you the blackest kind of ingratitude in not sending you any 'puppies' in return. . . ." And now stop nagging me and don't ask for any puppies. [That is, I should stop nagging and not ask.] Oh no, *Papochka!* You speak of yourself very modestly and most delicately, but in my opinion that was not "black ingratitude" but something more—much more. Good Lord! In his granaries he has heaps of "fragments" and art songs (though let's say I could do without the art songs) and he writes at the rate of seven a week—that is, he doesn't just write but composes, creates—and he doesn't even have the time to send me a fragment or two. And yet I would very much like to see your fragments. I was very interested in one little thing you said; namely, that some of them were "very risky." You may not like them now, and may be afraid to send them, but that means nothing. When I sent you my puppies they were still warm, and I didn't like them very much. But since I had promised, I kept my word (!!) and, after copying them, sent them off kicking and protesting to Oranienbaum. Then, while they were en route, they caught my fancy and I came to like them.

Incidentally, as regards property rights: if a "puppy" bears the inscription "à M. Miaskovsky, P," that means it was written for M. Miaskovsky, and was dedicated to M. Miaskovsky, and belongs to M. Miaskovsky, so that there is nothing to discuss.

I have a rather ordinary little "puppy" that I am copying and want to

---

* Evgeny Baratinsky (1800–44), friend of Pushkin and, next to him, the best poet of Russia's so-called Golden Age. (Translator's note.)

send to you, but I won't send it until I receive some fragments from you. [My difficult temperament made itself felt even in dealings with Mia-skovsky, toward whom I tried to be pleasant.]

[That piece has not been preserved. It was in E-flat minor, and gloomy. In the second theme I tried to combine a minor accompaniment with a melody built on a whole-tone scale:

I can understand how pleasant it must be to study with dear Alex-ander Nikolayevich [Kobylyansky]. He has long been known for his fifthomania (fifthism) and uses up to ten fifths [I had the statistics at hand!] in a chorale of medium length. All I have heard of his works are a few art songs and a few fragments. One of his art songs, "The Bird Cherry's Boughs Are in Blossom" (No. 7, I believe it is), is rather nice.

I am now working on *Undine* (I have begun a new scene) and some "puppies" for piano from time to time. As for the sonatina, I just haven't managed to complete the Finale.

Best wishes to you. I'm looking forward to a letter, but even more to the fragments.

I tried in vain to puzzle out your letter, written in a highly rhetorical diction and an Asiatic hand. I had to make a Russian translation of it, puz-zling out each word and immediately jotting it down. After that I could make sense of it, and am now replying to it.

Best regards,
S. Prokofiev.[107]

60

At about that time I had a letter from Morolev, sent from his new home in Nikopol. He was delighted at having been transferrred from the dusty village of Grishino to a town on the banks of the Dnieper. But he didn't send me his chess moves, his pretext being that he had no chess set handy. This letter also marked the beginning of a long correspondence, although not nearly so long as with Miaskovsky. Morolev's epistolary style was less elegant and witty than Mia-skovsky's. Also, whereas I learned a lot from Miaskovsky, with Morolev I was doing the teaching. Morolev's first letters to me have not been preserved, but my replies have been.

The "nice, trifling little song" composed for the Rayevskys' governess in 1904.

Nikolai Rimsky-Korsakov, Anatoly Lyadov, and Alexander Glazunov, in a photograph taken in 1905.

One of the cartoons that appeared in 1905 when Rimsky-Korsakov was dismissed from the Conservatory. (He holds the Conservatory under one arm and the scores of his operas under the other—Editor's note.)

Сравненіе флотовъ различныхъ государствъ.

Всѣ суда я дѣлю на слѣдующіе 5 классовъ: 1) новѣйшіе эскадренные броненосцы; 2) болѣе слабые эскадренные броненосцы и очень сильные броненосные крейсера; 3) броненосные крейсера по-слабѣе и старые броненосцы, а также сильные броненосцы береговой обороны; 4) слабые броненосцы береговой обороны и сильные бронепалубные крейсера. 5) слабые бронепалубные крейсера. (Строющіеся суда не счисляются.)

	1	2	3	4	5		1	2	3	4	5
Россія (до войны)	7	9	15	18	7	Италія	2	13	4	5	8
Японія (до войны)	4	10	1	—	16	АвстроВенгрія	—	4	10	2	8
Великобританія	15	32	26	48	79	С.А. Соединенные Штаты	8	7	4	11	16
Франція	9	19	20	15	21	Швеція и Норвегія	—	—	15	—	1
Германія	15	—	15	8	17	Голландія	—	—	6	1	7

Notebook page categorizing by country the number and classes of warships each possessed.

Page from the author's notebook. The last row of ships, under the command of Admiral Rozhestvensky, includes the Borodino, *second from left.*

<u>Какія вещи я слышалъ</u> въ концертахъ и на кон-
цертныхъ репетиціяхъ въ сезонъ 190 5/6 года.

Вещи, слышанныя на репетиціяхъ помѣчены крестиками:* –

		Балл вещи
1. Увертюра къ оперѣ „Князь Игорь"....	Бородина	2+
2. Романсъ f-moll.........	Чайковскаго	4+
3.	Вагнера	4-
4. Симфонія № 9*	Брукнера	3+
5. Академическая увертюра*	Брамса	3-
6. Весна.*	Глазунова	4-
7. Концертъ № 4 d-moll*	Рубинштейна	4-
8. Изъ сюиты „Млады" — „Шествіе князей"*	Римскаго Корсакова	4-
9. Изъ сюиты „Млада" — „Шествіе князей"*	Римскаго Корсакова	4+
10. Сюита „Млада"*: Вступленіе, Дыня рядовая, Литовская пляска, Индійская пляска.	Римскаго Корсакова	4+
11. Вступленіе къ „Гунтрамъ"*	Штрауса	3
12. Концертъ для струннаго оркестра d-moll: Larghetto affettuoso		3
Allegro ma non troppo		3
Allegretto	Гендля	4-
Allegro molto vivace		5-
Adagio con fuoco		5-

Notebook page listing compositions heard during the 1905–6 season.

Статистика задачъ и ошибокъ при занятіяхъ контрапунктомъ у А.К. Лядова въ 1905 году.

	кв. окт.	кв. окт.	Диссонансы			недоборъ							Число задачъ	Число ошибокъ	Число задачъ	Число ошибокъ	Всего		въ этотъ урокъ	Вообще
			2	4	7								за этотъ урокъ		среднее					
1. 2 ноября.																				
Асафьевъ	—	1	—	—	—	1	1	—	—	—	—	10	9	10	3	0,30	0,30	2	2
Прокофьевъ	—	1	—	—	—	—	—	—	—	—	—	7	1	7	1	0,14	0,14	1	1
2. 9 ноября.																				
Асафьевъ	5 -2	1	—	5	—	—	1	—	—	2 1		24	17	17	10	0,79	0,59	2	2
Прокофьевъ	5 2	—	—	—	—	—	2 3	1				16	13	12	7	0,81	0,66	3	3
Шписъ	1 -2	—	1	6	2	—	—	—	1	—		24	13	12	7	0,54	0,54	1	1
3. 16 ноября.																				
Канкаровичъ	1 -2 1	1	1	9	5	—	2	—	—	—	2 —	19	24	19	24	1,26	1,26	4	4
4. 23 ноября																				
Канкаровичъ	-2	—	—	—	—	—	1	—	—	—		5	3	12	14	1,17	1,12	4	4
Прокофьевъ	1 3 1 4	—	—	6	—	—	3	—	—	1 3	—	28	22	17	12	0,78	0,71	3	3
5. 30 ноября																				
Асафьевъ	-1	—	—	1	—	2 3	—	—	1			18	8	18	10	0,44	0,56	1	1
Канкаровичъ	-2 1	—	—	—	—	1	—					6	7	10	11		1,15	2	4
Прокофьевъ	--1 1	—	2	1	2	—	1	8				12	16	16	18	1,33	0,82	4	3
Шписъ	1 -3	—	—	4								11	8	18	11	0,73	0,60	3	2

". . . next year I'll keep account of all mistakes in counterpoint from the very beginning." Page of statistics for Lyadov's class, during November 1905, from the author's notebook.

After a dancing lesson, 1905. The author at far left in the second row.

Morolev and I playing chess at his home in Nikopol, 1909.

Второй матчъ В.М.Моролева и С.С.Прокофьева

Июль-Авг. 1906

Побѣдителемъ считается тотъ, кто первый выиграетъ 6 партій. Ничьи въ счетъ не идутъ. Изъ каждыхъ трехъ пар-тій, В.М.Моролевъ играетъ бѣлыми 2 разъ, а С.Прокофьевъ одну партію. Матчъ признанъ ничьимъ, т.к. оба партнера выиграли по 5 партій: В.М.Моролевъ 2ю, 4ю, 5ю, 10ю и 11ю; С.С.Прокофьевъ 1ю, 3ю, 6ю, 7ю и 12ю; 2 партіи (8я и 9я) были ничьи.

Первая партія.

Отказанный королевскій гамбитъ.

В.М.Моролевъ — С.С.Прокофьевъ.

1. e2—e4, e7—e5; 2. f2—f4, d7—d6; 3. f4—f5,
g7—g6; 4. f5:g6, h7:g6; 5. Kg1—f3, Cc8—g4.6.
Cf1—c2, Kg8—f6; 7. 0—0, Kf6:e4;

Конецъ партіи (см. діаграмму)

1.	Фg3—g2	4. c2—c3	Фa1—b2+
2. Rd5:c7 (?)	Фg2:f1+	5. Фa4—c2	Фb2:c2+
3. Kpd1—d2	Фf1:a1		сдался

Page from the notebook. The heading reads, "Second match of V. M. Morolev and S. S. Prokofiev."

> From me to Morolev at Nikopol.
> Sontsovka. July 28 (August 10), 1907.

Amiable Uncle: [At that time I was fond of old-fashioned words.]

I congratulate you upon your phenomenally happy situation on the Dnieper Flood. The gentleman is so happily situated, and describes it all so finely, that I have become envious. But I am amazed: "No chess set, so I'm not sending my moves." You could have borrowed a set from a neighbor—leaving something in pledge, if necessary.

And what shall I do with your *Sad-Sadko?* Send it by mail, perchance? Write me and tell me. [Because I had not bought *Sadko* as Morolev had suggested, he had sent me his piano score.] I am playing the crowd scenes for the most part—the first and second scenes. They are very well done.

All the way back from your place I kept hearing—and I can still hear —Wagner's *"Liebestod,"* which you played beautifully (very!). [Before Morolev's departure for Nikopol we had been at his place, and while I played chess with a doctor who had stopped by to see him, he played *"Isoldens Liebestod"* with much feeling. It was too bad I had to be playing chess with the doctor while listening to it: that may have been one of the reasons for my losing. Here is what actually happened! Morolev, seeing that he had begun to lose to me lately, unleashed Dr. Zavitayev on me. The doctor was a rather good player, and to the accompaniment of Wagner's music I lost the first game. The next two ended in a draw. I was vexed at not being able to win. Morolev rubbed his hands at his victory, even though it had been won by someone else's brains.] I heard that played with Nikisch conducting, but he dragged out the tempo, and I didn't like it. [There is a compliment for you, Vasily—the result of a comparison with one of the best conductors of that time!] I haven't yet begun to miss you very much, but I soon will. The Devil made you go to Kolyepol! [Kolya=Nika] We all send you greetings.[108]

In answer to my letter of July 22, Miaskovsky wrote me promptly and sent me a dozen short piano pieces under the collective title of *Flofion.**

> From Miaskovsky to me at Sontsovka.
> Oranienbaum, July 26 (August 8), 1907.
> Received July 30 (August 12), 1907.

[For some reason he had addressed the envelope "The Right Honorable Sergei Sergeyevich Monsieur Prokofiev." "Right Honorable" was an accepted form of address then, but the "Monsieur" must be accounted a joke.]

---

* M. Kozlova says *inter alia* that this word was probably coined by Miaskovsky and meant "miniatures or trifles." (Translator's note.)

Light of My Eyes:

If you are so eager to get my trash [*Drebeden*—trash—was one of Miaskovsky's favorite words, and he used it all his life], I will send it in the very near future. Unfortunately—or perhaps fortunately—I have only one copy, and thus things will remain: so help me, I don't have the strength to make another copy. Consequently, perhaps you will not deprive me eternally of these "creations," as you call them, but will bring them with you next fall and either give them back to me for copying or give them back for good, since in any case I do not regard them as worthy of you. There are risky moments in only two of them. It's too bad you didn't promise to send me the sonata and the sonatina: I am especially greedy for that kind of music. Perhaps you can wrap up some of it and send it to me.

I am desperate because I'm not managing to write anything worthy of my descendants. I have again tried a sonata, but this time in smaller form; that is, if you will allow me to say so, it is a sonatina, but—as if in mockery of my earlier quasi-sonatas—it is in four movements, of which I have already knocked out three. It has a profoundly passionate Largo and a wildly bold Scherzo—in a word, just what is needed for a sonata. Now I'm worried about the Finale. And it looks as though, like you, I will not finish it—at any rate judging from the fact that I have started it five times with no results. Only today did I come up with something, and I stopped there. But I get the feeling that the rest of it will be such trash that I'll probably discard it again. [Almost forty years later Miaskovsky published that sonata, with some reworking, as Opus 64, No. 1.]

You are making a mistake in declining my art songs. Some of them are very sweet, which is why I gave them to Asafyev. Incidentally, that unfortunate young man (unfortunate, of course only in his devotion to children's operas) has not only begun his second opera but almost completed it. At any rate, when I was at his place about ten days ago he had already finished three scenes out of the six, amounting to 160 pages of music. When I saw them, I gasped. But in the last analysis it's too bad that he is spending so much effort on what, in the best case, will be no better than something like *Askold's Tomb*.[109] [What follows is a prophecy that was fully borne out.] Another bad thing is that because of this he will never get away from elementary harmonies and naïve melodies. This is an absolute necessity—especially for him, since what he is now writing "for adults" is unbearably banal. He showed me one art song of that kind. [Thirty-four years later I showed those lines to Miaskovsky, saying, "What a murderously accurate prophet you turned out to be!" As he read them, he murmured something and smiled.]

But I have been torturing you, although I tried to write at least in the American style if not in the European. Don't be angry, little Angel.

Goodbye for now,
N. Miaskovsky.[110]

61

From me to Miaskovsky at Oranienbaum.
Sontsovka, August 4 (17), 1907.

Nikolai Yakovlevich, My Treasure:

I was madly happy to get your ultra-amiable "puppies." I didn't at all expect to get so many and to get them so soon. Please send more!

As for those I received, I delved into them, and here is my opinion on each of them. (Sit down, please, and don't curse me out!) The first is *sympathique* but no more than that, The ending, at any rate, is bad. You can write much better. I don't like the second one. I simply don't like it, that's all—except to mention that there is much imitation of various composers—especially Rimsky-Korsakov—that just isn't your dish of tea. The third is a very charming waltz à la Chopin-Scriabin. It is the most naïve of all your puppies, but I say again that it is very charming. The fourth, the *Berceuse,* is very good, and I liked it terribly much from the very beginning. If the ending were longer, the impression would be ruined. Although it is in E minor, there is so little of it in that key that you didn't even put an F-sharp in the signature. I don't like the fifth one, although the theme itself (the first four bars) is good. But what an idea to choose such vulgar subjects for music! I understand "He sits on a chair and grumbles." But perhaps from the viewpoint of *"Il est mécontent"* [this was the title of Miaskovsky's piece] it is even expressed colorfully. The sixth, *Aux champs,* is simple but very pretty. It should, however, be marked *allegretto* rather than *molto lento;* otherwise it drags far too much. I don't like the seventh: I don't like the seventh: I don't like that kind of harmonies. The eighth is good at the beginning, but the second half is somehow strange—only the end is not so bad. The march in Russian style [the ninth] is very good. When I play it, I can't help thinking of the subordinate theme of your sonata in E minor. I especially like what follows the reprise. Counterpoint in a march à la Rimsky-Korsakov! What if in the last four bars you used a pedal point on D in the small octave? Or would this sound too much like Rimsky? The tenth is very charming right up to the reprise. From there on you imitate the chirping of sparrows and other birds very well. But what can be musical about that chirping? Surely you will agree. The eleventh, the barcarole, is very, very good. The combining of counterpoint with melody, first ascending and then descending, is beautiful and very unexpected. But the fifth, sixth, and seventh bars sound a bit thin. I liked the twelfth, the scherzo, even before I played it, when I was just looking it over. It is a very vivid and original piece. I don't like the ending (or perhaps I don't know how to play it). And I would advise you to mark the long section at the end *senza replica;* otherwise there are too many repetitions of the same thing.

My opinion about all of them considered together is that there is a great deal in them that is good, although some of them were written too rapidly and without having been sufficiently thought out. The waltz, the *Berceuse, Aux champs,* the march, the barcarole, and the scherzo I consider your best and equal to your sonatas. Please forgive my harsh and overly frank judgment. If it displeases you, burn it and forget it.

I am so eager to see the sonatas! Please think up a name for the "puppy" in E-flat minor that I am sending along with my sonata.[111]

From Miaskovsky to me at Sontsovka.
Oranienbaum, August 10 (23), 1907.

Dear Sergei Sergeyevich:

I will no doubt send you the sonatas, since I am not playing them at all: it is not only the one I recently put together that sickens me but the earlier one as well. Still, the first one is somewhat better than the second, except for the fugue in the first. [Unlike Miaskovsky, I always liked that fugue.] The second one is eclectic, much of it was written without having been well thought out, and the Finale isn't worth a damn, even though I rewrote it five times. Even worse, it does not tie in well with what went before because it is in a minor key. (B major does make its appearance toward the end, but only belatedly, and there is too little of it.) For that matter, for the first movement to be in a major key and the Finale in a minor key is an unprecedented phenomenon. So I'm thinking of renaming the whole thing—calling it a *Sonate-Fantaisie.* The first sonata is more unified and more vivid.

Your sonata is impressive despite some motions that don't seem quite right, but I would say that everything from the start of the development on is better than what comes before. (Still, the subordinate theme of the exposition is pretty good and, most important, it is very fresh.) I see you decided to keep the outrageous episode in the introduction. [He is referring to the first twenty or twenty-six bars, which shocked him when I showed him the sonata in the spring. I had not discarded those measures, as he advised, but merely reworked them somewhat. Later, when the sonata was transformed into Opus 28, I revised them even more, so that the tendency toward triteness which had shocked Miaskovsky seemed to vanish entirely.] But thank God that episode doesn't show up again in the reprise—something of which I am very glad. I am not entirely happy with some of the sloppy figurations, the *haphazard* scattering of the voices, and the occasional awkward figures; for example, the closing theme in the accompaniment:

would be better if written thus:

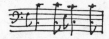

etc.,

which would not do any over-all damage. Then it sometimes wouldn't hurt to supplement your upward skips with octaves. This:

could, for example, be written thus:

since otherwise in crescendo these bits sound too thin and piercing. [I did not agree with Miaskovsky, and that fall I convinced him that I was right.] In conclusion I note that, although you used imitation [based on the theme e-c-h-e-] in stating your subordinate theme, it doesn't sound that way at all but rather like a unified melody. I especially like the way you handled the reprise: it is gay, vivid, and fresh.

62

From me to Miaskovsky in Petersburg.
Sontsovka, August 23, 1907.

Amiable Nikolai Yakovlevich!

I received your sonatas and immediately gobbled them up.

Contrary to your instructions, I began with the B major, and by now I have thoroughly relished and digested it. Also the other, but not yet thoroughly. (Incidentally, your G major sonata is actually in G major and not in E minor.) First, the matter of what to call your [B major] sonata: a fantasy, a sonata, or a sonatina? In my opinion, you should simply call it a sonata. In terms of form, its regularity rules out the label of "fantasy." As for calling it a sonata, except for the main theme à la Mozart there is nothing sonatina-like about it. I don't like the way you have built the development section. There is no development in it, no counterpoint, and yet it is terribly —or, if not terribly, then somewhat—long. It has no closing theme. Perhaps it doesn't especially call for one, but one could be successfully built on a pedal point on C-sharp. The first part of the subordinate theme is very good (although I do not entirely approve of the middle part):

etc.

. . . It is especially good in the minor (in the development section). In conclusion I should say that the first movement is very monotonous despite the diversity of rhythms. This is because the development is not done interestingly. Also, the reprise in no way differs from the exposition. Nor do I like the transition from the development section to the reprise: it is too unexpected, too sudden. I'm not saying you should employ the kind of *fermate* I use in my sonatas, but you should stay in the dominant a bit longer.

The second movement is *impressive* but by no means fresh. In the first place, it begins like Kontchakovna's cavatina from *Igor:*

The first theme (the Beethovenian one) is very good; it's too bad there isn't more of it before the modulation to F major. The second theme, the F major one, reminds me of an art song. I can't say which one, because it reminds me of several all at the same time. You have repeated it four times, and each time in its entirety. That's too much! In general, the F major section is too protracted. The reprise and codetta are very good.

The third and fourth movements are much better than the first two: they are vivid and original. As to the chords in the Scherzo, I would advise you to write those not marked with the letter A [not so marked in my manuscript] a whole octave lower: this is both more beautiful and more convenient. There is much elegance in the bit right after the first repeat:

etc.

I'm coming to Petersburg at the end of August. If you're in town, I'll run over to see you. If you're still in charming Oranienbaum, when you do get to Petersburg look in on me *without fail,* at Apt. 3, 30 Sadovaya (near the Church of Intercession).[112]

63

Morolev's departure for Nikopol had left me without a chess partner. The monthly supplement to the magazine *Niva* had a chess column. I couldn't wait to get my hands on it, but it was rather slight: one or two games, one or two news items from the world of chess, and sometimes the results of tournaments (which I especially prized).

I wrote the editors asking for the names and addresses of French and German chess journals, since there were no Russian journals at that time. In late August I received a postcard from Karlsbad with the information I had requested. It was signed with the initials "M. Ch.," and I surmised—although not immediately—that the editor of the chess column was Mikhail Chigorin, the famous Russian chess expert, who at that very time was playing in an international tournament at Karlsbad. Chigorin! How excited I had always been when following his successes and failures and replaying his games! And now I had a postcard from him! I proudly showed it to my parents, and shortly thereafter I subscribed to one of the journals mentioned in it. This was the *Deutsche Wochenschach,* the only weekly journal. The others came out once a month, but I didn't have the patience for that. I still have the postcard from Chigorin.

64

In giving an account of that summer, I have been recalling through the prism of my correspondence. And in fact letter-writing did come into my life in a rather important way and took a prominent place among my quiet pursuits at Sontsovka. This was especially true, of course, of the correspondence with Miaskovsky, which got me involved in numerous tasks of composing and introduced me, as it were, into the world of real musicians. Because of intellectual demands, I had less contact with my country friends. Although we still had tournaments and matches on stilts, and tournaments involving duels with toy pistols, I devoted less time and zeal to them than I had in previous years.

Stenya, the heroine of *The Giant,* was already over fifteen and had gone to the city to learn the trade of seamstress. Her place was taken by Serezha Khristianovsky, the son of the new priest. The latter had replaced the aged Father Andrei—the one who had buried my grandmother. Father Andrei had four grown sons, all of whom had become priests, and in the course of his long life he had saved up 4,000 rubles for them. My father advised him not to give the money to his sons while he was still alive. But Father Andrei kept imagining a touching scene in which he, surrounded by his sons who had come from various corners of the province, was giving each of them a thousand rubles. All this did in fact take place. But what my father had feared also took place: once they had the money, the sons forgot about their father.

Father Andrei was retired for reasons of old age, and took lodgings with a peasant family. When riding my bicycle through the village square I would often see him sitting on the mound of earth along the wall of the peasant's cottage—a lonely old man, forgotten by everyone, whose appearance was vaguely reminiscent of Leo Tolstoy.

In addition to the village children, I was friends with Dr. Reberg's daughters—Vera, Nina, and Zina. It was the kind of friendship that is formed between well-wishing neighbors, with no tinge of the romantic. Sometimes on Sundays our whole family would go to see the Rebergs in Golitsynovka, twenty-five kilometers away, or else, as previously arranged, we would send a carriage for them. Some Sunday mornings I would go to my father and ask him to let me use the horses so I could go to Golitsynovka, and he never refused.

The spring before, in Petersburg, a tailor had made me an olive-green khaki jacket—a great novelty in those days—and a pair of black twill trousers.

"Veh-ehry fine twill," the paunchy salesman had said distinctly, spreading the cloth out on the counter before my mother and me. "I strongly recommend that you buy it."

Mother bought it, and from then on I never forgot that I was wearing trousers made of very fine twill.

In the course of telling about all these trivia I failed to mention the most important thing for me that summer—or at any rate, the thing that took up most of my time: the lessons in academic subjects with my parents. They consumed many hours—even more than the year before. My father, in particular, pedantically hounded me in Russian language, grammar, and syntax. True, the letters I sent Miaskovsky that summer had more than an occasional grammatical error. But Father did manage to foster in me a fondness for correct spelling and punctuation. In a word, my parents taught me, "not out of fear but out of conscience," and I am grateful to them. But how I would have liked to have a free summer after studying all winter!

On my father's birthday, in July, I gave him a walking stick I had chosen earlier in Petersburg. When I conferred with my mother about getting it, she said, "Just don't buy a thin one. Your papa has to walk through the snow and mud at Sontsovka. He needs something to lean on. And there are lots of dogs around there."

65

Finally the day came when he got from the storeroom the large trunk we used for carrying things on our trips to Petersburg, and put it on two chairs in the bedroom. Before, when Mother had spent a long time in the country, she would get out the trunk and put it on the chairs almost a month before it was time for us to leave. She was so bored in the country that she liked to get ready to leave well ahead of time, and the presence of the trunk seemed to make life less dull at Sontsovka.

It was a strong trunk, and very large. After being double-locked, it would be wrapped in sailcloth and then tied with a heavy rope. The rope was so thick that my youthful imagination took it to be a ship's cable.

When my father was going on a trip he would draw up a list of the things he needed. I liked the idea, and I always intended to do the same when, in later years, I traveled a lot, concertizing. But I never managed to do it.

Upon our arrival in Petersburg, three important events took place. First, I passed the entrance exams for the sixth form (eighth, according to the Soviet system). Second, a tailor made me a black suit of the kind worn by students at academic high schools. It fitted me rather well, the shoulders were padded, and on the belt buckle was engraved SPC, meaning St. Petersburg Conservatory. Third, I began to keep a diary.

I was a bit apprehensive about the diary and began it as follows: "I am beginning these notes, a kind of diary . . ." That is, not simply a diary but a "kind of diary." I was beating around the bush, so touchy was I about it. I didn't write fluently, and it was not until several years later that I developed a more literary style. At first I vacillated between writing it in ordinary Russian or using a cipher—replacing each letter with a symbol I had thought up. I had devised alphabets before, but this time it was clear to me that the symbols had to be simple and clear so as not to hamper the writing. The idea that no one could read the diary was enticing, but there was another danger: I might get bogged down with the code—especially at first. Also, the desk had a good lock on it, so I discarded the idea of using a code.

(Now that I am writing my autobiography I should be glad if, after covering the period for which there is no diary, I could finally fall back on accurate dates and an accurate record of events. But the diary is not available to me, and that fact puts me in a difficult position.

If I write without having a diary to depend upon, many dates and events may prove to be not quite accurately set down, and if the diary should show up sometime, it would turn out to be my accuser on a charge of conveying inaccurate information. Strictly speaking, the charge would not be all that serious, since the inaccuracies would not be all that great and the important things would have been said in any case. But the trouble is that if a writer lies once and is caught at it, he will be disbelieved in a thousand other instances.

I vacillated for a long time and broke off work on the autobiography for several years. But then I decided that the inaccuracies would probably not be very numerous, and that in any case well-wishing readers would forgive me, if only for the sake of those works of mine that they liked. Readers who didn't like my works would not read the autobiography anyway. Incidentally, to begin with

I have four months of the diary transcribed in abridged form. It makes things much easier, if only for that period of time.)

66

I did very well on the academic exams for the sixth form: five A's and four B's. The inspector for academic subjects congratulated me and said that in the sixth form—the one I was entering and that at the Conservatory was the highest one—I would take classes at the Conservatory rather than being tutored at home, as had been done during the preceding years.

At first I was upset about this, since I had a scornful attitude toward the "scholars." But then I weighed the circumstances and discerned certain advantages: only two hours a day, the prospect of a free summer, and . . . a whole flock of girls I would get to know.

During my three years at the Conservatory I had not gotten to know a single girl. Those in Winkler's class were uninteresting, besides being several years older than I, and hence did not come within my purview.

In the meantime I had received a letter from Miaskovsky in reply to a note I had sent him asking whether he was in Petersburg and, if so, whether one could see him.

Very Much Esteemed and Cherished Sergei Sergeyevich [he wrote]:

I would be ineffably glad to see you. Unfortunately, I have not yet ventured to undertake the journey to Sadovaya [the street where I lived], since I have not yet fully recovered my health after a slight illness. But to lay eyes on you at my place . . . would be most unusual, and would throw me into the wildest transports. As you can see, I am in the city.[113]

I went to his place on Suvorovsky Prospect. He lived with his father, who had a fine apartment with sunny rooms and high ceilings.

Miaskovsky showed me to his room, where he announced that he had completed his string quartet.

"I wouldn't even try to write a quartet," I said.

"That's all right," he replied easily. "When the time comes, you'll write one."

(In my diary, after recording this conversation, I wrote: "I would have written a lot, if I had had a free summer!")

In reply to Miaskovsky's question as to what I had done during the past month, I said that I was completing my fourth sonata. He advised me to write a contrapuntal development section and to develop the themes a little more.

"What do you mean by 'develop the themes'?"

"When you introduce the theme into the development section, you don't leave it unchanged. Instead, you lengthen it, shorten it, add things to it, change the intervals, and thus it comes out the same but not the same. In a word, it is developed into something very like but different."

I was intrigued. "That's very interesting. I must try it. But first of all, how difficult it is to compose a good theme! I should learn that first. . . ."

"But you have no reason to complain about unsuccessful themes!"

I was flattered, and started to play the sonatina I had written that summer, which I had brought with me, and the subordinate theme I quoted a bit earlier. But Miaskovsky was not excited by them.

"You shouldn't try to write simple things," he muttered. "Complex and inventive things are much more your dish of tea."

For my part, I was rather critical of a sonata of his that he played for me. Then we started talking about whether one could or should write one-movement sonatas. We decided that one could, although one shouldn't necessarily do it.

We were called into the dining room for tea, and Miaskovsky introduced me to his father, the general, who was somewhat deaf but amiable. His mother had died, and her place in the household had been taken by an aunt—a lady with her hair cut short. Also at the table were his three sisters—younger than he but older than I—and the husband of one of them. The sisters struck me as uninteresting, as did the husband.

After tea we returned to Miaskovsky's room, where we sat down at the piano and played a four-hand arrangement of Dukas's *Sorcerer's Apprentice*. We had heard it two years before at a Siloti concert and liked it very much. The augmented triads were pleasantly abrasive, as were some of the other unexpected devices.

67

Classes at the Conservatory got under way gradually, with no hurry. Winkler alone was punctual—to the point of pettinesss. When I saw him, I hid. By mid-September, Rimsky-Korsakov had not yet met his class in orchestration. Lyadov's fugue class met on the seventeenth.

"Ah, the fugue students!" he said as he came in. "Well, gentlemen, we'll meet on Wednesdays and Saturdays at one. Goodbye."

Lyadov's bleary-eyed indifference was simply amazing. He might at least have shown some interest in what his students had composed during the summer. I recalled that the spring before, irritated by a good deal of sloppiness in our assignments, he had said, "If I had money, do you really think I'd be teaching you? But I'm employed by the Conservatory, so I have to fuss over your mistakes."

There were seventeen girls and three boys taking the academic courses. I was like a monk who found himself in a nunnery instead of a monastery. Having decided that I would soon get to know the girls, I behaved in a reserved, business-like manner. For that matter, the number of boys in attendance at the next class sessions had risen to nine. They all had improbable names, like islands in the Pacific Ocean.

I should mention that there was a considerable difference between the boys and the girls as to social standing. Most of the former were the sons of orchestra musicians who had neither the money nor the time to give them a good upbringing. These boys often showed up in scuffed boots and fringed trousers. They made crude jokes and were poor at their lessons.

Most of the girl students were more refined. Some had come to the Conservatory from other educational institutions—academic high schools and institutes —where they had shown musical ability and then transferred to the Conservatory—often getting the same teacher who taught in both places. In our class there were two girls, Eshe and Glagoleva, who behaved like fine young ladies and did not mix with the other students—especially the boys. I have already mentioned the Eshe girl in connection with the piece based on a theme using the letters of her last name. She was rather attractive. She was not very talkative, never ran through the corridors, and did her lessons well. Leonida Glagoleva was altogether beautiful, although her features were somewhat irregular. She was slender, tall, and dark "as the ace of spades." Her behavior was also strict, although it cloaked a temperament that was really quite fantastic.

On the first bench sat three girls whose names began with A: Abramycheva, Anisimova, and Alpers. Abramycheva received a lot of attention from the others because she was the daughter of an inspector. Anisimova was short, mischievous, and cute. (At first I was interested in her and devoted a whole page of my diary to her.) Alpers, of whom I shall tell more later, was a quiet girl "with a face that was pale even before she was born," as someone said of her. Among the others were Nodelman, an activist in various social movements, insofar as that was possible in those days; and Bessonova, a giddy girl who was always rushing off somewhere. She made eyes at the boys and got D's.

The boy who sat closest to me was Gvirtsman, a violinist. He was handsome, with wavy hair. Although he had nothing else to distinguish him, the girls liked him. In short, he was a big frog in a small puddle. Next to him sat Michel Piastro. He was a fat boy with a round head and a profile that reminded me of a chess pawn. Piastro was good-hearted and ruddy-checked.

When I entered the classroom, I modestly took a seat in the second row and tried to assume a serious air. At first no one paid any attention to me—or perhaps only pretended to pay no attention. Between classes I met up with my old acquaintance Akhron, whom I mentioned earlier. Akhron was one class below me and was studying piano. He was terribly impudent, with a ready tongue, and was rather good-looking except for his long nose. I once heard some of the girls saying, "A nose like that makes kissing impossible!"

"What are those initials on your belly?" he asked, jabbing a finger at my belt buckle.

" 'St. Petersburg Conservatory.' "

"Were you instructed to wear it?"

"No, I thought up the idea myself."

"You didn't exactly think it up," he corrected me. "You got it from the high school students. For example, some of them wear 'S.P. 10 G.,' which means 'St. Petersburg 10th Gymnasium.' But people take it to mean 'That Suckling Pig is Ten Years Old.' "

"Well, mine can be read as 'Sergei Prokofiev, Composer.' "

"By the way, are there any capable people in your composition class?"

"So it seems."

"I doubt it. They're proud to call themselves fugue students, but they can't compose." Akhron took on a dreamy air and added, "I have an older brother who is a real composer."

"Really?" I asked ironically.

"He has one violin sonata that has been published and is performed at concerts. And he has done all kinds of transcriptions for violin and piano that have been published too. He lives in America."[114]

Akhron cast me a proud glance and, satisfied that he had impressed me, walked off. "That Akhron is strange!" I wrote in my diary, after recording the above conversation.

It is curious, however, that ten years later I met that brother in New York. He actually did compose violin pieces that were not at all bad and very literate. Thanks to the fact that he concertized and taught violin, his pieces often appeared on programs. The moral of all this is: if you want to brag about something, do it in a serious and modest tone, otherwise it may turn out that no one believes you.

68

Despite the conversation that had taken place the year before, when Tcherepnin asked me if I wanted to study conducting and I stupidly gave him a vague answer, it turned out that I was registered for the conducting class. This time I was glad and went to the first class with pleasure.

Tcherepnin began by again explaining what was demanded of a student taking that course. He should have a background in theory; he must, in particular, know orchestration and form; he must be able to play the piano decently—to read piano music in general and orchestral scores in particular; he must learn his orchestral scores well, both for symphonic conducting and conducting operas with soloists and a chorus; and parallel with this class, he must punctually attend orchestra class, choral class, opera class, etc.

I got the impression that the standards for this course were so rigid that only one and a half persons would take it. But a lot of people showed up for the class—more than a dozen. Yet we had only a few instruments to work with: only one orchestra, which each of us would be able to conduct maybe once a month.

Tcherepnin first explained what a preparatory upbeat was. Any musician playing a wind instrument must take air into his lungs before playing a note. Therefore a conductor must first of all raise his baton while the musician is taking air into his lungs, then bring it down for the first beat, when the musician plays his note. Big wind instruments—for example, the tuba—require a longer preparatory upbeat, so that the player can take in more air. But for smaller instruments—e.g., the piccolo—a short silent upbeat is enough. And stringed instruments don't require any—just a little warning.

"For example, Borodin was once called upon to conduct the overture to *Ruslan and Lyudmila.* The piece is simple, and he undertook it, although he had never conducted before. He came to the rehearsal, went up to the podium, raised his arms, and brought them down immediately. But no one started to play. 'Attention!' he shouted, and again did the same thing. And again no one started to play—only a few scattered sounds were heard. The problem was that Borodin did not give them a preparatory upbeat, so that none of the wind instrument players could play the note."

With this historic anecdote, the lesson was over. Most of the students chatted about music for a while, then dispersed.

Tcherepnin, who loved to talk (and talked very interestingly, it should be noted), announced, "I am thinking of using natural horns in my new piece. It seems to me that that would be very fresh."

I was tempted to comment, "The tale is a fresh one, but hard to believe."* But I restrained myself in time.

Of all my teachers, Tcherepnin was the liveliest and most interesting musician, although he was entirely made up of contrasts. His talks about conducting were always lively and meaningful, but when he went up to the podium the orchestra fell to pieces under his baton. His talk about the future of music was no less interesting. For example, he would strike an E major chord, and then some short chords in B major. "In the end, they will write all white and all black notes." (At this, he would spread his left hand over the white keys as far as he could, and his right hand over the black keys.) "Then they will see there's no place to go."

* A familiar quotation from Alexander Griboyedov's great comedy *Gore ot uma* (1824), perhaps best known in English as *Woe from Wit.* (Translator's note.)

I don't know how right he was, since the development of music doesn't lie merely in the order of written notes. But at the time he struck me as such an innovator that it made my head swim.

69

Although Rimsky-Korsakov was the most interesting person among the teachers at the Conservatory, his class was by no means the most interesting. This was due to the way he taught it. As had been the case the year before, he had a lot of students—enough for two classes—and taught them at a session lasting twice the usual time; that is, four hours in a row.

Tremendous fervor was required to concentrate throughout those four hours. Unfortunately, I possessed no such fervor—all the more so, since Rimsky-Korsakov did little explaining, and most of the four hours was spent correcting assignments.

We orchestrated Beethoven sonatas for chamber orchestra (at least this was more interesting than the four-hand marches of Schubert we had the year before), then went on to various pieces that we scored for full orchestra. It seemed to me that if he had told me to orchestrate my own pieces, and had explained why such-and-such a passage should be scored in such-and-such a way, I would have been excited by his teaching.

One day when he had my assignment on the music rack in front of him, Rimsky-Korsakov turned to me suddenly and asked, "Why did you give the melody to the oboe here?"

I was stunned by such a point-blank question and said confusedly, "Because . . . it seemed to me . . . I thought that the timbre of the oboe . . ."

"And why not the clarinet? It looks as though, instead of feeling the tone color, you were playing 'she-loves-me, she-loves-me-not' on your fingers: oboe . . . clarinet . . . oboe . . . clarinet . . ."

He screwed up his eyes and, wrapping one finger of his right hand around a finger protruding from his left hand, he suddenly brought both hands together. And as finger told off finger, he exclaimed, "Right! The oboe! And so you're in a hurry to use the oboe. But for pity's sake! Is that really acceptable?"

I stood there, overwhelmed by the sudden attack. And I remembered Tcherepnin's saying recently that the oboe has a more distinctive tone than the clarinet, while the clarinet is a more versatile instrument than the oboe.

"I like the oboe," Tcherepnin continued. "It has a nasal tone with bright coloration. But Rimsky-Korsakov, for example, prefers the clarinet. He feels that its tone is velvety and softer, so that it blends in with the orchestra better. The oboe doesn't blend in so well, but for that reason it stands out better."

Rimsky-Korsakov turned the page of my manuscript and again asked me in a disgruntled voice, "Why do you have a cello playing solo here, instead of all the cellos together?"

I was starting to get cramps somewhere inside because I felt he wasn't so much teaching me as nagging me. I replied bluntly, "I wrote it for solo cello because I don't like the sound of all the cellos playing in unison."

He jumped up. "You don't like it? Why don't you like it?"

"For example, in that Sibelius symphony they all play together for a very long time, and the sound isn't good." (I don't remember whether that was in the *Third Symphony,* which I had heard recently, or in another symphony by the same composer.)

"Then why try to learn from Sibelius? And what about *Ruslan*—the second theme of the overture. Perhaps that doesn't sound good, either?"

I looked around in the hope of catching someone smiling as if to say, "Look, the old man is getting angry." The other students were standing in a half-circle around the piano, and the light was such that I could see their faces clearly. There stood Miaskovsky, and there Zakharov. But no one was smiling. They all wore serious expressions, and I could find no sign of sympathy.

Rimsky-Korsakov picked up my score and passed it back over his shoulder, saying, "Next!"

That incident was clearly etched in my memory, and to this day I don't know to what extent I was right or wrong.

About one thing there is no doubt: at that time I was poor at scoring, and my choice of the oboe instead of the clarinet was due to thoughtlessness. But my choice of a solo cello rather than all of them was made deliberately, precisely because the part for the cellos in the Sibelius symphony had, as a matter of fact, not sounded good.

Rimsky-Korsakov was right in pointing out the magnificent singing of the cellos in the overture to *Ruslan and Lyudmila.* But it would have been better teaching if, instead of shouting, he had had a talk with the student and explained the matter at hand as Tcherepnin often did—for example, in the conversation mentioned before.

At the next lesson it wasn't I that the lightning bolt struck, but . . . Peter Ilich Tchaikovsky. One of the students—I believe it as Asafyev—had brought the score of his *First Symphony.* Placing it on the music rack in front of Rimsky-Korsakov, he asked how the flutes got down to B-flat. Rimsky-Korsakov looked at the score, twisted his beard and pulled at it, and then said with a little smile, "M-m-m, yes . . . Peter Ilich got something wrong here . . . French flutes go down to C. German flutes—the kind we use—go down to B. But no flutes go down to B-flat. Of course right here it's not especially important if the flutes don't play the note. But if they can't play it, why write it?"

He was obviously pleased at having found a mistake, and gave a little laugh as he handed the score back to its owner.

At this point I remembered another of Tcherepnin's anecdotes about Rimsky-Korsakov—this time about his amazing capacity for work. "He'll spend the whole morning at a rehearsal," Tcherepnin said, "and then go home to lunch. But right while they're serving lunch, he sits down at the table and orchestrates a little chord. In the fall when everyone comes back from summer vacation, Rimsky-Korsakov will have a thick portfolio of music under his arm: 'That's a new opera I've written.'"

At the next lesson, Rimsky-Korsakov was late. And the next time the inspector summoned us and said that Rimsky-Korsakov had caught a cold and would give the lesson in his apartment. Malko had already been there and showed us the way. We went through the gate in front of a building on Zagorodny Prospect. I was amazed, I had thought Rimsky-Korsakov would have an apartment with a street entrance. His apartment, however, did prove to be spacious. On either side of the entrance hallway was a big room with a grand piano in it—the wing in one corner and the keyboard facing the middle of the room. On both of these pianos lay opera scores—Rimsky-Korsakov's own works, for the most part.

I don't remember the lesson itself, but I do remember that afterward Rimsky-Korsakov came out to the vestibule with us. I liked that, and when we were out in the street, I mentioned his courtesy to Malko.

"He's always like that," Malko said. "Sometimes he holds students' coats for them." Then he laughed and began to tell the following anecdote:

"One day he was showing his students to the door. 'No, no. Allow me,' he said to one puny little student, taking his coat and holding it for him. Meantime, he himself was continuing a conversation with another student standing behind him. He was talking over his shoulder, don't you see? Of course Rimsky-Korsakov is tall, and the first student was short. Also, out of absentmindedness Rimsky-Korsakov kept raising the coat higher and higher, so that the armholes were already above the student's head. The student was terribly pleased that Rimsky Korsakov was holding his coat for him, and started jumping so that he could get his arms in the armholes. Meantime, Rimsky-Korsakov was still talking over his shoulder and never noticed the young man's difficult position."

"Well, what happened?" I asked, when Malko had stopped.

"Oh, he got into the coat somehow."

70

Miaskovsky had at first criticized me for the "overly simple" style of my sonatina. Then later, having kept the music with him, he declared that "one should also analyze a simple thing." Now he found the first movement of the sonatina by no means so bad, "and perhaps even rather good." I was glad to hear this and played him my *Fourth Sonata* (old numbering), which I had just completed, or almost completed.

The main theme:

The subordinate theme:

The second movement was already written too, and the third sketched out. The manuscript was lost during the Revolution, and the above specimens, which I am now reconstructing from memory forty years later, may not be entirely accurate, though they are undoubtedly close. Miaskovsky listened to it, smiling at various contrivances, and was in general pleased with the sonata, though he found it was not entirely uninfluenced by Scriabin's *Satanic Poem*.

When I asked him to recommend something amusing and very pianistic in lieu of the *Satanic Poem*, he suggested Nikolai Medtner's *Zwei Märchen* (Opus 8). By way of confirming his recommendation, he played a few measures of the introduction:

I liked the introduction tremendously. At the time Medtner was a young Moscow composer of twenty-five and little known in Petersburg. I bought the sheet music. The *Fairy Tales* did in fact turn out to be splendid—especially the second, written in the form of a sonata allegro. In the first place, because of the meter—3+2+3=8 eighth notes in a measure—which I had never encountered before. Second, because of its general shape. But it was hard to play, although everything was pianistic; i.e., all the notes were right there under your fingers. In general, it was very typical of Medtner's piano technique that all the notes should be right there under your fingers. I hoped that someone would play me that *Fairy Tale* in the right tempo, but there was no such person, so I had to work at it quite a lot in my spare time. It wasn't until many years later that I finally mastered it and played it at a concert somewhere in America.[115]

One day after Tcherepnin's class I was looking for Miaskovsky at the Conservatory. We ran across Kankarovich, and I asked him, "Have you seen Miaskovsky?"

"Yes, of course I've seen him."

"Where is he?"

"Where he always is."

"Meaning?"

"When Tcherepnin's class is over, and his wife comes to get him, Miaskovsky goes down to the cloakroom and looks at her."

I went to the cloakroom but found no one. I knew that Tcherepnin's wife, a beautiful woman, was called *"La belle Marie Tcherepnine."* But I was never able to find out whether Miaskovsky actually liked her. If so, it would have been the first time in my experience that Miaskovsky was interested in a woman.

From me to Miaskovsky in Petersburg.
Petersburg, September 26 (October 9), 1907.

Poor Nikolai Yakovlich:

Today when Saminsky came to the Conservatory, he said you were sick. This made all of us sad. How is it that you, a prudent man, didn't manage to take care of yourself? Then, too, at four o'clock yesterday, when we had lunch, you looked so ruddy and healthy. . . . I am very sorry for you, dear Nikolai Yakovlevich, and hope that you will soon be as healthy and amiable as before.

I didn't get to *Kitezh*. I asked those profiteers for tickets ten times, but didn't get one.

Well, so long, and please get well soon.

Your loving,
S. Prokofiev[116]

But Miaskovsky did not follow my suggestion: he had appendicitis, and his cecum had to be removed. The operation went off well, and I was able to visit him on October 18.

"Why are you so hard on Rimsky-Korsakov?" Miaskovsky asked me. "That's not good."

I felt offended (I was easily offended in those days) and objected testily, "I'm not at all hard on him. He's the one that's hard on me."

Sometime later, when Miaskovsky was recovered, he and I were walking down the street when a beggar came up and asked him for alms. He reached into the pocket of his military greatcoat, took out a whole handful of copper coins, and put them in the beggar's outstretched hand. I was amazed. Later I had the naïve idea that he had to be that generous out of respect for his uniform.

71

My father arrived from Sontsovka and when he noticed that I had down on my cheeks, he said, "That's good, but don't shave. That way your beard will grow to be soft, and it's pleasant to have a soft beard. But if you have been shaving for a while, it will be bristly, and there's nothing good about that."

But I didn't heed his advice, since I couldn't imagine myself with a beard.

Of course Father was chiefly interested in how my academic classes were going at the Conservatory. I was able to boast of a rather successful essay I had written on *Boris Godunov,* for which I had gotten an A. But in general he was dissatisfied with the way the subjects were taught at the Conservatory—that way being much more negligent than he had supposed. Also, needless to say, a great deal of time was spent on special musical courses and preparing for those classes, so that there was little time for academic subjects.

About that time I began to fuss with my handwriting. The thing was, I had noticed that many young people retained a quasi-childish way of writing for a long time, while others quickly developed a style that was firm, confident, and distinctive.

I was in a phase where letters and the way they were written were very important to me. The way the thought was expressed, the handwriting, and the kind of paper that was used—all these things struck me as very important, and when I got an "interesting" letter I would analyze it in detail. So I began to devise a kind of penmanship that would be firm and distinctive.

The above specimens of letters were deliberately chosen as examples of a style that stuck with me even after the folly had left me.

My father strongly disapproved of my project. "What's good about that?" he asked. "It's not penmanship. It's a deliberate contrivance. It's as though you wanted to call attention to the letters rather than to the content—as though you'd given everything to them and left nothing for the content."

But I didn't listen to him because I liked the idea of introducing more and more new ways of making letters. In my diary for that period, one notebook differs from another, as though each had been written by a different person.

Father himself wrote in a fine, slanting hand. But he was not a good letter writer, and kept trying to get by with clichés. Thus his letters to us always began with "Dear Manyusha and Sergunya" and ended with "Your sincerely loving and fully devoted." By contrast, Mother had a vigorous and beautiful handwriting, and her letters were almost always interesting.

72

About this time I heard Wagner's *Siegfried Idyll,* and went into raptures over that entrancing music. I was no less excited by Rimsky-Korsakov's piano concerto, which was being rehearsed by students at the Conservatory: Lemba played, and Malko conducted. I have adored both of these compositions ever since. But the performance of the concerto left something to be desired and provoked several comments from me. Those comments, however, were greeted with shrugs. Lemba and Malko were seniors and hence ranked higher in terms of Conservatory achievements, whereas I was still only halfway up the totem pole, and it wasn't my business to judge whether they performed well or badly.

I wrote in my diary: "No doubt I would make a good daily critic, and a real bastard at that." And a further note: "I went to the Maryinsky Theater to see how Tcherepnin conducted *Kitezh.* In my opinion, he conducted badly."

There was also a benefit concert for the student restaurant at the Conservatory with a program of Glazunov's works. The *Seventh Symphony* seemed pallid to me: made but not composed. But Rimsky-Korsakov, who was sitting in the front row at the rehearsal with the score in his hands, was delighted and kept praising it. (I must admit that later, when I played a four-hand arrangement of it with Miaskovsky, I liked it better—especially the first movement.) Glazunov conducted. Despite his huge size and corpulence, he adored conducting, although he was by no means brilliant at it. His appearance was especially curious when he was conducting something in fast 4/4 time, blessing the orchestra by making little signs of the cross somewhere under his nose. But he had great prestige with the orchestra, so the musicians were attentive and tried to play well.

Taneyev gave a chamber music concert in the Small Auditorium: string ensemble and piano, which he played himself. He asked me to turn pages for him, and I accepted with a feeling of pride. Before the concert he gave me a long and thorough explanation of how to turn pages. "Two bars before the end of the page, stand up and grasp the upper corner of the page. At the end of the last bar, turn the page quickly and straighten it out, but not in such a way as to screen the upper bars from the performer with your hand."

In my diary: "In general, Sergei Ivanovich (Taneyev) is wonderful, and Lyadov is not to be compared with him."

Another piece of music I got to know—and didn't like at all—was Richard Strauss's opera *Salome*. Miaskovsky had given me the piano score with a smile, saying it was the most modern of modern compositions. But I didn't understand it, and took no pleasure in all the scratches and scribbles, so I returned the score to Miaskovsky. The "private viewing" had been a failure.

At this point we come to an event that, although a slight one, represented a little step forward in my musical life. An announcement was posted on a wall at the Conservatory stating that on December 17, 1907, there would be a gathering of "beginning composers" for the purpose of making their works known, and that later, those works which proved worthy of it would be performed publicly.

Those students at the Conservatory who were composers were invited to attend. This event was being organized by a woman named Ranushevich, who had completed the course in theory of composition the year before. I had heard little about her except that she was a woman of some years, but the promise to perform "worthy works" sounded enticing, and I went. About fifteen people were there. I played *Reproach, Fairy Tale,** and *Fantome*. As I recall, *Badinage,* later included in Opus 3, had also been composed as a part of this group, but I decided not to play it: it was too bold and not solid enough. As I put it in my diary, my pieces provoked "animated discussions." The other composers played too, but it was bad. A week later we convened again, but this time there were fewer of us. I was asked to repeat the pieces I had played the time before. This time they were praised with no strong "buts." However, I was disillusioned with these "beginning composers." They couldn't do anything, and nobody went to hear them. What a circle!

The Ranushevich woman said to me, "You know, there is already a legend about you: that Prokofiev can't bear to hear two true notes in succession. That's because his piano at home is out of tune, and he's used to it."

My most regular correspondence in the second half of 1907 was with

* Sometimes referred to as *Story*. (Translator's note.)

Morolev. I exchanged two pairs of letters with him per month, since we were playing four games of chess simultaneously by mail. Chess was, so to speak, the main business, but to the chess moves were added talk about music and the usual chitchat of a sixteen-year-old boy.

It is curious that I was very seriously addicted to the publicity in favor of Beethoven and Wagner.

> Make sure to buy the second volume of Beethoven symphonies for four hands [I wrote to Morolev][117] Even every beginner should know it.[118] Start with the *Seventh Symphony*. [Here I made a few comments.] The first two movements are remarkable, and come out well on the piano. The third movement is also good, but it's difficult to render on the piano, since the purely orchestral effects don't come out. In the third movement, pay attention *inter alia* to the trio (D major). The note A runs like a red thread through almost all of the trio:

> which in the orchestra is given to the tuba and from time to time produces an effect so unique that you almost stop breathing. The Finale is weaker and rather trite. After the *Seventh Symphony,* go to the sixth. The ninth is the most famous—Beethoven wrote it when he was already deaf—but it is very difficult until you have heard it played by an orchestra.[119]

This fondness for Beethoven's symphonies is somewhat surprising, but it does show that the classics were always dear to me.

In another letter I wrote:

> I would very much like to see you get to know Wagner better: you'll see his work in an entirely different way. When you get to know him, you will like him, and you will stop swearing by all those Rubinsteins and Chopins. [I particularly despised Chopin at that time. I considered him cloying—especially in the nocturnes and waltzes—and didn't notice all the new things he had contributed. Rubinstein is not worth talking about.
>
> I was very insistent about the *Ring of the Nibelung,* which fascinated me at the time.]
>
> *Das Rheingold* costs only two rubles, and the others two rubles and seventy kopecks each [I wrote].[120] But what music in them! If you're still interested in piano concertos, buy Rachmaninov's No. 2: very beautiful.[121]

In general, this was the period when I was discovering a new kind of music, piano concertos. Student performances were given regularly in the Small

Auditorium. If a student had studied a piece thoroughly and played it well, he would be chosen to play it at a student evening that would be attended by everyone from the Conservatory. By going to these performances, students became familiar with the classical repertory. My attention was drawn to a genre that I had known little of before: the piano concerto. I suddenly discovered that it included a vast amount of beautiful music, and that the concertos were very interesting technically. I listened and listened, and constantly commented on their merits.

I especially liked the concertos of Beethoven, Rachmaninov, Liszt, Rimsky-Korsakov, Tchaikovsky's *First,* Saint-Saëns' *Second* and *Fourth* (Tcherepnin had called my attention to the fact that Saint-Saëns was particularly skillful at combining the piano and orchestra), and others. I was less enthusiastic about the concertos of Chopin, Schumann, Brahms, and Scriabin. Chopin's concertos struck me as being not so much concertos as piano pieces to which the orchestra had been added. I adored his E minor theme, but one could get along very nicely without an orchestral accompaniment for it. The Schumann concerto was charming music but not interesting technically. And Brahms simply floated past my ears. I wrote about my fondness for Beethoven and Rachmaninov in my letters to Morolev, advising him to buy the concertos and get to know them.

In these letters, serious comments on music were often accompanied by childish amusements. One letter was written on a round piece of paper, and the lines formed spirals, as on a phonograph record. When you got to the center you had to "crawl into the hole" (there actually was a hole in the paper). On the reverse you had to follow the spirals from the center to the edge. This little joke provoked some indignant remarks in Morolev's reply.

In a more serious vein, I wrote to Morolev that at the Conservatory I was busy learning scales in double thirds (an entire branch of mathematics—one had to learn a whole system of fingering). But it was something very important: it meant that I was getting ready to move on to the advanced course—actually the only significant dividing line in the study of piano at the St. Petersburg Conservatory. Those who had met the requirements for technique before moving on to the advanced course concentrated, thenceforth, largely on the artistic aspect.

Only a few postcards have been preserved from my correspondence with Miaskovsky, which was much less extensive than that with Morolev, since Miaskovsky and I were living in the same city.

On one postcard I wrote: "My fine fellow, I knew that already, and I dislike you very much." This is followed by Miaskovsky's penciled notation: "Was he perhaps offended by my arrival?" On another one, dated December 28, I say in a postscript: "I have written *Snow* and *Autumnal Sketch.*[122] This refers to the fact that Miaskovsky and I had agreed that each of us would write a piano piece depicting falling snow. Miaskovsky depicted "very repulsive snow—stinging, with a strong wind," as he expressed it. By contrast, I evoked snow falling gently in large flakes:

The piece proved to be pleasant and gentle despite the parallel seconds and the parallel chords. But I did not, in later years, include it in Opus 3, which comprised pieces from that period, since it seemed to me that *Snow* lacked thematic material and was more of an experiment than a piece. The manuscript later got lost, and the specimens quoted above have been reconstructed from memory.[123]

In general, memory is a strange and wonderful thing: pieces written forty years ago can be reconstructed rather easily, while those written five or six years ago are just as easily forgotten. Miaskovsky's piece was preserved, and after slight reworking was included a good while later in his album *Reminiscences,* Opus 29, No. 2.

Snow stirred up quite a bit of interest (and not only on Miaskovsky's part), chiefly because it offered something strange: parallel seconds, yet they had a gentle sound. Word about it soon got to Lyadov.

"What's this I hear about you?" he asked me in his usual querulous tone. "They tell me you've written a piece in which the voices always move in seconds,

seconds, and more seconds." As he said this, he stuck two fingers in the air, first bending and then unbending them, to illustrate seconds.

"But it seemed to me that could be done very harmoniously," I replied, somewhat embarrassed.

But Lyadov wasn't listening: apparently he required no reply. He turned to another student and began talking to him.

The second piece mentioned in the postcard to Miaskovsky was *Autumnal Sketch*. If I'm not mistaken, it was he who thought up the title. I have no memory of what the piece was like, and the manuscript has been lost. The symphonic sketch I wrote three years later, also titled *Autumnal Sketch,* has nothing in common with the other piece: only the title was retained. Obviously, I liked the title, but I wasn't satisfied with the music in the first variant, so I came back to the theme later.[124]

73

As I come to the year 1908, I again note rather bitterly my lack of materials. The abridgment of the diary, which I drew upon for 1907, does not go beyond that year. And very few letters have been preserved. At the time I wanted to keep a complete set of letters: those I had written and those I had received. For that purpose I started using copying paper. But the copying paper didn't take the impress of the pen well: when I used the necessary pressure, the pen point spread, and the copy was hard to read. And keeping my own rough drafts was a bit like accumulating dirty linen. So for a whole year I put off assembling my correspondence, and I lost the letters sent to me. The few dates I have had available were either those of concerts or those which come to mind automatically, or virtually so. I am trying to utilize them insofar as possible, and to relate whatever I remember of the events of that time.

As early as 1919, having an autobiography in mind, I began to jot down all kinds of events—and even expressions—that I remembered, and to sort them by years. I have by now accumulated more than a thousand such jottings, and they have of course come in handy as materials—all the more so since it often happens that one event or expression brings to mind others associated with it.

Even without any such jotting, I remember that the Conservatory Ball was held on January 2. It had not occurred to me, before going to the ball, to buy new gloves (in those days it was *de rigueur* to wear white gloves for dancing— no doubt so as to avoid soiling the lady's dress), or a new collar, or a boutonniere, or even to shine my shoes. I had made an attempt to look presentable, but in general I was dressed pretty much as I was every day. For that matter, most of the students were not of the propertied class, so that only a few were elegantly attired. But this did not dampen the spirit of gaiety.

There was a huge crowd at the ball. It was held in the Small Auditorium, which accommodated 600 or 700 persons on concert evenings. But on this evening the chairs were removed and the standing room—i.e., the space for dancing —was much greater. Japanese lanterns were hung (not without a certain naïveté) in the adjacent corridors, and several classrooms were used as "drawing rooms," being provided with divans and armchairs taken from God knows where. All in all, there must have been more than a thousand persons at the ball.

It began with a concert, and the concert itself began with a trio by Glinka called *Doubt,* performed by two other students (a violinist and cellist) and myself.

Afterward, some students shouted at me, "Come here, and we'll put a red ribbon on you!"

"Where?"

"On your arm, of course. Did you think we were going to put it around your neck?"*

The Nodelman girl came up to me, holding a big, bright red armband of the kind worn by a master of ceremonies. The Bessonova girl, who was hovering about, took me by the arm and we went strolling through the corridors and the "drawing rooms."

The concert didn't last long, thank God! Soon, from the Small Auditorium, we could hear the strains of a military band. They were playing a popular waltz —*On the Hills of Manchuria,* I believe it was. Even now, forty years later, I still hear that waltz from time to time.

After several dances (I didn't dance very well), the Bessonova girl and I went back to one of the "drawing rooms" and got into conversation. "Three of my admirers have come to the ball," she told me. "They see I am busy, and are watching me from a distance. That would be all right, except that one of them is a very determined man. The day before yesterday he told me if things went on the way they are now, he would kill me. Now I'm so afraid! . . ." Etc., etc.

The above is a condensed account in a mere three lines. Actually, she talked for more than an hour, and in my naïveté, I believed everything she said. The next day I wrote in my diary: "I don't understand people like that. They come to a ball and stand in a corner like wallflowers, waiting patiently for something to happen."

Meantime my siren had moved on to loftier themes. "What is your notion of friendship between a man and a woman? At what point does it become love?"

But her shot missed its mark. Instead of being captivated, or alarmed by her fate, or proud that she was devoting her time to me, I just sat there listlessly and dozed while she, melancholy and garrulous, went on talking.

But finally a young man came up to her, and she excused herself and went off. I heaved a sigh of relief and looked around me. Standing a few paces away from me was Sonya Eshe, the younger sister of Elizabeth Eshe, whose name I

---

*I.e., as if it was a decoration bestowed by the government. (Translator's note.)

had once used as the basis for composing a piece of music, and who had introduced me to her sister. Whereas Elizabeth's behavior was always dignified and reserved, her younger sister (at fourteen or fifteen, she was scarcely more than a child) was entirely different.

Sonya was a brunette with a rather low but prominent forehead, slanting eyes that often gave you a distrustful look, irregular but pretty features, a slender and supple figure, and a tongue sharp as a razor: a very interesting little she-devil. In a word, the child was frisky but charming. At the moment she was holding an orange. She inclined her head slightly and gave me a rather tender look, like a little monkey.

"Why are you wearing such a long face?" she asked me, raising her eyebrows high.

"No doubt I'm overwhelmed by my responsibility for the conduct of the ball," I said, touching my armband and remembering for the first time that I was master of ceremonies.

"In that case shouldn't we go and put some life into this ball?"

I glanced at the Bessonova girl. She was sitting in a corner talking to the same young man. "With the greatest pleasure," I replied. Then I added (using an expression I had picked up from Shurik Rayevsky), "I am extremely flattered by your attention."

I proffered my arm, and we headed for the auditorium, where the dancing was in progress. On the way Sonya made all kinds of witty remarks, some of which were rather daring. For instance: "The one in green is his wife, and the one in lace is his spare wife." Or: "Just look how her face is rouged. That's called sandalwood red. But the good thing about that rouge is that it doesn't come off when you're kissing."

I was an innocent lad, and all I could do in response to her remarks was to stammer, "Wh-where did you learn all that?"

But I enjoyed myself in her company. My ears were buzzing with her comments, but at least I didn't have to ponder whether there could be friendship between a man and a woman, and just how friendship becomes love.

I don't remember how the evening ended. But I got home after three in the morning, tired and yet contented, since this was my first ball on the grand scale.

74

Another large gathering I had occasion to attend—a much stuffier one, by the way—was my cousin Katya Rayevskaya's wedding, which took place a week after the Conservatory Ball. Katya was marrying Paul Ignatyev, a junior captain in an engineering battalion of the Guards. Ignatyev was handsome, with a neat little reddish-brown beard. He carried himself well and in general was elegant.

In thanking someone, he said, *"Blagodarstvuite"*—a form whose grammatical origins were unclear to me. A good many officers in various handsome Guards uniforms showed up at the wedding on his behalf.

The Rayevskys' guests included generals of the civil service in black frock coats and white waistcoats, with broad red and blue ribbons worn diagonally across the chest (like the way a bishop moves in chess), and Gentlemen of His Majesty's Bedchamber in white trousers and a gold key embroidered on their full-dress coats.

Katya Rayevskaya (thenceforth Ignatyeva), who was very fond of me, had invited me as best man, and I was to take turns with Shurik Rayevsky and four other young men in frock coats, in holding the tiara over her head during the ceremony proper. My suit was by no means fine enough for such a splendid occasion. Even high school students who wore a black jacket like mine had special full-dress coats for such formal occasions.

The Rayevskys had cautiously asked my mother if I couldn't wear my old dark blue suit, which was something like a sailor suit. But I was almost sixteen, and, taking advantage of the fact that the coat was out at the elbows, I protested. The Rayevskys did not object, and I wore my black jacket. To make my attire look more formal, I even wore starched cuffs. But I neglected to make sure they were fastened to my shirt-sleeves. And just when I was taking Katya around the lectern, holding the tiara over her head and being very careful not to step on the long train of her wedding gown (I had been particularly warned about that), the sleeve of my jacket slid back and the unfastened cuff shot out and stopped only when it reached my fist. In short, it wasn't enough that my attire was lacking in smartness: this disgraceful little incident had to happen too!

Katya's and Ignatyev's marriage was not a happy one. She soon had to use her small dowry to pay his gambling debts. And it later developed that he was having an affair with Countess T., the wife of a fellow-officer who, since he was having affairs of his own, did nothing to stop it. Katya and Ignatyev separated several years later, although she loved him to the end of her days.

I, too, was involved in an unpleasant incident with him. One Sunday when I came to the Rayevskys' for dinner, I was informed that dinner had been delayed for an hour.

"Today I got very tired at the rehearsal," I said to Katya.

"Since it will be another hour before dinner is served, why don't you go and lie down?" she said. "You can use my old room. No one is using it now."

I went in and stretched out on the bed. I had just begun to doze off, when Ignatyev came in, whistling and jingling his spurs. When he saw me, he was surprised. "What are you doing here? Sleeping?"

I sat up on the edge of the bed. "What a slob you are, Paul!" I said. "When you come into a room and find somebody sleeping there, it's better to leave without starting a conversation."

(I had learned the word "slob" from Zakharov, and I liked it.)

"I must ask you not to call me names," Ignatyev replied, and left.

I was by then completely awake and couldn't get back to sleep. A short time later I went out to dinner. During the pause between the soup and the next course (gray hen), when no one at the table was saying anything, Paul turned to me and gave me a whole lecture on manners. "You see, my friend Serezha," he said in a rather acid tone, "I wanted to tell you something." Then he proceeded to give me a long and boring lecture in front of everyone at the table.

I was at first embarrassed, then angry. I formulated a full-dress reply, but finally got so confused I didn't voice it, which was too bad. That reply was more or less as follows (I had intended to stand up while delivering it): "I very much apologize for my rudeness, and promise to refrain from it in the future. At the same time, in view of the change in our relationship, I consider it appropriate to switch from the second person singular to the second person plural, and must ask you, if you find it possible, to do the same with respect to me."

All this had been thought out on the spot and in rather precise expressions, but at the last moment I hesitated. Meantime the conversation at the table had shifted to other subjects having nothing to do with our "business." I became completely confused and let the moment slip, so that I left his remarks unanswered. My relations with Ignatyev remained proper but very cool.

Once he chanced to mention Miaskovsky, who was likewise an engineering officer but not in the Guards Regiment. "I ran across Miaskovsky a few days ago," he said. "Is he a classmate of yours at the Conservatory?"

"Yes."

"I simply didn't recognize him. He used to be a good-looking chap, but now he's sloppy-looking and sluggish as a fly in the fall."

I mentally sent Ignatyev to the Devil. I knew that Miaskovsky got up late and made his own hard bed, that he was often sluggish and rather sleepy. But that would not appear to be any of Ignatyev's business.

Sometime later Ignatyev's rating with me dropped even further because of a scandalous incident with a cabdriver. At that time, cabdrivers in Petersburg would quote a fare they thought profitable. Some prospective passengers would bargain with them; others, being grander persons, would simply get in and ride off. The Guards officers naturally considered themselves grand. But Ignatyev was poor, and on this occasion he paid the cabdriver a mere pittance. The latter started to grumble.

"Quiet! Don't argue!" Ignatyev shouted.

The cabdriver started to swear. Ignatyev rushed at him and began to beat him with his saber, which was still in its scabbard. The cabdriver, a muscular man, managed to whip up his horses and drive off. But Ignatyev got the number of the cab and called the police. Three days later he was visited by a rather poorly dressed woman who proved to be the cabdriver's wife. She said her husband was being banished from Petersburg, and begged "Your Honor" (Ignatyev) to forgive him and intervene.

Ignatyev replied that he wouldn't even think of it. The cabdriver, he said, was impudent, yet she was asking him to straighten out his affairs. The woman fell on her knees. Whereupon Ignatyev shouted, "Get out!" and left the room.

My mother related all this when she came back from the Rayevskys' one day, confused and upset. I too got upset, and my father was indignant. "Oh, naturally," he said, "the high and mighty officers must be given special respect. They must not be touched, and they must be allowed to do whatever they like." And he walked out, slamming the door behind him.

Things went badly between Katya and Ignatyev: first she would leave him and come to her parents, then she would go back to him. Three years later they separated for good. After the Revolution, Ignatyev emigrated to Yugoslavia, where all sight of him was lost.

Katya suffered a good deal, believing her life to have been a failure. Moreover, her hearing was getting worse because of her nerves, and she was threatened with ultimate deafness. On one occasion—I don't remember exactly when—she again asked me to write an art song. "I have run across a good poem," she said, "that could be set to music with great feeling. But write it clearly and simply so that I can sing it before I go deaf."

I was sorry for my cousin and complied with her wish. I tried to be simple, melodious, and expressive, using an idiom I had abandoned three years before. The problem was with the accompaniment: it involved a good many skips, and I lacked the technique to write it well. In certain spots it was never really completed, and when I showed the song to Katya it was a rather sloppy rough draft. I never got around to making a fair copy and completing the accompaniment, and Katya never had occasion to sing it, since at that time her family troubles intruded.

I have quoted the song from memory. My reconstruction of the melody and the words (whose author I don't remember) is accurate. But here and there in the accompaniment I had to complete what I had left unfinished—to plug up the holes in the piano part, so to speak. In my other works, written "for myself," I sought more complex harmonies and tried to think up something new and unexpected. (I was extremely concerned with this "something new.") But I wrote the song for Katya Ignatyeva in a simpler vein, trying to please my cousin.

75

The classes with Lyadov went along rather regularly, except for those weeks when he was too lazy to show up. In addition to fugues, he would sometimes ask us to bring him piano pieces in binary or ternary form. These pieces had to be written simply and clearly (like the one for Katya Ignatyeva). One could not devise complex harmonies or (God forbid!) use dissonances, otherwise he would get furious and even stamp his feet. So that the music we brought him was more conservative and serene, but perhaps much more shapely, if it be regarded from the viewpoint of the strict style and strictness of form. But sometimes we would slip into innovation in some of the pieces. When we did, Lyadov would thrust his hands into his trousers pockets and say, "If you want to compose that kind of music, why do you come to my class? Go to Debussy—go to Richard Strauss!" And it sounded as if he were saying, "Go to the Devil!"

His attitude toward the fugues we brought him was demanding and even captious, and he would allow no clashing between the voices. Nevertheless, some of the students got some selected pieces by Bach out of their portfolios, and showed him examples like the following:

where one voice is ascending the melodic minor scale while the other is descending, so that they hit different notes.

"And so?" said Lyadov. "That's not the best passage in Bach. But he wrote so many unfathomable things, and had such vast technique, that he could sometimes allow himself such tricks. Take Beethoven, for example. All his life he worked at counterpoint, but he was never able to master it properly. Most of his fugues are heavy; you can find clearer examples in them than what you are showing me here. But Mozart's light touch in counterpoint was something innate. And Chopin—what purity of voice-leading! In neither Mozart nor Chopin will you ever find any sloppiness."

"And contemporary composers?"

"Among contemporary composers, Scriabin's voice-leading is the purest. Only . . . only in some of his most recent works he has penetrated into such thickets that I simply refuse to analyze those works."

Lyadov was by nature a petty individual: it is surprising that he even went so far as to praise the early Scriabin. But those early works were short pieces for piano with a slight aroma of Chopin. When Scriabin began to write huge, complex, and more modern things, Lyadov turned away from him in annoyance: Scriabin, you see, had plunged into the thickets.

After a pause he added, "As for fugues, I would single out the young composer Pogozhev. At the Belyayev Publishing House, we recently put out a selection of his fugues for piano. You should get to know them. They are very well done, and will be useful to you."

He gave a little laugh. "And they were published as Opus 1! If a composer lists a selection of fugues as his first opus, it means he really loves fugue."

A quarter century later I chanced to recall that conversation and asked Miaskovsky if he had bought the opus Lyadov recommended on that occasion.

"Yes, I bought it and played it."

"How was it?"

"Boring," he drawled, "and not very interesting from the viewpoint of composition."

Lyadov loved to say, "That is tastefully done," when in fact there was but little there that was tasteful. He sometimes adored strange things. Once when I was praising a work by Rachmaninov, he said, "How can you say that? If it's young composers you're interested in, you'd do better to take a look at Vassilenko."* But apart from his charming setting of a poem by Blok (a song about ships returning to port), Vassilenko hadn't done anything.

On another occasion Lyadov was annoyed by the poor voice-leading of one student—this time quite justifiably. "What if you had to orchestrate this thing? What would you get? Here—pooh, there—pooh, and there—pooh . . ."

He uttered each "pooh" at a different pitch, representing first one instrument and then another. As he did this, he would first puff up his cheeks like a *Posaunenengel,* then suck them in like a flutist spitting a note into his instrument. The idea was that when one of the musicians had hit that note he couldn't go on, and the following note had to be given to another player.

Lyadov was not very pleasant during class. About the only times we liked him was when, in order to demonstrate some modulation, he would improvise at the piano in a strict four-voice style. He did this gently, beautifully, and "tastefully," keeping all four voices well defined and singling out the one we should pay special attention to.

In any case, the greatest "monument" to our classes with him were the pieces in binary and ternary form, since that did involve composing. Later I selected the most successful of these, developing and polishing them. Such were the origins of the *March, Gavotte,* and *Scherzo* in Opus 12, and the scherzo of the Opus 14 sonata.[125] But these pieces were expanded and complex by comparison to those I brought to class.

About ten years later, Asafyev told me, "Lyadov used to tell me, speaking of you, that although he found your music repellent, you were nonetheless talented and would develop your own mature style. Miaskovsky made fewer mistakes in his assignments, but for some reason Lyadov did not believe in his future as a composer. 'It looks as if in time Prokofiev will develop his own mature style; that he will find his own kind of voice-leading and orchestration.' And then he added, 'But I don't understand why he studies with me: I tell him A and he says B.'"

I told Asafyev, "It's a good thing he did say A and I answered him B: that meant progress in music."

"It's not likely that Lyadov had that in mind."

But to return to the fugue class. Upon getting to know the students in that class, one could see that some of them were composers and others were quasi-composers. The quasi-composers solved problems but rarely composed. The com-

* Sergei Nikoforovich Vassilenko (1872–1956), composer and conductor. (Translator's note.)

posers solved problems too—some of them well, others badly—but they were eager to write music and get out of the stuffy atmosphere of Lyadov's class and be on their own. Once Asafyev brought Maikov's* poem "The Venerable Thick-Branched Oaks" to class with him and said that it should be set to music.

"Well, I'd like to set it," Miaskovsky said.

"I too," I chimed in eagerly.

And Saminsky put in, "If it's all right, I'd like to try it myself."

With Asafyev, that made four of us. We copied out the poem, and a week later, when we came to the next class, each of us had written an art song. When the lesson was over we stayed in the classroom and played our new compositions to one another. At first each one would play through his own song, then we went through all of them again. Miaskovsky's was the most interesting—something that everyone confirmed. And Asafyev's was successful and charming. Mine was less good. I depicted the "venerable oaks" with a series of chords in the lower register, and the "playful stream" mentioned later in the poem with a passage in which a series of chords twined their way downward. My song looked like a serious piece of work, but it was not the best of my compositions for that period. Moreover, there was more emphasis on the piano accompaniment than on the voice part. Saminsky's piece was completely uninteresting. The music was rather colorless throughout, and it ended on an augmented triad with the figuration built on it rocking in the right hand—altogether too simple.

"And that's the way it ends," he said, triumphantly glancing around at his listeners.

No one said anything except for an "Mmm" here and there.

Finally, having decided that Miaskovsky's song was the best, we declared our "competition" over and went our separate ways. The songs also went their separate ways: at any rate, mine eventually disappeared without a trace, as did Miaskovsky's.

A curious thing happened many years later, when Asafyev was already famous. He was very sick, and I went to visit him at his apartment near the Bolshoi Theater. As we were reminiscing about things shrouded in the mist of the past—things that happened at the Conservatory and other events of our youth—he said, "Do you remember that time we decided that each of us would set the same poem by Maikov? Later I was given some kind of certificate for that competition. . . ."

I was at first amazed, then slightly embarrassed. Apparently Asafyev's memory had betrayed him. There had been no such "certificate." And even if we had thought one up, neither Miaskovsky nor Saminsky would have been inclined to manufacture such a document. That left me, since at the time I enjoyed drawing diagrams of chess and stilts tournaments. But in that particular case, I too would have been disinclined to proffer a certificate for the competition. And besides, it was Miaskovsky and not Asafyev who had won. Switching the topic

---

* Appollon Nikolayevich Maikov (1821–97), a minor poet and member of the Russian "Parnassian" group. (Translator's note.)

from the certificate to the matter of the songs themselves, I reminded Asafyev that it was he who had suggested setting Maikov's poem to music.

"Yes," he said, "I was very fond of Maikov."

After that competition we continued to bring fugues to Lyadov's class. But I wanted to compose, so I proposed we all write a violin sonata together. With the sonata, however, things went worse. Hardly any of us had mastered the form and were ready to undertake such a complex piece. I announced that I would write the first movement. After all, I had written a violin sonata five years before, under Glière's supervision. At the next class Miaskovsky said he could probably write the finale, and Kankarovich said he would do the minuet. I don't remember who promised to write the andante, but at the time it looked as though we had lined up a composer for each movement of the sonata.

I got to work on my sonata allegro and brought it in two weeks later.

The main theme:

The subordinate theme:

The subordinate theme was given to the piano alone, without the violin. I don't remember whether I planned it that way or whether it just came out that way, but for all my wanting to work the violin into it, I couldn't.

"And what about your finale?" I asked Miaskovsky, who had heard my allegro and in general praised it.

"I've sketched out one little theme," he said unhappily, "but beyond that it just won't work right."

Kankarovich never did write his minuet, nor was the andante ever written. Under these circumstances it seemed to me that, with the momentum I had gained in writing the first movement, I could finish the sonata on my own. But the momentum petered out, since I viewed the undertaking basically as a "group" composition. Left to my own devices, I couldn't come up with either the andante or the finale, and the "group" sonata gradually got bogged down. A year later, however, I used the subordinate theme in my opera *Maddalena*.[126]

76

About this time I chanced to meet up with Chernov—the same Chernov who, at Glazunov's suggestion, had given me lessons in theory of composition before I entered the Conservatory. At the time, my mother was none too pleased that he took little interest in my compositions, and in her letters to my father she complained that he made no effort to see that anyone got to know them. No doubt Chernov had heard something about Mother's criticism of his teaching, since when we met he asked me straight out, "Well, how are things with you? What are you composing? Who has seen your compositions?"

"I've shown them to Miaskovsky."

"Miaskovsky? Who's that?"

"A student in our class. He's an excellent musician."

"And to whom else?"

"In December there was a gathering of so-called beginning composers organized by Ranushevich. I played them a few things, and I was promised that they would be given a performance, but all that has gone down the drain."

Chernov frowned. "They aren't really in a position to arrange for recitals. They talk about it and then drop it. But I'll tell you what: I'll introduce you to a society called 'Evenings of Contemporary Music.' It is headed by very avant-garde people who love contemporary music and give several concerts every year featuring new music. These concerts are attended by almost all the musicians in Petersburg, and in any case by all the critics. If your music is to their taste, they are in a position to present it to the public in the right way. They gather every Thursday to listen to new music and select future programs. Come for me next Thursday, and I'll take you to them."

I was deeply interested, and on the following Thursday I went to pick up

Chernov. He was in shirt-sleeves, brushing his teeth. Next he combed his hair carefully, got a new jacket out of the closet, and said, "Let's go."

It was clear that he had great respect for the leaders of "Evenings of Contemporary Music," and I was ashamed that I had come straight from the Conservatory without having groomed myself as he had.

They met in a big room at the Becker piano factory, located in the center of the city on Morskoy Boulevard (now Herzen Street). As a friendly gesture, Becker had made it possible for them to gather there and make music. By day the store did business. At night it was closed, and the musicians gathered in that dark room where only one light was burning.[127] Chernov introduced me to the leaders. There were five of them, all middle-aged. Alfred Nurok, a man with a bald and rather knobby head, was the liveliest and most vigorous. Walter Nouvell, a short man who dressed more neatly than the others, had a rather sharp tongue. Vyacheslav Karatygin, an unattractive, almost ugly man, was serious and known as one of the best music critics in the capital. These three were the most important ones.

Nurok was in some way associated with a famous textbook for learning English: either he had written it or his father or uncle had. Nouvell had a position in some ministry—foreign affairs, I believe—and hence was more formal than the others. If I'm not mistaken, he had some French blood in his veins. Karatygin taught music theory and wrote reviews for a big newspaper, *Rech*.[128]

I started playing my compositions: *Snow,* then those which were later included in Opus 3 (*Fairy Tale, Badinage, Fantome*) and some that went into Opus 4.

Karatygin, Nouvell, and especially Nurok were really very excited. They praised the pieces and asked me to play them again. When I had used up my whole stock, Nurok shouted, "Beautiful! Very, very interesting! What's more, you play the piano splendidly. You must by all means play your pieces at a concert of ours this spring."

"The programs have already been drawn up," Nouvell said.

"Well, in the fall, then. Yes of course, in the fall. Play *Snow* again."

I had never before experienced such immediate enthusiasm.

Then they began an animated discussion. Karatygin felt that my music was the antithesis of Scriabin, and thanked Heaven that such an antithesis had appeared. "It's a compound of Reger, Moussorgsky, and Grieg," he added. "Those are the elements it was born from."

"Come here every Thursday."

"Play that once again."

When I came back the following Thursday I found Miaskovsky there. He had been brought not by Chernov but by Krizhanovsky, one of the five, with whom (as I found out) he had studied harmony before taking Lyadov's class. They liked Miaskovsky's work and promised to program some of his art songs for a fall concert.

Nurok said to me, "I'd like you to write the music for a pantomime. Come to my place, and I'll read you the script."

His lodgings consisted of two rather modest rooms with photographs and sketches on the walls. One of the sketches showed a lion mounting a lioness. When I saw the king of beasts so engaged, I felt embarrassed and walked away. But then I came back again: the lion wore an expression of concentration, and the features of the lioness were dissolving in ecstasy.

Nurok sat me down on the divan and read me the pantomime. It offered all kinds of things for musical depiction: the sounds of an approaching hunt, a heroine on a white horse ("Splendid!" Nurok exclaimed, and chuckled); a declaration of love as the lady is being handed down from her horse; a curse on the hero (if his beloved gives herself to him, he can possess her only once in his life); etc.

Nouvell and Kryzhanovsky, who were also there, applauded the reading. But I was reserved and said I would have to look more closely at the script, which struck me as a halfway decent concoction. Nurok gave it to me, and I took it home feeling that I would have to write a great deal of music, and wondering if that made sense. In any case the music would play a secondary role, and the pantomime would not be produced more than once or twice.

That was the last time I saw them until the following fall.

77

The word was getting around at the Conservatory that Wagner's *Ring of the Nibelung* was being rehearsed at the Maryinsky Theater. Previously, the Maryinsky's productions of Wagner had consisted chiefly of *Tannhäuser* and *Lohengrin,* so the *Ring* was a welcome novelty. As I have already mentioned, I was interested in Wagner. Naturally, I began asking when and how they were rehearsing it, and whether anyone was allowed to attend. Someone told me that they were now rehearsing *The Rhinegold* almost daily, with Blumenfeld* conducting, and told me at what time rehearsals were being held. He said they were strictly private, but if you said, "Blumenfeld sent me," they would let you in.

The first thing I did was to go to the music library at the Conservatory and ask for the orchestral score of *Das Rheingold.* The chief librarian was one Fribus, who was called "Diminished Fifth" because he was short and had a big hump on his back.

"Sorry, old chap," Diminished Fifth said. "The score of a Wagner opera is such a precious thing that we can't let you have it."

"Then who can get it?"

"Well, Director Glazunov, or perhaps Rimsky-Korsakov."

"And I?"

---

* Felix Mikhailovich Blumenfeld (1863–1931), conductor, composer, and pianist. (Translator's note.)

"Someone will have to vouch for you. Bring a note from the director. But then he won't give you a note."

"How can I bring it to you? Glazunov isn't seeing anyone today, and I want to take the score to the rehearsal."

"Are you going to the rehearsal?"

"Yes."

Fribus relented. "All right, here's pen and paper. Write out a request, I'm going to see Glazunov on Conservatory business in a moment, and I'll slip it to him. But I'm telling you that nothing will come of it."

I wrote a brief note, trying to be musically learned in explaining my request, and Fribus took it and left. When he returned a half hour later he had a look of amazement on his face. "He gave permission for you to have it anyway," he said.

"Thank you very much," I said, bowing and scraping.

"I had nothing to do with it. He just told me to let you have the score— why, I don't know."

He ducked behind a bookstack and emerged with a huge tome with a brownish cover. I took it and headed for the Maryinsky Theater. The man at the box office asked, "Who sent you?"

Aha! His question called for the reply suggested to me at the Conservatory. "Blumenfeld told me to come to the rehearsal," I said.

The man whispered with another usher and then let me in. On the stage they were rehearsing with the orchestra but were not in costume. Sitting in the dim, almost empty theater were a half-dozen singers who did not have to be on-stage at the moment, and a few other people, among whom I recognized Rimsky-Korsakov. I chose the best-lighted spot I could find, under a dimmed light from a chandelier near the entrance, sat down, and opened the score. On the left side of the stage stood a group of actors, apparently quarreling in recitative with another group on the right, who likewise answered in recitative. Between them an actor lively as quicksilver was twisting and turning. I didn't know the score of *Das Rheingold* well enough to realize that all those people in jackets were German gods, and that the wriggling actor was the crafty Loge, the incarnation of Fire. The role was being played by Ershov, a singer with a powerful but somewhat constrained voice and a fine acting talent. I had already seen him as Grishka Kuterma in *Kitezh*. But now he was literally enhancing the entire *Ring,* playing the roles of Loge, Sigmund, and Siegfried by turn.

I tried to find the passage in the score that was being rehearsed, but didn't succeed right away. Meantime there was a break in the rehearsal for intermission, and some of those listening moved toward the exit to go out for a smoke. Rimsky-Korsakov was heading the group. As he passed by me, I stood up and bowed.

He stopped and asked, "What's that fat tome?"

"The orchestral score of *Das Rheingold*. I got it from the Conservatory library."

"Do you know the opera well?"

"Not really as well as the other operas of *The Ring*."

"In that case you'd do better to bring a piano score. With a piano score you can grasp all the music right away. But the orchestral score is so complex that you'll keep trying not to lose your place, and you'll never pay attention to the music. Bring the orchestral score when you know the music better."

At first I was afraid Rimsky-Korsakov would notice that the score wasn't opened at the right place, but he paid no attention.

"I have the piano scores for the other operas of *The Ring;* now I'll get the one for *Das Rheingold*," I said obediently.

He nodded and walked away.

When the rehearsal resumed, I found that I liked *Das Rheingold* less than *Die Walküre* or *Die Götterdämmerung*. A few days later the Maryinsky Theater announced that tickets for *The Ring* were on sale: a subscription for all four operas. I hurried to report this to my mother, and we subscribed—but not without difficulty, since at the box office there was a tremendous line of people who wanted to hear Wagner.

There is no doubt that I was greatly impressed by those four productions. I loved *Die Walküre* and *Die Götterdämmerung*. In Siegfried I adored the forging of the sword: that struck me as very operatic. In *Die Götterdämmerung* I especially liked the part where Siegfried journeys down the Rhine with the sound of horns and shouts coming from the bank: that wild whirlwind captivated me. But I shall not undertake to discuss *The Ring* here or the impressions made on me by those four productions, since the next year we subscribed again, and the year after that we subscribed a third time, so that now, so many years later, I have confused the details of my reactions to those three series. All I can say is that Wagner had a tremendous influence on me at that time.

For the moment, descending to a lower plane, I should like to take the liberty to tell about something very funny that happened at a performance of *Siegfried* after Ershov had killed the dragon and was hauling it into the cave. At that point the music is quiet, and the audience can hear every word uttered.

When Ershov had dragged—with considerable effort—the huge stuffed dragon into the cave, his angry whisper suddenly came from within: "Damn it, this thing is *heavy!*"

To which someone replied, cautioning him, "Quiet, Ivan Vasilyevich! The audience can hear you, and things could get awkward."

I had heard both remarks. I forgot the drama onstage and had a good laugh.

One day at the Conservatory, Leonida Glagoleva came up to me and asked if I could tell her about *Die Walküre,* because she was going to it that night at the Maryinsky. I was flattered by her request and tried to tell her everything I knew: about the German myth of the stolen ring; what happens in *Die Walküre,* one of the four operas; and about Wagner's excellent method of composing an opera using leitmotifs; etc. We went to the library to see Fribus, and got from him the piano score of *Die Walküre* "for five minutes." (Unlike orchestral scores, piano scores were something that Fribus would let you have without objection, provided it was for a short time.) Then we went back to the classroom where we had been sitting before and which was now empty. There I showed her what leitmotifs were, and what she should pay attention to that night. In a word, I was not found wanting, and she was overwhelmed with my erudition. When we parted she thanked me for the lecture, which she said she had not counted upon, and from then on our relations were friendlier than they had been before.

The only thing I can't ascertain with precision is whether that happened in 1908 or a year later.[129]

78

Exams at the Conservatory began early, even before the end of March. First came those in academic subjects. I was completing my academic course and decided to do it well. Also, to jot down the results in all the exams, and then make a diagram, as is done in chess tournaments. Actually, my marks were very good to start with. And if there had been an exam in French (which I knew better than the other students), I no doubt would have been ahead at the end. But I had finished my French requirement the term before, and in the other subjects I was overtaken by two or three girls—including Glagoleva and Eshe, as I recall.

Since I was finishing my course in the Russian language, I decided to introduce something new into spelling (my own, of course). It seemed to me that in the final analysis there was no sense in having two symbols to represent the letter *u*. I decided to use the Roman *i* everywhere. Of the two, it seemed to me that it took up less space and was more eye-catching, and besides it was found in the alphabets of other peoples. So I chose it. Then years later the government legitimatized the other symbol: *u*. Nonetheless, the *i* continued to exist in my writing for about thirty years. Then, when I saw that the *u* had been firmly established in the Soviet Union, I switched to it.

The technical exam to qualify for the advanced course in piano was held on March 31. As I said before, the qualifying exam was in two parts (days).

One was technical and involved the playing of scales and arpeggios, scales in double thirds, and études: trill studies, octave studies, and a competitive étude. The other involved performing a piece in public. The most disagreeable thing in the first exam was the scales in double thirds, for which you had to memorize a huge number of fingerings, major and minor, for major and minor thirds.

The students started learning them a year in advance and hardly memorized them by the time of the exam. Strictly speaking, these scales in double thirds had no practical application, but the training of the fingers and the memory was very useful. The competitive étude was a very serious matter. For this the professors chose something from among the obscure études of obscure composers. They made their choice at a late date and in secret. Then, based on the number of students, they would place an order with a music store, which would in turn order the required number of copies from abroad. When the students finally got the sheet music, they would begin to work on it intensively. That year the étude consisted of rapid passages with unexpected (but not exactly beautiful) modulations. The students memorized it and tried very hard to make sure that in their excitement they would not trip up on the modulation and get into the wrong key.

Finally the exam was held. Winkler, as a meticulous German, gave me the following evaluation in the class journal: "Very capable, but not too diligent in his work; made very good progress; B+." Glazunov was kinder: "Brilliant technique, beautiful tone; got an A on the technical examination and an A on the public examination." I don't know where Glazunov got the idea that my tone was beautiful. Even fifteen years later, as I recall, tone was by no means my best quality. My technique had been developed on the new Ratke concert grand that my parents had bought me that winter. That piano had a resonant, rather sharp tone that was somewhat muffled by the overstuffed furniture in our drawing room, where it took up one third of the space because of its huge size. It had not cost my parents too much, because the manager of the Ratke store had taken our old grand as a trade-in and had also given us a discount on the new one, since it had once been used at a concert.

"It weighs 1,260 pounds," I wrote to Morolev.

The public examination, which involved playing a piece, was held three weeks after the technical one. Back at the beginning of the term, when Winkler had told me that I should prepare myself for moving up to the advanced course, he had said one should play Bach at the public exam. When I ran across Taneyev, who had come to Petersburg, I reported this to him and asked his advice.

"I'll tell you what," he answered. "They always play Bach. But you play something older—say, Buxtehude. When Bach was a young man, he walked all the way to the next town to hear him. For some people his music will be a novelty—even at the Petersburg Conservatory."

"Did Buxtehude write any piano pieces?"

"He wrote pieces for organ. You can transcribe one for piano. The transcription won't involve much work, and the piece will be fresh and not threadbare."

Without saying a word to Winkler, I went to the Jurgenson music store and bought a few albums of Buxtehude's organ pieces. I chose one and transcribed it for piano without any trouble.

"What's that?" Winkler asked, when I played it at the lesson.

I told him, not forgetting to mention that Taneyev had suggested it.

Winkler smiled, "Well, go ahead and play it. The examiners will be interested to hear it."

For my other piece he gave me Tchaikovsky's very lively *Scherzo à la russe* —one of his early opuses. I don't remember in detail how the exam went, but I got an A and was moved up to the advanced class.[130]

This is perhaps a good place to note that the Buxtehude fugue in question was not the one I transcribed fifteen years later to play at my American concerts, which was published.[131] At that time I simply recalled the composer that Taneyev had recommended to me, of whom I had a pleasant memory. And since in America the audiences were getting tired of programs consisting entirely of my own works and demanded that part of the program be devoted to classics, I preferred to choose classics that would at the same time be novelties—if only because of their decrepitude.

79

The next exams were in orchestration. Those of us who had spent two years with Rimsky-Korsakov felt we were skilled in the art of orchestration. Relatively skilled, I should add. For the exam, they gave each of us something selected from a batch of piano pieces, relatively new and little known to us. I got Grieg's *Humoresque* in D major—a piece that was not very well known.[132] Moreover, it was a motley work, and one that didn't much call for orchestration. In a word, it was not Grieg's best. It began more or less as follows:

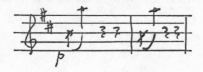

No matter how hard I tried, I couldn't imagine how it should be done. I went to consult Kankarovich, who was doing his orchestration problem in the next classroom.

"Well, it could be done in various ways," he said, displaying good taste. "For example, you could give the first bar to the first violins, and the second to the second violins. You must realize, you'll be conducting to the left for the first bar, and to the right for the second." (Kankarovich viewed everything from the conductor's standpoint.) "And the triangle should be struck in every bar. It rings out, and the sound is prolonged, as with the pedal on a piano."

I thanked him and went back to my classroom. I can't say, though, that his advice helped me. I dragged my way through the whole piece: it was like hauling a cart uphill.

The oral exam on orchestration was held the next day, with Lyadov and someone else presiding.

"Tell us, for instance, about kettledrums," Lyadov said.

I liked the question. I told how kettledrums were made (like big kettles with skin stretched over them), and how they are tuned. I went on to say that in the days of Haydn and Mozart the orchestra usually had two kettledrums tuned to the tonic and dominant, but that today three or even four are used. That they are divided into low ones, from F to B, and high ones from C to F; and that Rimsky-Korsakov had even introduced a little one. Also, that a tremolo is often written for them as a trill, but it amounted to the same thing; that a kettledrum could be retuned while a piece was being played, but you had to allow time for that, and the interval should not be a big one, etc.

Lyadov praised me, and after asking a few more questions (about the clarinet and bassoon, I believe), he dismissed me.

I don't remember what mark I got—a B or B+, as I recall. But on the written work of the day before I got a C. That really wasn't important, however: I might have failed. I was saved by the yearly grade on classroom work from Rimsky-Korsakov. He gave all of us B's. His comment on both me and Zakharov was: "Capable, diligent." On Miaskovsky: "Rather capable, very attentive, diligent." On Asafyev: "Capable, sluggish, fairly diligent."

Thus when they totaled up the yearly grade on classroom work, the oral answers, and the written exam, they found it possible to give me a B, and I passed the orchestration course. But it wasn't until five or six years later, when I was composing one orchestral piece every year, that I learned to score decently. Although I was sincerely fond of Rimsky-Korsakov, I was not able at that time to take advantage of the splendid knowledge emanating from him.

80

The last exam was in fugue. It was May, and already warm outside. But they shut us up in separate rooms, gave us a theme from Handel's *Messiah* and told each of us to write a four-voice fugue on it.

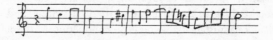

What had me worried the most was that Lyadov was always criticizing us for a lack of style in our fugues. I thought to myself: Maybe if I try, in my fugue, to use several sequences within the same scale that I'm in—that is, the kind of sequences where the repetition occurs in the same key but merely on a different scale degree—I can give it a more antiquated flavor and hence more style."

Miaskovsky had promised that, if he finished ahead of me, he would visit me in my classroom and see how I was making out. Visits of this kind were not strictly legitimate, but the professors didn't make much fuss about them. When I was just about through, he showed up.

"There is a story about Mozart," he said. "They say that when he was writing his examination fugue, he knocked way ahead of time on the door of the room in which he had been shut up. The people standing guard thought he needed something, but it turned out that he had already finished. That's facility!"

Miaskovsky took a cursory look at my fugue and, finding that everything seemed to be in order, wished me luck and left. It was already rather late, but I ate the sandwich I had brought from home and went on working for another hour and a half. Finally I brought the completed fugue to the deputy inspector on duty.

I can't say that the fugue was written very convincingly, but only a very few mistakes were found in it. The last five bars were as follows:

The deputy inspector took the manuscript[133] and said, "Come back in a day or two for the results."

I gasped, "But I'm leaving for the Caucasus tomorrow!"

"Oof! What are we going to do? Well, all right, we'll write you."

"Do you think I'd go away without knowing whether I'd passed?"

"I see what you mean. In that case, I'll show your fugue to Glazunov tomorrow morning. If he looks it over, he'll no doubt tell you how you made out."

When I came back the next morning, I found Glazunov sitting in his armchair with my manuscipt in his hands. One of the instructors in theory of composition was hovering nearby.

"Your fugue is written quite properly," Glazunov said. "If you want, I can even tell you your mark: it's B+."

"Thank you, Alexander Konstantinovich. So I can leave with my mind at ease?"

"Of course," he said with a smile.

When we had chatted a bit about the course in form that I was to take the following autumn, I took my leave of him and raced home, since my mother was literally sitting on our assembled baggage.

At this point I would like to say a few words about my *Sonata* in C minor, No. 5 in the numbering system I employed in my youth, which was reworked into *No. 4*, Opus 29. I have preserved no indications as to when it was "first" composed. It was only when I reworked it into *Sonata No. 4* (Opus 29) that I noted the year of composition: 1917 (1908); that is, the first version in 1908 and the second in 1917. It can hardly have been written in the fall of 1908, since at that time I was busy composing examples of musical forms for Wihtol,* including the *Sonata* in E minor (No. 6). Nor was it likely that it was written in the summer, since I was then working on my *Symphony* in E minor. Hence it must have been composed in the first half of 1908.

That sonata was written more seriously and—if one may so express it— more thoughtfully than its predecessor, No. 4 (old numbering). There was less seeking after novelty in it, but it was more concentrated. When I reconstructed it nine years later, the first movement and the Finale were but slightly reworked. Some parts of the Andante were discarded and replaced by others, but of that more later. At the time of which I am writing—that is, the first part of 1908—I had by no means finished it, although I had written quite a bit of it. No doubt the exams interfered and besides, I was preoccupied with the idea of writing a symphony.

Miaskovsky and I agreed that each of us would write a symphony during the summer and this became a goal of which we never lost sight.

81

Olga Smetskaya continued the friendship she had first struck up with my mother back in their high school days, and often invited her to come and stay at the Smetsky estate on the shore of the Black Sea, near Sukhumi. Weary of the cold in stern forests of their Kostroma estate, the Smetskys had gone to the sunny Black Sea area, bought a large tract of land, built a house, and settled there in the south. That had happened fifteen years before, when the Black Sea littoral was still rather wild, and you had to root out tenacious bushes before planting your own greenery. This proved to be just the right hobby for Smetsky,

* Joseph Ivanovich Wihtol (1863–1948), Latvian composer. Started teaching at the St. Petersburg Conservatory in 1886 and founded the Latvian Conservatory in Riga in 1919. (Translator's note.)

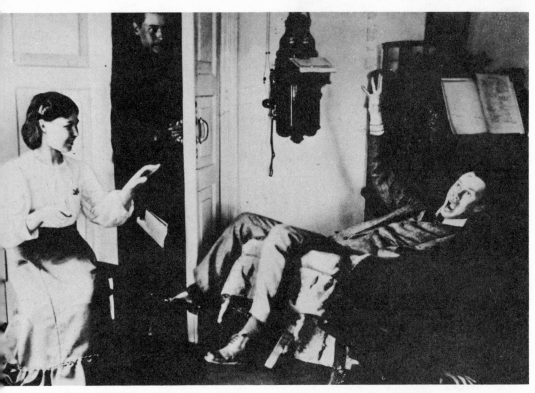

From the series "Dramatic Situations"—scenes posed and photographed at the Rebergs' when I was sixteen or seventeen.

A photograph taken at Golitsynovka (near Sontsovka) at Dr. Reberg's home in 1908 or 1909. Two photographs were taken, one from behind, one from in front; they were then cut out and pasted together. (Front view seen here.)

Vera Alpers with her mother, 1908.

"Miaskovsky showed up at the Conservatory in the uniform of a lieutenant in a battalion of engineers."

Glazunov with Irena Eneri.

"At the time, Medtner was a young Moscow composer . . . I bought the sheet music. The Fairy Tales did in fact turn out to be splendid."

"Of all my teachers, Tcherepnin was the liveliest and most interesting musician. . . ."

"Anna Esipova, the famous pianist, was considered the best teacher at the Conservatory."

Josef Hofmann.

Max Reger.

The influential critic Vyacheslav Karatygin.

Felix Blumenfeld.

Hugo Warlich, conductor of the Court Orchestra.

Alexander Scriabin.

Richard Strauss.

Ida Rubinstein.
Portrait by V. Serov.

Ivan Ershov in the role of Siegfried.

a man who was wealthy, childless, and idle. Taking advantage of the warm climate, he began to send for seedling trees from all parts of the world: rare kinds of eucalyptus came from Australia, and palms, agaves, and cacti from South America. By the time we arrived the hills around the house were covered with wild beauties that had gained in both height and breadth.

My mother, busy in recent years with shuttling between Sontsovka and Petersburg, and getting settled in the city, had not been able to plan a trip to Sukhumi. But this May she had decided to spend a month with her friend Olechka (Olga) before going to Sontsovka—all the more so, since the latter, very fond of music, had asked her to bring both me and Aunt Tanya, whom she had known since girlhood.

So it was that on June 1, as soon as I had wrapped up my affairs at the Conservatory and Aunt Tanya's vacation had begun, we set out in fine spirits. We had to take the train via Moscow and Voronezh to Novorossisk, then travel by steamer to Sukhumi. At Sukhumi, which we reached in the evening, we were met by Olga Smetskaya in a barouche. The south, the June night, the dark sea, the marvelous scent of the southern trees and plants, and the brightly lit port— all this was delicious.

The Smetsky estate, located about one and a half kilometers south of the city, extended to the very seashore. At first it followed a flat stretch of beach. Then, abruptly, came a low hill, on top of which stood the rather elegantly built house to which we were going. The second house—the gardener's—was situated farther down the hill. After the Revolution, when the Smetskys' estate had become government property, they were allowed to keep that house for the rest of their lives as a reward for having beautified the region. Since they had had a good gardener to take care of their palms and eucalypti, and had seen to it that he had a decent house, they themselves later profited from this indirectly.

En route to the Caucasus I sent Miaskovsky a letter I wrote on the train. It was rather sloppily written, since the train was lurching, and the paper was lurching, and I was lurching and leaping for joy because of the successful exams and the interesting trip to a new kind of country.

82

Zverevo Station
May 20, 1908.

Dear Nikolai Yakovlevich:

I'm very sorry things worked out so that we didn't see each other again and parted God knows how.

I can't tell you anything in particular about the exams, since after I had requested it they relented and graded my fugue ahead of time, whereupon I immediately headed for the train. I know only my own marks, but that's not enough for me. I'm very, very sorry to say that I can't tell you what marks Saminsky got. Don't fail to send me your compositions (by registered parcel). For my part, I won't hold things up. I have come up with a theme for my symphony. [The first theme of the Andante.] How is yours? Make sure you write *it*, rather than that vile quartet. [At that time I loved symphonies and sonatas and was rather cool toward quartets.] I wish you all the best. I'll expect a letter at Sukhumi. And once again, dear Nikolai Yakovlevich, I apologize for not being able to tell you what marks Saminsky got.[134]

These remarks about Lazar Saminsky were due to the still-unfriendly relations between him and me, which in turn were due to jealousy as regarded Miaskovsky.

On one occasion when Saminsky and I went to a crowded rehearsal in the Big Auditorium, we both noticed at the same time that Miaskovsky was in the audience, sitting in the middle of the auditorium, and that the seat next to him was empty. Grasping the situation, we both headed for that seat, Saminsky going down one aisle and I down another. As it happened, Miaskovsky was sitting midway between the two aisles. When we reached the row he was sitting in, we went along it toward each other, approaching the empty seat. Since it was on my side, and Saminsky could not get to it without squeezing past Miaskovsky, I naïvely supposed that Miaskovsky would block Lazar's way, if only by putting out a foot in jest. But Miaskovsky just sat there like a graven image and Saminsky, hopping over his feet, plumped down in the empty seat. But I lost no time and plumped into it from the other direction, so that the two of us sat down together.

Enraged, I dug my nails into my rival's hand. Lazar howled and began to "unscrew my hand." At this point the symphony that was being played went from *forte* to *piano*. People in the audience began to look around and hiss—especially at Saminsky, who was uttering sharp little wails. Finally he jumped out of the seat and, stumbling over people's outstretched legs, hurried along the row of seats and out of the auditorium.

Forty years later Miaskovsky told my wife of this incident, saying that he remembered every detail of it. Gradually I reconstructed the details from his account.

My second letter to Miaskovsky was from Sukhumi.

Sukhumi, May 31, 1908.
Much-Adored Nikolai Yakovlevich:

According to the scanty information I have had from Petersburg, you got an A and I got a B+. In general, it seems that our whole class distinguished itself and did beautifully in the exams. As for the course in forms, I tried to get a hint out of Glazunov; but he said rather categorically that now, having completed fugue, we would go on to forms, which would be taught in great detail. I knew that before. But apparently one still has to go through it.

How is your health? You say you're freezing? Here it's hellishly hot, so that we have to stay in the house all day. Like you, I'm doing nothing, except greatly enjoying learning Korsakov's concerto—spending up to two hours a day on it. They have a splendid Bechstein here. It's very good for playing Wagner, but I just can't compose on it—Lord only knows why. So I have put off writing the symphony until fall, even though I very much want to compose.

You are doing the right thing in lightening your sonatas, but please send something. Don't be a *fortepyashek**—send an art song.[135]

In temporarily digressing from my correspondence with Miaskovsky, I should like to tack on at this point a few fragments of the letters I wrote to Morolev that spring. In those letters I had begun to be a bit rude on occasion, and he replied with dignity that he was organizing a whole concert at Nikopol, having learned a series of pieces, including the waltz from *Onegin* as arranged by somebody-or-other. To this I responded indignantly that his next concert was apparently going to be "an evening of dancing." Morolev sometimes used the salutation "Dear Senor," to which I would reply, "Dear Mandarin," having in mind a Chinese mandarin; then, in the next letter, "Charming Fruit," having in mind the mandarin (tangerine) as a fruit.[136]

83

At the Smetskys' I was given my own room in the upper house. It had high ceilings, comfortable furniture, and several copies of pictures and works of sculpture that the Smetskys had brought from abroad. When I first came into the room I noticed two naked Venuses by different sculptors, and saw a small revolver on the night table.

"Do you know how to shoot?" came Olga's voice from behind me. "This is not a quiet part of the country, and it's better to have a revolver by your bed. But don't let it worry you too much. Nikolai is an excellent watchman. He patrols the grounds with a double-barreled shotgun, and once he almost fired it when some savage tried to climb the fence. Later you can look at the revolver, if you'll do it cautiously. It has a safety catch: learn how to use it. The most shameful thing is to sleep so soundly that you don't wake up in time and get killed with your own revolver."

When she had left I gingerly picked up the revolver, aimed it at the wall, and clicked the safety catch off and then on again. I was proud to have a real weapon.

But Aunt Tanya sounded the alarm. "Marie," she complained to my

* An apparently untranslatable coinage based on *fortepyanist*—pianist. (Translator's note.)

mother, "a person just can't get any sleep here. They gave Serezha a revolver, and he'll just shoot all of us. For that matter, he doesn't know how to shoot."

Olga spoke up, trying to reassure her guest. "We have special wires running throughout the house. If you look you'll see that in every room—by the bed in your room, for instance—there is a special switch. If you pull it, you will immediately hear a deafening sound ring out in both this house and the lower one. And of course all the watchmen will show up, because they know it's an alarm."

One of the guests who had come that day said, "Very interesting!" He looked closely at the switch and reached out a hand toward it.

"Careful! Don't touch it!" Olga shouted. But he paid no attention to his hostess and pulled the switch.

"Oh my God!" she screamed, beside herself.

The guest turned and gave her a smile. Everything was quiet. There was no alarm. For a time, no one said anything.

"It's been five years since the electricity was installed," Olga finally said, in some embarrassment.

"Then it's a good thing I checked the equipment," the guest said.

We spent three or four weeks with the Smetskys, but there was no more talk of an attack by bandits. Smetsky himself, a gray-haired, pink-cheeked old man with very youthful looks (in general, I don't like it when people of fifty of fifty-five are called "old men," as in Turgenev, for example), would spend the whole day hopping about on the hillside, where he had his plantings.

Smetsky loved to make puns. "Careful!" he would say. "Don't go outside at sunset—the house painter (*maylar*) is in the bushes."

This meant one could catch malaria, which was still endemic in uncleared regions but was supposed to disappear when new shrubs were planted.

Another time, when someone asked if there was a doctor in Sukhumi, Smetsky replied seriously, "There are three doctors: Dr. Zhivotsky, Dr. Bryukhanov, and Dr. Puzinelli."*

Everyone laughed, because no one could imagine there was a Dr. Puzinelli in Sukhumi. Later I found out that Dr. Puzinelli actually existed. He lived, however, not in Sukhumi but in Germany, where he was known for his published correspondence with Wagner.

The Smetskys took us to the neighboring estate, which they had also bought, and where they were building a tuberculosis sanatorium. Olga said, "Kukula [i.e., Smetsky] plans to build a series of sanatoriums. That one there, which we call Gulripsh, has already gone into operation. Another one, Agudzery, is being built over there and the next one is in the planning stage."

Gulripsh was attractive—especially in the undeveloped area of Sukhumi. Later Smetsky gave all three sanatoriums to the city of Moscow, expressing the

* The pun involves three words meaning "belly": *zhivot, bryukho,* and *puzo.* (Translator's note.)

wish that they be used chiefly for ailing schoolteachers. After the Revolution, in recognition of his gesture, he and Olga were given government pensions. Their park, now maintained by the municipality, was used for botanical field trips. And Gulripsh appeared on postage stamps in 1948.

We had scarcely returned to the dacha when an automobile came up the drive. Autos were a rarity in Russia in 1908, and even more so in Sukhumi. A rather well-built man of about fifty hopped out of the car. This was the Smetskys' neighbor, Myatelev, a wealthy landowner. With him was a pretty young woman. As Olga explained later, she was a rather well-known violinist, née Prokopovich, who had given up concertizing when she married Myatelev.

"Serezha," Olga asked me, "do you read music well?"

"Not badly," I answered, sure of myself.

At this she began entreating Mme. Myateleva to play a concerto, with me accompanying her.

"I don't have my violin with me," the latter said. "But if you'll come to our house, I'll be glad to play."

The next day we went to the Myatelevs'. I don't remember whose concerto she chose—something by a composer of violin pieces, and rather complex. She played with considerable brilliance but paid little attention to the accompaniment. Although I didn't know the music, I was able to follow her during the first two movements. But in the Finale she rushed ahead like a whirlwind, no longer paying any attention to the ensemble. I scarcely managed to turn the pages, I would skip bars, lose her for a time, and then catch up with her again. But we did hit the last chord together.

Our listeners applauded. Smetsky said—using his favorite expression—that it was "fabulous."

Back at the Smetskys' house, Olga said, "Myatelikha played brilliantly, but Serezha's accompaniment was rather mediocre."

It was characteristic of her to express herself directly and frankly. But she never noticed that "Myatelikha" had not followed the accompaniment.

A few days later we went by carriage to Navy Afon, located about twenty kilometers north of Sukhumi. The monastery stood on a steep hill on the very edge of the Black Sea, and offered a view of the sea that was marvelous. The monastery buildings themselves looked less like a holy place than a tourist attraction.

At seventeen I was far from religion. I was busy reading some German poetry with great relish when the others, somewhat embarrassed by my behavior, pointed out the buildings and the view.

Another trip we made was through a gorge in the interior in the direction of Klukhori Pass and Teberda. It was said that this was the place where the Venetians defeated Tamerlane in the fourteenth century. It seems more likely that they merely stopped one of his detachments, since the Klukhori Pass was apparently the only means of access to the Black Sea from the Northern Caucasus.

Ten years later I approached it from the north but didn't reach the summit—as, indeed, I did not on this occasion.

When I first saw this marvelous landscape, I noted in my diary that I was little attracted to nature, being more interested in people. But as we went farther the gorge, with its overhanging cliffs, made a strong impression on me, and I fell silent and began to daydream. It was only much later, though—at thirty-five or forty—that I became fond (really very fond) of nature and the countryside in general. I liked, for example, the crowing of roosters, the smell of smoke, the smell of horses mixed with that of shag tobacco, etc. But at seventeen I was in fact indifferent toward nature and the countryside.

84

About June 20, Aunt Tanya got ready to go back to Petersburg, because her vacation was nearly over. Mother was staying on with the Smetskys for a while. But since I was going to Sontsovka, she let me start off with Tanya. (Up to that time I had been considered a "little boy" and was not allowed to take dangerous trips on a train or steamship alone.) Tanya and I arrived safe and sound at Rostov, and there we parted company: she got on a train for Petersburg, and I got on another, which took me to Zhelannaya Station, twenty-three kilometers from Sontsovka. I was met at the station by our phaeton, drawn by four horses but looking very antiquated, and by the coachman, Ivan, who announced it was "hot as blazes." Then we set off along the very broad road that used to be called "the cowpath," as I later learned from my father, who had been waiting for me and pining away in his solitude.

A pall was cast over my first trip alone by the news of Rimsky-Korsakov's death. I had bought the St. Petersburg papers at the station, and in them I read of his funeral.[187] It made me very sad: my heart ached. I was very fond of Rimsky-Korsakov's music—especially *Kitezh, Sadko, The Snow Maiden,* the piano concerto, *Capriccio Espagnol, Scheherazade,* and *The Tale of Tsar Saltan.* As it happened, I never got to know him really well: there were lots of students in his class, and he never singled me out. The last time I saw him (in May, I believe) was at the Conservatory. He had just come back from Paris, where he had gone for a production of *The Snow Maiden,* as I recall.[188] He was standing with someone in the corridor and animatedly talking about something—no doubt the brilliant reception that had been accorded him in Paris. His face was radiant and handsome . . . yes, handsome. Or, more accurately, picturesque. In my diary I wrote: "I feasted my eyes on him and thought: 'There is a man who has achieved real success and fame!' "

Not long before that, Tcherepnin was saying, "When a French orchestra was rehearsing *Snow Maiden* in Paris (or perhaps it was Monte Carlo), the musicians were so delighted with the festive scene in the sacred wood, when Lel takes Kupava to Berendey and kisses her to the strains of a marvelous melody, that when it came time to play the melody again they suddenly put down their instruments and sang it. That was a really exciting moment."

I wanted to honor Rimsky-Korsakov's death by composing some kind of piece. That fall, as a matter of fact, Steinberg's* *In Memory of Rimsky-Korsakov* was performed at a Siloti concert, and pieces by Lyadov and (I believe) Glazunov were performed at Belyayev concerts. But all that was pallid and negligible. As I planned it, my piece would have a dramatic introduction, followed by Rimsky-Korsakov's gentle and charming theme from his *Tale of Tsar Saltan,* as though characterizing the man himself:

Then more dramatic music, leading into the funeral passage.
Not a bad plan, perhaps, but unfortunately, it was never carried out.

85

I came back to Sontsovka in the last part of June—that time of year when everything there was warm and green. After Petersburg and the Caucasus, Sontsovka was pleasant—all the more since this was my first summer without the drudgery of lessons in academic subjects. True, my father still gave me lessons in certain subjects—e.g., mathematics and history—because he felt they weren't adequately covered at the Conservatory. But I had plenty of time to get started on my symphony; i.e., to carry out the plan Miaskovsky and I had agreed on.

I abandoned *Undine.* It had been written over too long a period—a period when my idiom was gradually changing—and I didn't want to go on with it. Moreover, its lyrical elements were not appreciated by those who heard it. But the idea of writing a symphony struck me as completely fascinating—*a fortiori* since the form didn't frighten me: I had, after all, written quite a few sonatas by that time. When it came to orchestration, however, things weren't so good: I had gotten a C in the exam, and when I sat down to write an orchestral score I felt awkward.

But Tcherepnin had once told me, "You compose easily. Write an orchestral piece every year, and in a few years you will have mastered scoring, and at the same time you will have developed your own idiom. This will be more interesting than memorizing a tone on orchestrating by Gevaert, or even Rimsky-Korsakov, and getting into the habit of scoring *the way it is taught* instead of following your own ideas."

* Maximilian Oseyevich Steinberg (1883–1946), composer and teacher. (Translator's note.)

I can't say that I promptly followed that advice. But it stayed with me, and I did in effect proceed as Tcherepnin had suggested. I very much wanted to write pieces for orchestra, and it pained me that I couldn't deal with the orchestra easily.

I set to work on my symphony shortly after I got back to Sontsovka. The main theme and bridge passage were easy to compose. I had trouble with the subordinate theme, because I wanted to make it a bit more significant than usual. For the second movement—the Andante—I had material written in Petersburg that past spring.

At that point I was amazed by a letter I had from Miaskovsky. He had already written more than 100 pages of his orchestral score. Since he had gotten that far with his scoring, it meant that the music of his symphony was almost completely composed.

> From me to Miaskovsky.
> Sontsovka, June 27, 1908.

Dear Nikolai Yakovlevich:

You really flabbergasted me with your 120 pages. In the ten days that I have been here, I have got halfway through my subordinate theme. There's no hurry. I am composing slowly, as my heart wills—perhaps too lazily.

I am very saddened by your (as you put it) *Longueurs,* and the 120 pages. Really, what can be worse than a long symphony? In my opinion, the ideal length of a symphony is twenty minutes, or thirty at the most; and I am trying to make mine as compressed as possible. I am penciling out the slightest redundancies in the most ruthless manner.

I am writing as simply as possible. Probably the scoring, too, will be simple—a step backward in all respects [I was afraid of Glazunov]—but I am very satisfied. I am sending you bits of the main theme, the subordinate theme, and the bridge passage, all of which (I note) will be beneath all criticism in this version. So please play some of it and write me whether anything in it is stolen. . . .

I'm expecting all kinds of news from you.

> Yours,
> S. Prokofiev[139]

First movement, introduction:

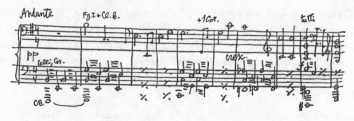

First movement, main theme:

First movement, bridge passage:

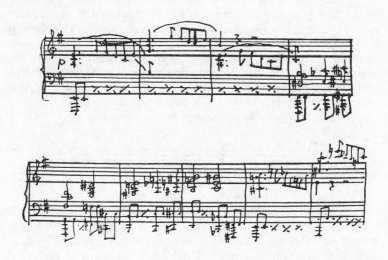

First movement, subordinate theme:

In subsequent work on the subordinate theme I added some two-voice counterpoint in quarter notes in the small octave.

From me to Miaskovsky.
Sontsovka, July 11 (24), 1908.

Dear Nikolai Yakovlevich:

I am very glad that you and I have a stimulating effect on each other. After getting your letters, I too am in better spirits for composing. Such was the case just now.

I congratulate you upon the completion of your first symphony, since by the time you get this letter you will have brought it to completion. [I was distressed and envious that he had gotten ahead of me.] Thanks for the little themes you sent me. The main theme of the Finale is very good—fresh and spirited. But the subordinate seems to ruin everything: from whatever angle you look at it, it is uninteresting throughout. If you change it you won't lose anything, since you couldn't compose worse no matter how hard you tried. The closing theme should sustain the mood.

You criticized my main theme in the violin sonata:

but you yourself (very successfully) wrote something of a similar character.

Now for the first movement. I still don't fully approve the serious main theme, although somehow it seems to me that I should like it. But the subordinate theme is very good. [I still think this is one of the best themes in Miaskovsky's symphonies.] *Throw out* the first closing theme: it is wretched. That's all I can say about it. The second closing theme is very good, but I don't understand why rhythmically it is a copy of the subordinate theme. In general, however, I am pleased. Just one thing, old chap: cut as much as possible! Really, it's boring when a symphony is long.

Now send me some bits from the middle—some with interesting harmonies, for example. Incidentally, the way you combined the themes in the Finale made me furious. Moderation in all things—after all, you're writing a symphony! It is pleasant when two themes are combined, as for instance in *Die Meistersinger*. But four themes! For whom is that? For Lyadov, maybe? I swear, it has a catastrophic effect on the beauty of the individual themes themselves, which is much more important than four bars or so that no one will understand or appreciate. Just remember the Finale of the *Seventh Symphony* [of Glazunov] that you love so much! [Irony: Miaskovsky felt it was too heavy.]

So much for that.

Send me a few more themes. I'm dissatisfied with my Finale. There's a good chance that I'll rewrite it from scratch, since it isn't finished yet. I have begun the reprise of the first movement. Although you write that the themes in the first movement are tasty, they are quite indigestible: they are heavy, inflexible, and don't fit into the development.

I often get despondent because of my symphony and then I can find encouragement only in your letters and the selfish thought that I might not finish the symphony by fall.

But never in my life will I again undertake such a thing!

> Your devoted
> S. Prokofiev[140]

I enclosed in that letter the themes of the symphony's second movement, the first of which was used in its entirety in my *Fourth Piano Sonata* (Opus 29), so that I am not quoting it here. Instead, I shall quote the subordinate theme of the first movement as it appears in the recapitulation:

From me to Miaskovsky.
Sontsovka, August 4 (17), 1908.

Dear Nikolai Yakovlevich:

Forgive my brevity, but if I don't write you now I won't manage it for a whole week.

The fact that you are in such miserably low spirits after writing your symphony makes me very sad. If it really is as you describe it, I suppose there is good reason for being horrified. But it doesn't make sense that a person capable of writing very fine things should, for his debut (so to speak), produce "a barren wasteland" [a quote from Miaskovsky's letter]. Even supposing that I don't believe you—you have a trait that is the opposite of Wagner: that of always being dissatisfied with yourself (if it isn't coquetry)—I do not approve of you and am not pleased with you.

I am getting toward the end of my symphony. The fourth movement has been orchestrated. I am sending along some themes.

The Finale is amazingly laconic:

Main theme – 13 bars.
Bridge passage – 10.
Subordinate theme – 20.
Closing theme – 8.

But it will have a coda of decent length which will comprise themes from all the movements.

I very much like the first theme of [my] second movement: it is by no means cold, although somewhat solemn in character.[141]

From me to Miaskovsky.
Sontsovka, August 12 (25), 1908.

Dear Nikolai Yakovlevich:

[I have received] your letter of August 7, and was terribly moved by your concern for my offspring. I have no intention of abandoning it, and will of course complete it by fall. All the themes have now been composed. I now have to finish up the reprise and the coda in the Finale, and complete and score the second movement. I have just now struggled with, and vanquished, a passage where five or six themes are woven into one. The Devil only knows how I combined them: there is no contrapuntal skill involved. But that's why what is built against the background of an expanded second closing theme sounds so animated.

They say you are horrified at the thought that I'll be a composer of piano music. You can stop worrying. I was upset by the symphony because it's boring to write a long piece of absolute music if you like program music. [Later my opinion changed.] That's all there is to it. And now that my darling is almost finished, I have ceased getting angry at her.

In the matter of showing our symphonies to people, you amaze me with your question about Lyadov. You want to know how we are going to show them to him? Very simple. We'll carry them with us, and when we meet up with Lyadov somewhere in the corridor, we'll say, "Look here, we've written these. . . . Would you please let us show them to you? . . ." And he will be pleasantly surprised.

Your Largo did not put me in a rage: I liked it very much. It merely induces a gentle melancholy which would be even better if it were free—if it were not encumbered by the shackles Lyadov managed to put on you.

[A continuation of the attack in the letter of July 11 on Miaskovsky's attempts to build his themes so that they could be combined.][142]

Finale, main theme:

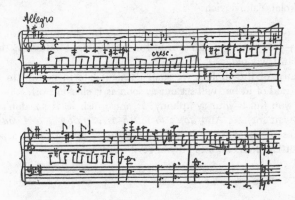

Finale, bridge passage:

Finale, subordinate theme:

On September 15, 1908, I completed the score of my symphony. The day before, I had written in my diary:

> Yet one more page—the last—
> And my symphony will be complete.*

That page had a pleasing, lacy look. But when I heard it later, it didn't sound as finely wrought as I had imagined it to be.

From me to Miaskovsky.
Sontsovka, September 15, 1908.

Dear Nikolai Yakovlevich:

Today I completed my symphony. It came out to 131 pages (57+19+55), with enough music for twenty-eight minutes; that is a bit longer than I wanted.

Because of the cholera we shall be a bit late in getting to Petersburg. We are afraid of it, but will set out as soon as it slackens off.

Did you finish your symphony: If not, finish it. If so, don't show it to anyone—wait for me. And *don't so much as mention it to Lyadov,* because there's no sense in showing it to him. Glazunov may arrange a performance for us. But Lyadov? . . . He'll just revile us.[143]

86

In any case, I was glad I had finished the symphony. I had labeled "First Symphony" the other one (in G major) that I had written six years earlier, under Glière's supervision. But I didn't call the new one my "Second Symphony" since I had obviously moved into a completely different phase of creativity and was using a different idiom. On the other hand two "first symphonies" wouldn't sound right, so I simply called it "Symphony."

In addition to the symphony—while scoring it—I wrote some piano music: two rather stormy pieces. One of them, that fall, was given the title *Despair,* at the suggestion of Nouvell and Karatygin, since in their opinion that was precisely the title and piece called for. While I was playing the other, Nouvell jumped up and shouted, "That's a kind of diabolical suggestion [*navazhdeniye*]!"

And so it was called *Navazhdeniye*[144]—but not without a rather long discussion as to whether the word should be spelled *navazheniye* or *navozhdeniye.* It seemed natural to spell it with an "o," but we found that Dostoyevsky had written it with an "a." Also, Nouvell had found out somewhere that this word

---

* A paraphrase of the first lines spoken by Father Pimen (the scene in the monastery cell) in Pushkin's *Boris Godunov.* (Translator's note.)

was derived from the old verb *vaditi*,* the root of both *navazhdeniye* and *povadka*.† Thus *Navazhdeniye* was inscribed on the manuscript as a title that sounded good and looked more original. But then it turned out that as a typically Russian word it was not translatable into French. We had to have something diabolical, since such had become the mode in piano literature after Liszt's *Mephisto Waltz* and Scriabin's *Poème satanique,* so we finally called it *Suggestion diabolique.*

By way of concluding my account of that summer at Sontsovka I should say a few words about what was happening around me.

My childhood friends had grown up and gone off to nearby towns and villages. The only one left was Serezha Vlasov—he of the big head, with whom I had walked on stilts to the neighbor's orchard and back. All in all, we covered a distance of three kilometers, which is not easy when you're walking on stilts. When I noticed that he was courting a pretty Ukrainian girl named Grunya, I began to ask him sly questions about her. (Grunya had huge, wide-set eyes and a beautiful complexion.) But he remained sullenly silent, not telling me anything so I decided not to plague him with questions.

At home I read all six of Turgenev's novels in a row, and my reaction to them was rather indifferent. I like *Fathers and Sons* the best, but I was irritated by the overly detailed descriptions of the death from blood poisoning. I also read several novels by Scheller-Mikhailov,‡ but for the most part they put me to sleep.

Sontsov's older son came to visit us, and for some reason tried to belittle me. But my experience in Petersburg, and my association with older classmates at the Conservatory, prompted me to respond in the same manner. I did this so often and so pertly that my father had to take me aside unobtrusively and tell me, "You shouldn't talk back to him like that. After all, he's your senior in years."

"In years" but not "in status." I appreciated my father's motives, however, and the gentle tone he used with me. Sontsov's son was in fact twice as old as I. So from then on I used a more polite and indifferent one, and he did likewise.

At about that time his father, by now an old man, divided the estate into three equal parts: one for himself, and two for his sons. The younger son, who was a vice-governor somewhere, had decided to sell his share, and had entrusted my father with the negotiations. The older son had at one time served in a regiment of the Guards but was now doing nothing. He wanted to increase his income, and hence he started coming to Sontsovka from time to time to talk with my father about such things as whether it was advisable to buy a steam-powered plow—an expensive implement but one that undoubtedly plowed better and

* To entice. (Translator's note.)
† Habit. (Translator's note.)
‡ Alexander Konstantinovich Scheller (1838–1900). His more or less radical "purpose" novels were written under the pen name of A. Mikhailov. (Translator's note.)

faster that one could plow with oxen. He and Father would hole up in the latter's study and talk there for hours.

In the evening my father and mother would sit side by side on the sofa in the drawing room. Once I heard my mother ask him if he ever thought about death.

"Of course I think about it," Father replied. "But I'm used to it, and more or less undisturbed by it."

Both were atheists, but my father was probably more serene in these matters than my mother.

She said, "If I should die, don't remain alone."

An on another occasion, I heard her say, "I don't like the dawn. For me it is always associated with some kind of anxiety: either someone is dangerously ill, or people are getting ready for a long trip, but the train leaves early. . . ."

My mother often had headaches and I remember that as a child I often saw her with leeches on her temples. . . .

In September we went back to Petersburg. It is clear with the passing years that my relations with Sontsovka were fading. Or rather, I was losing my interest in it.

Petersburg was gradually claiming me—because of both friends and music. At that age I was still indifferent to nature, although I must say that a summer in Sontsovka offered many marvelous things. But Morolev had left, and my childhood friends had flown off in different directions, like flocks of sparrows.

87

When we came back to Petersburg in September 1908, I was concerned with two important things as regards music. First, to show my symphony to Glazunov and entreat him to have it "tried out" by an orchestra. A "tryout" was a special expression, and it had a magical sound. And why shouldn't it be?

What a joy for a young composer to hear an orchestra play his own piece, even if it was not accepted for public performance. The second matter was the course in musical forms we were going to take. We had finally mastered the harmony, fugue, and counterpoint we had been studying up until then, and were to go into free composition. Previously the second half of the composition curriculum—three years of "free composition"—had complemented the three years spent on theory proper; i.e., harmony, counterpoint, and fugue. But now the composers were being divided into two groups. First, the "composing composers." (For these students there was a professor who might work with them to some good purpose and teach them something.) Second, those who did not compose or who composed in such a way that you couldn't teach them anything. We were so regarded by Lyadov, who that year was taking over the course in free composition.

I nonetheless felt it necessary to have a persuasive talk with Lyadov, entreating him to take me into his class in free composition.

"But what would I be able to teach you?" he asked. "With the kind of things you write, if I did give you any advice, it wouldn't lead to anything anyway."

"In other words, you think I'm on the wrong track. But that's just why I need help to get off it and onto the right track, instead of being told, 'You've got off the track, so go away.'"

I was very pleased I had thought up that argument. It seemed to overcome all Lyadov's objections.

He held out for a while longer and finally said, "Well, let's try a few lessons. But I'm convinced nothing will come of it."

We had two lessons, and then Lyadov "got sick." That is, he missed a lesson or two under that plausible excuse, after which the lessons somehow stopped of themselves. I no longer insisted—all the more so since I had already started taking classes with Wihtol, who was teaching form.

Joseph Wihtol was a rather well-known Latvian composer who had become a friend of Glazunov and Lyadov and followed their school. He had a broad, kindly-looking face with a reddish-blond beard, and a deeply receding hairline. Instead of a necktie he wore a white scarf—apparently in order to give himself an artistic look.

Wihtol rarely explained the forms themselves, and sometimes he didn't explain anything.

88

When Miaskovsky finished his symphony (he had first written the score in pencil and then gone over it in ink), he didn't wait for me to arrive from Sontsovka but went ahead and showed it to Glazunov. Glazunov liked it, and suggested that Miaskovsky come to see him a couple of times so that he could get to know the symphony better and offer whatever advice about it seemed desirable.

At first I felt that I had been offended by Miaskovsky. The two of us had thought up the idea of writing a symphony apiece. We had written them over the same period of time, although at opposite ends of the earth, and throughout that period had shared our impressions and themes. Then suddenly, as we reached the finish line, Miaskovsky had gone ahead and shown his symphony to Glazunov without waiting for me to get back to Petersburg.

Miaskovsky argued, "What do you want of me? You will play your symphony beautifully, but I'll stumble through mine at best. You have a great advantage. And in order to have an even chance, with you, I had to play mine before you got here from Sontsovka—all the more so since before the start of the term Glazunov has more free time and can pay closer attention."

I was not completely satisfied with his explanation (the fact remained that it had destroyed my summer illusions), but I dropped all further discussion of the subject and started trying to wheedle Glazunov into letting me show him my score. A little note that I wrote to Miaskovsky has been preserved: "I waited 29 minutes for you. You stayed a horribly long time at Glazunov's. I wanted to find out how you fared, and talk about how I would." (That is, how Glazunov had received Miaskovsky, and what I should do so that Glazunov would receive me.)[145]

At that time, telephones were little used in Petersburg. I took my score and went to Glazunov's home behind the Kazan Cathedral. I was told that he was not there. When I went back the next day, I was told he was at his country place. Then I went back a third time. In a word, I was stubborn and importunate.

Finally, I managed to see him. I asked him politely and respectfully if he would look over my score and give me advice. Actually, what I wanted was not so much his advice as his help in getting my symphony played by an orchestra. But I didn't tell him that at first. He gave me an appointment, and a few days later I went to his home with my score.

He sat down at the piano with me, and went over the score carefully, in two sessions. Right off, he expressed amazement at a chord in the introduction:

"It's rather harsh," he muttered.

I can't say that he made many comments. Also, since I am writing this forty years later, I can't remember all of them. Apropos of the Finale, written in 12/8 time, he made the following practical comment. "Since you are writing the basic division of your measure as ♩. , the corresponding rest should be written 𝄽 · that is, a quarter rest with a dot rather than with an eighth rest, (𝄽 𝄾). That will simplify your score and make for less strain on the eyes."

I liked that suggestion and have used it ever since.

I corrected other things in accordance with his suggestions, but I left unchanged the specimen quoted above. The C major with the F-sharp in the base struck me as pleasantly dramatic and not at all "harsh."

Toward the end of this talk with Glazunov I timidly brought up the most important thing: "Alexander Konstantinovich, what would you think of arranging . . . well, a tryout of my symphony? You realize how essential that is for a beginning composer."

As always in such cases, Glazunov muttered something unintelligible. "I'm thinking of that myself. But who could do it? The Sheremetyev Orchestra? The Court Orchestra? They're tied up with their work, and it's hard to get them interested in something from the outside."

This conversation as I was taking my leave of Glazunov lasted a rather long time but didn't get anywhere. Finally I realized it was time to leave, so I thanked him and went out, taking with me his promise—or better, his half promise, or crumb of a promise—that he would think about a performance.

In general, Glazunov's attitude toward me was changing. His interest in the boy whose parents he had persuaded to send their son to the Conservatory was giving way to an irritating impression produced by that adolescent who had grown into a young man and begun to compose very unseemly pieces. On one occasion when my mother saw Glazunov at a concert, she went up to him (after some hesitation) and asked him what he thought of her son's symphony.

He replied, "What can I tell you? It's written with verve, but there's a bit too much dissonance in places, and the orchestration is palish." (Glazunov was fond of words ending in "-ish.")

Justice had compelled Glazunov to mention the verve, and irrationality had compelled him to mention the dissonances.

For my part, after having first enjoyed Glazunov's symphonies, I was losing interest in his work. From that time on it seemed boring and not new, and his fame was fading. People ceased to expect anything much from him. That season, for example, he wrote the music for a production of Oscar Wilde's *Salomé*. It was produced by one Ida Rubinstein, a dilettante. She had the money for the production and wanted to act and in general be on the stage. Her looks were interesting: she was tall and thin, although not very pretty. Serov did a famous charcoal and chalk drawing of her on the kind of bright blue paper they used to wrap sugar in.

When the production of *Salomé* was banned because of the story, Glazunov decided to conduct the music he had composed for it at a Siloti concert. (Ida Rubinstein came to a rehearsal: tall, thin, in a big hat and a slinky black dress. Glazunov navigated up to her and kissed her hand.) But his music was pallid and worthless.

Glazunov's popularity was still great—not because of the music he was writing, however, but because of the great attention he devoted to students at the Conservatory. For instance, he would go to see the Public Prosecutor, Korsakov, to intervene for a student about to be expelled for revolutionary activity. Or he would request that a residence permit be issued to a talented Jew. (In those days, it was not every Jew who was granted a permit to reside in the capital.) Or again, he would contribute his director's salary to the scholarship fund. One anecdote had it that at a session of the arts council he asked that his salary as director be increased, citing all the kinds of work he had to do. Everybody understood that he wasn't requesting the increase for himself (he was wealthy, as it was) but to increase the scholarships for needy students, so the pay raise was granted.

89

As soon as I found out that Karatygin, Nurok, and Nouvell were resuming their Thursday gatherings at the Becker store, I went to see them to show them the things I had composed during the summer: the symphony in E minor and the piano pieces. They liked the piano pieces, accepting them as they had the pieces they had heard the spring before, but even more warmly. As I have already recounted, these "Modernists"* immediately thought up titles for them (*Despair* and *Suggestion diabolique*) and they included them in the program for my upcoming performance.

"We can already give you the date: it will be December 18."

"In the meantime," said Nurok, "don't forget to obtain permission from the Conservatory for a public performance."

"Is that necessary?"

"Without permission—and written permission at that—you can't perform."

Then I played the symphony. It was a disappointment for me: I was already so used to joyous exclamations of praise from Nurok and Nouvell that I was dismayed by the indifferent expressions on their faces after I had played the symphony.

"Well," said Nurok, "of course it's very nice—very smooth and neat. But it's not nearly so original as your piano pieces. Besides, they have so much fire and so much invention! But during the playing of the symphony one was rather inclined to doze off than to leap up from one's seat, as happened when we heard your piano pieces."

I was inwardly offended and I decided to make a notation—somewhere in a corner of my memory—to remind me to be wary of these "Modernists."

At the Conservatory I first went to see Glazunov to ask for written permission to perform my pieces under the auspices of the "Modernists." He gave me the authorization with complete indifference, and without even glancing at the music. He took no interest in the pieces, but he didn't want to put obstacles in the way of a young composer. And Wihtol had much the same attitude. So I was in very good spirits when I went to see Winkler. But as a scrupulous German, he told me, "Good. But first you'll have to play them for me. I'll make some suggestions as to how they should be played, and if they go off well, I'll give you the permission you're asking for."

* I.e., members, "Evenings of Contemporary (Modern) Music." (Translator's note.)

So I had to play them. But it was useful, since there were things about my execution that needed correcting before I performed. Winkler made a few comments. There were two times when he put on his pince-nez and told me to use the pedal, and two others when he advised me to learn the passage work better so I wouldn't hit any wrong notes. But in general he didn't condemn me for modernism, and at the end he gave his permission.

90

At about that time Miaskovsky's father, the Civil Service general, got a rather large government-owned apartment on the Sadovaga (No. 8), and moved there with his family from Suvorovsky Prospect. It was in the very center of the city and made it very easy for Miaskovsky and me to resume our practice of getting together to play four hands. For want of a telephone, we sent postcards to each other indicating where and when we would get together to make music, and what the program would be. I have preserved several of them, like the following one from me to Miaskovsky.[146]

> The fates have willed that tomorrow (Saturday), evening I will be free, at home, and entirely alone. Whether you can or not, please do not fail to come: I shall be infinitely happy.
> Bring:
> 1. Miaskovsky, *Quartet*.
> 2. Wagner, *Faust*.
> 3. Glazunov, V, and whatever else you want. [I. II. o8][147]
> Or:
> *Venez, mon cher, demain mercredi soir: nous jouerons le Reger, le Glasounoff (No. 6) et la symphonie domestique. Venez absolument. Serge.* *
> [I. III. 09][148]

As before, the Glazunov symphony was one of the pieces we played. But the glory of Glazunov's symphonies, and especially of his grand finales, had (as they said) "already ceased to resound" in his work. And if it was still resounding in certain homes, it was chiefly because of momentum or habit. Of course there was a certain kind of mastery in those finales (though rather academic) and a quasi-antiquated grand manner. But we young people were more attracted by (for example) Scriabin, with his poems and flights of fancy. No one (especially Miaskovsky) denied the sturdy quality of Glazunov's symphonies and their irreproachable counterpoint. But we wanted something new and unexpected— something that "took wing." So it was that at first we were interested in Glazunov and enjoyed playing four-hand arrangement of his music (it was so conveniently at one's fingertips). But finally, while Miaskovsky remained among

* In the original the French is in Russian transliteration. (Translator's note.)

his followers, I began to get irritated, seeing Glazunov's music as obsolescent and devoid of invention but music that was nonetheless taken as the creativity of a leading composer.

Our fellow-student Zakharov soon joined our ranks. He was a man of great charm and a decidedly good musician, although he lagged behind us in appreciating new music. He sight-read fluently, more "fluently" than either of us, although sometimes he lost his place; e.g., when we were playing Richard Strauss or Debussy.

His father was a big merchant dealing in wood, and had his own town house (not, it is true, in the center of the city). Boris had a comfortable room with a broad sofa on which one of us would loll while the other two were playing. The room had excellent acoustics for the new Steinway his father had recently given him because of his progress at the Conservatory. During breaks between symphonies tea would be served, and a servant would bring in a huge bowl of sandwiches.

Zakharov's favorite composer was Rachmaninov, and sometimes he would play us his *Second Concerto,* which he had learned at the Conservatory. Miaskovsky's favorite Rachmaninov piece was his *Second Symphony.*

"I recently bought a postcard with a photograph of Rachmaninov on it," he once said, shrugging his shoulders. "I looked and looked at it, unable to decide whether his face was that of a genius or a criminal. . . ."

It seemed to me that in Rachmaninov's music there were certain melodic turns typical of him that were extraordinarily beautiful. But all in all there weren't many of them and once they had been found, they were repeated in other works. As compared to Scriabin, he struck me as a composer who strove less for novelty and harmonic invention. Someone once said (rather venomously) of his melodies that they were mostly written for a voice with a very small range. And yet sometimes he managed to fit amazingly beautiful themes into that small range; for example, in his *Second Concerto.*

It was about the time of our evening of music-making that Miaskovsky resigned from the army and became an official in some elegant ministry. The minister himself was Taneyev: not the composer Taneyev whom we all knew but another Taneyev, also a composer, whom none of us knew. He was attached to the court, and Miaskovsky had to have a frock coat made for himself before he could be presented to this Taneyev.

Once when Zakharov and I went to Miaskovsky's, we found him with a headache. He explained that the evening before he had attended a farewell *souper* with his comrades-in arms. (I don't recall whether it was in honor of his own retirement or that of someone else.)

"And you drank?" asked Zakharov.

"We drank champagne."

"Did you drink a lot?" Zakharov persisted.

"Oh, about a bottle apiece."

Zakharov threw up his hands. "Good Lord, Nikolai Yakovlevich! You're turning out to be a drunkard!"

"Only rarely," Miaskovsky corrected him.

Actually, in later years too Miaskovsky always liked to drink a little in friendly company at a pleasant *souper*.

91

I liked very much going to Tcherepnin's conducting class. Here it gradually became clear that the practice of constantly studying scores and then working with the orchestra in preparing them for performance was not only useful in terms of conducting but a help to me in learning more about orchestration.

As Tcherepnin and I were sitting side by side with the score in front of us at one of those endless lessons, rehearsing the student orchestra, he would say, "Just listen to how marvelous the bassoon sounds right here!" And I gradually developed a taste for the scores of Haydn and Mozart: a taste for the bassoon playing staccato and the flute playing two octaves higher than the bassoon, etc. It was because of this that I conceived or thought up the *Classical Symphony,* although that was five or six years later.[149] Right here I should note that, although I didn't learn all that I should have about orchestration in Rimsky-Korsakov's class, I made up for it in Tcherepnin's class.

That year the so-called little student orchestra began to function. In the basic Conservatory orchestra, the so-called big orchestra, the students worked as an ensemble, performed at concerts and in operas, and then left the Conservatory and disappeared. Every year it was necessary to replenish the personnel of that orchestra. For that purpose it was desirable to have musicians who, although but slightly experienced, were not the kind who had no notion of how to play in an orchestra. It was in order to provide such musicians that the "little student orchestra" was formed. It included students who in some cases even played their instruments rather badly and had no notion of an ensemble or what a conductor was. In a year or two they would acquire a certain degree of skill and transfer to the "big orchestra." Also, those of us who had recently joined the conducting class were given the opportunity from the outset to work with the little orchestra, to make contact with orchestra musicians, and in general to learn how to "beat time."

A rather disturbing incident took place at the second or third lesson. One of the students who had just joined the orchestra played very badly and was quite unable to count measures or rest.

"Why are you coming in now?" shouted Tcherepnin, stopping the orchestra. "You have two more bars of rest. Draw glasses for yourself." ("Draw glasses for yourself" was an expression used by orchestral musicians. It meant circling in red pencil a passage when one did not play.)

They began the passage again, and again the young bassoonist came in early.

"The same passage over again!" shouted Tcherepnin.

This time the bassoon didn't come in at all. Tcherepnin came down from the podium. A hush reigned.

"Can you count bars?"

Silence.

Tcherepnin raised his voice. "What is your name? I'm asking you."

Silence. The student sitting next to the bassoonist stood up. "His name—if you will forgive the expression—is Parshin."*

Tcherepnin exploded and shouted furiously, "What do you mean, 'forgive the expression'? Everyone bears the name of the family into which he was born. Sergei Sergeyevich (he always addressed students in the conducting class by their first names and patronymics), sit down next to the bassoonists and count the bars for both of them!"

I quickly went over to the orchestra, sat down between the two bassoonists, and started counting measures of rest for them. Since I wasn't accustomed to this kind of situation, it wasn't really so easy. Furthermore, if in that situation I made a mistake I too would get a tongue-lashing. And there would be some jibes at the education (or lack of same) of conductors. Little by little, we got through the piece and in a half hour or so the class was over.

Tcherepnin called the watchman of the Small Auditorium (where the class met) and ordered, "Bring me a big cup of black coffee with lemon." Then, seeing that the watchman was amazed, he added, "Today the orchestra played so badly that I have a headache. And black coffee with lemon is the best thing for it."

I went up to Tcherepnin. "He can't play his instrument at all," he muttered, nodding toward the erring student.

I put in: "Tell him to practice counting up to twenty every night. Otherwise he'll never be able to count bars of rest."

92

After Tcherepnin's class that day I walked home with Kankarovich. He was talking constantly about a conductor's techniques. Sometimes he would stop in the middle of the street and make the gestures of a regular maestro, by way of explaining what he was saying. As he had done before, he declared, "Either I'll become a conductor, or I'll put a bullet in my head."

I said I did not intend to become a conductor, but that I would of course have to conduct my own works, which was why I was taking the course in conducting, although I hadn't yet figured out how to practice. Tcherepnin advised

* *Parsha* means "mange" or "scab." (Translator's note.)

us, "Practice at home." Or else, when he was in a good mood, he would say, "Get a cat and box its ears, acquiring the habit of making your blows sharp and rhythmic." But none of that helped much.

"If you want," said Kankarovich, "come to my place, and I'll gladly show you how I practice. Tcherepnin is always being dragged around by the ears by all kinds of mamas and aunties and friends, so his head spins. It's easy to see why he isn't always capable of teaching."

Kankarovich often repeated that remark.

Actually, Tcherepnin taught the musical aspect of his subject very well, but he was sometimes remiss when it came to the strictly technical aspect of conducting.

I thanked Kankarovich for the invitation, and the next day I showed up at his place at the appointed hour. He lived with his older brother in an apartment that seemed to me almost elegant. In his own room he had a music stand for conducting, which he promptly brought out. After choosing one baton from a collection of them, and giving me another, he struck a pose before the music stand.

"Now," he said, "first of all you have to feel that you're in rapport with the orchestra sitting around us. Without feeling that rapport, you won't be able to do anything as a conductor."

He worked with me for about an hour. He would have me stand behind the music stand and practice the most complex meters like 6/4 or 12/8. I felt it was very useful, and told him so as I left, thanking him for his "enlightened friendship."

I certainly don't mean to say, however, that Kankarovich's teaching was useful and Tcherepnin's wasn't. I learned a great deal from Tcherepnin but it was chiefly about music in general, on which subject he was much better than Kankarovich. Granted, it would have been more to one's liking if Tcherepnin had worked in greater detail with each of us, explaining techniques for dealing with the orchestra, etc. But his strictly musical explanations were always interesting.

I once met up with Tcherepnin at a rehearsal for a Siloti concert when they were playing the Brahms *Violin Concerto*. It was the first time I had heard the concerto, and I didn't think much of it.

Tcherepnin was amazed. "What? But you learned the Brahms *G minor Rhapsody* for a student recital[150] and told me that you liked Brahms's music."

"I liked the *Rhapsody*, but I know too little of 'Brahms's music' as such. Now as to the violin concerto. The harmony? Rather ordinary. The counterpoint? It's there in outline, but there is very little actual counterpoint. The orchestration? Interesting in places, but in general not vivid. Melody? Only rarely."

"You'll have to hear the concerto again, listening closely and following the score. Then you'll realize that this is absolutely pure music. You mustn't take it apart, screw by screw, and then examine each screw to see whether it is good or not. You must realize that this is music of crystalline purity that flows like a spring."

That explanation impressed me. I began to pay closer attention to Brahms, and gradually I came to like him precisely for the purity of his flowing music.

93

Some of my other interesting talks with Tcherepnin had to do with Tchaikovsky, in connection with a production of his *Eugene Onegin* at the Conservatory the year before.

"Turgenev was very fond of Tchaikovsky's music," he said. "But how he reviled him for the libretto of *Eugene Onegin*! In his opinion, Onegin himself was not characterized at all in the opera, which should have been called *Tatyana Larina* instead of *Eugene Onegin*. Nor was Lensky anything like the character Pushkin had created. In one rough draft Pushkin even called Lensky a "bawler," but Tchaikovsky makes him into something like strawberry jam! And that aria of Lensky's, with such feeling and seriousness! But in Pushkin's poem he is a kind of caricature of the confused poet of those times. ('So he wrote, obscurely and limply.')."*

"And Tatyana?" I asked.

"Tatyana is well realized, except for 'Let Me Perish,' which is more suitable for a music-hall singer than for a girl from a decent family."

After a certain lag in the conversation I came back to the subject, which had aroused my interest. "Also, that depiction of rustic life in the first scene is not very Russian."

"What don't you like about it?"

"Take the first four bars—the ones leading up to 'Have You Ever Heard?' They're from the first movement of Saint-Saëns' *Second Concerto* (where they introduce the reprise in that movement). They're even in the same key of G minor, and have the same tinge of melancholy."

"But did Saint-Saëns write that concerto before Tchaikovsky's *Onegin?*"

"Ten years before. I checked in the encyclopedia. And then after 'Have you Ever Heard?' when the ensemble sings 'Habit Is Given Us by Heaven'—that, too, is not very Russian but rather Italian. And then that scene where Tatyana visits Onegin's empty house. To my mind, that's the most poetic scene in Pushkin. But Tchaikovsky just left it out. . . ."

Later I came back to that idea more than once: I wanted to write the music for the scene in Onegin's empty house—in Tchaikovsky's vein, naturally.[151]

* The quote is from Pushkin's *Eugene Onegin,* and characterizes Lensky's farewell letter to Tatyana. It is this letter that serves as the basis for Lensky's (second) aria in Tchaikovsky's *Eugene Onegin.* (Translator's note.)

At the next lesson we talked about Tchaikovsky some more. Tcherepnin said, "Tchaikovsky's early work—the first two symphonies, *Cherevichki,* and some of *Eugene Onegin*—shows a remarkable line of development with some very enticing harmonies and melodies. Then, at the midpoint of his life, it began to disappear."

Left to myself, I thought for a long time about what moments Tcherepnin was talking about. Eventually I decided they were: the introduction in the *First Symphony:* the subordinate (syncopated) theme in the Finale of the *Second Symphony:* "The Apple Tree Has Bloomed in the Orchard" and "What Are My Mother and Father to Me?" in *Cherevichki* (the latter was used in the overture, but very awkwardly, with too much condensation: that is, it lacks something that might have let it unfold to the full); in *Eugene Onegin,* the first part of the opera, and the first part of the "letter"* (in C major) and its last part (in 3/4 time).

When I mentioned *Cherevichki* to Tcherepnin, he said (referring to a conversation we had once had), "All his life Rimsky-Korsakov wanted to write an opera based on that subject, but he held back. He was apprehensive because the subject had already been used, and he was afraid he might offend Tchaikovsky, who had written two versions of an opera based on that story. Then, when Tchaikovsky died, Rimsky-Korsakov immediately set to work on *The Night Before Christmas.* And what were the results? It turned out that in his opera all the fantastic scenes were more interesting, but that in Tchaikovsky's music the lyrical passages still had more warmth."

"Then one should pick out all the lyrical passages from Tchaikovsky's music and leave all the fantastic ones as composed by Rimsky-Korsakov. The result would be a marvelous opera from beginning to end."

Tcherepnin didn't say anything. He just smiled the way people smile at a youthful adversary.

Finally he said, "I don't think the two halves would fit together." Then he changed the subject.

94

In Winkler's piano class, things went on just as if there had been no frightful exams the spring before. But the technical exercises had been useful to me: they had strengthened my fingers, and I could undertake more interesting pieces. Winkler was attentive to his students, and musical, but I sometimes felt that, if I had not outgrown him, at any rate I had grown up to him. He was an excellent musician. But as a professor he lacked both the technique and the subtlety of phrasing necessary to teach the more advanced students.

He soon informed me that on December 5 I was to perform three pieces at

---

* Tatyana's famous letter to Onegin. (Translator's note.)

a student recital: Chopin's *Etude No. 1,* Brahms's *Rhapsody in G minor,* and a C major étude by Rubinstein—(with staccato chords)—which, incidentally, I played rather dashingly. I had never used the wrist staccato, which seemed to me not to be trusted, so I played the chords with an absolutely stiff wrist. Winkler came up to me, first from the right side and then the left, observing how I played the Rubinstein. Then he said, "All right. Play it that way if it works for you."

When I went onstage the evening of the student recital, I was a bit nervous, but not for long. I was reassured by the fact that I had learned all three pieces well. The one I played best of all (most assertively) was the Rubinstein étude. The stiff wrist did the trick. There was a good-sized audience, and I went over.

Zakharov took me by the arm and led me off to one side. "There's nothing more for you to do with Winkler. You should study with Esipova."

Anna Esipova, the famous pianist, was considered the best teacher at the Conservatory. Zakharov himself had recently switched to her class and was very proud of it.

"She was sitting in the first row, and she smiled while you were playing," he went on. "I imagine she'll take you, although in general it's devilishly hard to get into her class."

At that moment Winkler came up and congratulated me on a successful performance. He was beaming, as though reflecting the success of his pupil. I felt guilty, as if I were betraying him.

But the next day Miaskovsky told me, "They say you played splendidly at the recital. It's time for you to leave Winkler. He won't teach you anything. Zakharov is on good terms with Esipova. Let him ask her whether she will take you. Winkler is better suited for the counterpoint students who can't flex their fingers at the keyboard." (Some of the harmony and counterpoint students were taking supplementary piano lessons from Winkler.)

"But you have to remember that he makes a lot of me. Supposing that after this successful performance I turn my back on him and switch to another class. Would that be nice?"

"When you're marching toward your goal," Miaskovsky said, "you mustn't look at the corpses you have to walk over." Then he shrugged and moved away.

When I told my mother about the possibility of switching from Winkler to Esipova, she said, "Don't make any decision until you've consulted your father."

I wrote my father about it in detail, and the tone of his reply was one of indignation. In his opinion it would be very inconsistent to switch from one teacher to another, all the more so since Winkler had already shown that he was interested in me. Also, why should I make an enemy when I still didn't know anything about Esipova? Meantime, while Father and I were exchanging letters, I had gradually come to favor the idea of switching. I wrote Father (without indicating Miaskovsky as a source): "When you're marching toward your goal, you mustn't look at the corpses you have to walk over."

In reply to this second letter, my father wrote: "But the trouble is, the corpses sometimes rise up and club you in the back of the head."

Meantime, in Petersburg it had become clear that Winkler, although a good man, was not an important one, and was hardly any kind of pianist; that he carried more weight as a theoretician than a teacher of piano. (Also, when he had to perform with an ensemble, he got such stage fright it was terrible to look at him—something I had observed recently when he performed with a trio.) But Esipova was world-famous, and her class was the elite one at the Conservatory.

I wrote my father that we could settle matters in the spring, and that in the meantime we could put off our discussions until he came to Petersburg from Sontsovka.[152]

95

As I have already mentioned, the "Soiree (or Evening) of Contemporary Music" at which I performed was given on December 18—in the rather modest concert hall of the Reformatsky School. It was the forty-fifth concert given by the Evenings of Contemporary Music, and this was their eighth season. The first part of the program consisted of posthumous works by Grieg. In addition to Miaskovsky and me, the second part included pieces by my professors: Wihtol, Tcherepnin, and Taneyev. Works by Scriabin and Medtner had also been scheduled, but they were not performed, owing to the illness of the pianist. My first number was *Fairy Tale* (later included in Opus 3). It was followed by *Snow* (which by now had half melted), *Reminiscence, Elan, Despair,* and *Suggestion diabolique* (pieces that later made up Opus 4), and *Entreaty,* of which not a trace has remained and which I cannot now remember. I played rather well—in any case, jauntily. My success was rather great and, I should say, no doubt unexpected. After the concert lots of people came to the green room to shake my hand. But my chief concern in those days was to improve my piano technique, and I had been more elated by the successful performance I had given for Winkler, with everybody from the Conservatory present, than by this performance somewhere in the Reformatsky School before "moderns" and musicians for most of whom I had already played my pieces.

Nonetheless, this was my first appearance as a composer, and reviews of it soon came out in the newspapers. (Naturally, no one reviewed the recitals at the Conservatory.) On December 20, 1908, the newspaper *Slovo* published a review[153] signed "N. Sem"—the pseudonym (as someone explained to me) of one of the promoters of Evenings of Contemporary Music, who had thought it advisable to give me support:

S. Prokofiev's short piano pieces, performed by the composer himselt from manuscript scores, were most original. This young composer, who has not yet completed his musical education, belongs to the extremist school of Modernists, and in his daring and originality goes far beyond the contemporary French composers. All the oddities of his rich creative fantasy evidence a big and indisputable talent. It is a talent that still lacks equilibrium, yields to every impulse, and is given to extravagant combinations of sonorities, but one that very adeptly finds a logical basis for the most daring modulations. The pieces vary greatly in mood—from the impetuously stormy (*Despair*) through the serenely meditative (*Reminiscence*) to the fantastic (*Snow*). Or again, one is stunned by a wild, unbridled play of fantasy (*Suggestion diabolique*). Sincerity, the absence of contrivance or a deliberate seeking for harmonic novelty, and a really outstanding talent are manifest in the logical development of ideas, form, and content. The composer's tremendous powers of fantasy and invention provide him with a superabundance of creative material.

In the following—from *Rech* for December 22, 1908—my self-esteem was a bit wounded:

> As for the pieces by S. Prokofiev, they are above all very miniature in form. The composer is a very young high school student. He is undoubtedly talented, but there are many oddities and contrived effects in his harmonies that go beyond the bounds of the beautiful.   G.T.

"G.T." was Timofeyev, who alternated with Karatygin in writing for that paper but was much less influential than the latter.

The following is from the *Peterburgsky listok* (an unimportant paper) for December 24, 1908. Here, too, my vanity was a bit wounded:

> This same program included an entire series of short piano pieces by Prokofiev, a composer who is still very young. They were titled *Fairy Tale, Snow, Reminiscence, Elan, Entreaty, Despair,* and *Suggestion diabolique,* and were performed by the composer himself. If one views all these generally rather confused pieces (or, more accurately, rough drafts and sketches) as the composer's first steps in his career, one may perhaps find in them occasional gleams of a certain talent.

Finally, the German paper *St.-Petersburger Zeitung* for December 24, 1908, published a knowledgeable review[154] that was not signed but was in fact (as I found out later) written by Winkler:

> In the second part of the program, devoted to Russian composers, the talented Conservatory student Prokofiev played several of his own short piano pieces, which met with a favorable reception. Mr. Prokofiev is still very young and still in his *Sturm und Drang* phase, while also being under the influence of the very recent Decadent trend in art. But when he has left

his developmental phase behind him, we can expect the very best fruits from his unique talent. The pieces this reviewer liked the best—the most interesting harmonically, and most successful structurally—were *Fairy Tale, Reminiscence, Elan,* and *Despair.* The very decadent *Suggestion diabolique* has the advantage that it was truly created for the piano. [It is impossible to understand what it was that Winkler found "very decadent" in *Suggestion diabolique,* a limpid and purposeful piece. But it was significant that this term was promptly applied to everything new, even though it was not at all decadent. And things went on that way for a long time!]

Morolev, who had chanced to come to Petersburg from Nikopol, was at the concert. In his memoirs[155] he writes:

Justice compels me to note that along with S. S. Prokofiev, other young composers were on the program, and their works were coldly received by the audience. The entire first part of the concert was rather colorless and boring. The audience came alive only in the second half, after Sergei Sergeyevich's performance. The piano was resonant, the sonorities were entrancing, and pianistic technique was compelling. The success was complete. It seemed there would never be an end to the applause.

Here Morolev exaggerates a bit. Moreover, that "boredom" had nothing to do with Miaskovsky's art songs, which were performed following my appearance. Miaskovsky himself was not present. Just before the concert he had fallen ill (or else he had been so nervous he pretended to be ill)—of which he informed me.

My reply to Miaskovsky before the concert.
Petersburg, December 17, 1908.

My Dear Fellow:

If only you could imagine even slightly how sorry I am for you! (This in case you are *really* having a bout of influenza. . . .) In order to console you a bit I am sending you the program; and the day after the concert I will send you the most detailed review *of everything.* I hope you will soon send your guest to the Devil.

s. pv.[156]

After the concert.
Petersburg, December 19, 1908.

Also:*

Let me begin by telling you that Mme. Emtsova also got sick, so that the seventh section of the program [Scriabin, Akimenko, Medtner] was dropped, and your songs came at the end. Karatygin played the accompa-

* In German in the original. (Translator's note.)

niments to your songs, and I must give him his due: he accompanied beautifully—especially the last two numbers. Likewise, Demidova sang rather well. In my opinion, their tempo for *Moon and Mist* was a bit fast. On the other hand, I am now convinced that the song is somewhat too long, and that with a slower tempo it would be boring. Also, the accompaniment should have been a bit more tender more "misty." I am less familiar with *Contradiction,* and so can't judge of it in the same way. I'll say only that I myself liked the end very much; but the audience was left somewhat perplexed and didn't applaud for several seconds, since they were obviously waiting for a continuation. *Blood* was beautifully performed, and I frankly enjoyed it. But so far as I could gather, the audience liked it less than the others. The fact remains, however, that they applauded every song boisterously.

I must tell you the singer's opinion. She said your songs seem to have been composed for a machine rather than for a singer.

Of myself I can tell you that I played much better than at home, so that both the "Moderns" and Winkler liked me as an executant.

People clapped when I appeared on the stage. They clapped again after every piece (except *Snow*) and quite a bit at the end. The pieces they liked best were *Reminiscence, Despair,* and *Suggestion diabolique.* And now we're going to hear abuse from the critics, about six of whom (so I gather) were there.

Please get well! I'm very sorry to hear from you that your illness is contagious so that I can't visit you.

Yours,
S. Prokofiev

The only other composer there was Chesnokov.[157]

96

Josef Hofmann, the famous pianist, came to Petersburg in October or November. Hofmann was still very young then. He did in fact play superbly, but the most important thing was that he had an excellent memory and an inexhaustible repertory. When I met him in New York many years later, I asked him, "In what city did you give the most piano recitals?"

"I guess it was in Petersburg in 1908."

"About how many, in your recollection?"

"Something like twenty-six in succession."

"And how many programs did you play in succession?"

"Something like twenty."

They say that when Hofmann, in his evening clothes, would walk out on the stage, the program for that evening's recital would be on the music rack—a program of whose contents he knew nothing. He would pick it up, glance through it, and then play the whole thing from beginning to end.[158]

Quite separately from his other programs, Glazunov asked him to play a special one for the Conservatory students—a big program of "classical" music. It was hastily reproduced on a hectograph and distributed among the students so that they could get an idea of the music to be played. At the time I was in a phase of great fondness for Schumann, and I especially wanted to hear his *Concerto sans orchestre*. I scarcely knew it, but I liked its first bar very much, as I did the "speculative" A-double flat on the first page. Hofmann was playing a great many things, and I could scarcely wait for the Schumann concerto. Finally I heard what, according to the program, was supposed to be Schumann and what sounded like Schumann. I listened to it with pleasure, though I was amazed by its brevity. Then I headed for home, where someone was waiting for me, in a great rush. But as I was leaving the Conservatory, someone told me that Hofmann had not yet played the Schumann. He was still playing Chopin—the *Etude on the Black Keys*.

I went home embittered by my own mistake. When I found out that Hofmann was soon to play six recitals with new programs, I decided to attend the one that featured Schumann in abundance.[159]

At the recital, after I had bought my program and studied it closely, I looked around and saw a very pretty girl in a light blue blouse sitting behind me. She was very young and had sultry, wide-set eyes, like a Ukrainian girl. I ogled her for about a minute, unable to tear myself away. But then I had the feeling that my gaze was a bit importunate for her. So I turned quickly around and tried to interest myself in something else.

The recital began. I buried myself in the program and felt restless. In the first place, I had a strong urge to look around at the pretty girl. In the second place, Hofmann was playing one of those endless Beethoven sonatas in which the Andante goes on for a half hour. Finally he finished the sonata, which ended that part of the program. I glanced over the program again, and then started to get up to go and stretch my legs. At that moment someone tapped me on the shoulder from behind. "Would you by any chance have a program?"

When I saw it was the girl in the light blue blouse, I jumped to my feet and proffered my program.

"Oh, thank you," she said, and then vanished almost immediately. But not before she had said over her shoulder, "I'll give it back to you after the intermission."

That gave me an excellent pretext. I immediately decided that before the next part of the program began I would have to get lost in the crowd so that the girl couldn't see me. Then when the music started again, I would sit down next to her. (We were in the balcony, which was not crowded.) This I proceeded to do.

"So there you are!" she said, with a surprised movement of the shoulders.

By way of stimulating the acquaintance, I launched into a conversation about the music: about the program, Hofmann's playing, and that it was said he put his hands into boiling water before coming onstage, which explained why they were so red. But she interrupted me with, "Quiet! He's already begun."

We sat together during the rest of the recital. Afterward I took her home in a hansom cab—something considered rather elegant by Conservatory students. She told me what days she came to the Conservatory, and what her name was: Katyusha Borshch. I didn't much like it because its sound, although unexpected, was not very pretty.[160]

The next day before class, when Miaskovsky and I were standing on the steps in front of the Conservatory, waiting for Wihtol to arrive, Katyusha Borshch came by at a fast gait, her high heels clicking on the sidewalk. I greeted her, and she replied.

"Is that a new acquaintance of yours?" Miaskovsky asked. He rarely asked that kind of question, but it was plain to see that Katyusha appealed to something in him.

"I happened to be sitting next to her at the recital last night. She's very pretty, don't you think?"

Miaskovsky looked at her again. "And what eyes! . . . How sultry!"

With that, our talk about Katyusha came to an end. It had been something rare, since Miaskovsky almost never talked about women.

My acquaintance with Katyusha Borshch gradually grew, but not to the extent I had hoped for. She proved to be a very talented pianist, but there didn't seem to be much more to her. She didn't know how to talk about music, and in general took little interest in it. She came from a rather uncultivated family and was not remarkable for her good manners. Whenever I took her for a ride in a hansom cab (I sometimes had enough money for such a fling), she liked it but in general she felt drawn, not so much to me as to a different circle of people. Just what kind of circle that was, I never managed to find out. Even on the basis of friendship, our relations followed a kind of zigzag pattern. Sometimes we would go to concerts together. On other occasions she would say she was busy, and I would go alone, only to be surprised by finding her there in the company of someone I didn't know.

97

From me to Glière in Moscow.
Petersburg, December 29, 1909.

Dear Reinhold Moritsevich:

On December 18 I made my debut as both composer and performer at a concert of Contemporary Music. Of the pieces I played, you know all but the first and last: I played the others for you last fall. They went over well, and the critics' attitude toward them was peaceable. I am sending you the very first review—the one that appeared in the *Slovo*.

Right now I'm trying (as I have been all this fall) to get my symphony performed. Needless to say, everything depends on Glazunov: on his access to the Court Orchestra, the Sheremetyev Orchestra, and that at the Conservatory. But in order to get him to do anything, I constantly have to nudge him. I have therefore made more than fifteen raids on him [a very importunate young man], with the result that a performance of the Finale is assured. Probably of the Andante, too; but as for the first movement, there has as yet been little talk, since he doesn't like it. He says it's harsh—including the introduction, which you (contrariwise) found much to your liking. However, I hope to arrange for the performance of the first movement, too; i.e., of the whole symphony.

Naturally, he has never seen or heard of the "Modernist" pieces.

Yours truly,
S. Pv.[161]

Nothing was being done about getting my symphony performed (Miaskovsky's wasn't performed until much later), and I could find no peace. Hence my importunate visits to Glazunov.

98

One day Aunt Katya Rayevskaya said to my mother, "Marie, I'd like to have you meet my girlhood friend, Maria Pavlovna Korsak, a very nice woman. Unfortunately, with the passing of years she has begun to have attacks of congestion in the head. She spends many evenings just sitting at home feeling bored. If she could talk with you, she would no doubt appreciate your liveliness and intelligence. If you want, we can go to see her tomorrow."

So they went, and my mother and Maria Korsak, who was married to the Public Prosecutor, took to each other. Mme. Korsak had a higher social position than my mother, but Mother was a livelier conversationalist. Sometimes she would make witty remarks that were, shall we say, hardly suitable for government circles and the kind that shouldn't be uttered in the presence of the Public Prosecutor's wife. But Mme. Korsak would only smile.

Having heard of the "talented Serezhenka," Aunt Marie Korsak (so she always called herself, although this kinship remained somewhat dubious) listened to my music. And whether she understood it or not, she exclaimed, "We really must arrange for a performance of his symphony! My husband was recently appointed Chief Prosecutor here in Petersburg. Glazunov is always coming to see him about Conservatory matters, intervening for a violinist from Odessa, a boy from Berdichev, and so on. In a word, we do a lot of things out of respect for Glazunov."

At that moment the Prosecutor came into the room. "Unfortunately," he said, after bowing to the ladies, "we can't get anywhere with Glazunov for the time being. He's just gone to Riga."

Then, smiling at me, Korsak asked half jokingly, "Do you know what it means when people say Glazunov has gone to Riga?"

I was confused.

"Well, now!" Korsak smiled. "Every student should be educated with respect to his director." And he added didactically, "Glazunov sometimes likes to drink a bit of white wine—a bit too much, in fact. When he is sitting at home in a semiconscious state, asking for more and more, his acquaintances are told that he has gone to Riga. Then, when his mama notices—yes, it turns out that he does have a mama—when she notices that the critical period is almost over, she tells the servant to put water in the wine, adding more each time. Well, with this Glazunov comes around. So they put him in a carriage and take him for a ride around the islands. At this point it develops that he is returning fom Riga."

Korsak gave a deep-voiced laugh and added, "As you see, you can learn things from me that they haven't taught you at the Conservatory."

"Fine," said his wife. "But what about the symphony?"

"Talk to Ruzsky. He'll take care of everything."

A week later, at Mme. Korsak's invitation, I went to her home and was introduced to Nikolai Pavlovich Ruzsky. He was a very nice man—a rich businessman who played the cello well and liked to organize chamber ensembles. Ruzsky was close to Glazunov and, at the same time, was on good terms with Korsak. Probably it was through him that Korsak heard gossip like that I have just mentioned about Glazunov.

He was accompanied on this visit by Ossovsky* and Siloti. The latter seemed to me the most important person, since he directed the concerts with the most interesting and most modern programs. In the past he had been regarded as a favorite pupil of Liszt, who was supposed to have called him Silotissimo.

Ossovsky, the critic, later in the course of his long life became an academician. In the days of my youth he always helped me in musical matters when he could.

I began playing my symphony in E minor. Siloti sat there curled up in his chair pulling at his beard. (Like Liszt, he had a beard that covered his face with it luxuriant growth.) Ruzsky and Ossovsky had words of praise for me at the end of each movement.

"All my programs for this season have already been lined up," said Siloti in the classic phrase. "And your symphony is too immature for a debut before a big audience. Write some more, and then we'll see."

---

* Alexander Vyacheslavovich Ossovsky (1871–1957), musicologist, corresponding member of the Academy of Sciences, U.S.S.R. (Translator's note.)

I left with an outward show of gratitude and inner feelings of disillusionment. The people who had heard me play were both important and nice but as for my symphony—back in the drawer, please!

A few days later Mme. Korsak came to see us. "My husband," she said, "has been given an automobile in connection with his official duties, and I've come to take Serezha for a ride."

In those days, an automobile was a great rarity in Petersburg. And this one was bigger than the one I had seen the summer before in Sukhumi.

Mme. Korsak turned to my mother. "Maria Grigorevna, will you come along with us?"

My mother agreed. My father, who was in the city at the time, did not consider it suitable to go for a ride in the Prosecutor's car: he stayed behind in our apartment, where we could glimpse his face in the window. Mme. Korsak, my mother, and someone else got into the back seat, while I got into the front seat next to the chauffeur. Then off we went, going very fast by the standards of those days.

It was my first ride in a car, and when we were seemingly about to collide with a hansom cab, I didn't believe the chauffeur could stop the car in time. Or when we had to turn into a side street, I was sure that at any moment the chauffeur would drive up on the sidewalk, which was full of people. At such time I put my feet in front of me to brace myself.

That's the way things were when we started out. But on the way back I looked around quite unconcernedly, and for the first time I took pleasure in the ride.

I have noted down these reactions simply because this was my first ride in an automobile.

99

After meeting Katyusha Borshch, I tried to remember the Glagoleva girl. She was older, with more polished manners, and in that respect more interesting. But she was a bit of a madcap—something I noticed in her behavior toward a young man a little older than she who was in love with her, and on whom she played a rather nasty trick.

With me (since the time of my lecture on Wagner) she was rather consistently amiable. When we chanced to meet, she would exclaim, "Ah! Monsieur Prokofiev! How very pleasant to see you!"

Since I wanted to get to know her better, as soon as the first snow fell, I asked her, "Do you skate well?"

"More or less, but rather less."

"Let's go skating together. I'll teach you."

"We'll go sometime."

I could skate better than she and on the slick ice she had to do what I said, and lean on me, whether she liked it or not. But she accepted my suggestions, and we went skating a half-dozen times.

On one of these occasions, she asked me, "Are you familiar with Assyrian music?"

"What kind of music could they have had? Probably drums or some kind of tambourines . . ."

"But why don't you know it? You're supposed to know everything—at least in the field of music."

"Do you have to know right away?"

"No, tomorrow is all right."

"Fine, I'll tell you tomorrow at the Conservatory."

The next day I went to see Fribus at the library. "Do you know," I asked, "whether there is any Assyrian music?"

"Like what—*La Reine de Saba?*"

"What's that?"

"An opera by Gounod."

"Do you have a score?"

"Yes." And he gave me one.

In a hallway of the Conservatory, I met up with the Glagoleva girl and gave her *La Reine de Saba.* "That's the most Assyrian thing in the world," I said with a crafty look. She was overjoyed.

"Ten days from now, we'll have a talk," she said.

I was even intrigued.

100

In addition to Leonida Glagoleva and Katyusha Borshch, I should like to mention Vera Alpers, who sat next to me in aesthetics class.

Aesthetics was taught by Professor Sakketti, who in the distant past had been an Italian. He was a very old but picturesque man. On the subject of aesthetics, however, he babbled such frightful nonsense that everyone whispered for the sake of diversion. Or else they just yawned. But the course had to be taken, as did the examination, so the students worked at it little by little.

Vera Alpers was a girl of sixteen and a half with a neat figure and a face rather pale for her age. She behaved very properly and, unlike Katyusha Borshch, loved to talk about music. Her father, a civil engineer in the employ of the railroad system, often had to travel in connection with his duties and in his free time he composed, for which he possessed some technique. He had musicians as friends, including Byelsky (the librettist of *Kitezh* and the *Cockerel,* who had a huge bump on his head) and Ossovsky. I told Vera that I knew Ossovsky, and she verified it at the first opportunity. It was verified for her by the ever-amiable Ossovsky, who said "Oh, yes. He once played us a symphony that was not bad." After that, Vera decided to be more attentive to me, and even to persuade her parents to invite me to their home sometime.

Many years later she showed me her diary for that period. Some of it was interesting, and I asked her to copy out certain excerpts for me. (I had my auto-biography in mind.) Having received her permission, I shall quote some of the most pertinent material, while condensing other things.

From Vera Alpers' diary.
December 1, 1908.

I very much like going to the Conservatory. During the time I have spent there I have "made friends" with Prokofiev. I have frequent, long talks with him. Some of my friends among the girls make fun of me: Ksyushka, Ida, Bessonova, and, in a word, many. At first they said all kinds of bad things about him, but now he has suddenly become good. It's very interesting to talk with him. He behaves well, and is very different from all the Conservatory brats.

Prokofiev has become popular. At one rehearsal for a concert he called attention to my long fingers. He took my hand, studied it, and said it was pretty. I was embarrassed. And when he saw I was blushing, he himself got embarrassed. . . . All in all, I don't understand why he attracts me. In the first place, he is frightfully egotistical; in the second place . . . he has many unlikable things about him in general, but at the same time . . .

December 6, 1908.

Today I'm in some kind of terrible mood. I suppose Prokofiev is the cause of it. Last night I went with my brother Boris to a student recital . . . [I have already told of that recital with the Rubinstein étude.] Prokofiev played last night, and played very well. But after his performance he got frightfully excited, and I was afraid for him, thinking he might faint or have an attack of nerves. He rushed off the stage and sat down on the steps, unable to recover his breath for a long time. Then he jumped up like a madman, and on his way through the green room he bumped Esipova (who was standing there) with his arm. Then he went out, slamming the door. During intermission I looked and saw that Prokofiev had reappeared. When he saw me he smiled politely, as though he had not seen me in a long time. . . .

I very much like the way he played. He plays so attentively and with so much meaning, and somehow becomes one with the piano and the music. He is definitely talented. I would very much like Mama to see how he behaves with me.

101

From the diary of Vera Alpers.
January 4 (17), 1909.

. . . Last night at the Conservatory soiree I was terribly happy. I don't know why, and I don't want to know. I spent a greater part of the evening with him.

. . . And yet he very much likes pretty faces, and that means a lot to him. Apparently he is not used to denying himself anything; and the Conservatory girls he knows—the ones he is attracted by, such as Eshe, Sadovskaya, and Glagoleva—are rather free in their behavior.

For my part at about that same time I wrote somewhere (in my diary, I imagine) something rather stupid about Vera Alpers: "Verochka is not very pretty, but from the back she looks very neat."

That was the night of the annual ball for those graduating from the academic course.

102

The news that Scriabin had composed a big new symphonic piece stirred up a lot of interest. Rumor had it that the piece was written for a huge orchestra and was more avant-garde than *The Divine Poem.*

Miaskovsky said, "Tonight let's go and hear Scriabin's *Poem of Ecstasy.* That's what his new symphony is called."

"But its first public performance in the Belyayev series has been announced for February 16."

"Yes, but it seems that although the score had already been published, Blumenfeld didn't manage to get the Belyayev Orchestra to learn the piece. So Warlich has taken it on. Also, tonight's concert will be private—with admission by pass—so that there won't be any *first* performance that is *public.*"[162]

Warlich, conductor of the Court Orchestra, was an elegant-looking man—rather old but lively. The Court Orchestra played for balls at court and was relatively free the rest of the time. Therefore, a series of symphonic concerts "for the general public" was organized, chiefly in order to keep the orchestra in form. Both the orchestra and the conductor were good. But the concert hall, converted from what had formerly been the Czar's stables, was too small and had bad acoustics—something all the more noticeable when a piece for a big orchestra was being performed.

Miaskovsky and I had adjoining seats, and we gulped down *The Poem of*

Ecstasy with great interest, although in some places we were perplexed by the novelty of the music. We had expected an improvement (so to speak) on *The Divine Poem,* which we knew very well and loved. But both the harmonic and thematic material, and the voice-leading in the counterpoint, were completely new.

Basically, Scriabin was trying to find new foundations for harmony. The principles he discovered were very interesting, but in proportion to their complexity they were like a stone tied to Scriabin's neck, hindering his invention as regard melody and (chiefly) the movement of the voices. Nonetheless, *The Poem of Ecstasy* was probably his most successful work, since in it all the elements in his manner of composing were apparently balanced. But it was hard to imagine, at first hearing, just what he was trying to do.

On February 16 the *Poem* was again performed in the Hall of Columns, with Blumenfeld conducting.[163] Whereas Miaskovsky and I had come away from the first performance (in the Czar's stables) perplexed and trying to understand where Scriabin's creativity was taking him, after the second performance (in the Hall of Columns), when Scriabin's orchestration, new in its design, had unfolded before us in all the breadth of its sonority, we came away exclaiming, "What a work of genius!" But later, when the intellectual coldness of some of Scriabin's "flights" became discernible, that opinion had to be downgraded a bit.

103

One day in January 1909 the deputy inspector summoned me and said, "The director wants to see you."

That could be either good or bad. I took my time walking to Glazunov's office.

As usual, he spoke in a low voice and not very clearly: "I have managed to find a way to have your symphony performed. In a month Warlich is going to conduct the Court Orchestra in a performance of my new piece. Half of their rehearsal time will be spent on it. Warlich can use the other half for your symphony. Have the parts been copied?"

"Not yet, but I can probably do it."

I knew that it would cost a lot to have the parts copied, but my parents had promised to pay for it.

"Be careful," said Glazunov. "After all the parts are copied, check them and count the measures between the numbers. The copyists often mess things up. If they do, instead of enjoying hearing your symphony you will be bitterly disappointed when the musicians play false notes or when they are not together."

"Yes, of course," I replied, agreeing to everything. "And what copyist do you recommend I give the score to?"

"I suggest you give it to Kek. He is an experienced copyist who worked for

Rimsky-Korsakov more than once. You can get his address from the Conservatory doorman."

I thanked Glazunov and felt as if I were walking on air as I hurried to get my symphony and take it to Kek. He proved to a cheerful man and a knowledgeable copyist, although he was extremely expensive. He copied the music accurately and clearly, but he hadn't heard my name before, so that on some of the parts he wrote "Prokhorov's Symphony." It was a good thing that in earlier days he had written "Rimsky-Korsakov" and not "Ippolitov-Ivan,"* otherwise Rimsky-Korsakov might have gotten angry.

Kek was punctual, and he soon delivered half of the parts for me to proofread, then the other half shortly thereafter. But at this point I caught a cold and went to bed with a temperature. Miaskovsky came to my aid and undertook to proofread some of the parts. He was meticulous and fast, in which respect he distinguished himself from certain other composers; e.g., Stravinsky and Scriabin. In Scriabin's case, I recall that in one of the first opuses of his that I got to know—*Ten Mazurkas*—I found a lot of misprints. And this kind of thing was always happening with Stravinsky. On one occasion, ten days after one of his big works had been published, it was necessary to print an errata sheet to be pasted in the score; and a few weeks after the errata sheet had been pasted in, it was necessary to print errata for the errata.

> From me to Miaskovsky.
> Petersburg, January 1909.

I have a terrible case of the glanders, with a headache and watering eyes. It looks like I'll have to stay home for several days. Thanks much for the help in proofreading.

> Yours,
> S. P-v.

Dear Monsieur Prokhorov (thus does your last name appear on some of the parts):

Since you are ill, I shall drop in at your place on Wednesday at about seven-thirty with the finished parts and the coda of the score. If, contrary to expectations, you are well and not at home, I have the following to request: 1. Prepare the first part of the score (to return to me), the first and second movements—if, of course, you have finished proofreading the parts you have. If you have not finished, give me the parts you have checked, and I will leave with you the ones I have finished. (Thus you will get, as your share of the work, everything that has to do with the first two movements, and I'll get the Finale.) 2. My little art songs, which are of no use to you. I will pick all this up.

---

* Pseudonym of Mikhail Mikhailovich Ivanov (1849–1927), composer and conductor. (Translator's note.)

I must say that the proofreading is not a burdensome task, since the copyist is apparently skillful. In places he has even corrected your own errors and, so far as I have been able to verify, everything is correct.

Hoping you get well soon.

Yours,
N. Miaskovsky

A week after all the parts had been proofread and I had informed Glazunov of it, he told me that the symphony would be played at a private rehearsal on February 23 (March 9), and that I could invite close friends and relatives (not many). The score had to be delivered to Warlich ahead of time so that he could study it.

In my naïveté, I never asked myself what considerations had prompted Glazunov to give my symphony a fillip at last. He had arranged things, and I was grateful to him. That was all there was to it. But perhaps he had asked a favor of Korsak, and the latter had expressed an interest in how things were going with young Prokofiev's symphony—merely expressed an interest, nothing more—whereupon Glazunov had taken the hint. Or perhaps some help had come from Ossovsky, who on several occasions in my lifetime has given me a hand in musical matters. If he told Glazunov that the symphony was interesting, and that it would be useful to help a composer whom Glazunov himself had sent to the Conservatory, it is possible that Glazunov followed his advice because he wished to do a favor for Ossovsky (and not me). . . .

What is less likely is that the initiative was wholly Glazunov's, since those pieces of mine that were being performed at the "Modernists'" concerts were of a type that were clearly beginning to annoy the venerable composer. . . . In a word, I still don't know who provided the fillip for getting my symphony performed.

As for Miaskovsky's symphony, it wasn't performed at that time. It wasn't until several years later, when he had already written his second and third symphonies, that it was played by an orchestra.

When I met Warlich at a concert, I asked him when I should give him my orchestral score. He replied, "You can bring it to the rehearsal at which we're going to play it. I have conducted from many unfamiliar scores, and no doubt I can sight-read yours."

This amazed me, and at the same time I was glad to hear it. What a skillful conductor! Yet the performance would probably not catch all the nuances in the music. . . .

The performance was attended by my father, who had just come to Petersburg from Sontsovka; my mother; her sister, Aunt Katya Rayevskaya; Cousin Katya Ignatyeva; Cousin Andrei Rayevsky (in earlier days he had "produced" my *Giant,* with himself taking the part of the orchestra, and was in general a musically gifted person); and, of course, Miaskovsky and Zakharov, with whom I had become closer friends recently. Glazunov was there too, sitting in the second row. I myself was sitting near Miaskovsky farther back in the hall.

Warlich conducted the symphony in the proper tempi (he had asked me about the tempi in advance), stopping when the players weren't together. But there were absolutely no dynamic shadings or other nuances in general: under his baton the symphony sounded rather coarse.

The next day I wrote a rather detailed account in my diary of how the symphony was performed and how it sounded, but by now I have forgotten the details. I recall only that the counterpoint in the subordinate theme, which I had given to two trombones, sounded horribly harsh, as though they were pounding in nails. Glazunov even stood up and asked the trombonists to play a bit less loudly. I had given an indication in the score to that effect, but neither Warlich nor the musicians in the orchestra paid any attention to it.

The last page of the Finale, which I had considered lacy, was played *mf* instead of *p,* so that my intention was not realized. Zakharov nudged me in the side during the bridge passage from the main theme to the subordinate theme in the first movement: he liked that passage, with its parallel four-three chords. But the most pleasant surprise was that when the symphony was over they played it through again from beginning to end. ("I hung on every note," I wrote in my diary.)

It was not for me that they repeated it, but for Baron Schtackleberg, the musical director of the orchestra, who had come into the hall toward the end of the rehearsal.

General Schtackleberg was an elegant, rather lively man with a drooping mustache and easy manners. When I went to thank Glazunov, he introduced me to the general, whispering, "First thank the baron for the performance, then Warlich."

This I did. But later, when I saw Schtackleberg at another rehearsal, the sporty general walked through the audience from one end of the hall to the other, bowing to the left and right, without even noticing me, so that I was unable to say hello to him.

After the rehearsal, Zakharov asked me, indicating Andrei Rayevsky, "Why is that man with the mustache à la Wilhelm? Why did he go up to Glazunov and the orchestra?"

"That's my cousin, Rayevsky."

"Does he understand music?"

"More or less."

On my way home I asked myself: What was the result, for me, of hearing my symphony played? Probably more or less as follows. I realized that the orchestra was good, but I also realized they had played coarsely. I realized that the symphony was not really badly orchestrated, and I also realized that if it had been rehearsed with close attention and understanding, those places could have been made to sound perfectly all right. But how much more naïve it was than

Scriabin's *Poem of Ecstasy*! In a word, I returned home dissatisfied and not at all beaming with joy.

I would have to write a new symphony.

104

On one occasion Karatygin told me that a very capable pianist by the name of Iovanovich had made his appearance on the scene; that he was going to perform at a concert; and that they had recommended he play a group of my pieces. He said I should give him the music right away; that we would meet in a week; and that Iovanovich would play for me so as to determine the way the pieces should be performed.

And indeed, I soon received the following letter:

Dear Sir:

V. G. Karatygin has no doubt informed you that we are to meet at his home on Monday evening. I shall be very interested to learn your wishes as to how your very, very interesting pieces should be played.

Respectfully,
M. Iovanovich.[164]

I went to Karatygin's and there, along with all the "Modernists," I met a tall, thin fellow in a rumpled suit with stubble on his cheeks. It was Iovanovich, who proved to be of Serbian origin. He said he had not yet thoroughly worked up my pieces but had only looked them over. "Play them anyway," I replied. "It will be a pleasure to hear them." After a while he sat down at the piano.

"Now you'll hear," Nurok said in an undertone.

And Nouvell added, "He also sings a beautiful falsetto, although that has nothing to do with your pieces."

Iovanovich played *Fairy Tale, Suggestion diabolique,* and something else. The playing was by no means on the concert level but rather mere sight-reading. In particular, *Suggestion diabolique* did not sound impetuous and was not played with the rather dry, vigorous touch that I had imagined and with which, apparently, I played it myself.

He finished, and I remained silent. He said, "I haven't yet learned these pieces."

"In that case, allow me to show you in what direction you should work."

Somewhat jarred by this, he yielded me his place at the piano, and I started playing excerpts—chiefly from *Suggestion diabolique*—while explaining what he had done wrong and what he should strive for.

The door leading to the next room opened, and Karatygin's head appeared in it. He said, "Iovanovich is an excellent pianist. Will everyone please come to the table for tea?"

Having said this, he went up to Iovanovich and, taking him by the arm, led him into the dining room as if they were "the lead pair," gesturing to the rest of us to follow.

I realized that I had said too much, and that from then on Iovanovich would not heed my suggestions, although actually I still had a lot to say.

A few days later I received the following letter from Nurok. It was haphazardly written, and the hand was obviously that of an agitated person.

Dear Sergei Sergeyevich:

If you have not already done so, I entreat you, immediately upon receipt of these lines, to write a few words to Iovanovich saying you are sorry about last night's "misunderstanding."

I consider this absolutely necessary not only with a view to keeping your pieces in the program for the concert but simple as an act of justice and politeness toward a man and artist whom you have offended—something he in no way deserved.

Yours sincerely,
A. Nurok.[165]

I was upset: I had never expected such a dressing down from Nurok. Relations with the "Modernists" were obviously on the decline: first the praise for my piano pieces, then the restrained quasi-approval of my symphony, and now this direct attack in defense of Iovanovich. This was unacceptable. What I had to do was attack Nurok in my turn, because actually Iovanovich had not so much played my pieces as pecked away at them, and it is a composer's duty to show how pieces should be played so that they will not be compromised in the eyes of the public.

In talking with my parents, I improvised a rather impudent reply to Nurok. But my father said, "They have been rather decent to you so far, and they arranged a rather good public appearance. So it's not worthwhile spoiling relations because of some Iovanovich who can sing a good falsetto. . . . If you don't want to apologize to him, write him a few kind words. Nurok will be satisfied with that."

From me to Iovanovich.
Petersburg, February 11, 1909.

Dear Mladen Emmanuilovich:

I am sending you the ending of my *Fairy Tale,* which is intended to replace the last two bars. I trust that in this version, plus your execution, my *Fairy Tale* will gain in quality.

I wish you all the best. If you are angry, please don't be so because of my violent attacks on you at Karatygin's last Monday.

Sincerely,
Prokofiev.[166]

My father was more or less right: although Nurok did take my pieces off the program (perhaps Iovanovich realized that he didn't play them very well, and there wasn't enough time to learn them), no squabble with the "Modernists" occurred. As for the amazing pianist, Iovanovich, far from making a big name for himself he gradually faded from the musical horizon of Petersburg.

105

Meantime, the worm of discord was gnawing away somewhere in the depths of my relations with Winkler. The latter, pleased with my playing of the Rubinstein étude, had put me on the program for another student recital—this time assigning me the Schumann toccata.

I have already mentioned that at this time I had a great fondness for Schumann. I undertook the toccata eagerly: it demanded good technique and posed quite a number of challenging musical problems. The technique involved much that was pleasurable for the fingers, and gradually led me to compose my own toccata.[167] Although with its chromaticism it did not rise to the level of Schumann's diatonism, it was consistently successful with the public.

Shortly before I was to perform the Schumann toccata, I sent the following notice to the Glagoleva girl:

Petersburg, February 18, 1909

Dear Leonida Mikhailovna:

The days have now become a bit brighter, but the walls of the Conservatory are dark and gloomy. . . . Nonetheless, on Friday I am playing a toccata at the soiree—something of which I humbly inform Your Grace.

With sincere respect,
S. Prokofiev.[168]

Her reply, written in green ink and with the Church Slavonic ligature, arrived a day later:

Petersburg, February 19 (March 4), 1909.

Slave of God Sergei, son of Sergei:

Be apprised that it liketh us to visit that house of music men call Conservatory and listen, with particular attention and ear most assiduously bent, to that toccata of which mention was made. Accordingly, so that obstacles and impediments not be set in our way at the entrance, we require *two* passes on white paper, inasmuch as lacking them we will not be allowed access to the hall. And if it should be the case that a pass on white paper is not to be found, then let it be on some other paper. [If you had a pass written on white paper, you were allowed in the orchestra; those with passes "on some other" paper were sent to the balcony.]

We send you our most humble greetings, and herewith affix our signature spelled out in full.

Leonida[169]

Petersburg, February 20 (March 5), 1909.

Most Gracious Madame:

Since when have you begun sitting on two chairs at once?

I shall struggle desperately and entreat all the saints of the Conservatory with a view to obtaining a fourth and fifth pass, since the three allotted to me have already been taken. If I should obtain them, I shall leave them with the Conservatory porter in your name.

I send you herewith my archepiscopal blessing.

I, Prokofiev[170]

Meantime, Zakharov was striving to enlist me as a student for Mme. Esipova. She liked pleasant young people of Zakharov's type, and Zakharov, who knew how to charm people, had become one of her favorites. One day, at a convenient moment, he told her with a charming smile (his smile was a delight to the heart): "Anna Nikolayevna, young Prokofiev—a very capable student of Winkler—is hoping to get into your class. Incidentally, he is completing theory of composition, and composes rather well. . . ."

Esipova was silent for a time, ruminating. Then she said, "I heard Prokofiev when he played that Rubinstein étude at a recital. I would probably take him. But he is Winkler's favorite pupil, and I know Winkler is proud of him. So it would be best if he first settled things with Winkler and then came to me."

I was exultant. But at the same time it would be terribly awkward to tell Winkler of my intention to leave him. I had to make an effort and recall Miaskovsky's saying, "When you are marching toward your goal, you must not look at the corpses over which you are walking."

As Winkler was walking through the hall on the way to class, I struck up a conversation with him. I stammered, girded my loins, and tried to swallow the conversation at one gulp, like bad medicine.

Winkler flushed as he listened, but kept his equanimity. "Take the spring examination with me, and I won't hold you back. What would you like to play for the exam?"

"If possible, I would like to play the Rimsky-Korsakov concerto."

"Why not? It's a good choice."

We went into the classroom, and Winkler began to work with me. I don't remember what the piece was, but he gave it particularly close attention, noting how I used the pedals and my fingers. In a word, it was a very detailed lesson. A couple of weeks later I brought the Rimsky-Korsakov concerto in. Winkler said that at the exam I would be accompanied. I very much enjoyed working on the concerto: there was something extremely good and picturesque about it. Before the exam Winkler arranged for a rehearsal in the Small Auditorium (he accompanied me in a rather pallid manner). After the exam his pupils gathered around him, and he told them what marks they had received (I got an A) and discussed in detail what each of them should work on during the summer.

Since I was leaving his class, this didn't concern me, so I stood off to one side, feeling a bit like a traitor. Finally Winkler turned to me with a weak smile, and said, "Here is your passport." Then he gave me a note saying he had no objections to my switching from his class to Esipova's. I thanked him and left in a hurry.

On my way down the stairs I decided that during the next summer I would write four technical études for piano and dedicate them to him.[171] They would serve to commemorate the time I had spent in his class.

106

The classes with Wihtol were rather colorless. Although Miaskovsky and I wrote quite a few things, we had the impression that Wihtol's teaching was weak.

Asafyev had dropped out of the class. Apparently he had decided to graduate from the university that spring and was carving out some time for the exams. He had had a talk with Rimsky-Korsakov about this, and the latter had opposed such a step in such a hostile manner that he had offended Asafyev, who for a long time thereafter was cold toward his great teacher. I don't know whether Asafyev was ever graduated from the Conservatory.

Our other classmates had a hard time composing, and Wihtol had to explain to them what was meant by the rondo form or the sonata allegro form. But Miaskovsky and I had already composed several sonatas apiece, and we composed rather rapidly. Consequently, Wihtol merely listened to our pieces, making a negligible comment from time to time. Nonetheless, each of us considered it his duty to write a piano sonata. Mine (No. 6 according to the numbering system I used at the Conservatory) was a rather variegated piece in terms of idiom, so that during the next few years I made no attempt to rework it. And later—apparently during the first months after the Revolution—it was lost. But I can still reconstruct its materials from memory.

First movement, main theme:

The subordinate theme represented a kind of alternation between the major and minor that especially annoyed Wihtol.

"Rather in the vein of Reger," opined Miaskovsky with a smile, when he heard it. "It confirms Karatygin's comment that you have been somewhat influenced by Reger."

Sergei Rachmaninov.

At the piano. (The score is Wagner's Die Walküre—*Editor's note.)*

Sergei Prokofiev in 1909.

Morolev and I at Nikopol, 1910. The piece on the music rack is apparently my sonata, Opus 1, dedicated to him.

A cartoon on a postcard that I sent to Morolev in November 1912. The inscription reads: "Morolev. Prokofiev. (Ten years from now.)"

A friendly caricature: Sergei Prokofiev and Max Schmidthof.

Boris Zakharov. Taken in Vienna in 1914, when he was twenty-seven.

Terioki, August 1913, after the premiere of my Piano Concerto No. 2, Opus 16. *Boris Zakharov and I at the seashore. (I was twenty-two, and he was twenty-six.)*

First movement, main theme:

The subordinate theme represented a kind of alternation between the major and minor that especially annoyed Wihtol.

"Rather in the vein of Reger," opined Miaskovsky with a smile, when he heard it. "It confirms Karatygin's comment that you have been somewhat influenced by Reger."

"If possible, I would like to play the Rimsky-Korsakov concerto."

"Why not? It's a good choice."

We went into the classroom, and Winkler began to work with me. I do[n't] remember what the piece was, but he gave it particularly close attention, noti[ng] how I used the pedals and my fingers. In a word, it was a very detailed lesson. [A] couple of weeks later I brought the Rimsky-Korsakov concerto in. Winkler sa[id] that at the exam I would be accompanied. I very much enjoyed working on t[he] concerto: there was something extremely good and picturesque about it. Befo[re] the exam Winkler arranged for a rehearsal in the Small Auditorium (he accom[-] panied me in a rather pallid manner). After the exam his pupils gathere[d] around him, and he told them what marks they had received (I got an A) an[d] discussed in detail what each of them should work on during the summer.

Since I was leaving his class, this didn't concern me, so I stood off to on[e] side, feeling a bit like a traitor. Finally Winkler turned to me with a weak smil[e] and said, "Here is your passport." Then he gave me a note saying he had no ob[-] jections to my switching from his class to Esipova's. I thanked him and left in [a] hurry.

On my way down the stairs I decided that during the next summer I woul[d] write four technical études for piano and dedicate them to him.[171] They woul[d] serve to commemorate the time I had spent in his class.

106

The classes with Wihtol were rather colorless. Although Miaskovsky and [I] wrote quite a few things, we had the impression that Wihtol's teaching w[as] weak.

Asafyev had dropped out of the class. Apparently he had decided to gradu[-] ate from the university that spring and was carving out some time for the exam[s.] He had had a talk with Rimsky-Korsakov about this, and the latter had oppos[ed] such a step in such a hostile manner that he had offended Asafyev, who for [a] long time thereafter was cold toward his great teacher. I don't know wheth[er] Asafyev was ever graduated from the Conservatory.

Our other classmates had a hard time composing, and Wihtol had to [ex-] plain to them what was meant by the rondo form or the sonata allegro form. [But] Miaskovsky and I had already composed several sonatas apiece, and we co[m-] posed rather rapidly. Consequently, Wihtol merely listened to our pieces, mak[ing] a negligible comment from time to time. Nonetheless, each of us considere[d it] his duty to write a piano sonata. Mine (No. 6 according to the numbering [sys-] tem I used at the Conservatory) was a rather variegated piece in terms of id[eas,] so that during the next few years I made no attempt to rework it. And later— [ap-] parently during the first months after the Revolution—it was lost. But I can [re-] construct its materials from memory.

The second movement:

There was still another Andante, written in the second rondo form early in Wihtol's course, that I intended to substitute for the Andante in C major in case Wihtol didn't like the latter. But since he expressed no opinion, the sonata was presented for the examination with two Andantes—the main one and a spare.

The spare Andante for Conservatory Sonata No. 6:

For the main theme of the Finale I took the theme of the Finale of my second Conservatory sonata, although I set it in E major instead of F major, and "modernized" it a bit. The rest of the material in the Finale was different from that in the Finale of my second youthful sonata, but I have forgotten it.[172]

After writing our sonatas, Miaskovsky and I consulted with each other on what to write next. He decided to write a string quartet, and I opted for an operatic scene.

At the time a string quartet, as a form, struck me as too dry and strict, but for an operatic scene I had ready at hand an old acquaintance: the end of Pushkin's *A Feast in Time of Plague*. When I had been writing *A Feast in Time of Plague* under Glière's supervision twelve years earlier, he had suggested that I depict the priest against a background of liturgical organ harmonies—which I now proceeded to do. At this time, looking at what I had composed so long before, I felt that the priest was no easygoing churchman in gorgeous garb but a medieval prelate who foamed at the mouth as he railed against the feasting sinners, and that therefore the entire scene should involve raging and gnashing of teeth. This gave me a justification for building it with many dissonant chords. But at the same time my striving for the dramatic made the vocal part insufficiently vocal. To make a long story short, when I presented this scene at the exam, the entire Conservatory council gasped and raised a hue and cry.

For his quartet, Miaskovsky used sketches he had already made. Later he himself told me that in the Finale he had used a chord he had found in Roger Ducasse. "But," he added, "in the Ducasse work that chord is a result of the general voice-leading, whereas I used it for its sonority. Just at that time Glazunov came into Wihtol's class, so that I played the entire Finale of the quartet with him present. I stumbled over the chord, and he asked, 'What kind of a chord is that?' I couldn't explain. Then Glazunov muttered in a vexed tone, 'Up until now, everything has been going along smoothly with you. But now you've run smack into those unacceptable harmonies again. . . .'"

Later, after fundamental reworking, Miaskovsky published that quartet as his tenth.

In March my mother had a letter from my father, saying business matters would not allow him to come to Petersburg for Easter, so we decided to go to Sontsovka.

From Miaskovsky to me at Sontsovka.
Petersburg, March, 23, 1909.[173]

Dear Serge:

Since your departure, nothing has happened and nothing has changed. Since my vacation begins tomorrow (today being Monday the 23rd), it will soon be time for the *reduction* to four hands of your gloomy Adagio. [Miaskovsky had promised to make a four-hand arrangement of my symphony —of one movement at least.] I have recently come into possession of some amazing music paper. So it is that I now find extremely attractive everything that makes it necessary to use that paper.

Rimsky-Korsakov's *Chronicle of My Life in Music* has just been published. Lots of interesting stuff about his method of composing and things in general.

Apparently my unfortunate operatic scene has gotten completely bogged down. Of the themes that occur to me, each is worse and more wretched than the one before.

Just look how much I've written you, although I definitely had nothing to say.

Holiday greetings,
N. Miaskovsky

From me to Miaskovsky in Petersburg.
Sontsovka, March 25, 1909.

Please accept my assurances as to my compliments; also my Easter
greetings with the appropriate wishes.

I am chiefly engaged here in developing myself aesthetically—a very
boring business. [I was preparing for the exam in aesthetics.] The weather
here is vile; the orchard is "something in gray" [a reference to Leonid
Andreyev's play][174]; in a word, everything is splendid. I often play my
Feast, which I like very much; I am trying to compose material for a sinfonietta,[175] and I am waiting for letters. On Thursday I shall return to the
capital, so that on Friday I can display my knowledge of aesthetics. Behind
that looms the history of music.

And what about my symphony? Just play it—it's not bad.

Did you get Shelley? [Shelley: Miaskovsky was about to start work on
Silence.]

So long,
P.[176]

At Sontsovka I finished the operatic scene from *A Feast in Time of
Plague*[177] and made a fair copy of it, but on my way back to Petersburg I lost the
fair copy. Fortunately, I had the rough draft (very sloppy) with me. From it I
had to make another fair copy to present at the exam.

107

We had come back to Petersburg in April for a stay of a month so that I
could take the exams. One was with Wihtol in musical forms. (With that we
completed the Conservatory course in the theory of composition, since Lyadov
didn't want to teach us free composition. Nor could he have taught us much: he
himself could no longer compose big works, and we no longer needed instruction in small forms. . . .) Another was piano with Winkler (in order to get his
permission to switch to Esipova). In addition, there were two trivial exams: one
in history of music, and one in aesthetics.

I remember the first question in the music history exam: "When was
Glinka born?"

"In 1804."

"Correct."

On both of those exams I got an A. I have already told of the exam with
Winkler.

The most poisonous was the examination in musical forms. It consisted in
appraising the works we had written in the course of the year. The compositions
presented were divided into two groups: the first by students of Wihtol whom
he had gotten from Lyadov, and the second by students from Solovyev's class. At

this time those students who were more inclined to compose were taking Lyadov's class, and those less inclined were taking Solovyev's.

The greatest furor at this exam was provoked by my sonata and my *Feast in Time of Plague*. Lyadov was especially exercised. When, after playing both pieces, I had left the director's office, I could hear his howl (through the half-opened door): "They all want to be Scriabins! But what do they bring for the exams?"

I couldn't hear Glazunov through the door, but his hostile mood was evident.

Wihtol himself was apparently remaining neutral: he neither defended his students nor attacked them. Probably he could do neither one nor the other, since for the past year he had taught all his classes with passive indifference.

They decided to punish us by applying a leveling policy. We were told that we were all being graduated from the Conservatory and were being given diplomas as Free Artist, but that all of us—both those who could compose and those who could not—were being given a B on the examination in form. This upset us. But when we met up with Solovyev's students, they said, "Why are you so annoyed at not getting an A? We all got a C, and we don't know whether we have been graduated from the Conservatory, or whether we'll still have to do some finagling before they'll consent to regard us as graduates."

Getting a bit ahead of the story, I might mention that Miaskovsky nonetheless took Lyadov's course in free composition, studying with him for two years. He then received an offer of the post of director at a music school in Voronezh, but turned it down. As for me, I no doubt profited more from my continued work in Tcherepnin's course than I would have from Lyadov's classes. For that matter, it shouldn't be thought that Lyadov and I parted violent enemies. Three or four years later we met up with each other several times at the home of Ruzsky, a wealthy, hospitable man who gave marvelous dinner parties. At about two o'clock one morning, Lyadov, who had a glass of Benedictine in his hand and was swaying slightly, came up to me and asked, "Is it true that you play chess pretty well?"

"Yes, I play, Anatoly Konstantinovich."

"And you played to a draw with Lasker?"

"Yes, at a simultaneous session."

"I used to know both Chigorin and Schiffers. [He pronounced "Schiffers" very harshly, with a Russian e, just as he pronounced *"seksta"* and *"tertsiya."*] Sometimes I played with them. But I have given it up."

Thirty years later I had a dream about Lyadov. He was sitting in some kind of amphitheater, and I was sitting behind him, a bit higher up, with my elbows on his shoulders. Wanting to annoy him, I said, "The sad thing was that we all counted on your being an innovator, but you turned out to be terribly conservative."

108

One evening that spring I went to the Small Auditorium at the Conservatory to hear a public student recital of the kind at which I had played the Rubinstein étude the December before. I noticed Vera Alpers in the balcony and sat next to her.

She was concentrating hard. "The next number," she told me, "will be played by two students from our class. Please listen to them closely."

Vera was studying with Mme. Ossovskaya, the wife of that Ossovsky I have already mentioned. She was a very nice lady but only so-so as a teacher.

Her two girl students came onstage, accompanied by a boy of about sixteen, who took his seat between them. They played some suite for two pianos (hence the use of a score), and he turned pages, first for one and then for the other. I was interested in his looks. He had a huge, rectangular forehead and a rather handsome though somewhat flattish face. His behavior was free and easy.

"Well, how do you like the way our students played?" Vera asked.

Having been caught completely unawares, I mumbled, "All right, I guess. But who is that young man with the easygoing air who turned pages?"

"That's Max," Vera said. Then she rushed off to congratulate her friends.

"Max" could have been a first name, but it also might have been a last name. I started for the green room, thinking as I went about what I would say to Mme. Ossovskaya (whom I knew) about the performance of her two students. When I got there I found her surrounded by all her students, with whom she was carrying on a spirited discussion of the performance. I went up to her and congratulated her upon how well her students had played. She and the two girls listened to my comments, thanked me, and introduced me to someone, but they left Max standing to one side. I went up to him and said, "You turned pages most artistically." The tone was lightly ironic but pleasant.

"What, sir?" he asked. "Oh, that. I did my best. Thank you."

I don't recall how that acquaintanceship developed, but with the coming of sunny weather that spring, the three of us—Vera Alpers, Max, and I—started taking little walks through the city.

From the diary of Vera Alpers.
April 20 (May 3), 1909.

Serezha was rather irritable today. He chatted with Max. In general I am displeased that he got acquainted with Max, because Max obviously wants to start us quarreling. No doubt he is portraying me to Prokofiev in an unfavorable light. . . .

If he succeeds, it will be a bad thing for him too, since my feeling for

Serezha has developed to a sufficient degree . . . and such quarrels will have consequences.

During the walks with Maximilian Anatolyevich Schmidthof (for such was his full name), he and I exchanged a good many caustic remarks, going into great detail. He was witty and loved to cavil at words. For my part, I was fond of attacking, and in those verbal battles I sought out areas where he was the weaker. Music was one such area. Although Max was musical and had a wonderful memory, I knew more than he in that field. For his part, if I constructed a sentence wrongly, he would immediately seize upon my mistake and hang on as long as he could.

On one occasion I got tired of trying to beat off his attack and fell silent. Whereupon Vera said sympathetically, "You're probably tired."

I couldn't forgive her for that. In general, she said nothing during most of the time of those walks. But she regarded herself as an arbiter, or the one being courted by both of us, or the one in whose honor those cockfights were being fought. That was not true. No one was courting her. We took her along on those walks as a female partner—someone who understood music and was pleasant to have along on an excursion.

"Do you want me to give you some good advice?" Max asked me one day.

"Please do," I replied.

"Make a transcription of the 'Polovtsian Dances' from Borodin's *Igor*. But do it in such a way that it comes out a bit more complex— à la Liszt, for example."

"I'll think about it. It's a good piece of advice."

His suggestion really did interest me, although I never carried it out.

For his part, Max found an area where he could attack me: quotations from Schopenhauer. Either I wouldn't know how to object or the replies that I improvised would not always be successful.

"Can it be that you haven't read him?"

"That's right, I never have. But I know from my parents that to read through Schopenhauer is like taking a cold bath in pessimism."

"I took that bath two years ago," Max said. (He liked the expression "take a bath.") "And on the bottom I found some brilliant ideas."

The fact that he had mastered philosophical theory at fourteen or fifteen (he was a year younger than I) engendered in me a certain respect for him.

"Have you learned to play chess?" I asked.

"Yes, I have."

"We can play a game by correspondence this summer."

"All right. That will give us a reason to continue our exchange of opinions at the same time."

And that was the way things went during our walks along the streets and quays of Petersburg in the spring of 1909: rather roughly but quite gaily, as things tend to go when one is seventeen.

109

From the diary of Vera Alpers.
May 15, 1909.

Serezha is going away soon, and it looks as if we won't make up. It's all my fault.

May 19, 1909.

I haven't seen him for three days. Saturday, at the exam, we sat together and had a very friendly talk. But he suddenly broke off, as though a fly had bitten him, and disappeared. And I haven't seen him since. Actually, I don't agree with Prokofiev's politics.* For some reason he has begun to drift away from me. Perhaps he is bored with me. But why spoil a relationship just before leaving for the entire summer?

May 20, 1909.

What a beautiful night! A bright, fresh May night! Serezha has already gone to the station, and in another half hour he'll be on his way to the country—to the scents of spring and the song of the nightingale. The lucky fellow!
The train goes clickety-clack on the rails, and through the open window one can feel the fresh evening breeze on one's face. And he is perhaps recalling the distant Conservatory—or, more likely, is playing chess with a fellow-passenger.
Today he made me laugh because of the suit he was wearing. A gray suit, a red tie, and yellow shoes. But for that matter, the suit becomes him.

(My black jacket, which I had worn every day, was pretty well worn out and threadbare at the seams. Since I would soon be eighteen and had a diploma as Free Artist, I hinted to Mother that it wouldn't be a bad idea to have a real adult's made for me. A gray one, for example.
"All right," she agreed. "On Nevsky Prospect, across the Gostiny Dvor, there is a nice store. Ask Shurik Rayevsky to go and pick out something suitable for you."
Shurik Rayevsky always dressed foppishly, and he gave me a little lecture: "A suit should never fit you as if it were poured out of a mold. It should not cling closely to your torso as if you were a wooden mannequin. That's the way the German tailors make them. Now you take the English—they really know

* *Politika,* which can also mean "policy." (Translator's note.)

how to tailor clothes! With them everything allows for free movement. Yet how well their suits fit them!"

At the store recommended by Mama we looked over a half-dozen suits and finally chose a gray one. It fitted me rather well, although the sleeves were short. But there was extra material, so the sleeves could be lengthened. I brought the suit home, but with the realization that I needed lots of additional items: colored shirts, ties, cuff links, and yellow shoes. My mother agreed that I really needed such things for the suit, and gave me some money for the extra purchases.

This time I asked Miaskovsky to go with me. In choosing shirts and the ties to go with them, he showed a rather strange taste. "I would choose cuff links with spiders, but they don't have any here," he said.

"With spiders?"

"You see, every cuff link has the form of a little box into which some kind of liquid is poured. And in that liquid is a spider—a real one."

"Alive?"

"Of course not. That is, the spiders are quite real, but I don't know what is poured into the little box. Perhaps it's alcohol. And since the spiders have died, the alcohol is used simple to preserve them."

We chose more ordinary cuff links—not the zoological kind. Then, no longer accompanied by Miaskovsky, I went to buy a pair of shoes. When I had changed into the whole new outfit, I went to show it off to him.

He laughed. "Oh me, oh my! Sergei in yellow shoes!"

But when he had made me turn around, he decided the effect wasn't bad; and most important, that it was a very jolly landscape.)

It was getting close to the time when I would be leaving for Sontsovka. I was going alone, since my mother was remaining in Petersburg to make the move to a new apartment we had found at 7 Bronnitskaya Street. It was bigger than the one at 90 Sadovaya, and I daresay more elegant, with a doorman and carpeted stairs. Unfortunately, one had to walk up those carpeted stairs to the fourth floor. But at age seventeen, and with a healthy heart, one could overlook that.

110

When I got back to Sontsovka I set to work on my sinfonietta, for which I had already thought up several (about five) themes that spring. The incentives for this were: first, the work I had done on classical scores in Tcherepnin's course; second, Kankarovich's suggestion that it be performed in Voronezh. Kankarovich had been graduated from the Conservatory with a major in conducting, and had been engaged to conduct summer concerts in Voronezh. He took advantage of this to suggest to a few composers that he conduct their pieces, and they were naturally pleased and shook hands on it. Finally, early in the year

I had heard Rimsky-Korsakov's sinfonietta,[178] and that genre struck me as very charming, gentle, and attractive. Therefore I chose the sinfonietta form and set to work with great enthusiasm.

It was the first time in my life that I had been promised that a piece of mine would be performed by an orchestra while still in manuscript. Theretofore, the idea of a performance had hovered somewhere between a possibility and a suggestion.

> From me to Kankarovich in Voronezh.
> Sontsovka, May 27 (June 9), 1909.

I have now been in the country for a week. I am completing the orchestral score of one movement of the sinfonietta. I plan to complete the entire score by the beginning of July, and send it to you so the parts can be written out. I'll come to Voronezh myself in the second half of July. I hope this will be a convenient time for the performance of the sinfonietta, and also of the Korsakov concerto. I have bought the orchestral score and the parts. [I wanted to play the concerto with his orchestra, since I had worked it up for my last exam with Winkler.] I would also like very much to hear my symphony performed, but I'm afraid that would be asking too much. As for its difficulty, it is by no means as difficult as you think. The Court Orchestra sight-read it *without once stopping.*

Well, what's new? How do you like Voronezh? What kind of concerts are you giving? I'm very interested in the make-up of the orchestra.

So long, and all the best to you. I'm waiting for your answer.

Prokofiev[179]

> Kankarovich to me in Sontsovka.
> Voronezh, unspecified date in June, 1909.

Dear Friend Prokofiev:

I apologize profusely for having delayed my reply to you for so long. The reason: a mountain of work that exhausts me terribly and gives me not a single minute of rest.

With respect to performances of your works, I cannot say anything definite yet. The thing is that most of the members (about thirty) of our orchestra are Jews who, not having permits to reside in Voronezh, have been ordered to leave the town. At the moment efforts are being made to obtain permission for them to stay. But if those efforts should not be crowned with success, the orchestra will break up *volen snolens* and cease to exist.

In any case, when your sinfonietta (I gather that's the way it should be spelled, should it not?)[180] is ready, write me. And write me in general—I'll be very glad to hear from you.

Yours,
A. Kankarovich[181]

From me to Kankarovich in Voronezh.
Sontsovka, June 14 (27), 1909.

Dear Anatoly Isaakovich:

Your letter alarmed me very much. Can it be true that your impending summer experience as a conductor, and mine as a listener to my own music, is going to the devil?

I very much hope that all your troubles will vanish, and that everything will go as it should.

Write and tell me about the make-up of your orchestra. Also (providing your affairs get straightened out) about how much it will cost, and how much time will be required, to write out the parts of the sinfonietta: eighty pages for the smallest orchestra (for single trumpet and one trombone only from time to time). I may use a harp in one movement; but if you don't have a harpist, there's no great harm done.

So write me soon—right away—about how things are going with you. Either comfort me, or kill me with one blow!

I'm waiting.
Prokofiev[182]

From Kankarovich to me at Sontsovka.
Late June 1909.

Dear Friend Prokofiev:

Things have been straightened out here in Voronezh. Our orchestra has three trombones, a harp, etc.

I should say we can get your sinfonietta copied out rather quickly. One of the orchestra members is a good copyist. Write. I'll be glad to hear from you.

All the best.
Yours,
A.K. [183]

From me to Kankarovich in Voronezh.
Sontsovka, July 4 (17), 1909.

Dear Anatoly Isaakovich:

I'm glad your affairs have been straightened out. My sinfonietta is just about completed. So tell me very definitely whether your orchestra will be able to perform the symphony, the sinfonietta, and the Korsakov concerto.

For my part, I have drawn up the following play. On July 25 I will send you the orchestral score of the sinfonietta so that the parts can be copied out. That should take about ten days, and somewhere between August 5 and August 10 I shall arrive in person. Naturally, I should like to spend the shortest possible time in Voronezh: time for two or three rehearsals and the concert.

I am now waiting for you to send me any corrections in my plan, *accurate* data, and your opinion.

And please write a bit more!

Best regards,
S. Prokofiev.[184]

My father said, "I'm curious to hear the sinfonietta you're composing. When you know the date of the performance for sure, I'll try to arrange my affairs so that I can go to Voronezh on the day of the concert."

From Kankarovich to me at Sontsovka.
July 9 (22), 1909.

Dear Friend Prokofiev:

I have just had your letter.

Whether or not you swear at me, punish me, call me a liar, a man of no conscience, etc., I make haste to give you some news that is unpleasant for both you and me. The thing is that I am cutting loose from Sokolovsky and leaving Voronezh. The circumstances and reasons are as follows.

When I was on my way to Voronezh, Sokolovsky paid me all kinds of compliments, promised me heaps of gold, and in general held out the promise of many enticing things in the sense of conducting. But upon my arrival in Voronezh, when he noticed the rather good reception I got from the public, the press, etc., he backtracked (as the expression goes) and gave me nothing but trash to conduct. For almost two months now I have been conducting Eilenberg, Blok, and Company. My patience has given out and I have categorically decided to leave. [Kankarovich's patience often gave out in the course of his musical career, which was why it was not successful.] I am leaving on the 14th or 15th. I'm thinking of going abroad, but I don't yet know for sure.

I apologize from the bottom of my heart for not having been able to keep my word. I blush and feel ashamed.

But what can I do? . . . We merely propose, but Fate disposes.

I'm very sorry, and once again I apologize.

All the very best to you.

Yours,
A. Kankarovich.[185]

Thus all the hopes I had placed in Voronezh were dashed (partly because Kankarovich had proven to have such a vile character). But on the positive side of things, I had almost completed the sinfonietta. It was written for an orchestra of the size used by Mozart and consisted of five movements. The first, third, and fifth were pastoral in character and were related in terms of materials and tonality, while the second and fourth contrasted with them. My correspondence with Miaskovsky dealt in greater detail with the sinfonietta, as with other musical matters.

III

From me to Miaskovsky in Petersburg.
Sontsovka, June 3 (16), 1909.

Lieber Kola:

I am sending you one of the five movements of my sinfonietta. Look it over and send it back within three days, since I have to revise it, recopy it, and send it to Voronezh. By the way, do you think it needs recopying or not?

I am now starting on the Scherzo [it was an intermezzo] and am writing the first theme entirely in pizzicato. But I'm afraid the cellos will play badly and too slowly—especially in places like this:

Did you get my circular letter [I had reported the publication of Scriabin's *Fifth Sonata* and told where it could be obtained] from Moscow indicating one should go to Jurgenson's for the Scriabin? I like the sonata, although it is too morbid, and want to learn it by heart.

I'm not going to learn the Glazunov sonata, although I enjoy playing it. But tell me: What state of beatific simplemindedness did he fall into on page 37?

Zakharov has reached Italy, and has already sent me three (!) letters in a row. This is a bit out of character. The climate must be having its effect.

Well, I've got nothing more to write about. Write and tell me what you're doing. Is it really true—O bliss!—that my elder child will be returning to me in four hands, together with the younger one? [This refers to Miaskovsky's promise to make a four-hand arrangement of my symphony.]

Your P-v.[186]

From Miaskovsky to me at Sontsovka.
Petersburg, June 8 (21), 1909.

Dear Serge:

I must finally write you, if only a rather disappointing note. My spirits have sunk so low that for some two weeks I abandoned music entirely and did not come near the piano. So your symphony is still lying there. As soon as I am again in a mood for playing and composing, my capacity for working will return, and along with it, the desire to transcribe the symphony. But until that time comes, I am not undertaking anything. Your manuscripts have compelled me to sit down at the piano, and I believe I have fully understood them.

I didn't much like the art song. [I don't recall what song that was, But it is true that at that time I often showed little concern for the vocal part.] The vocal part is completely unsatisfactory—the declamation hasn't been thought out at all. The music proper is better. The *agitato* is quite good, but only in a musical sense. "Oh, Why?" is also quite good. But I find the beginning and the end unsatisfactory. Those melodic shouts demand a completely refined harmony and not an empty fifth; otherwise you get a kind of clumsy primitivism and complete vagueness, especially in connection with the vocal part.

The Intermezzo is really quite good and fresh, although somewhat pallid. I made some comments on it in the score. I especially disliked the C-A-C-A episode: the melody is frightful, and the harmony is nothing more than an intellectual game.

[By way of explaining what the "C-A-C-A episode" was, I shall try to reconstruct it (from memory) as it was in the first version of the sinfonietta.

In it, the theme is first set in C major, then in A major, followed by C major and then A major again—which is why Miaskovsky called it the "C-A-C-A episode."]

The scoring, both here and elsewhere, is very monotonous: always the rocking figure in the violas, the first figure always given to the woodwinds. That's so boring! The harmony of the piece suffers from the defect imputed to Rachmaninov: too much use of pedal points. Good: the beginning up to the pedal point on A, which is somewhat boring although it seems it will soon pass; then the transition to the sixth chord combined with the main theme. Not bad: the episode with the main theme of the first movement, and the codetta; the dying fall is very pleasant. In general, almost everything. Yet I can't get away from the idea that this is not so much a genuine composition as the orchestration of an improvisation.

In conclusion I want to say that I prefer works of yours like the operatic scene to such simplicity, where you almost fall into primitivism à la Sibelius. The "CACA" episode definitely makes you look bad: it is just too homely. And I would say that your other kind of music is more convincing even for Lyadov.

Don't be too angry with me for my forthright response, and send me your next offspring.

N.M.[187]

From Miaskovsky to me at Sontsovka.
Petersburg, June 25 (July 8), 1909.

My Precious:

Why have I heard nothing from you? Can it be you are sulking because of my caviling at your Intermezzo? If so, you are quite wrong, although my completely sincere opinion is that the melody of the middle of the c-a-c-a spoils the piece. But it does not follow from this that your music does not attract me. It's not my fault if I prefer your complexities to your simplicities, because the former display not only your fiery temperament but your purely external technical virtues, without which music for me has only half its value.

Nonetheless, I am hopefully waiting for your next sending—or, in any case, an epistle.

Up to the time when I got your letter I had not yet resumed working at music; and it was only ten days ago that I got back to it. I have now got hold of the Scriabin sonata. I find it extremely attractive and, finally, really Scriabinesque, like *Ecstasy,* with no more traces of Wagner, thank God! I don't like the introduction and the last few bars; they don't tie in with the rest. I believe I have understood the musical idea in this passage; but I don't much like the way it is expressed. Besides, it is hard to play in such a way as to make the thread understandable. But the thought, in my opinion, is:

that is, as a cadential fourth. On the other hand, what spendid pages at the end of the development section!

If you have not yet started learning a sonata for Esipova, take the last D minor. Its first movement is written with great perkiness, and the last movement consists of very grateful variations—unlike the big C major, Opus 53.

But, my precious angel, I am still waiting for your letters and even sendings. It will soon be time for me to work on your E minor [my symphony], since I have already got back to composing and am working steadily.

Unfortunately, I can't send you anything, since this opus of mine promises to be another massive one and—most important—I will be working at it for an infinitely long time.

The piece is an orchestration of Edgar Poe's story "Silence," which I once thoughtlessly suggested to you—to no purpose, fortunately. I am incredibly fascinated by the story line. The work is already planned: all the tempi have been selected; the music is half composed (without polishing), taking up some forty or fifty pages of normal length score. The orchestra will be very large, no less than threefold in the woodwinds; no doubt an extra pair of horns, harps, and, I imagine, a male chorus. I'm afraid I won't complete it by autumn.[188]

In the music I have gotten as far as the cursing of the Devil. Next the howling beast comes onstage, followed by the storm. But I have not yet thought up anything for the Silence. The end has likewise been sketched out. There will not be a single bright note in the entire piece: all will be Gloom and Horror. How it will come out, I don't know. So far it is rather monotonous and melancholy. I beg of you, please send me a manuscript I can have some fun with.

Yours,
N. Miaskovsky

My precept for you is: write complexly—that's your element.[189]

From me to Miaskovsky in Petersburg.
Sontsovka, July 6 (19), 1909.

Lieber Kola:

Not for one minute was I "sulking" at you because of your infamous deed in the matter of my sinfonietta. I fully understood your state of mental incompetence, your revulsion from everything and toward everything; and I was not offended in the slightest. It was just that I decided to wait for the time being and not disturb you until you came out of it. Now, however, permit me to explain to you what an Intermezzo is. An Intermezzo is an interlude for relaxation. Thus it must be: 1) simple; 2) not long and not varied, so that it will not compel the listener to strain his attention; so that he can relax, especially when the Intermezzo comes between two such movements as my Scherzo and Andante will be. This I believe I have attained.

As for the "c-a-c-a episode," I like it so much that I shall include all of it in the Finale, perhaps twice. My first movement has proved to be very pretty and even subtle. The second and fourth movements have been half completed—at great risk, but with some beautiful scoring. The Finale will be a different version of the first movement. All in all, the score will run to about 110 pages.

I very much like Scriabin's Fifth Sonata (= an improved Fourth Sonata). I even want to learn it by heart. But ultimately its unrelieved morbidity for nineteen pages is alone enough to exhaust one and make the piece pall on one. It seems to me that the sonata is too sprawling, and loses its form. The end of the development section is very good. But the high point of exaltation is the frenzy of the last page, *estatico*. Have they published *Extase?*

Have you decided to begin your *Silence?* Well, keep quiet, then. The *theme* is not good but the *themes* are good—especially those of the man and the snail:

I don't understand the Devil's grumbling in the bass. To me, all such grumblings are alike.

For that matter, such an opinion is superficial.

Please send me the orchestral score of my symphony immediately. I have to look it over and correct it in case it is performed at Voronezh. The procedure for making the mailing parcel is as follows: put the score between two pieces of thick cardboard which overlap one centimeter on all four sides; then put a wrapper around it. Rolling it up telescopewise is categorically prohibited. After the way you rolled up the Intermezzo, it is like nothing I've ever seen. It makes me weep just to look at it.

Now don't get angry and sulk. I wish you success in your vow of silence. So long.

Your devoted Free Artist,
P-v.

1909
O, write![190]

PREFACE TO THE NOTES

Sergei Prokofiev's "Notes from Childhood"* represents an unusual departure in autobiography. Here is a unique story of a life in which the author functions not only as a memoirist but as a writer, supplementing his reminiscent narrative with details of life in the Russian city and country as it was lived at the end of the past century and the beginning of the present one.

On many pages the author also functions as a critic of his own compositions dating from his childhood and youth. But the chief thing that makes his autobiography unusually reliable is the publication of original documents (diaries, letters, reminiscences, newspaper reviews), accompanied by the author's detailed commentaries. Yet for all that, the book's structure has been brilliantly worked out: the materials chosen by the author, despite their diversity and variety of form, make an organic whole with the fabric of the reminiscences.

The author's manuscript of his autobiography and all the materials pertaining thereto, together with many of the documents here published, are deposited with the Central State Archives of Literature and Art USSR (TsGALI), in the S. S. Prokofiev Personal Collection.

Sergei Prokofiev's attitude toward writing his "biography of himself" is clearly formulated in the Introduction—and Apology.

As one can see from that introduction, the autobiography was conceived long ago, and the materials were gathered little by little. In his autobiography Prokofiev says, "As early as 1919, having an autobiography in mind, I began to jot down all kinds of events—and even expressions—that I remembered, and to sort them by years." This is borne out by the numerous notebooks, writing pads, and separate sheets of paper on which he jotted down biographical facts, fragments of conversations, notes, and memos to himself. He devised a plan for sorting the materials by years and included excerpts from various sources.

On one page of a notebook we find: "Began to jot down materials for a biography (individual reminiscences) in 1923." And another page bears the amusing notation: "An idea: snip out a piece from each costume and glue it in the album. I know the costume, so I'll associate it with the particular period and events."

* Presently titled *Prokofiev by Prokofiev*. (Editor's note.)

"Autobiography" was the author's own title, as is "Childhood," the title of the first part. Although the maturation of the ideas and the collecting of materials went on over a period of many years, the date when the writing of the autobiography actually began can be fixed as June 1, 1937. This is the date on the first page of the holograph manuscript. The rough draft of it consists of seventy-two sheets plus verses, with numerous paste-ins and insertions in Prokofiev's scarcely legible shorthand, in which the vowels are omitted and unusual abbreviations are used.

The specimens of music quoted in the text were copied out by the author himself, as were the few schemata and sketches. The only musical specimen lacking is that for *Indian Galop* (the first composition in the text). In the place where it was to appear were the words "Specimen 1 (the entire piece)." It may be assumed that this specimen was copied out on a separate sheet that was not preserved. Also, in the text of the author's manuscript, following the description of his first musical manuscript, the author made the following notation: "Photograph of the first manuscript." This testifies to the author's obvious wish to make a photocopy of that manuscript as an illustration.

The rough draft manuscript of "Childhood" was deciphered and retyped while the author was still alive. The typescript consists of eighty pages. At the top of the first page is a heading that was lacking in the rough draft: "Sergei Prokofiev. Autobiography. Part One: Childhood." The date given on the first page of the rough draft ms.—June 1, 1937—is lacking in the typescript. Also, in the course of the typing, certain phrases (or sentences) were omitted, some words were read incorrectly, and some abbreviations were expanded while others weren't. The specimens of musical text were copied from the author's ms. by P. A. Lamm. Also included was a specimen of *Indian Galop,* which was lacking in the rough draft.

In 1939, after he had completed the first part of the autobiography and written several chapters of the second part, he stopped working on it, since at the suggestions of the editors of *Soviet Music* he had begun to write a condensed version of his autobiography.

This was titled *A Brief Autobiography,* and included the chapters headed "Youthful Years," "Upon Graduation from the Conservatory," and "The Years Abroad and After Returning to the Homeland." The first two chapters were published in *Soviet Music* in 1941 and 1946. *A Brief Autobiography* was published in its entirety in the miscellany *S. S. Prokofiev: Materials, Documents, and Reminiscences,* edited, with an Introduction and Notes, by S. I. Schlifstein, 2nd ed., Moscow, 1961 (1st ed., Moscow, 1956).

In 1941, after writing three chapters of *A Brief Autobiography* and bringing his life story up to 1936, Prokofiev abandoned the book and never came back to it. But after a break of six years—1939 to 1945—he again set to work on his detailed autobiography, and during the next six years (with a break in 1947–48) he worked on the second part, which he called "The Conservatory."

In his subsequent work on his autobiography (after the six-year break mentioned previously) Prokofiev was actively assisted by M. A. Mendelson, who had become his wife. Sergei Sergeyevich would remember something and dictate it, and she would write it down. At his instruction she copied out excerpts from letters, reviews, and memoirs. All the rest of the text of the autobiography is in the hand of M. A. Prokofieva (Mendelson) and fills eight notebooks. The last notebook, only half filled, consists of sixty-five sheets, the first of which bears the holographic notation "Sergei Prokofiev: Autobiography. Ninth Notebook. Written by M. Mendelson, taking dictation from S. Prokofiev. (Partially transcribed from his rough drafts.) Notebook begun on August 28, 1950." No date of completion is given, since the work was discontinued. The author breaks off his account of his life after quoting the text of a letter from himself to Nikolai Miaskovsky written on June 6, 1909.

The Prokofiev archives contain many materials that one can assume were used by the author in writing the autobiography as basic or supplementary materials to which he sometimes makes reference and at other times does not mention at all.

Those sources not mentioned by the author include, for example, *Recollections of the Childhood of S. S. Prokofiev,* written by his aunt, E. G. Rayevskaya in 1924; *Recollections of Conversations Relative to the Origins of the Zhitkovs (Shilins),* written by Prokofiev's second cousin, S. A. Sebryakov, in the middle Twenties; the reminiscences of other relatives—K. K. Sezhensky and N. P. Faleyeva; and correspondence with relatives and acquaintances of his parents.

One of the sources that Sergei Prokofiev cites and partially includes in his autobiography is *Recollections of the Childhood and Youth of Sergei Prokofiev,* written—or, more accurately, dictated—by his mother, Maria Prokofieva in 1922. These recollections were taken down and transcribed on the typewriter by B. N. Bashkirov. Sergei Prokofiev made many corrections in the typewritten text of those recollections, and the excerpts from them quoted in his autobiography are from the edited and corrected version. This same version of the *Recollections* was published in the miscellany *S. S. Prokofiev.*

The Recollections of Serezha Prokofiev, written in 1946 by the veterinarian V. M. Morolev, a friend of the Prokofiev family, consists of seven holograph pages in a small hand with no paragraphing for dialogue.

The childhood diary in which Prokofiev made daily entries between July 15, 1909, and the end of that year was included by him in his autobiography (with some small gaps). Unfortunately, of the 110 pages (on sheets of various sizes) in the penciled holograph of the twelve-year-old Serezha Prokofiev, the first six are now lost. The first page that has come down to us is dated July 26 and begins with the words "Got up early . . ."

Among the documentary sources closely related to the diary were two notebooks with various entries which provided the author with abundant material for his reminiscences. These notebooks have been preserved. One of them, consisting of 370 pages in a speckled chartreuse binding, has the following inscription on the first page: "Begun in 1904. February 15." The other notebook— 180 pages in a speckled black and white binding—bears the inscription "Begun on June 29–30, 1905." Judging from the entries, they were made up until the middle of 1907. In his autobiography Prokofiev tells in considerable detail of the content of these notebooks and quotes excerpts from descriptions of mock battles on stilts and croquet games. Several pages from these notebooks have been reproduced as illustrations to the autobiography.

Prokofiev's letters to his father during the years 1902–6 have been preserved. He wrote often and in great detail. Also preserved from this period are letters from Maria Prokofieva to her husband in which she too gives detailed accounts of the circumstances of her son's life.

For 1907 and the following years, no letters from Prokofiev to his father have been preserved. Prokofiev notes in his autobiography that the letters from those years had been collected, numbered, and made ready for binding, but that they were lost. Therefore, in relating events of those years he utilized letters from other people and rough drafts of his own letters that had been preserved.

These include, first, rough drafts of letters to V. M. Morolev, with whom Prokofiev played chess by correspondence. In these letters he gives the latest news about music in the capital, tells of his plans for composing, and writes of his classwork at the Conservatory. Some of these letters are written in pencil in a few columns on large sheets of paper and are very hard to make out. (The "Prokofievan" shorthand had not yet been fully developed.)

In telling of his friendship with two girl classmates in his "academic" courses at the Conservatory—Leonida Glagoleva and Vera Alpers—Prokofiev quotes from correspondence with Miss Glagoleva. It should be noted that, whereas the friendship with the latter lapsed after his graduation from the Conservatory, that with Vera Alpers continued for the rest of the composer's life. While she was at the Conservatory, Vera Alpers kept a diary. When Prokofiev was writing his autobiography, she showed him the diary and gave him permission to make excerpts, which he quoted in the text. Today those excerpts are not to be found in the Prokofiev archives: apparently they were returned to Vera Alpers, together with her diaries, after the composer's death.

From the correspondence with B. S. Zakharov during the summer holidays, Prokofiev selected only a few letters. On the other hand, virtually all of the 1908 correspondence with another Conservatory student, the conductor A. I. Kankarovich, was included in the autobiography. Letters to Prokofiev from his friends are quoted from the originals; his replies are quoted from existing rough drafts.

The correspondence between Prokofiev and Nikalai Miaskovsky occupies a very special place in the autobiography. The creative letters of these two budding composers are exceptionally interesting and pithy. Detailed accounts of their work alternate with circumstantial critical analyses of each other's works, and all this is abundantly illustrated with musical quotations.

Diverging from the autobiography for a moment, one may note that the correspondence between Prokofiev and Miaskovsky continued throughout the lives of both composers. Certain letters from that correspondence were published in the miscellany *S. S. Prokofiev,* and in the second volume of the two-volume miscellany *N. Ya. Miaskovsky: Articles, Letters, Reminiscences,* edited by S. I. Schlifstein (Moscow, 1959, 1960). (That edition—the second volume—will be cited here as the miscellany *N. Ya. Miaskovsky.*)

Prokofiev's letters—carefully preserved by Miaskovsky, judging from the notations—were made available to him for work on his autobiography and for possible publication. Today those letters are deposited at the TsGALI as part of the Miaskovsky archives.

Miaskovsky's letters to Prokofiev have been deposited in the archives of the addressee and also contain the rough drafts of some of his replies. As a rule, there are no discrepancies between the fair copy of a letter and its rough draft. However, while Prokofiev noted, in the rough drafts, the date and place of writing, in the fair copies he gave only the year, omitting the month and day.

Some of the youthful compositions of Prokofiev and Miaskovsky that they mention in their correspondence have not survived, while others, after reworking, became part of new opuses of later times. But the sketches of musical themes and the analyses of various works (or merely their mention) in the letters enabled the author to "reconstruct from memory" many compositions dating from his childhood and youth, quotations from which are given in the autobiography.

Other sources for reconstruction from memory or simply for quotations of music are discussed in detail. These include the manuscripts of compositions written in his childhood. It must be regretfully stated, however, that several of these works from the childhood years which Prokofiev described in detail in the autobiography are not to be found in the composer's archives today. Notes have been provided on these lost manuscripts, as on all those mentioned in the autobiography.

Prokofiev makes frequent mention of a *Catalogue of Childhood Compositions,* which he began to draw up in 1902 (apparently) and in which he entered his compositions from the years 1896–1903, giving their titles and first few bars. The entries in this catalogue were not very accurate. Thus for certain works whose title is given, a space was left but no quotation of the music is given. Judging from the handwriting, some of these blank spaces were filled in by the author at a later time—no doubt during the writing of his autobiography.

Prokofiev quotes from yet another interesting document, naming the author but not identifying the source. This is an unstitched notebook on the first page of which is written: "A List of the Manuscripts of S. Prokofiev in the Custody of B. V. Asafyev (Years of Childhood and Youth: 1896–1910)." This list, drawn up by Asafyev, contains a detailed description of Prokofiev's manuscripts, giving the titles, keys, and dates of composition. It also includes analyses and descriptions of compositions, and insertions of musical themes, viewed by Asafyev as sources, later developed in Prokofiev's work. This document is valuable both as a "sketch" of Asafyev's musicological work and as testimony to the existence of certain of Prokofiev's compositions that have not come down to us. The list was turned over to Prokofiev, along with the manuscripts returned to him, and is to be found in his archives.

Such are the chief sources upon which Prokofiev based his autobiography, in which they are quoted abundantly.

From the above description of the sources of the autobigraphy and of its constituent parts, one can see what a complex and many-layered work it is. Hence the preparation of his work for publication was likewise complex and was carried out in several stages.

Before undertaking the editing and unification of the text, it was necessary to establish a single text, subjecting it to textological analysis. This, in turn, was preceded by two kinds of preparation.

The first involved establishing a single text for the autobiography from the manuscripts and typescripts (in various forms) written by Prokofiev or authorized by him.

The second involved identifying, ascertaining, collating, and ensuring the accuracy of those documentary materials whose texts Prokofiev included in his work. This presented complexities of its own. Almost all the documents were archival materials difficult of access. And the fact that for more than a hundred excerpts the author either gives no accurate dates or gives incorrect dates in his references, making the finding of them even more difficult. When a single text had been established for the autobiography, it was edited and harmonized. However, the fact of heterogeneous documentary sources, and the author's varying approach to them, made it impossible to adhere to one single principle in preparing and editing the text.

At first, the typescript of the first part, "Childhood," was taken as the basic text for publishing purposes. But when it was collated against the author's rough draft manuscript, it was found to have many inaccuracies, with the omission of entire sentences and with incorrect spelling out of abbreviations.

The entire text was verified and established on the basis of the rough holograph, which must be considered as the basis of the published book. In deciphering Prokofiev's shorthand (words that were abbreviated or that lacked their vowels; numbers used in place of letters), we departed from the generally accepted rules for editing, which require that all restored omissions be put in square brackets.

The same principles in the preparation of the text were employed in deciphering the fourteen sheets that constitute the first section of Part II, "The Conservatory." The other text used as basic in preparing this part for publication was that of the notebooks in the handwriting of M. A. Prokofieva (M. Mendelson), as dictated by the author, with his corrections and additions.

The preparation of Prokofiev's childhood diary for publication presented some special problems. The author's cuts in the text of the diary entries are not indicated, since they are explained by the author himself: "To begin with, I shall quote some of the entries in full. Later on, I shall delete matters that are simply not interesting." However, several of those entries that were "not interesting" from the author's point of view may nonetheless be of factual interest and are given in the Notes.

When quoting texts of letters in his autobiography, Prokofiev provided them with headings indicating the sender, addressee, place from which the letter was sent, and destination. But he quotes about a hundred letters without providing them with headings and without dating them. For purposes of providing more accurate information and ensuring uniformity, all letters quoted by the author (in full or in part) have been annotated. The Notes indicate whether the letter was quoted in full or in part (*"from* a letter"). They identify the sender and the addressee and give the date.

With the exception of *Indian Galop* all musical excerpts in the text are facsimiles of authorial holographs.

Prokofiev strove to be accurate in setting forth the facts and events in his autobiography, but in some cases when he was unable to verify them from documents, his memory played him false and the facts and events were somewhat displaced in time. He foresaw the possibility of inaccuracy, and on one page he permits himself the following digression:

> But the trouble is that if a writer lies once and is caught at it, he will be disbelieved in a thousand other instances.
>
> I vacillated for a long time, and broke off work on the Autobiography for several years. But then I decided that the inaccuracies would probably not be very numerous, and that in any case well-wishing readers would forgive me, if only for the sake of those works of mine that they like. (Readers who didn't like my works would not read the Autobiography anyway.)

Actually, the inaccuracies are not very numerous, but they exist. Patent errors in dates have been corrected in the text and explained in the Notes. Likewise corrected in the text are those errors that may be attributed to slips of the pen; for example, when the Brahms G minor *Rhapsody* is referred to as a "ballade"; when the Grieg *Humoresque* from which the author gives a musical quotation is called (in German) a *novellette*.

Other types of mistakes—shifting events from one year to another or lumping several events into one—have not been corrected. This applies, for example, to the account of the piano exam at which Prokofiev played the Buxtehude fugue, and which he moves up two years. Again, Josef Hofmann's concert tours are moved up a year or two. And the concert (attended by Prokofiev) at which Scriabin's *Poem of Ecstasy* was performed could have taken place only on January 31, 1909, and not February 16, as Prokofiev would have it. And there are other inaccuracies of a similar nature. Thus he has his father talking, in 1904, about the doctor's degree that Glazunov received in 1907. Again, he says that in 1906 he had two detailed conversations with A. P. Maksutova, who died in 1905. And he writes of Ya. D. Becker as a living person in 1908, although he died in 1901. The Notes contain explanations of everything it was possible to ascertain and correct. But these time shifts in no way detract from the importance of the incidents and the virtues of their detailed and colorful description. And the author begs the "well-intentioned reader" to forgive him if at times his memory has played him a bit false.

It is hoped that the reader will likewise forgive those slight discrepancies existing in the text of the autobiography. They are not substantive and hence were not corrected or explained. No great harm is done because on one occasion Prokofiev says the distance from Sontsovka to the local hospital was twenty-five kilometers, and that to the post office was eight kilometers, and later gives these distances as twenty-three kilometers and seven kilometers, respectively. After all, the book was not completed—which explains unresolved discrepancies in the details. But this does not apply to the repetitions that one finds in the text. With respect to the same facts, events, and people, Prokofiev sometimes repeats himself, but not out of forgetfulness or because these are unresolved discrepancies in work that was not completed. This is a peculiarity of his narrative manner, and each repetition has a new shading and carries its own cargo of ideas. These repetitions, like certain typically Prokofievan turns of phrase and verb forms, and other stylistic traits of Prokofiev's diction, have been safeguarded against editorical correction.

When Prokofiev mentions certain of his works (e.g., the *Classical Symphony*), he states that he will have more to say of them later. But since chronologically his memoirs break off too early for this, several excerpts that appear in the composer's *Brief Autobiography* and that refer to those works have been given in the Notes.

In the Notes use is made of materials from the TsGALI USSR: the personal archives of Prokofiev: materials from the archives of B. V. Asafyev (f. 2658), N. Ya. Miaskovsky (f. 2040), R. M. Glière (f. 2085), and S. I. Taneyev (f. 880); materials from the archives of the publishers P. I. Jurgenson (f. 952) and A. S. Gutheil (f. 953); a collection of programs (f. 993) and materials from other collections. We have also used the collection of programs and certain other materials from the archives of the A. B. Goldenweiser Apartment Museum (a branch of the M. I. Glinka Central State Museum of Musical Culture).

The Notes include some excerpts from S. I. Taneyev's *Diary,* deposited at the P. I. Tchaikovsky House Museum in Klin. Extracts from the *Diary* were made available by L. Z. Korabelnikova from the edition she is preparing, which is to be published by the Muzyka Publishing House. Also, mention is frequently made in the Notes of Rimsky-Korsakov's book *A Record of My Musical Life* (the 1955 edition published by Muzgiz). With the exception of the afore-mentioned miscellanies, *S. S. Prokofiev* and *N. Ya. Miaskovsky,* the titles of other published sources are given in full whenever they are referred to.

All dates in the Notes are given Old Style, as was the accepted practice in dating events that happened prior to February 1, 1918.

The present edition* of Prokofiev's autobiography is its first publication as an individual book. A condensation of Part One, *Childhood,* was published in the second edition of the miscellany *S. S. Prokofiev;* and excerpts from Part Two, "The Conservatory," were published in the journal *Soviet Music* (*Sovet-skaya muzyka*) (1963; No. 3; 1972, Nos. 3, 4, and 6), and in the journal *Muzy-kalnaya zhizn* (1966, No. 8).

M. KOZLOVA
(Soviet Editor)

* The Soviet edition.

NOTES

PART ONE

1. Prokofiev's parents were actually married on August 27, not April 27, as indicated by a following documentary notation on the notary's copy of his mother's birth certificate:

> The bearer, the maiden Maria Grigoryevna Zhidkova [sic], daughter of the serf Grigory Nikitin Zhidkov [sic], did on April twenty-seventh (27) legally espouse, in her first marriage, the honorable private citizen Sergei Alekseyev Prokofiev.

This birth certificate of M. G. Prokofieva, together with certain other documents, including a notary's copy of Prokofiev's own birth certificate, was acquired by the TsGALI in 1968.

2. Yuzovka was renamed Stalino in 1924 and Donetsk in 1961.

3. ". . . their only good friends were the doctor and the veterinarian." Dr. A. E. Reberg, his wife Maria Iosifovna, and their daughters Vera, Nina, and Zina, who lived twenty-five kilometers from Sontsovka, were frequent guests of the Prokofievs, who maintained good relations with two veterinarians: N. Ya. Klenov and V. M. Morolev.

4. Tchaikovsky's *Fifth Symphony* was written in 1888, and his *Sixth* in 1893.

5. Prokofiev gives the date of his birth as April 11, 1891. But on his birth certificate the date is given as April 15, which corresponds to April 27, New Style.

6. *Indian Galop, allegro,* F major. The original has not been preserved. All that survives are three bars in the *Catalogue,* where the work is designated "Indian Galop, 1896, late summer." On the *Catalogue,* see Preface to the Notes.

7. *Waltz, moderato,* C major 3/4; six bars in the *Catalogue. March, andante,* C major, 4/4; four bars in the *Catalogue. Rondo, allegretto,* C major, 3/4; ten bars in the *Catalogue.*

8. *March, allegro,* B minor (D major), 4/4; five bars in the *Catalogue.*

9. *March* for four hands, *andante,* C major, 4/4; five bars in the *Catalogue.*

10. This album is not to be found in the S. S. Prokofiev Archives.

11. *Waltz, allegretto,* G major, 3/4. The holograph described by Prokofiev is not in the composer's archives. There is only an entry in the *Catalogue* consisting of six bars, including five bars of the introduction in C major.

12. An untitled piece for four hands, fast, F major, 2/4; holograph; first page inscribed: "To my dear, nice Mother from Serezha Prokofiev in 1899." (Opus 1, ed. khr. 199.) Nine bars are entered in the *Catalogue.*

13. On the *Catalogue,* compare the Preface to the Notes.

14. Twelve nonsequential pages of the holograph piano score of the opera, with an explanation of the first two acts, have been preserved. They are in a red cardboard portfolio on which is stamped in gilt: "The Giant, An Opera in Three Acts, composed by Serezhenka Prokofiev."

15. All that has survived of Prokofiev's opera *Desert Islands* are the entries in the *Catalogue:* five bars of the overture, thirteen bars of Scene 1, four bars of Scene 2, and five bars of Scene 3.

16. Several fragments of the piano pieces have been preserved. One of them bears a later notation by Prokofiev: "Apparently the period between *The Giant* and *Desert Islands.* SP." (Opus 1, ed. khr. 200.) The piece from which Prokofiev quotes one bar has not been found.

17. The piece for piano (four hands) and zither, *maestoso,* G major, 4/4 (no ending), has been preserved.

18. On the basis of the story line as recounted by Prokofiev, the first scene of his opera *Desert Islands* resembles the prologue of Borodin's opera *Prince Igor,* and not its first act (as Prokofiev has it).

19. The first of Prokofiev's operas to be staged was *The Love for Three Oranges,* an opera in four acts composed in 1919, with a libretto by the composer based on an entertainment by K. A. Bogak, V. E. Meyerhold, and V. I. Solovyev, which was in turn based on Carlo Gozzi's play. It was premiered on December 30, 1921. The stage director was P. (*sic*) Coini, the sets were designed by B. I. Anisfeld, and the composer conducted.

20. The ms. of this untitled piece has been preserved.

21. In the summer of 1915, on commission from S. P. Diaghilev, Prokofiev began to write the music for the ballet *The Buffoon (Chout),** for which he had written a libretto based on two Russian tales collected by A. N. Afanasyev. The final redaction of the ballet was made in 1920.

22. In the ms. of the autobiography the date reads: "November 18 (December 1), 1902." In dating the letter quoted below these words, Prokofiev repeated the incorrect date given at the beginning of the letter.

23. Ibid., 1, 1 ob.†

24. From a letter from M. G. Prokofieva to her husband, dated November

* This French title of the ballet, frequently used in the literature, is simply the French transliteration of the Russian *Shut* (Buffoon). (Translator's note.)
† This is a Russian archival reference.

17, 1902. The statement that the letter was "of that same date" is incorrect. Compare note 22 above.

25. Seventh ditty of the first series, *allegro con fuoco,* C major, 4/4.

26. In his reminiscences of Taneyev, Prokofiev mentions *Four Etudes for Piano,* Opus 2, in connection with this episode. (The miscellany, *S. S. Prokofiev,* p. 239.)

27. From a letter from Prokofiev to his father, dated December 14, 1902.

28. From a letter from Prokofiev to his father, dated December 17, 1902.

29. First ditty of the second series, C minor, 3/2.

30. Sixth ditty of the second series, *grave,* D major, 4/4. (Ibid. 11, 41 ob.–43 ob.) This same piece exists in a transcription for orchestra: *lento maestoso,* D major.

31. Seventh ditty of the second series, *lento,* E-flat major, C.

32. Eighth ditty of the second series, *presto,* C major, 4/4. There is also a holograph of this piece.

33. Second ditty of the second series, *andante,* A-sharp minor, 7/8. The holograph of this piece bears a notation in the hand of R. M. Glière: "2 methods."

34. All that has been preserved of Prokofiev's opera *A Feast in Time of Plague* are the entries in the *Catalogue:* nine bars of the overture in a four-hand arrangement for piano, and fifteen bars of the subordinate theme in the composer's later handwriting.

35. All that has been preserved of the orchestration of the piece *Warum?* from Schumann's cycle *Fantasiestücke* (Opus 12, No. 3) is nine bars entered in the *Catalogue.*

36. Piece for violin and piano, *lento,* D minor, 4/4. The copy that is mentioned in the autobiography as having been made is not in the composer's archives. There is only a penciled sketch with the notation "Ditty with violin. July 8, 1903. Dedicated to dear Papa," and six bars entered in the *Catalogue.*

37. Ninth ditty of the second series, *moderato,* A major, 4/4. There is also a holograph of this ditty.

38. *The Root of Evil: A Historical Tale Retold for Young Readers,* by P. N. Polevoi. St. Petersburg: 1893.

39. Tenth ditty of the second series, *prestissimo,* D-flat major, 4/4. The rough-draft holograph of this piece is marked "*presto,* D-flat major, 4/4.

40. *Vanity of Vanities: A Historical Tale from Russian Life in the Past Century for Young Readers,* by S. A. Makarove. St. Petersburg: 1901 (previously published in 1887).

41. Piano sonata in B-flat major; first movement, *presto,* B-flat major, 2/4; second movement, *vivo,* F major, 3/8. Preserved only in the form of twenty bars entered in the *Catalogue,* of which sixteen are in the composer's later handwriting.

42. *The Adventures of Rougemont, a New Robinson of the Nineteenth Century,* a tale by L. Rougement (no date).

43. "To the New World for Happiness," a narrative by the geographer and traveler N. I. Berezin in the magazine *Yunyi Chitatel.*

44. Eleventh ditty of the second series, *andante,* F major 4/4. The holograph has also been preserved.

45. *Tell Me, Twig from Palestine (Twig from Palestine),* an art song by S. S. Prokofiev for baritone and piano, F-sharp minor, 4/4, to words by M. Y. Lermontov. A rough sketch has been preserved.

46. The date and day of the week—"Monday the 20th"—is given in accordance with the calendar for 1903. In the ms. of the autobiography, Prokofiev repeated the error he had made in his diary, where some jottings for October are mistakenly headed "Sunday the 20th," "Monday the 21st," "Tuesday the 22nd," "Wednesday the 23rd," and "Thursday the 24th."

47. Twelfth ditty of the second series, B-flat major, 4/4.

48. *Dubrovsky,* an opera by E. F. Nápravník, was produced at the Bolshoi Theater in 1895.

49. *Nero,* an opera by Anton Rubinstein, was staged at the Solodovnikov Theater on October 24, 1903, by N. N. Arbatov. The sets were designed by A. A. Svedomsky, and S. P. Barbini conducted.

50. Fifth ditty of the first series, *maestoso,* C major, 4/4.

51. *I'm Not the Same,* an art song by S. S. Prokofiev to words by Pushkin (*lento,* E-flat major, 3/4). Two penciled sketches have been preserved, one of which is inscribed "Dedicated to dear Mamochka, December 25, 1903."

52. In his diary Taneyev wrote as follows about the visit to him mentioned by Prokofiev, which took place on December 12, 1903: "At three o'clock, Mme. Prokofieva and her son Serezha, age twelve. He brought the score of his opera, *A Feast in Time of Plague.* He has made great progress. His teacher, Glière, also came. I gave Serezha the score of *Ruslan.*"

53. *The Lamps of Truth: Sketches and Scenes from the Lives of Great Men,* by Al. Altayeva (M. V. Yamshchikova). St. Petersburg: 1903 (1st ed., 1900).

54. From a letter from M. G. Prokofieva to her husband, dated March 8, 1904.

55. The copy of the variations on the theme of *Siskin* is not to be found in the Prokofiev Archives.

56. *Undine,* a tale (narrative poem) by the German poet Friedrich de La Motte-Fouqué, was translated by V. A. Zhukovsky in 1837.

57. Prokofiev worked on *Undine* for several years in succession, as he tells us in the second part of his autobiography. The composer's archives include 109 pages of the piano score with the vocal parts, dated by the composer (apparently at a later time): Act III, Scene 1, "The Courtyard of the Castle with the Well,"

bears the date "July 15, 07" on its first sheet; Act III, Scene 2, "The Boat on the Danube"; Act IV, "The Great Hall in Ringsteten Castle," bears the date "26/M 07" on the first page, and "30 June 07" at the end.

58. The actual title of the book is *Mikhail Ivanovich Glinka: Founder of Russian Opera: A Biographical Tale for Young Readers,* by V. P. Avenarius. St. Petersburg: 1903.

59. Letter from Prokofiev to his father, dated March 17, 1904.

60. From a letter from Prokofiev to his father, dated March 18, 1904.

61. *March No. 2,* second ditty of the third series, E-flat major, 4/4.

62. Piece for symphonic orchestra by S. S. Prokofiev; penciled sketch; piano score with indications for orchestration.

63. From a letter from M. G. Prokofieva to her husband, dated March 8, 1904.

64. ". . . he did send me the orchestral scores of Glinka's *Valse-Fantasie* and his *Kazachek.*" A patent error. This should read: ". . . he did send me the orchestral scores of Glinka's *Valse-Fantasie* and *Kamarinskaya.*" In 1902, Rimsky-Korsakov and Glazunov had edited (with a view to a new edition) Glinka's *Valse-Fantasie* for orchestra and his *Kamarinskaya,* a fantasy on themes from two Russian songs for orchestra, the orchestral scores of which were published by Belyayev that same year. It is natural to assume that Glazunov would give Prokofiev classical works in whose publication he was directly involved.

65. It is likely that Prokofiev's father's reply as to Glazunov's doctorate was made not in 1904 but later. Prokofiev "shifted" the events somewhat ahead in time, not taking into account the fact that Glazunov received doctorates *honoris causa* from Oxford and Cambridge universities in 1907, on the twenty-fifth anniversary of his creative activity.

66. On the notebook mentioned by Prokofiev, see the Preface to the Notes.

67. *March No. 3,* sixth ditty of the third series, *allegro,* E-flat major, 2/4, with the notation "Dedicated to my dear Papochka by S. Prokofiev. 28.3.1904." There also exists a holograph orchestral score of this march for band, with the voices recopied. (Op. 1, ed. khr. 206.) In the "Asafyev List" there is a note on this March: "Rhythmically, almost a prototype of the F Minor March, Op. 12."

68. *Vivo,* eighth ditty of the third series, G minor, 2/4, with the notation "Dedicated to my dear Papochka on his birthday, July 8, 1904."

PART TWO

1. From a letter from M. G. Prokofieva to her husband, dated August 23, 1904.

2. From a letter from M. G. Prokofieva to her husband, dated September 2, 1904.

3. From a letter from Prokofiev to his father, dated September 8, 1904.

4. From a letter from M. G. Prokofieva to her husband, dated September 9, 1904. The letter was published in the miscellany *S. S. Prokofiev*.

5. ". . . the things I had written this year." *Undine:* see Note 57 to Part I. *Vivo*, see Note 68 to Part I. *March No. 2*, see Note 61 to Part I. *March No. 3*, see Note 67 to Part I. *March No. 4*, seventh ditty of the third series, *allegro*, F major, 4/4. A note in the Asafyev List reads: ". . . it is curious that one finds typically Prokofievan harmonic logic in this march. (Harmonization of the leading tone as the basis of a chord and not as a third in the dominant.)" *Variations on Siskin*, see Note 55 to Part I. *Romance No. 1* for piano, fifth ditty of the third series, *andante*, E-flat minor, 4/4. *Allegro*, third ditty of the third series, *allegro con fuoco*, D-flat major, 4/4. A note in the Asafyev List reads: "The exposition differs from that of the preceding pieces by the development of the music and tendencies toward tonal variety (sequence-like ascensions and intensifications). Distinct 'Prokofievan' contrasts (*chiaroscuro*) make their appearance." *Presto*, fourth ditty of the third series, C major, 4/4.

6. The incident involving Rimsky-Korsakov, here recounted by Prokofiev, was related in the miscellany *S. S. Prokofiev*, p. 634.

7. From a letter from Prokofiev to his father, dated September 9, 1904. This letter was published in *S. S. Prokofiev*, pp. 630–32.

8. Cf. Note 4, above.

9. Cf. Note 7, above.

10. Cf. Note 4, above.

11. From a letter from M. G. Prokofieva to her husband, dated November 1, 1904.

12. According to the canonical text, the beginning of the prayer is: "We thank Thee, Christ our God . . ." Checked against *The Condensed Prayer Book*, published by M. O. Volf (no date).

13. S. A. Prokofiev died of cancer of the liver on July 23, 1910.

14. M. A. Schmidthof, a pianist and Prokofiev's fellow-student at the Conservatory, killed himself early in the morning of April 27, 1913. (He shot himself in the woods not far from Teriod.) That same day Prokofiev received a note from him which read as follows: "Dear Serezha. I am reporting the latest news to you. I have shot myself. Don't grieve overmuch. Just take it in your stride: it doesn't merit anything more than that. Farewell, Max. The reasons were not important." This undated note was apparently written on April 26, the day before the suicide. The envelope was stamped "27.IV.13.—8" by the receiving post office, and postmarked by the Finnish Postal Department (name illegible) "9.IV.13." Prokofiev dedicated the following pieces to the memory of M. A. Schmidthof: *Allemande*, a piano piece from Opus 12; *Piano Concerto No. 2*, Opus 16; and the *Second* (Opus 14) and *Fourth* (Op. 29) *Piano Sonatas*.

15. From a letter from Prokofiev to his father, dated November 7, 1904.

16. From a letter from Prokofiev to his father, dated November 10, 1904.

17. The Russian Musical Society or RMO (IRMO beginning in 1896) was

in existence from 1859 to 1917. It was founded in St. Petersburg and headed by a committee of directors. In 1859 the RMO opened a music school in St. Petersburg which served as the base for the Conservatory, founded in 1862. The RMO organized symphonic and chamber music concerts. It had branches in St. Petersburg, Moscow, and other Russian cities.

18. The Siloti Concerts. Such is the name that has been given, in the history of Russian music, to the symphonic (and, later, chamber music) concerts organized by Alexander Siloti in St. Petersburg in 1903. Siloti often performed at these concerts as pianist and conductor, but his chief contribution consisted in organizing them: in drawing up interesting programs, inviting composers and performers, concluding contracts with orchestras, renting concert halls, etc. The Siloti Concerts existed until 1917.

19. From a letter from Prokofiev to his father, dated November 10, 1904.

20. *Mlada*, a collaborative opera-ballet by Cui, Moussorgsky, Borodin, and Rimsky-Korsakov, based on a scenario by S. A. Gedeonov (text by V. A. Krylov) was composed in 1871–82 but was not completed, since the Directorate of the Imperial Theaters, which had commissioned it, refused to produce it. Of the music that was composed, the following excerpts were published individually: the first act of the opera, by Cui; a *March* and *Night on Bald Mountain*, by Moussorgsky (reworked by Rimsky-Korsakov); and a *Finale* by Borodin (scored by Rimsky-Korsakov).

Later the story line was used by Rimsky-Korsakov, who in 1890 wrote a mythical opera-ballet with the same title, *Mlada*.

The concert whose rehearsal Prokofiev attended was given on November 13, 1904.

21. The concert in which Possart took part was given on November 27, 1904. He read Schiller's "Elysian Holiday" and E. Wildenbruch's "Song of the Witches," with music by M. Schillings, who also took part in the concert, conducting his own works.

22. The holograph of the farcical song for high voice and piano, *Oh, No! Neither Figner nor Yuzhin . . .* (G-flat major), has been preserved.

23. *March No. 6*, twelfth ditty of the third series, *tempo di marcia*, A minor, 3/4.

24. *March No. 5*, ninth ditty of the third series, C minor, 4/4. (Ibid., 11, 21–22.) In the Asafyev List it is noted that "this march is in ternary form, and variegated in terms of modulation (harmonic and rhythmic development with fanfares within)."

25. *Romance No. 2* for piano, tenth ditty of the third series, *allegretto con espressione*, F minor, 2/4.

26. *Grande Valse*, eleventh ditty of the third series, *allegro con brio*, D major, 3/4. From the Asafyev List: "This waltz is curious by reason of its harmonic feeling-out of directions."

27. From a letter from M. G. Prokofieva to her husband, dated January 10, 1905.

28. A reference to the firing upon a peaceable demonstration of workers on January 9, 1905, which marked the beginning of the Russian Revolution.

29. From a letter from M. G. Prokofieva to her husband, dated January 13, 1905.

30. From a letter from Prokofiev to his father, dated January 12, 1905.

31. From a letter from Prokofiev to his father, dated January 16, 1905.

32. From a letter from M. G. Prokofieva to her husband, January 16, 1905.

33. *Romance No. 3* for piano, second ditty of the fourth series, *lento*, D minor, 2/4.

34. Third ditty of the fourth series, *allegretto*, A minor, 3/4.

35. From a letter from Prokofiev to his father, dated February 5, 1905.

36. From a letter from Prokofiev to his father, dated February 9, 1905.

37. The beginning of the excerpt from Prokofiev's letter of February 9, 1905, is not quoted accurately. In the ms. it reads: "At the Conservatory some students are still on strike. They gather together in bunches and make a hubbub. They have been offered an explanation . . ."

About six hundred persons attended the student meeting at the St. Petersburg Conservatory on February 10 that Prokofiev mentions. In addition to Conservatory needs, they discussed the "Declaration of the Moscow Composers and Musicians" published in the newspaper *Our Days* on February 3, 1905, demanding freedom of thought, of conscience, of speech, and of the press. By a majority vote it was decided to adhere to the "Declaration of the Moscow Composers and Musicians" and declare a strike to close the Conservatory until September 1, 1905.

The subsequent development of events was as follows. On February 18 there was another student meeting, at which the decision to close down the Conservatory was confirmed. At a meeting of the Artistic Council of the Conservatory on February 24, Rimsky-Korsakov, Glazunov, and certain other professors and teachers supported the students' demand that the Conservatory be closed until autumn. But the Conservatory's director, A R. Bernhard, with the agreement of the St. Petersburg Directorate of the IRMO, which administered the Conservatory, ordered that it be opened, and classes resumed, on March 16. By way of response to this order, Bernhard was sent a collective letter signed by Rimsky-Korsakov, Glazunov, L. A. Sakketti, A. A. Petrov, Lyadov, I. I. Zeifert, N. A. Sokolov, and F. M. Blumenfeld:

As a consequence of receiving notice that classes will be resumed at the Conservatory on March 16 (by order of the St. Petersburg Section of the Russian Musical Society), we the undersigned teachers, who at a session of the [Artistic] Council on February 24 voted for suspension of classes until September 1, hereby declare that we have not changed our opinion, finding it impossible for us to resume classes in view of the circumstances which will be inevitable if the Conservatory is reopened prematurely. —N. A. Rimsky-Korsakov, *Complete Collected Works* (Moscow: 1963), II, 221.

38. From a letter from Prokofiev to his father, dated February 13, 1905.

39. From a letter from M. G. Prokofieva to her husband, dated February 13, 1905.

40. At the eighth Symphonic Assembly of the IRMO, on February 19, 1905, with A. B. Khessin conducting, Mozart's C minor Mass was first performed, together with Berlioz's *Fuite en Egypte* (the second part of the oratorio *L'Enfance du Christ*), and Franck's D minor symphony. Also premiered at this concert was Glazunov's *Concerto for Violin and Orchestra,* conducted by the composer, with Leopold Auer as soloist.

In 1905, Leopold Auer—an outstanding musician and professor at the St. Petersburg Conservatory—took a reactionary position vis-à-vis the progressive faculty members, who demanded that the Directorate of the IRMO grant autonomous rights to the Conservatory. In commenting on his own letter and saying that Auer was "hissed for political reasons," Prokofiev is getting a bit ahead of the story. The incident after which Auer was subjected to public criticism in musical circles and in newspapers took place in the autumn of 1905, when Auer undertook to conduct a concert at the third Symphonic Assembly of the IRMO (on November 12), in which many leading musicians refused to take part as a protest against the dismissal of Rimsky-Korsakov from the Conservatory.

41. *Ditty No. 40,* fourth ditty of the fourth series, *energico,* D minor, 6/8.

42. From a letter from Prokofiev to his father, dated February 23, 1905. The author has incorrectly quoted the penultimate sentence in the letter. In the ms. it reads: "I'm terribly sorry that I missed Lyadov's class. As you know, there was no class on Saturday the 19th, and Lyadov missed the one before that on account of illness. The question now is: Will there be on Shrove Saturday or not?"

43. On March 16, 1905, the St. Petersburg Conservatory was surrounded by police, and more than a hundred persons were detained and taken to the police station. By order of the director, all those detained were expelled from the Conservatory. On the next day, March 17, by decision of the Students' Committee, a number of students slipped through the police cordon and, in order to stop classroom work, created a so-called chemical obstruction, spilling a foul-smelling liquid in the rooms of the Conservatory.

44. The open letter from Rimsky-Korsakov to the director of the St. Petersburg Conservatory, dated March 16, was published in the newspaper *Russkiye vedomosti* on March 17 (reprinted on March 19 in the newspaper *Rus*).

45. From a letter from Prokofiev to his father, dated March 19, 1905.

46. *Ditty No. 41,* fifth ditty of the fourth series, *allegretto,* C minor, 2/4,

47. From a letter from Prokofiev to his father, dated March 20, 1905. Dated by Prokofiev on the basis of its content.

48. The events at the St. Petersburg Conservatory mentioned by Prokofiev developed as follows. After the clashes between the students and the police on March 16 and 17, a group of teachers at the Conservatory sent A. R. Bernhard a letter on March 18 demanding his resignation:

> . . . recently it has become very plain that there is total dissension between you, the director, and us, the faculty at the Conservatory. You have shown that you are completely ignoring the Artistic Council. Although you are its chairman, you have not only failed to defend its decision but have gone directly against the majority, which has declared that under present circumstances classes cannot be resumed before September 1. We trust that the events of the past few days have sufficed to show how right we were in insisting on suspension of classes, and how shameful were the consequences of your manner of acting.
>
> On the basis of the foregoing we have concluded that it is your moral duty to resign as director of the Conservatory. —N. A. Rimsky-Korsakov, *Complete Collected Works* (Moscow: 1963), II, 221.

On March 19, at a session of the Artistic Council, Bernhard demanded that the Conservatory be reopened on March 21, and insisted that a list of those students who had instigated the strike be sent to the police. The faculty, headed by Rimsky-Korsakov and Glazunov, prevailed in having classes suspended until September 1. After some sharp debates, the letter quoted above was handed to Bernhard. Glazunov was put forward as a candidate for the post of director.

On that same day, March 19, at a session of the St. Petersburg Directorate of the IRMO, Bernhard's resignation was accepted, and N. F. Solovyev was named interim director of the Conservatory. At the same time it was decided to dismiss Rimsky-Korsakov from the Conservatory faculty for having defamed the directorate and spoken out in the press. This decision was confirmed by the vice-president of the IRMO, Grand Duke Konstantin Romanov, and on March 21 it was conveyed to Rimsky-Korsakov. On March 24, in an open letter, he declared that he was relinquishing his honorary membership in the IRMO.

On March 24, Glazunov and Lyadov issued the following statement to the St. Petersburg Directorate of the IRMO—a statement that was published in the newspaper *Rus* on March 25, 1905:

> Having learned of the dismissal of N. A. Rimsky-Korsakov, Distinguished Professor of the Petersburg Conservatory, we have the honor to inform the Directorate that, to our great regret, we cannot continue our pedagogical activity at that institution after this accomplished fact.

The resignations of Esipova, Verzhbilovich, and Blumenfeld are mentioned in Rimsky-Korsakov's *Chronicle* (p. 230).

49. Letter from Prokofiev to his father, dated March 23, 1905.

50. From a letter from Prokofiev to his father, dated March 27, 1905.

51. From a letter from Prokofiev to his father, dated March 30, 1905. On Rimsky-Korsakov's letter see Note 44 of Part II.

52. From a letter from M. G. Prokofieva to her husband, dated March 31, 1905.

53. From a letter from Prokofiev to his father, dated April 3, 1905.

54. From a letter from M. G. Prokofieva to her husband, dated March 24, 1905.

55. From a letter from Prokofiev to his father, dated April 6, 1905.

56. From a letter from M. G. Prokofieva to her husband, dated April 7, 1905.

57. *Romance No. 4* for piano, seventh ditty of the fourth series, *allegro con fuoco,* B-flat major, 4/4. Asafyev's List reads: "It is in ternary form. The middle part is in A minor. The character of the music is agitated in a Schumannesque manner; there is impetuosity in it. But in general the feeling is still naïve and 'exalted.'"

58. On V. M. Morolev's *Recollections of Serezha Prokofiev* see the Preface to the Notes.

59. See Note 57 of Part II.

60. Eighth ditty of the fourth series, *presto,* A minor, 4/4.

61. Letter from Prokofiev to his father, dated August 28, 1905.

62. Postscript by M. G. Prokofieva dated August 29; added to Prokofiev's letter to his father, dated August 28, 1905.

63. In transcribing the text of fragments from his letter to his father dated August 31, 1905, Prokofiev exchanged paragraphs in certain places. In the middle of his letter, and at the end of the quotation from it, he put fragments from a letter from his mother to his father, dated September 1, 1905.

64. On the letter from M. G. Prokofieva that is quoted, see the preceding note.

65. From a letter from M. G. Prokofieva to her husband, dated September 7, 1905.

66. From a letter from Prokofiev to his father, dated September 11, 1905.

67. From a letter from Prokofiev to his father, dated October 10, 1905.

68. From a letter from Prokofiev to his father dated October 13, 1905. In this same letter he quotes the text of the letter from Vasily Shpis.

69. From a letter from Prokofiev to his father, dated November 16, 1905.

70. From a letter from M. G. Prokofieva to her husband, dated October 27, 1905.

71. From a letter from M. G. Prokofieva to her husband, dated October 15, 1905.

72. From a letter from Prokofiev to his father, dated December 1, 1905.

73. From a letter from M. G. Prokofieva to her husband, dated October 23, 1905.

74. *Ditty No. 42,* sixth ditty of the fourth series, *allegro,* A-flat major, 4/4.

75. From a letter from Prokofiev to his father, dated December 1, 1905.

76. The ditties of the fourth series. Ninth, *andantino,* D minor, 4/4. Tenth, *presto,* C minor, *alla breve,* with nine pages and not thirteen, as Prokofiev writes. Note in the Asafyev List: "A broad but nonetheless monotonous (harmonically and rhythmically) exposition. The feeling does not impress one, since the piece represents rather a searching for 'one's own' excitement, one's own symphonic development, than genuine passion." Eleventh, minuet, *allegretto,* F minor, 3/4. Twelfth (à la Mendelssohn), *moderato,* E-flat major, 4/4.

77. From a letter from Prokofiev to his father, dated January 18, 1906.

78. Prokofiev's penciled postscript, not to the letter he mentions but to a letter from M. G. Prokofieva to her husband, dated January 18, 1906.

79. *Scherzo,* second ditty of the fifth series, *allegro,* C major, 4/4.

80. First ditty of the fifth series, *moderato,* C-sharp minor, *alla breve.* In his list Asafyev notes its "ternary nature. Romantic feeling with the inevitable triples."

81. From a letter from M. G. Prokofieva to her husband, dated January 29, 1906.

82. Letter from M. G. Prokofieva to her husband, dated February 3, 1906. In quoting the text of this letter, Prokofiev changed the order of paragraphs here and there.

83. The actual title of the book by V. P. Avenarius is *Gogol's Student Years: A Biographical Trilogy: I—Gogol as a High-School Student; II—Gogol as a College Student; III—The Life School of a Great Humorist* (3rd ed.; St. Petersburg: 1904).

84. There is no book by Avenarius with the title *Pushkin's Childhood Years.* It is likely that Prokofiev is referring to that author's *Pushkin's Youthful Years* or *Pushkin's Adolescent Years.*

85. From a letter from Prokofiev to his father, dated February 3, 1906.

86. From a letter from Prokofiev to his father, dated February 9, 1906.

87. From a letter from Prokofiev to his father, dated February 12, 1906

88. From a letter from Prokofiev to his father, dated February 16, 1906.

89. *Ditty No. 51,* third ditty of the fifth series, *presto,* C minor, 4/4.

90. From a letter from Prokofiev to his father, dated April 27, 1906.

91. Prokofiev kept all letters addressed to him, along with copies of rough drafts of his own letters. When his archives were being prepared for transfer to the TsGALI for permanent deposit (after the composer's death, this work was completed by his wife, M. A. Prokofieva), the bound volumes of letters were unsewn, sorted by correspondents and addressees, and combined with more recent letters.

92. Eight ditties of the fifth series. *Waltz,* fifth ditty, *allegro,* G minor, 3/4. Asafyev's comment, quoted by Prokofiev, is taken from his List. *March,* sixth ditty, F minor, 2/4. Note in the Asafyev List: "This is the original version

of the March of Opus 12, still considerably more "rawish." Seventh ditty, *prestissimo,* D major, *alla breve.* A note on it on the Asafyev List reads: "The final cadence is a 'premonition' of the cadence of the March from *Three Oranges."* Eighth ditty, *allegretto,* A-flat major, 4/4, unfinished. Ninth ditty, *allegro con fuoco,* unfinished. There is neither a tenth nor an eleventh ditty. Twelfth ditty, *vivo,* C major, 2/4. A note on it in the Asafyev List reads: "Its ternary character . . . The Prokofiev manner: *élan,* impetuosity, compression, distinct accentuation, no decoration: only that which is necessary for finished utterance."

93. On V. M. Morolev's *Recollections of Serezha Prokofiev* see the Preface to the Notes.

94. M. K. Moroleva's *Recollections.*

95. See Note 92.

96. For details of the youthful *Sonata No. 2,* which Prokofiev called a *Grande Sonata,* see page 178. The original has not been preserved.

97. On the *Grande Sonata* in F minor see the preceding note.

98. The cycle—*Ten Pieces for Piano,* Opus 12—was put together by Prokofiev in 1913 from his works of 1906–13. No. 2, *Gavotte,* is dedicated to Boris Zakharov.

99. In addition to the art song mentioned by Prokofiev, Opus 9 (1910–11) included the song "There Are Other Planets," to words by Konstantin Balmont. The holographs of both songs were preserved in the archives of the Gutheil Publishing House.

100. The "thin music book with a bright green cover" has not been located in the Prokofiev archives. In the Asafyev List it is described in detail:

> A thin music notebook in a paper (chartreuse) cover. Twenty pages of holograph (in ink). Piano pieces as follows. *Reproach* (andante, 6/8, A minor). *Chant sans paroles* (penciled note, apparently in the handwriting of a stranger): *presto,* 6/8, D-flat major (middle part in A major, A-flat major). *Intermezzo, allegretto,* C, A major (middle in D-flat major). *Humoresque, allegro,* C. F minor. Next piece untitled, *molto energico,* B-flat minor 3/4 (middle part D-flat major, 3/4). *Oriental Song, andante,* G minor, 2/4. Untitled piece with no tempo indicaton: E minor, 6/8. On the cover of this cycle of pieces is a letter by the composer (in pencil):
> Dear Vasily Mitrofanovich!
> Herewith the pieces I promised. Look them over *before April 5th,* and send them to Sontsovka one way or another. Please be so kind as to think up a title for each and analyze all of their virtues and defects. But don't say something like "They're all pretty good" or "None of them is worth anything"—that's not interesting. Many greetings. Respectfully, S. Prokofiev. March 20, 07.

101. The new version of the *Piano Sonata No. 3,* in A minor with one movement, was composed by Prokofiev in 1917 as Opus 28, with the notation "From old notebooks" and a reference to 1907.

102. *Piece on the Theme of "Esche,"* C minor, 4/4. A holograph of this piece has been preserved. A note at the end reads "April 27, 1910."

103. For an explanation of the term "piano puppies" see p. 197.

104. The letter from Prokofiev to Miaskovsky dated June 26 was published in the miscellany *S. S. Prokofiev,* p. 262.

105. Letter from Boris Zakharov to Prokofiev, dated June 26, 1907.

106. The letter from Miaskovsky to Prokofiev, dated July 12, 1907, was published in the miscellany *S. S. Prokofiev,* pp. 263–64.

107. Letter from Prokofiev to Miaskovsky, dated July 22, 1907.

108. Rough draft of a letter from Prokofiev to Morolev, dated July 28, 1907.

109. *Askold's Tomb,* an opera by A. N. Verstovsky.

110. This letter from Miaskovsky to Prokofiev, dated July 26, 1907, was published in the miscellany *N. Ya. Miaskovsky,* pp. 245–46. The envelope described by Prokofiev has not been preserved.

111. This letter from Prokofiev to Miaskovsky, dated August 4, 1907, was published in the miscellany *N. Ya. Miaskovsky,* pp. 247–48.

112. This letter from Prokofiev to Miaskovsky, dated August 23, 1907, was published in the miscellany *N. Ya. Miaskovsky,* pp. 252–54.

113. Letter from Miaskovsky to Prokofiev, dated September 1, 1907.

114. Yu. Akhron, violinist; student of Leopold Auerbach (an émigré since 1922; in 1939 was living in the U.S.). In 1906–8 his compositions for violin were being published by the Yu. G. Zimmermann Publishing House.

115. Prokofiev played Medtner's *Märchen,* Opus 8, at the following concerts in America in 1920: April 8 (New York), December 7 (Chicago), December 14 and 16 (San Francisco). For several years thereafter he kept it in his concert repertory.

116. From a letter from Prokofiev to Miaskovsky, dated September 26, 1907.

117. From the rough draft of a letter from Prokofiev to Morolev, dated September 4, 1907.

118. From the rough draft of a letter from Prokofiev to Morolev, dated September 29, 1907.

119. From the rough draft of a letter from Prokofiev to Morolev, dated November 22, 1907.

120. Here Prokofiev quotes three fragments from the rough draft of a letter from him to Morolev, dated September 29, 1907. His quotation of the prices of the piano scores for the Wagnerian operas is not accurate. The ms. reads: "And how cheap the Wagner operas are! *Das Rheingold* costs only two rubles, and the three other operas about two rubles and seventy kopecks each. But how much music there is in them!

121. From the rough draft of a letter from Prokofiev to Morolev, dated November 22, 1907.

122. From letters from Prokofiev to Miaskovsky, dated January 3, 1908 (date as per the postmark), and December 28, 1907.

123. *Snow:* one sheet has been preserved on which Prokofiev jotted some of the music, reconstructed from memory, apparently in 1949. The verse has a sketch of the scene of Prince Andrei's delirium for the opera *War and Peace.*

124. *Autumnal Sketch,* a symphonic sketch for small symphony orchestra, Opus 8, 1910. Prokofiev came back to this work later: in 1915 he wrote a second version, and in 1934 a third. A holograph orchestral score from 1910 is in the composer's archives.

125. Opus 12, *Ten Pieces for Piano,* was composed by Prokofiev in 1913. Opus 14, *Piano Sonata No. 2,* in D minor, in four movements, was composed in 1912.

126. *Maddalena,* an opera in one act by S. S. Prokofiev, libretto by M. Lieven (Opus 13, 1911). In 1913, Prokofiev wrote a new version of the opera on the basis of an offer to produce it at K. A. Mardzhanov's Free Theater, but this production was not realized. In his *Brief Autobiography,* Prokofiev says:

> In the summer of 1911 I wrote a one-act opera, *Maddalena,* based on a play with the same title by Baron Lieven. I hoped it might be staged at one of the Conservatory concerts around which I, as a student in the conducting class, was always hovering, and at which operas by Conservatory students were occasionally produced amid all the classical things. But my hopes were not fulfilled. Baron Lieven turned out to be a young society lady, more pleasant in her social behavior than talented in dramaturgy. But *Maddalena,* set in fifteenth-century Venice, involved conflict, love, treason, and murder; and this meant that the composer had to face new problems relative to the anemic *Undine.* I wrote the music rapidly but orchestrated only one of the four scenes. In 1913 I revised *Maddalena,* but again I didn't score it. *S. S. Prokofiev,* pp. 144–45.

127. Ya. D. Becker died in 1901. In 1908 the owner of the music store at 35 Morskoy Boulevard and the Ya. Becker Company (which kept the name of its founder) was K. K. Schroeder, not to be confused with I. K. Schroeder, the owner and inheritor of the K. M. Schroeder piano factory, whose store was at 52 Nevsky Prospect.

In 1908–9 the Thursday gatherings of the "Modernists" ("Contemporaries")—which were private and preparatory in nature—were as a rule held in Hermann and Grossmann Hall at 33 Morskoy Boulevard, headquarters for the piano firms Steinway and Sons and K. Bechstein (and not at the Becker store, as Prokofiev writes). The directorate of "Evenings of Contemporary Music" had office space at the Ya. Becker piano warehouse (corner of Kazan Square and Nevsky Prospect, Nos. 18/27), where Prokofiev may well have been.

In those years the concerts of Evenings of Contemporary Music were given in the auditorium of the Reformatsky School, at 38 Moika.

128. Alfred Nurok was a bibliophile and music lover. The author of *A Practical English Grammar* (2nd ed., 1870) was his father, P. M. Nurok (pseu-

donym M. Nurok). Walter Nouvell was an amateur composer. Prior to 1917 he was an official *per procurationem* of the Office of the Ministry of the Court. Vyacheslav Karatygin made his debut as a music critic in 1906. He published in many periodicals and was editor of the music section of *Rech*. Beginning in 1915 he taught music theory at the E. P. Raphoff Music School, and in 1916, in addition, he was appointed to the chair of History of Music at the St. Petersburg Conservatory, where in 1919 he was made professor. In subsequent years he continued to combine his teaching with the writing of music criticism.

129. Prokofiev's talk with Leonida Glagoleva about *The Valkyrie* took place in 1908.

130. In his account of the examination, Prokofiev gets a little ahead of the story and confuses events of 1908 with events of 1910. In the spring of 1908, at the technical examination for piano, he played études by Clementi and Czerny. At the public examination on April 25 he played: *Etude* (F minor), by I. K. Kessler; *Fugue* (C minor, Vol. II), by J. S. Bach; and *Traumes wirren*, by Schumann.

It was in the spring of 1910, when he was already a pupil of Esipova, that he played Tchaikovsky's *Scherzo à la russe* (Opus 1) and Buxtehude's *Fugue* in A minor. His earliest mention of these pieces is found in the rough draft of a letter from him to Morolev, dated August 18, 1910, in which he mentions them among the pieces he has recently learned; also in a letter to Taneyev dated August 18, 1910, in which he writes:

> Last spring, following your advice, I played Buxtehude's A minor Fugue (which I had earlier transcribed for piano) for A. N. Esipova's examination. I got an A, and Anna Nikolayevna [Esipova] became very interested in Buxtehude's fugues. I know that later she got an entire volume of them from A. K. Glazunov.

131. Buxtehude's *Organ Prelude and Fugue* in D minor, in a transcription by Prokofiev, was first performed by him at a concert in Chicago on January 19, 1922. The transcription of this fugue was published in 1923 by Gutheil.

132. ". . . I got Grieg's *Humoresque* in D major . . . It began more or less as follows . . ." The music quoted at this point corresponds to the beginning bars of Grieg's *Humoresque No. 1* from his Opus 6. In the Prokofiev ms. there is a mistake: he had called this humoresque a novellette.

133. Four-voice *Fugue, moderato*, C major, 4/4. The rough draft of this examination fugue has been preserved. On the first sheet Prokofiev notes: "11 May, 08/10½ 3 p.m." and at the end "14 May 18/3 p.m."

134. From a letter from Prokofiev to Miaskovsky, dated May 20, 1908.

135. From a letter from Prokofiev to Miaskovsky, dated May 31, 1908.

136. From the rough drafts of letters from Prokofiev to Morolev, dated March 31 and May 12, 1908.

137. Rimsky-Korsakov died on June 7, 1908, and was buried on June 11.

138. *The Snow Maiden* was premiered at the Opéra Comique in Paris on May 7, 1908, with F. Ruhlmann conducting. Rimsky-Korsakov did not attend the premiere, since at the time he was seriously ill. Prokofiev's account of the circumstances under which he saw Rimsky-Korsakov, who was ". . . animatedly talking about . . . the brilliant reception that had been accorded him in Paris . . ." probably refers to the preceding year of 1907, since it was on May 24 of that year that Rimsky-Korsakov returned from Paris, where he had taken part in the "Russian Historical Concerts" organized by Diaghilev.

139. Letter from Prokofiev to Miaskovsky, dated June 27, 1908.

140. Letter from Prokofiev to Miaskovsky, dated July 11, 1908, published in the miscellany *N. Ya. Miaskovsky,* pp. 254–55.

141. From a letter from Prokofiev to Miaskovsky, dated August 4, 1908; letter published in the miscellany, *N. Ya. Miaskovsky,* p. 256.

142. From a letter from Prokofiev to Miaskovsky, dated August 12, 1908, published in the miscellany *N. Ya. Miaskovsky,* p. 257.

143. From a letter from Prokofiev to Miaskovsky, dated September 15, 1908.

144. Prokofiev's piano pieces *Despair* and *Suggestion diabolique,* written in 1908, were after revision included by the composer in his cycle *Four Pieces for Piano,* Opus 4: (I) *Reminiscence;* (II) *Elan;* (III) *Despair;* (IV) *Suggestion diabolique,* 1910–12 (1908).

145. Note by Prokofiev on one of Miaskovsky's calling cards, no date, with a notation in the hand of Miaskovsky: "IX/o8."

146. Among the rough drafts of letters and the postcards from Prokofiev to Miaskovsky, there is no postcard bearing the text quoted by the author. He is obviously quoting from material in the possession of the addressee.

147. This postcard from Prokofiev to Miaskovsky, mistakenly dated by him "(I.11.08)," was written on October 31, 1908, as indicated by the postmark ("I.11.o8"); the content: "tomorrow (Saturday)" (Saturday fell on November 1, 1908) and Miaskovsky's jotting "XI/o8."

148. Prokofiev's postcard to Miaskovsky, which he mistakenly dated "(1.III.09)," was written on March 10, 1909, as indicated by the content and the postmark ("11.3.09."). The *"Symphonie domestique"* mentioned in the postcard is a tone poem by Richard Strauss, Opus 53.

149. *Classical Symphony* in D major, Opus 25. Four movements: (I) *Allegro;* (II) *Intermezzo, Larghetto;* (III) *Gavotte, Non troppo allegro;* (IV) *Finale, Molto vivace.* 1916–17. Dedicated to B. Asafyev.

On the subject of this symphony, Prokofiev wrote the following in his *Brief Autobiography:*

> I spent the summer of 1917 near Petrograd. I had been thinking of writing an entire symphony without the help of the piano. In such a piece, the orchestral colors should be more distinct. Thus arose the notion of a

symphony in Haydn's style, since Haydn's technique had somehow become especially clear after my work in Tcherepnin's class; and in that familiar milieu it was easier to embark on a dangerous voyage without the piano. It seemed to me that, if Haydn had lived into our age, he would have preserved his own style of composing and, at the same time, have absorbed something from the new music. That was the kind of symphony I wanted to write: a symphony in the classical style. And when it began to hang together, I renamed it the *Classical Symphony*. First, because that was simpler. Second, out of mischief, to "tease the geese," and in the secret hope that in the end I would be the winner if the symphony really did prove to be a classic.

I composed the symphony while walking through the fields. The *Gavotte* was composed before anything else in the *Classical Symphony*. Then, still in the year 1916, I wrote some material for the first and second movements. But there was still quite a bit of work to be done in the summer of 1917. I discarded the first version of the Finale, together with all its materials, and rewrote it from scratch, *inter alia* setting myself the task of writing it without any minor chords whatsoever. —the miscellany *S. S. Prokofiev* pp. 158–59.

The *Classical Symphony* was premiered in Petrograd on April 8, 1918, with the composer conducting.

150. ". . . the Brahms G minor Rhapsody for a student recital . . ." Prokofiev played it on December 5, 1908. In the ms. of the autobiography, in the sentence quoted and in the text of the paragraph following it, Prokofiev made a mistake, calling the rhapsody a ballade.

151. In 1936, at the suggestion of A. Ya. Tairov, Prokofiev started writing the music for a production at the Kamerny Theater. On this subject he has the following to say in the *Brief Autobiography:*

The play *Eugene Onegin,* an adaptation by S. D. Krizhanovsky, emphasizes for the most part those scenes in Pushkin's novel [in verse] that were not used in the opera (I wrote in *Vechernyaya Moskva*). I think it would be very interesting to see, on the stage, Lensky arguing heatedly with Onegin over a bottle of Ay, Tatyana visiting his empty house, or Onegin "on the banks of the Neva." I have set myself the goal of penetrating as deeply as possible into the real spirit of Pushkin. I enjoyed composing the music for *Eugene Onegin,* and I feel I came up with a number of motifs that were right—although some were not quick in coming.—*S. S. Prokofiev,* pp. 195–96.

Owing to a change in the repertory plans of the Kamerny Theater, *Eugene Onegin* was not staged, and Prokofiev's work was not completed. The holograph for the orchestration of forty-four musical numbers from the music for the production has been preserved.

152. Prokofiev formally transferred to Esipova's class in the spring of 1909, and began working with her in the fall of that same year. He took the entire course in special piano with her, and took the graduation examinations in the spring of 1914. That year the five best Conservatory students, who had played at the graduation examination on April 22, were also entered in the A. G. Rubinstein Competition. Prokofiev played his own *First Piano Concerto* (D-flat major, one movement, 1911–12, published in 1913), being accompanied on another piano by V. A. Dranishnikov. He won first prize—a grand piano. On May 11, 1914, at graduation ceremonies, Prokofiev played the same concerto with an orchestra conducted by Tcherepnin.

153. The clippings from the newspapers *Slovo* (December 20), *Rech* (December 22), *Peterburgsky listok* (December 24) of 1908, with reviews of Prokofiev's first public performance from which he quotes excerpts in the autobiography, are preserved in the composer's archives.

154. Prokofiev himself made the translation from the notice in the newspaper *St.-Petersburger Zeitung,* which was published in Petersburg in German. The original notice (a clipping from the paper) is in the composer's archives.

155. On the *Recollections* of V. M. Morolev, see the Preface to the Notes.

156. Letter from Prokofiev to Miaskovsky, December 17, 1908, dated by the author on the basis of the content; viz., the concert of December 18, 1908. There is no date on the ms. of the letter, but there is a later notation in Prokofiev's handwriting: "16 (?) Dec. O. S."

157. Letter from Prokofiev to Miaskovsky, dated December 19, 1908.

158. Beginning in 1897, the Polish pianist Josef Hofmann repeatedly toured Russia, where his recitals were invariably successful. But Prokofiev could not have heard him in 1908, since Hofmann was not in Russia during the seasons of 1907/08 and 1908/09.

159. It seems likely that Prokofiev mistakenly assigned to 1908 a recital given by Hofmann on March 12, 1910 (when the program included works by Schumann, Liszt, and Chopin).

160. Prokofiev met Catherine Borshch a year later at a recital given by Hofmann in November 1909.

161. Prokofiev's letter of December 29, 1909, is quoted by Glière in his memoirs, published in the miscellany *S. S. Prokofiev* p. 365. The original of the letter is in the Glière archives, and the rough draft, which varies only slightly from it, is in the Prokofiev archives.

162. In speaking of a performance of *The Poem of Ecstasy* on February 16, Prokofiev is confusing events of 1908 and 1909, since the first performance had been announced for February 16, 1908.

163. Prokofiev applies the name "Hall of Columns" to the Great Hall of the Nobles' Club (now the Leningrad Philharmonia). The concert mentioned took place on January 31, and not on February 16 (see Note 162 above).

164. Letter from M. E. Iovanovich to Prokofiev, undated.

165. Letter from Alfred Nurok to Prokofiev, dated February 10, 1909.

166. Rough draft of a letter from Prokofiev to M. E. Iovanovich, dated February 11, 1909.

167. The *Piano Toccata* in C major (Opus 11) was composed by Prokofiev in 1912.

168. The rough draft of Prokofiev's letter to Leonida Glagoleva, dated February 18, 1909, has a correction. In the original version, the last sentence reads: "Nonetheless, on Friday I am making my debut with my toccata—something of which I am happy to inform Your Grace."

169. Letter from L. M. Glagoleva to Prokofiev, dated February 19, 1909.

170. Rough draft of a letter from Prokofiev to L. M. Glagoleva, dated February 20, 1909.

171. Prokofiev carried out his intention. The *Four Etudes for Piano*, which he composed in the summer of 1909 and included in Opus 2, were dedicated to Winkler. The first, second, and fourth études were premiered by the composer at the concert called "The Thirteenth Musical Exhibition," organized by M. A. Deishei-Sionitskaya and given on February 21, 1910, in Moscow. The holograph of the *Four Etudes for Piano* has been preserved in the archives of the publisher who issued them in 1912.*

172. The Prokofiev archives contain a sheet of music paper on which he wrote out the motifs of the first and subordinate themes of the first movement and two variants of themes from the second movement of the *Sixth Sonata*, (Conservatory) corresponding to the music he quotes in the autobiography.

173. This letter from Miaskovsky to Prokofiev is dated on the basis of content ("today being Monday the 23rd"). In the ms. of the autobiography Prokofiev mistakenly dated it March 24, 1909. The letter was published in the miscellany *S. S. Prokofiev*, p. 264.

174. The reference is to "someone in gray"—a character in Leonid Andreyev's play *The Life of Man*, written in 1906 and published in a series issued by the publishing house Shipovnik, No. 1, 1907.

175. Prokofiev twice came back to the sinfonietta he had composed in the summer of 1909, with the intention of having it performed at Voronezh that same year. After writing a new version of it in 1914, he included it in his list of compositions under Opus 5. In 1929 he reworked it again and assigned a new opus number (48) to the third version.

176. The original of Prokofiev's letter to Miaskovsky of March 25, 1909, is undated by the author, and Miaskovsky's dating ("27/III-09") is incorrect. It is dated on the basis of the rough draft, which gives the date.

177. There are no materials from the operatic scene from *A Feast in Time of Plague* in the Prokofiev archives.

* The publisher is not identified, the words "P. I. Jurgenson" having been deleted.

178. Early in 1909 (on January 31), Rimsky-Korsakov's A minor *Sinfonietta on Russian Themes for Orchestra* (Opus 31) was performed at the Second Russian Symphonic Concert, with Blumenfeld conducting.

179. From the rough draft of a letter from Prokofiev to A. I. Kankarovich, dated May 27, 1909.

180. In the text of the autobiography, the word "sinfonietta" is given in the spelling most commonly accepted by music publishers. In the mss. of letters by Prokofiev, A. I. Kankarovich, and Miaskovsky, and in the ms. of the autobiography, it is written variously as "sinfoneta," "sinfonetta," "sinfonieta," etc.

181. Letter from A. I. Kankarovich to Prokofiev, undated.

182. Rough draft of a letter from Prokofiev to A. I. Kankarovich, dated June 14, 1909.

183. Letter from A. I. Kankarovich to Prokofiev, undated.

184. Rough draft of a letter from Prokofiev to A. I. Kankarovich, dated July 4, 1909.

185. Letter from A. I. Kankarovich to Prokofiev, dated June 9, 1909.

186. Letter from Prokofiev to Miaskovsky, June 3, 1909. No date in the ms.; dated by the author on the basis of the rough draft. This letter was published in the miscellany *S. S. Prokofiev*, pp. 264–65.

187. The letter from Miaskovsky to Prokofiev dated June 8, 1909, exists in two versions that are very close in content, both written on the same day. Judging from the tone of the letter, Miaskovsky was in a rather distracted state and after sending the letter, he forgot that he had done so, and wrote another, again setting forth his ideas on the works Prokofiev had sent him. When working on his autobiography, Prokofiev chose the present version of the letter. The other version of it was published in the miscellany *N. Ya. Miaskovsky*, pp. 258–59.

188. After the words "I won't complete it by autumn," Prokofiev cut some material from this letter to Miaskovsky, omitting several sentences and a musical quotation: "I'm not writing anything for Lyadov. My themes are as follows:

This is almost all my melodic material."

189. Letter from Miaskovsky to Prokofiev, dated June 25, 1909; published in the miscellany *N. Ya. Miaskovsky.*

190. Letter from Prokofiev to Miaskovsky, July 6, 1909, dated by the author on the basis of the rough draft; published in the miscellany *N. Ya Miaskovsky,* pp. 261–63.

INDEX

Abramychev (deputy inspector), 109, 111

Abramycheva (student), 216

Adventures of Mademoiselle, The, 17

Adventures of Rougemont, The, 76

Aesthetics, 290, 305

Afanasyev, A. N., 329

Aïda, 30

Akatyev, Kolya, 173

Akatyeva, Mme., 173

Akhron (student), 108–9, 111, 216–17

Akimenko (composer), 283

Alekseyevka, 148

Alexander III, 12

Allegro. See Ditties

Allemande (Opus 12), 333

Alpers (Vera's father), 290

Alpers, Boris, 291

Alpers, Vera, 216, 290–92, 307–8, 309, 322

Alphabets, 92, 247

Altayev, 85

American flag, 18–19

Amishka (cat), 140

Andrei, Father, 12, 23, 211–12

Andreyev, Leonid, 305

Andreyevka, 67, 148, 179

Anisfeld, B. I., 329

Anisimova (student), 216

Appel, David H., explanatory note by, vii–viii

Apukhtin, Alexei, 186

Arbatov, N. N., 331

Arensky, Anton Stepanovich, 58, 80
death, 171

textbook, 44, 55, 103

Arithmetic, 154

Art Theater (Moscow), 81

Asafyev, B. V., 112, 118, 152, 156–57, 171, 181, 182, 184, 203, 220, 239, 326
and children's operas, 201, 206
Classical Symphony dedicated to, 344
drops out of class after talk with Rimsky-Korsakov, 301
and list of Prokofiev's manuscripts, 323, 324
Miaskovsky discusses, 206
mistakes in exercises, 130, 134, 140, 161
on Prokofiev ditty, 174
Rimsky-Korsakov comment on, 250
and "The Venerable Thick-Branched Oaks," 240

Askold's Tomb, 206

Assyrian music, 290

Auer, Leopold, 128, 131, 132, 136

Auerbach, Leopold, 341

Automobile, 289

Autumnal Sketch, 228, 230

Aux champs, 207, 208

Avenarius, V. P., 90, 169

Bach, Johann Sebastian, 248
Lyadov and, 238
Prokofiev plays for exams, 109, 150, 343

Index

Shilin family. *See* Zhitkov family
Shpis, Vasily, 112, 130, 140, 150, 152, 156, 161, 181
Shumeiko (chief overseer), 18
Shumeiko, Egorka, 18, 147. See also *Giant, The*
Shumeiko, Vanka (clerk), 15, 18
Shurov River, 8
Sibelius, Jean, 220
Siegfried, 246
Siegfried Idyll, 225
Sienkiewicz, Henry K., 146, 147
"Silence" (Poe), 317
Silence, 199, 305, 317, 318
Siloti, Alexander, 82, 118, 288
Siloti Concerts, 82, 118, 127, 162ff., 215, 259, 271, 277
Sinfonietta, Prokofiev's, 305, 310–11ff., 347
Sinfonietta on Russian Themes for Orchestra (Rimsky-Korsakov), 311
Siskin variations, 89–90, 99, 104
Skalon, Lelya, 161
Sleeping Beauty, 22, 171
Slovo, 281–82
Smetskaya, Olga Yureyevna (Olechka), 76, 123, 252, 253, 255ff.
Smetsky, Kukula, 252–53, 256–57
Smetsky family, 123, 252–53, 255ff.
Smirnov, Mikhail, 3
Smirnova, Ekaterina Mikhailovna (Catherine), 3, 61
Smirnova, Maria, 3
Smirnova, Nadezhda Alekseyevna, 3
Smirnova, Nadezhda Mikhailovna, 3
Smirnov family, 4ff., 22
Smolensk Province, 6, 7–8
Snow, 228–30, 243, 281, 282, 284
Snow Maiden, The, 89, 144, 159, 258–59
Sobinov, Leonid, 120
Soeur de Gribouille, La, 78

Sokolov, N. A., 335
Solenenkoi River, 8
Solfeggio, 104, 119, 126, 129, 195
Solodovnikov Theater, 21, 80
Solovyev (chess player), 42
Solovyev, N. F., 103, 108, 130, 136, 305–6, 337
Solovyev, V. I., 329
Sonatas. *See* specific composers
Sonatina, 200, 215, 221
Song form, 49–50, 53. *See also* Ditties
"Song of the Witches," 334
Song Without Words, 50
Sontsov, Dmitri, 7, 9, 10, 164, 179, 267–68
Sontsovka (Sontsov property), 7, 8–21, 22–42, 45–56, 61–78, 84–85, 88, 115–16, 120–21, 122, 140–48, 168, 174–79, 196–213, 258–68, 304–5, 310–18, 326. *See also* Prokofiev, Sergei Alekseyevich
  description of, 8–9
  disposition of, 164, 267
  and disturbances of the Revolution, 131, 148, 164, 179
Sorcerer's Apprentice, 215
Sour cream, 142
Sovetskaya muzhka (Soviet Music), 320, 327
Soviet Music, 320, 327
"Square" structure, 53
S. S. Prokofiev: Materials, Documents, and Reminiscences, 320, 321, 323, 327. *See also* specific subjects, works
Stalin, Joseph, 12
Stalino, 8
Stamps, 56
Steinberg, Maximilian Oseyevich, 259
Steinitz-Lasker chess match, 42
Steinway and Sons, 342
Stilts, 177, 178, 211, 267
Story. See Fairy Tale
Strauss, Richard, 226, 274, 344
Stravinsky, Igor, 294